Revolutionary Communist at Work: A Political Biography of Bert Ramelson

I dedicate this book to my partner Valerie, and all my children –
Sarah, Joseph, Rachel, Adam, Hannah, Judith, Miriam and Ben

Roger Seifert

My dedication is to Joan Ramelson, and to my grandchildren, Liam,
Patrick and Charlie

Tom Sibley

Revolutionary Communist at Work: A Political Biography of Bert Ramelson

Roger Seifert and Tom Sibley

London Lawrence & Wishart 2012

Lawrence and Wishart Limited
99a Wallis Road
London
E9 5LN

First published 2012

British Library Cataloguing in Publication Data.
A catalogue record for this book is available from the British Library

ISBN **9781 907103 414**

Text setting E-type, Liverpool
Printed and bound by Biddles, Kings Lynn

Contents

Foreword

I had the great good fortune of doing a series of taped interviews with Bert Ramelson towards the end of his life. He told me a fascinating story, spanning the anti-semitic pogroms of pre-revolutionary Ukraine and the hellish conditions of an Italian ship in the second world war, transporting thousands of prisoners of war from the battlefields of north Africa to the squalor of mass camps in Southern Italy.

Unfortunately the planned programme of interviews was not completed as Bert's health deteriorated in 1993, so for me the record stopped in 1945 with Ramelson leading the Troops Parliament in Deolali, India. This book's authors have done a great job in taking the story forward and bringing out the political significance of Bert's tremendous contribution to the British and international labour movement.

It is an inspiring story, and I was particularly struck by Bert's efforts as a mass educator in the prisoner of war camps in north Africa and southern Italy. These activities did much to raise morale among the troops concerned, and to make the case for a socialist Britain after the war. Bert was right to take great pride in these achievements.

Bert Ramelson is best known as the Communist Party's organiser during the days of the Wilson, Heath and Callaghan governments. With others on the left he helped to develop a mass movement based on organised workers that was strong enough to block anti-union legislation and protect workers' rights. We badly need another such movement today with an even broader canvas. Much can be learnt about how to build this movement from studying Bert's life.

Rodney Bickerstaffe

Note on Sources

Where possible we have used Ramelson's own words – from interview tape transcripts or from his writing and speeches – to support the arguments and interpretations used in this book. We have also been able to draw on Conference Reports, recorded interviews with comrades, friends and associates of Ramelson, and secondary sources. However, although this material is extensive, it cannot tell the whole story. People's memories are deficient and sometimes self-serving. There are gaps and instances where we have had to make judgements about Ramelson's position which are not fully supported by documentary evidence.

Ramelson himself kept no diary. Neither, as his papers show, was he a voluminous correspondent. His writings are extensive but limited to articles and pamphlets dealing with the urgent issues of the day. He wrote literally hundreds of articles for the Communist press, including theoretical journals such as *Marxism Today* and *World Marxist Review*. But he is probably best remembered as a writer for his polemical pamphlets, particularly on economic and industrial issues during the 1960s and 1970s.

Ramelson had a fairly small circle of political confidants, many of whom either predeceased him or had died before we started work on this book. For the last ten years of his life, beginning with his appointment to the Editorial Board of *World Marxist Review*, whose offices were in Prague, Ramelson had regular and often lengthy political discussions with Tom Sibley, one of this book's co-authors. When Ramelson joined the *WMR*, Sibley was working as the London Representative of the World Federation of Trades Unions and giving regular reports to that body's officials in Prague. From that time on, in either Prague or London, the two met on a monthly basis to talk about current political issues. These meetings were entirely informal, occasionally involved third parties, and were unrecorded. Towards the end they became increasingly difficult, as Ramelson's health deteriorated and his powers of speech and reading abilities declined, as a result of the stroke he suffered in 1990. During these discussions, particularly in the early years, Ramelson did most of the talking and Sibley was happy to do most of the listening. In this way the latter was able to form a view about what made Ramelson tick, and to develop an understanding of his approach to policies and events. These insights are used to inform some of the judgements attributed to Ramelson in this book.

The research for this book was largely based on unpublished materials. These were located in various archives: mainly the CPGB one based in the Manchester Labour History Museum and Ramelson's personal papers kept by his family; with additional material from secret service files at the National Archive, Kew (KV Series). Additional archival material was searched at Marx Memorial Library; through the internet with the archivist at Edmonton library in Alberta; Jimmy Reid papers at Glasgow Caledonian University; Lawrence Daly papers at the Modern Records Centre at Warwick University

Much of the evidence came from five sets of interviews with Ramelson himself: by the Imperial War Museum, whose transcribed tapes from the early 1980s were made available; by extensive interviews by Rodney Bickerstaffe in the 1990s when Bert was ill (transcribed with great care by Valerie Taylor); and taped interviews by Francis Beckett, Kevin Morgan and Paul Routledge that they had conducted for different purposes.

In addition we interviewed many of Bert's friends, family, colleagues, and comrades. Some interviews had been carried out earlier by Deanne and Charles Lubelski as part of their initial work on Bert's biography; others were conducted by the authors and Rachel Seifert.

In 1999: Beryl Huffingley; Bill Moore; Harvey Waggenheim

In 2004: Barry Bracken; Jack and Minnie Marks

In 2008: Vic Allen; George Anthony; Joan Bellamy; Ron Bellamy; Maggie Bowden; Anne Craven; Richard Craven; Ken Gill; Kevin Halpin; Betty Meth; Monty Meth; Jim Mortimer; Gordon Norris; Joan Ramelson

In 2009: Edna Ashworth; Ivan Beavis; Norma Bramley; Mick Costello; Geoffrey Goodman; Martin Gould; Charles Lubelski ; Deanne Lubelski ; Gordon McLennan;
Brian Moody; Derek Perkins; Mike Seifert; Ethel Shepherd; Simon Steyne

In 2010: Roger Bagley; Rodney Bickerstaffe; Philippa Clark; Mary Davis; Stan Davison; Paul Dunn; Noel Harris; Mitch Howard; Carolyn Jones; John Sheldon; Graham Stevenson; Mike Squires

In 2011: Jack Dromey; Ann Field

Written notes were sent to us by Joe Clark; Keith Baker; Lyndon White; Myron Momryk; Jim McCorrie; John Corcoran; Essop Pahad.

Acknowledgements

Many people have made this book possible. Bert Ramelson's family, in particular his wife of twenty-five years and widow, Joan Ramelson, helped with their encouragement and knowledge of Bert's life and work. Two of his old Yorkshire comrades, Charles and Deanne Lubelski, made their own considerable archive of articles, cuttings, interview transcripts and memories available to us. Rodney Bickerstaffe gave us access to the many hours of tapes he recorded with Ramelson towards the end of his life. Rachel Seifert gave great assistance in many of the taped interviews and carried out some of the archive research. Valerie Taylor transcribed interviews from both the Bickerstaffe and Lubelski tapes. This required great skill and patience as the quality was poor and the meaning sometimes obscure. Cheryl Coyne typed Tom Sibley's words with care, diligence and great accuracy, and Jennie Sibley compiled the index with great speed and accuracy.

We thank them all as well as all those interviewed, those that sent in written comments, and the archivists who assisted our research and made it considerably easier. The Nuffield Foundation awarded us a grant which enabled the work to be carried out more effectively and efficiently, and we are grateful to them.

A group of friends read some of the work in progress and made useful and telling comments to help clarify and improve our work. These included Mike Ironside, John Foster, Mike Squires, Graham Stevenson and Mick Costello. Sally Davison read and edited most of the book. She did an excellent job and we are very thankful to her for her patience, skill and dedication.

Abbreviations

ACAS: Advisory, Conciliation and Arbitration Service

ACTT: Association of Cinematograph Television and Allied Technicians

AEF: Amalgamated Union of Engineering and Foundry Workers

AEEU: Amalgamated Engineering and Electrical Union

AES: Alternative Economic Strategy

AEU: Amalgamated Engineering Union

AMICUS: formed by merger of MSF and AEEU in 2001 (became part of UNITE in 2007)

APEX: Association of Professional, Executive, Clerical and Computer Staffs

ASLEF: Associated Society of Locomotive Engineers and Firemen

ASTMS: Association of Scientific, Technical and Managerial Staffs,

AUEW: Amalgamated Union of Engineering Workers

BRS: British Road to Socialism

CBI: Confederation of British Industry

CEU: Construction Engineering Union

CIR: Commission on Industrial Relations

CND: Campaign for Nuclear Disarmament

CPB (M-L): Communist Party of Britain (Marxist-Leninist)

CPGB: Communist Party of Great Britain (mainly referred to as the CP and the Party in this book), founded 1920 and dissolved 1991

CPI: Communist Party of India

CPSA: Civil and Public Service Association

CPSU: Communist Party of the Soviet Union

CSEU: Confederation of Shipbuilding and Engineering Unions

CWU: Communications Worker Union

DATA: Draughtsmen and Allied Technicians Union

DEA: Department of Economic Affairs

EETPU: Electrical, Electronic, Telecommunications and Plumbing Union

EC: executive committee

ETU: Electrical Trades Union

FBU: Fire Brigade Union

FTAT: Furniture, Timber, and Allied Trades Union

GDR: German Democratic Republic

GMB: In 1982 the Amalgamated Society of Boilermakers, Shipwrights, Blacksmiths and Structural Workers joined the General and Municipal Workers' Union to form the General, Municipal, Boilermakers and Allied Trade Union, now GMB

IMF: International Monetary Fund

IMG: International Marxist Group

IS: International Socialists, later SWP

IWC: Institute of Workers Control

LCDTU: Liaison Committee for the Defence of Trade Unions

LRD: Labour Research Department

NACODS: National Association of Colliery Overmen, Deputies and Shotfirers

NALGO: National Association of Local Government Officers (since 1991 merged to form UNISON)

NASD: National Amalgamated Stevedores and Dockers Union, merged with TGWU in 1982

NBPI: National Board for Prices and Incomes

NCP: New Communist Party

NEB: National Enterprise Board

NEDC: National Economic Development Council

NEP: National Economic Plan

NIC: National Incomes Commission

NIRC: National Industrial Relations Court

NUDAW: National Union of Distributive and Allied Workers, later merged to form USDAW in 1947

NUM: National Union of Mineworkers

NUPE: National Union of Public Employees (in 1991 merged to form UNISON)

NUR: National Union of Railwaymen (now RMT)

NUS: National Union of Seamen (now RMT)

NUT: National Union of Teachers

OECD: Organisation for Economic Co-operation and Development

POEU: Post Office Engineering Union

PPPS: People's Press Printing Society

SCPS: Society of Civil and Public Servants (now part of PCS)

SLL: Socialist Labour League

SOGAT: Society of Graphical and Allied Trades union

SWP: Socialist Workers Party

TASS: Technical, Administrative and Supervisory Staffs.

TGWU: Transport and General Workers Union (after 2007 merged to form UNITE)

TSSA: The Transport Salaried Staffs' Association

TUC: Trades Union Congress

UCATT: Union of Construction, Allied Trades and Technicians

UCS: Upper Clyde Shipbuilders

UPW: Union of Post Office Workers

USDAW: Union of Shop, Distributive and Allied Workers,

WEA: Workers Education Association

WFTU: World Federation of Trade Unions

WMR: World Marxist Review

WNV: World News and Views

WRP: Workers Revolutionary Party

YCL: Young Communist League

Introduction

B ert Ramelson was a remarkable man who lived through remarkable times. Both an activist and a leader in the world struggle for a socialist future, he never lost his conviction that such a future would benefit the vast majority of humankind.

Ramelson's life was an extraordinarily full one, and it is impossible in a single volume to put every episode into its full context. For example, Ramelson was in Moscow in 1956 as part of the Communist Party of Great Britain (CPGB) delegation meeting Khrushchev and other Soviet Party leaders in the immediate aftermath of the Communist Party of the Soviet Union's (CPSU) Twentieth Congress, when Stalin was denounced. He was also the first British citizen to be told of the 1968 Soviet military intervention in Czechoslovakia. In 1956 he had been a member of a team involved in amicable discussions; in 1968 he was at the Soviet Embassy in London, strongly expressing his personal (and his Party's) opposition to the invasion. Although 1956 is of enormous importance in Ramelson's life, his personal contribution to political developments was much more significant in 1968. This, we hope, is reflected in the respective weights given to these two events in our account of Ramelson's life and times.

Our purpose in this book is two-fold: to trace Bert's personal contribution to the struggle, and to show how this related to and influenced developments within the broad labour movement. Along the way we aim to engage with the critics and commentators whose analysis of events and possibilities contradicted Ramelson's. In this way we seek to challenge the interpretations of recent accounts of the history of the CPGB that deal with the period of Ramelson's political activity in Britain between the 1950s and 1990s.[1]

Bert Ramelson's life took in many of the seminal political developments of the twentieth century. He lived through the first years of the Bolshevik revolution and the ensuing Civil War, during which members of his immediate family were murdered by counter-revolutionary forces in the anti-semitic pogroms of the period. As a young boy he heard Trotsky address mass meetings in Moscow, and on emigrating to Canada his family was nearly ruined by the 1929 Great Depression. As a young man and a zionist activist he gave up on a burgeoning law career to go to Palestine to work on a Kibbutz, only to be quickly disillusioned about the theory and practice of Jewish nationalism. He fought with bravery and distinction in the Spanish Civil War, and as a tank driver with the British Army at Tobruk. His biggest contribution was in the class struggle: for his entire adult life he put his considerable intellect, moral courage, and energy at the service of the labour and progressive movement.

From 1937 onwards, when at the age of twenty-seven he joined the International Brigades in Spain to fight alongside the Spanish people in defence of their Republic against Franco and Hitlerism, Ramelson was a professional revolutionary and an activist within the international communist movement. After nearly twenty years as a full-time Communist Party worker in Yorkshire, he was appointed as the Party's National Industrial Organiser, and it was in this position that he made his most important contribution to advancing the interests of the progressive movement. Arguably the most incisive pamphleteer of his generation, and almost certainly the shrewdest political strategist in the British labour movement between 1965 and 1977 (when he retired as Industrial Organiser), Ramelson was probably the single biggest influence in developing the trade union movement's campaign against wage restraint and anti-union laws during this period. As Ramelson himself would be the first to insist, however, his achievement belonged mainly to the work of the CPGB, which he served with tremendous pride and distinction for over forty years. Although we reject the 'great leader' theory of history – it is material conditions and mass movements that drive social change – we recognise that leaders can and do make a difference. Ramelson was an outstanding leader who contributed much to the labour movement in a period of industrial unrest and political uncertainty.

Ramelson died in 1994 aged eighty-four, a political activist until his dying breath. By then many of the political certainties that had helped him to play such a valuable role in struggles and campaigns to advance the cause of peace and socialism were disintegrating. The Party he loved, the Communist Party, was in disarray. The Soviet Union was no longer, and Ramelson's oft-expressed view, that despite all the mistakes and brutalities committed in the name of socialism the Soviet peoples, led by the working class, would never abandon socialism had proved to be altogether wrong.[2] So in many important respects Ramelson died a disappointed man. And yet he was never disillusioned. Despite the setbacks, he believed that humankind could only advance to a better, more secure and more fulfilling existence through socialist co-operation. He believed that the international working class, through struggle and experience, would one day build the necessary organisation and mass understanding to bring this about.

Over the years the capitalist media and anti-communist politicians have expended much energy in portraying active communists as robotic but clever fanatics without normal human feelings and aspirations. At the start of the Cold War, Dennis Healey set the tone in an article on world communism:

> The nucleus of every party was now a small body of devoted men whose spiritual personality had been obliterated by automatic conformity over two decades. The inhuman character of the trained Communist impressed all observers. The Communist elite was a secret army of intelligent and courageous robots, a religious society without God in which rationalization replaced nationality, the organised replaced the organic.[3]

As this book will show, Ramelson was no dull apparatchik simply carrying out the Party line. He was there at every turn, leading from the front, if necessary putting himself in harm's way to advance the cause. He lived and breathed politics every second of the day. All his friends were on the left and both the women he married were political (though it was not until he married Joan Smith in the late 1960s that he grew to appreciate the benefits of being a father and grandfather). All who knew him well testify to his warmth, his wit and his concern for the well-being of friends and comrades.

Ramelson read widely. Like most of us he preferred Coronation Street to Coriolanus, but he watched little television other than current affairs programmes. He had no interest in professional sport, and even as an adopted Yorkshireman remained baffled by the rules and technical sophistications of cricket. Despite this apparent narrowness of interests and lack of leisure activities, he was a man of enormous humanity who was deeply loved by his family, and highly respected by a wide group of political friends. Above all he was interested in people and what they did; particularly of course labour movement activists. In conversation with Ramelson, people with widely different backgrounds and experiences would sense that they were talking to someone who was more interested in listening to them than he was in getting his own views across. When in conversation with trade union leaders, including shop floor representatives, he would patiently listen before offering what appeared to be surprisingly tentative advice, giving options rather than answers. When they looked back a few weeks later, the shrewder amongst them realised that Ramelson had always convinced them to support the particular form of action which he himself favoured.

Ramelson was always anxious to encourage comrades in their work. As later recalled by his fellow full-time Party worker Bill Moore, in his early days in Yorkshire Ramelson was quick to praise initiative or steadfastness in carrying through tasks, while being a bit of a stickler for seeing that targets were met and decisions carried through.[4] This latter tendency could upset people – even hardened revolutionaries, but as he grew to national prominence, and away from the day-to-day job of managing a large Party District with seventy-odd branches, his style of work changed somewhat. The words of praise and encouragement remained, but the detailed and sometimes obtrusive checking of the carrying through of decisions fell away. Ramelson knew how to get the best out of people, and made it his business (though not always successfully) not to fall out with any potential allies. He also did his best to promote cadre development. For example, Graham Stevenson, now a very senior national official in Britain's largest union Unite, tells the story of how Ramelson raised the funds (presumably through Reuben Falber[5] and the Soviet Embassy) to finance a fortnight's trip to Cuba for a group of around ten young industrial workers, which included Communist education programmes during the day, and plenty of free time in the evenings and weekends.

Ramelson could at times seem overbearing. Novelist and political biographer Mervyn Jones spent some months sharing a bungalow (and Party membership) with Ramelson in Deolali, when they were both Non-Commissioned Officers serving in post-war India:

He had a dominating manner and was inclined to shout me down when we had a disagreement. But he also had a warm capacity for friendship and lively sense of humour. We got on well together. In the group of Communists which planned the activities of the Forces Parliament, Bert Ramelson was the leading spirit.[6]

The two men were of course of vastly different experiences and backgrounds. Ramelson was some ten years older, and had progressed from the ghetto to a distinguished if short-lived legal career, fought in the Spanish Civil War and been a prisoner of war; while Jones was a public school educated Communist in his early twenties, with little political activism behind him at that time. Ramelson's voice and debating style – developed when trying to get a word in edgeways as the youngster in a deeply political family – might well have appeared overbearing to Jones; and similar criticisms of his style have been made in subsequent years. It should be remembered that most of his public speaking techniques had been developed during the war in large open-air formal meetings where a loud voice was essential if the message was to be understood. Writing some forty years later, Nora Jefferys, a leading Communist and neighbour of Ramelson's, said of him: 'Notwithstanding his ability to shout, which he often did, carried away by his enthusiasm, he was a humble man, with a great appreciation of other people and of their needs.'[7]

Although Ramelson lived for more than twenty years in Yorkshire, and grew very fond of the area and its people, he never acquired the accent. His accent was as pronounced in 1980 as it had been in 1945. At public meetings c e rarely needed sound amplification even in large halls; and in relatively small co-op halls, which were characteristic meeting places for labour movement bodies during Ramelson's active political life, those in the know sat towards the back. In his fifties his hearing began to deteriorate, and it seemed to many that his speaking volume increased in inverse proportion to his partial but growing deafness.

Ramelson was above average height, straight-backed and broadshouldered. If he was physically imposing, it was his intellect and temperament which singled him out as a special person. He read voraciously, listened intently and was always prepared to openly debate and discuss political and social issues. Temperamentally Ramelson was almost always calm and open-minded. He bore no grudges and thought the best of everyone until proved wrong in his assessment. He saw people very much as products of their circumstances, and rarely spoke of people's personalities or peccadilloes. He did, of course, have his views about the personal dispositions of trade union and Party leaders, but these were seldom, if ever, expressed to others – at least while the individuals concerned were active in the movement. In his later years, and only when pressed, he might tentatively express views on these matters – that for example this trade union leader had had his head turned by the prospect of political influence, while another leader was, in a sense, corrupted by the trappings of office and, to a degree, the financial rewards that went with it.

Like the rest of us, Ramelson could be grumpy. He grew grumpier as the crisis in the CP deepened during the 1980s, and as he spent more time away from home during his sojourn as British representative on the board of *World Marxist Review* based in Prague. His grumpiness was generally short-lived, and seldom, if ever, resulted in expressions of bad temper or political pessimism. He was deeply disappointed with the split in the CPGB, and the tactics used by some of his former colleagues at national leadership level, who he saw as being prepared to traduce the Party's history and decry its achievements in order to prepare the way for its dissolution. On a personal level he was badly shaken, although not overly surprised, when the CPGB leadership refused to accept the re-registration of the members of his Sydenham Branch.

Before taking up full-time Party work in Yorkshire, Ramelson had been a Union of Shop, Distributive and Allied Workers (USDAW) activist. He had worked for Marks & Spencer as a middle manager, and was active in the union at branch, regional and trades council level. From 1946 onwards his Party responsibilities meant that he no longer had direct day-to-day links with the shop-floor, and his representation capacity was thus diminished; but Ramelson retained his links with his union branch, and continued to represent it at trades council level. He was subsequently elected as Vice President, and as trades council delegate to the West Yorkshire Association of Trades Councils, serving on its Executive Committee (EC).

Compared to most political leaders of his day, including those of the extra-Parliamentary left, Ramelson had extensive trade union experience. From 1953 he was in constant contact with workers' representatives in Britain's most important industries, particularly mining and engineering. It was here that Ramelson saw and promoted the benefits of a broad left approach in strengthening the trade union movement, both in organising for basic trade union demands and in widening the movement's political perspectives. Some commentators have intimated that it was the Electrical Trades Union (ETU) ballot-rigging scandal in 1961 that forced the Communist Party at national level to adopt such a strategy.[8] The evidence suggests that it was Ramelson's appointment as National Industrial Organiser, rather than the backlash from the ETU affair, that was the decisive factor in shaping a new approach to the Party's industrial work and its relationship to the trade union left, both at national union and rank-and-file level.

Ramelson was determined to translate his successes in Yorkshire to the national scene, and this would have been the case with or without the ETU debacle. Ken Gill explains Ramelson's ability to learn from others' struggles thus: 'You can be special without going through all the experiences oneself, but he [Ramelson] managed to maintain an intellectual clarity, not despite but because of, his experiences'.[9] It was a combination of a deep understanding of Marxism with an ability to listen empathetically to the views and hopes of those at the sharp end of the class struggle that singled Ramelson out as an outstanding communist leader. These qualities – allied to his experiences in the battle against fascism – made Ramelson a tough operator as well as a formidable intellectual force, in a labour movement that was sadly short of leaders with these attributes.

Ramelson's political work was almost all-consuming. He would spend long periods away from home, speaking at public meetings, attending evening and weekend committees, and from time to time representing the CP at events and Congresses at home and abroad. Despite this, his family members remember him only with fondness, as a loved and deeply admired step-father and granddad. A story told to us by Gordon Norris, a veteran of the 1966 seafarers' dispute, gives a clue to Ramelson's approach to family, and his deeply human concern for those sharing his life. Norris remembers being invited to a small party organised by Ramelson to mark the eightieth birthday of his father-in-law, Tom Jessop, who was a former Labour mayor of Leeds.[10] This was shortly after the death of Jessop's daughter Marian, Ramelson's first wife. At this event Norris, a London seaman, rubbed shoulders and discussed politics with progressive lawyers, surgeons and scientists, and all this made an impression on the rank and file leader. But he was particularly struck by Jessop's demeanour that night, and the way that Ramelson looked after his bereaved father-in-law. In Norris's view, Jessop deeply admired Bert Ramelson, and was extremely appreciative of his thoughtfulness and compassion in organising the event.

Above all else Ramelson was a Communist, an internationalist who sought to advance the cause of socialist revolution worldwide. Organisationally his primary attachment was to the CPGB, whose programme, *The British Road to Socialism*, originally formulated in 1951, set out both a revolutionary strategy and the conditions necessary for its achievements. The post-war British Communist Party went through a number of phases, and Ramelson could be critical of its positions if he felt it to be necessary. Between the last years of the second world war and the onset of the Cold War in 1948, its policies had been guided by what subsequent critics, including Ramelson himself, described as the Tehran illusion – that is, that the war-time big power agreements made by the United Nation (UN) Countries such as the United States of America (USA), the Union of Soviet Socialist Republics (USSR) and the United Kingdom (UK), promoting peaceful co-existence and co-operative relations, could be carried forward into the post-war world. Richard Kisch, quoting from the extensive correspondence between Ramelson and his friend Colin Siddons during 1944, argues that both men thought that 'the prospect of political miracles conjured out of the optimistic generalisation of the Big Three manifestos from Tehran and Yalta defied common sense'.[11] During this period the Communist Party made a bold but unsuccessful attempt to affiliate to the Labour Party;[12] and it also gave general, if critical, support to Attlee's domestic policies (though condemning its imperialist policies abroad); and it also put great emphasis on its electoral work, at some detriment to its industrial activities. But in 1948 there was a sharp turn to the left, partly in response to the Cominform's reappraisal of the world balance of class forces, but mainly because it was becoming more evident by the day that the Labour government was moving rightwards, and was to all intents and purposes now tied to the apron strings of the USA.[13] From 1948 onwards the Party placed its main emphasis on industrial work – although it continued to retain illusions about the possibilities of building an electoral base.

Like the rest of the international communist movement, the CPGB was badly shaken by the events of 1956 and 1968 (though substantial losses of membership as a result of these developments were fairly quickly reversed and by the mid-1970s membership had stabilised at around 28,000). Ramelson played a full part in the debates that followed on from these events, and in 1968 played a leading role in developing a more critical response to CPSU foreign policy. However these events and the debates they inspired led to wider divisions within the international communist movement. During the 1970s a Eurocommunist or neo-Gramscian current emerged, which placed more emphasis on social movements than on work within the trade unions, and sharply distanced itself from the international communist movement.[14] This current was strongly opposed by Ramelson, but by the mid-1980s it had become the main grouping in the British Party leadership, and in 1991 it successfully argued for the winding up of the CPGB.

For most of Ramelson's active political life, the communist movement spanned the world, and in many countries it formed the governing party, or was the main element within the socialist community. However, in Britain, unlike in many West European countries, the CP was always a small grouping, existing to the left of the much larger and electorally successful Labour Party. Yet it had many achievements. Unlike Labour, it was able to sustain a national daily newspaper (*Daily Worker*, later renamed as *Morning Star*), and to build Party organisation both at the workplace and within many national trade unions – and it was in this latter work, of course, that Ramelson's role was crucial. The CPGB was also very successful at building alliances and campaigns (for example the broad left in the trade unions; and CP activists' crucial role in the early development of the peace, anti-racism and women's movements).

The CPGB played an important role in British political life from its founding in 1920 to its demise in 1991. Its most successful achievement was its contribution to the trade union radicalism of the 1960s and 1970s, in which Ramelson played a major part. The achievements of the Soviet Union also still stand – particularly its huge contribution to the defeat of fascism, and its support for national liberation movements. For revolutionaries in particular, the setbacks during the period 1979-1994 (the year of Ramelson's death) were a sobering experience. Ramelson could nevertheless look back and reflect on a fulfilling life spent in the finest cause he knew – the struggle for a more just world and a socialist Britain.

NOTES

1. Andrews, G. *End Games and New Times: The Final Years of British Communism 1964-1991*, Lawrence & Wishart, London 2004; Callaghan, J. *Cold War, Crisis and Conflict – The CPGB 1951-6*, Lawrence & Wishart, London 2003; Thompson, W. *The Long Death of British Labourism: Interpreting a Political Culture*, Pluto Press, London 1993.

2. During the 1980s, Ramelson apparently changed his view on the Soviet Union and in a letter to his friend and comrade Colin Siddons he argued that by its actions the Soviet Party leadership abandoned its Socialist objectives in the mid-1920s. Ramelson family papers.

3. Healey, D. 'The Cominform and World Communism', *International Affairs,* 1948 24: 339-349; p. 341.

4. Bill Moore interview, 1999.

5. Graham Stevenson interview, 2010. Falber was responsible for the Party's finances and investments. In this role he liaised with the Soviet authorities to launder subventions received from the CPSU.

6. Jones, M. *Choices: an Autobiography*, Verso, London 1987; pp. 89-92.

7. Letter to Joan Ramelson in the Ramelson family papers.

8. Callaghan, op.cit. 2003, p. 246.

9. Ken Gill interview, 2008.

10. Gordon Norris interview, 2008.

11. Kisch, R. *The Days of the Good Soldiers: Communists in the Armed Forces in WII,* Journeyman Press, London 1985, p. 92.

12. A long term objective which Ramelson continued to strongly support into the 1990s – before New Labour.

13. The Cominform consisted of the ruling Communist Parties in Eastern Europe plus the mass parties of Italy and France. It was formed in 1947 in response to the Truman Doctrine and the Marshall Plan.

14. Some West European Communist Parties, led by the largest, the Italian Party, distanced themselves from the Soviet Union and emphasised the building of anti-capitalist alliances rather than class politics. This trend, which was not simply a European one, is probably best described as neo-Gramscian, although it is questionable whether Gramsci himself would have supported this general approach.

PART I

From the Ukraine to Yorkshire
via Canada, Palestine, Spain,
North Africa, Italy, and India,
1910-1965

1. Formative years, 1910-1946

THE EARLY YEARS IN UKRAINE, 1910-1922

Baruch Rachmilevitch (Bert Ramelson) was born on 22 March 1910
into a large Yiddish speaking and politically disputatious family. Like
most Ukrainian Jews of the time, his family lived in the ghetto quarters
of a small town. In the Ramelsons' case the town was Cherkassy (population in 1910 approximately 20,000) on the opposite bank of the
Dnieper River from Kiev. His father was a Talmudist scholar with the
qualifications of a rabbi, but with the role of a scholar rather than of
pastoral care and religious practice. This was an unpaid position,
although members of the Jewish community would usually provide
him with food and other sustenance on the occasions when he was
providing private tuition or leading discussion groups in family homes.
Ramelson's mother was the main breadwinner, and the bedrock around
which the family was sustained against the threats of poverty, civil war,
and the anti-semitic pogroms of the period. Bert Ramelson respected
his father and loved his mother. She ran a corner shop previously owned
by her father, which doubled up as the family home. Besides giving
birth to seven children and bringing them up, she made all the family
clothes and tended the kitchen garden, while her husband studied the
meaning of life and interpreted esoteric religious tracts.

The Rachmilevitch nuclear family brought up five girls and two boys. Bert was the sixth born, and one of two boys. When he was eight years old he witnessed the death of his elder brother in a swimming accident. This left him as the only boy in a large family and led, in his own words, to his 'being spoilt rotten'. Particular attention was paid to his education. When the opportunity came in 1922 to leave Cherkassy and emigrate to Canada, one of the main family considerations in taking the decision to leave was to protect their one remaining son from the perceived perils of an atheist education in a strongly secular state.

Ramelson's experiences as a youngster in the Ukraine did much to shape his political outlook in his adult years. There were three main influences – the family, the Yiddish school, and the events of the Russian revolution and the years immediately after 1917. Ramelson described his mother as apolitical, and his father as a social liberal – in favour of the Bolshevik revolution for the way it tackled anti-semitism and poverty in all its forms, but concerned about the socialist state's approach to religion and religious institutions. Above all it was Ramelson's older sisters who brought politics into the house. Three of the sisters were Bolsheviks, while another joined the Social Revolutionaries, and by far the biggest influence was Rosa, some seven years older than Bert. She was an active Young Communist (Komsomol) who at the age of seventeen married a young Red Army Officer and retreated with the Bolsheviks when the counter-revolutionary White Guards temporarily took control of Cherkassy during the first period of the Civil War.[1] Ramelson's enduring memory of his sister is of a young woman with a pistol in her waistband determined to rid her country of poverty, illiteracy and anti-semitism. It was Rosa, during the periods when the Red Army held sway in Cherkassy, who brought young women factory workers into the family home, where lively political discussions between Bolsheviks and other political tendencies ensued.

Ramelson's early education was also extremely rich in content. While the family was often short of clothes – particularly shoes – Bert's mother ensured that there was always food on the table, at least until the dislocations of the immediate post-revolutionary years. There were also books, and a love of learning, thanks to his father's influence. From the age of three Bert was sent to the Hebrew School (boys only), where he learnt the scriptures (by rote), and in so doing the elements of reading and writing. It was during the post-1917 period that the most important developments in Ramelson's early education occurred. The new Bolshevik government revolutionised every aspect of Ukrainian society. The Rights of Nationalities Act, drawn up by Joseph Stalin, legislated for equal opportunities in many spheres, including education. Other education reforms created new democratic rights for pupils and new higher education institutions for young adults. In Cherkassy this resulted in the creation of a Yiddish School, where Ukrainian and Russian were taught as second languages. For a short period pupil power was introduced to the schools. Ramelson recalls being elected at the age of eleven onto a twelve-member committee of pupils that had the power to discipline their teachers, and a big say in education issues at school level. Although this experiment in grass-roots democracy was quickly abandoned by Lenin, it gave Ramelson an almost unique experience in the exercise of power at a very young age. Another reform, which proved to be more long-standing, was Lenin's creation of a new tier of university teachers, drawn from the ranks of young Bolsheviks and sent on crash courses. This was a way of counteracting the influence of the old established professors with their pre-revolutionary mind-sets, as well as catering for a massive increase in educational provision. Ramelson's sister Rosa was a beneficiary of this scheme, and became what was known at the time as a 'Red Professor', in economics, at Sverdlov University.

Ramelson's early schooling did more than provide a formal start to his educational development. The new Yiddish school was by its nature a community school, incorporating the aspirations of the ghetto for a life free from the indignities of discrimination, which during the Civil War period had taken the form of anti-semitic murder, rape and pillage. So it was a school imbued with a democratic ethos and very much associated with hope for a new future linked to the socialist revolution.

The third thread of important influences on the young Bert Ramelson was the overall political background in the period between his birth in 1910 and his emigration in 1922. In some respects Ramelson's was a very happy childhood. He lived in the security of the ghetto and rarely left it, and his family was poor but not desperately so. In terms of the ghetto the Ramelsons were middle-income and well respected. In other ways these were horrendous times, particularly for the Jewish community. Denied most rights by the Czarist regime, the community suffered periodic pogroms, during which the people of the ghetto were seen as fair game for attack. These attacks peaked during the Civil War (1918-1922), and as a young boy Ramelson witnessed horrific events. He later recalled how his family suffered, how his grandfather, uncle and cousin were murdered, and how his father was protected by moving him into a hospital for incurable diseases to hide him from the White Guards. He also relates his personal experience of leaving his basement hiding place (aged eight) to see if it was all clear for the family following a night of looting and murder by the White Army. As he walked around the deserted ghetto streets early one morning he came across dozens of bodies lying dead where they had been struck down the previous night. He also describes witnessing how White Army troops held a pistol to his father's head while demanding money from his mother, who had hidden what they had in the dough prepared for the weekend bread making. Not surprisingly these events left deep impressions. As Ramelson himself put it, in summing up his political outlook when leaving Moscow for Canada as a twelve-year-old:

> I was a revolutionary. Rosa had a tremendous influence on me. Not only Rosa but the Jewish School ... the pogroms ... the saviours were the Red Army ... Communists were against anti-semitism. At the school they were all anti-Tsarist and anti-capitalist. So you had a tremendous environmental influence.[2]

By 1922 the family elders had decided to join Bert's paternal uncle in Canada, where he was a successful fur trader – 'ripping off the Indians' as Ramelson later put it.[3] His elder sisters preferred to stay in the Soviet Union. Rosa was already married, and all of them were supporters of the revolution. Ramelson's mother would also have preferred to stay, particularly since Rosa was now pregnant. His father was insistent on emigrating, almost certainly because he was concerned about the development of a militant state that would encourage atheist culture in his homeland, and the impact that this could have on his only surviving son. So the family were split. The parents and the younger children went off to live in a new world country, guaranteed financial support from the rich fur-trader uncle. Before they left for Canada the family spent three weeks in Moscow, where Rosa did her level best to inculcate her brother with the spirit of the revolution. Ramelson's own memories of 1917 Cherkassy are of exultant people on the streets of the ghetto tearing the epaulettes off police officers' uniforms and the badges from their caps. This was striking enough, but Rosa capped this. Not only did she take Bert to the Bolshoi to see the Spartacus ballet performed before an enthusiastic audience of thousands; she also took him to an enormous open-air public meeting addressed by Trotsky. Ramelson was off to a new life, but he took with him more than a small cardboard suitcase. By the age of twelve he had already lived an extraordinary life. Now he was fired by love and admiration for Rosa, his big sister, and the example of the Russian Revolution, with all the possibilities it appeared to open up for people like him.[4] Among his last acts in the Ukraine was an address to a school-leaving party arranged in his honour, at which he denounced his parents' decision to leave the revolution behind to emigrate to capitalist Canada.[5]

LIFE IN CANADA (AND PALESTINE), 1922-1936

When the Ramelsons arrived in Edmonton, Alberta, the centre of the fur trade in Canada, none of his immediate family spoke a word of English. They settled in comfortably enough. Ramelson's father was made a sort of non-executive, non-working director of his brother's company, and paid a good salary plus dividend earnings for doing very little. He continued with his studies and became a respected figure in the community, giving advice and spiritual guidance whenever asked. His mother, who had in Ukrainian times been a heroic figure central to the well-being and defence of her family, found it more difficult to adapt to her comfortable new life, but soon found a role as an allotment holder and gardener, providing fresh vegetables for the family and neighbours. Ramelson himself settled in very quickly. Within a year or so he had mastered the local language, to the extent that he won first prize in a school debating competition, and with some regularity he continued to win school prizes in a range of academic disciplines. At eighteen he gained a place at the University of Alberta, where he read law, and to nobody's surprise he took a first with honours. While at University he was conscripted to an Officer Training course, a half day a month exercise where he learnt to handle small arms and other military techniques, including man-management Army style. Years later, in 1966, the *Edmonton Journal* picked up on the news that Ramelson had been attacked by British Prime Minister Harold Wilson for his role in organising support for the seafarers' national claim, which was contrary to the government's wages restraint policy. It recalled that Ramelson was an Edmonton boy who as a young man had had a distinguished academic record, graduating from the University of Alberta with a bevy of honours. He had won the Chief Justice Gold Medal for leading his class over three years, the National Trust prize and the Carswell prize. The paper goes on:

> A search of university records and journal microfilm, and the memories of university classmates, paints a picture of a brilliant, admired and popular man, who couldn't make up his mind about what to do in the future … His classmates knew him as a Communist to his depths.[6]

The family fortunes had nose-dived with the 1929 Stock Exchange crash, and by 1930, when Ramelson became a university student, though not poor, the Ramelsons had to watch the pennies. This meant that in order to pay his way through university Ramelson had to seek paid work during the five-month-long university vacations. The family and business connections helped greatly. The family business had survived the Great Depression and remained a valued customer of Canadian Pacific Railways. Hence Ramelson was able to get a holiday job as a labourer loading freight trains with heavy goods. It was hard physical work and at first Ramelson was paid the student rate, 60 per cent of the union rate. When the union representative got to know of this he quickly got the matter put right so that Ramelson enjoyed equal pay and other rights with his fellow workers. This first lesson in the value of union organisation made a big impression on the young Ramelson. His next lesson was that with capitalism came unemployment, as the Canadian Pacific laid off all temporary workers when the depression deepened. While he learnt these lessons he was still undecided about his political position. After finishing university he did a mandatory year as an articled clerk with a local law firm, as part of his degree and qualification to practise law. At this stage he described himself as a Marxist zionist, and he was active in the zionist movement. The apparent contradiction between the nationalism associated with zionism and the internationalism which was so important to the international communist movement continued to worry the young man now in his early twenties. However, he was attracted by the Kibbutz movement in Palestine, where Jews from many parts of the world were coming together to build self-governing agricultural communities on a co-operative basis, and he decided to go to Palestine. Participation in the kibbutz required an initial investment, but thereafter full board and lodging was provided in exchange for work contributed. All decisions concerning the day-to-day running and investment policy of the kibbutz were made democratically, and policing, including defence against outside attack, was organised within the community. During this period Ramelson added to his knowledge of firearm use and defensive tactics, while participating in kibbutz activities.

Life in the Kibbutz started well enough. Ramelson enjoyed the comradeship, the debate and argument and the feeling of solidarity in working for a common purpose to build a democratic community. He soon realised that all was not as it first seemed. It became apparent to him very early on in his stay that the Arab people resented the increasing numbers of Jews being allowed to settle under the British mandate.[7] When the Jewish-based trade union Histradut began organising strikes against employers using Arab labour, Ramelson came to understand the divisive nature of religion-based nationalism. All this came to a head in 1936, when a wealthy US zionist, who owned a large orange grove employing 50 per cent Arab and 50 per cent Jewish labour, contracted from Ramelson's kibbutz, was faced with a Histradut-led strike, the chief demand of which was to replace Arab with Jewish labour. Ramelson saw this for what it was – a racist strike – and refused to participate. He later described this strike as a seminal event: 'That single strike in the orange grove was the catalyst'. Ramelson had become disillusioned with zionism, and from now on Marxism and internationalism were to be the key elements in his political outlook. By this time Mussolini and Hitler were in power in Europe, and fascism was threatening both Jews and the working class generally. At this stage: 'I could only see a solution to the problems through international terms, through a Marxist approach'.[8]

ON THE FRONT LINE IN SPAIN, 1936-9

Ramelson returned to Edmonton in 1936, with big decisions to make about his career and his political orientation. Zionism was no longer an option, and he now threw his energies into assisting the anti-fascist movement in Alberta. At the time the Canadian Communist Party was illegal, and what members it had worked in broad labour movement and progressive organisations, not in Party units. Ramelson may have met some of the individuals involved, but was not aware of having done so. He was also, in some senses, an outsider – a foreign-born intellectual, practising law, far removed from the working-class movement, and living in a province geographically remote from the main centres of Canadian political life. He had at last made his mind up about the central decision which was to shape the rest of his life. He now considered himself to be a Communist, and part of the same great movement as his sister Rosa back in Russia. By now he was a regular reader of Palme Dutt's *Labour Monthly*, a British-based journal which was distributed throughout the English-speaking world. He later recalled *Labour Monthly* as 'a very effective education into Marxism', singling out Dutt's notes of the month as being particularly important for readers trying to understand world events. [9] By the end of 1936, and entirely in line with *Labour Monthly*'s editorials, Ramelson had come to the view that events in Spain had taken on a universal significance: 'what was taking place in Spain was not a Civil War but was really a war waged by the fascists to prevent the development of a democratic Spain so as to establish a fascist regime'.[10]

The next decision Ramelson had to take was how best to support the anti-fascist struggle. Should he pursue a promising legal career, while putting all his spare energies into anti-fascist work in Canada, including the foremost task of building solidarity with the Republican cause in Spain? Or should he volunteer to fight in Spain alongside the Spanish people, and thereby help to highlight the Republican cause and its international significance? Here his political isolation helps to explain his decision to join the International Brigades. His disavowal of zionism had lost him some political friends in Edmonton, but it was his failure to link with the Communists, due to the Party's illegal status and Ramelson's lack of industrial roots, that finally tipped the scales. In Canada he was an isolated intellectual, who could make only a limited contribution to the central struggle of the time as he saw it. In Spain he could become part of an international force directly involved in the struggle to defeat fascism. Furthermore he knew that in Spain he would meet fellow Communists, and have the opportunity, at last, to join the Communist Party. So in 1936 Ramelson took the decision to go to Spain, to fight with the International Brigades in defence of the Spanish Republic. Aged twenty-seven, and with a smattering of military training, Ramelson started on his way to join what he later described as the first stage of the war against fascism in Europe.

His Spanish journey started in London. He had been given a few addresses by his anti-fascist friends in Canada, and in the early spring of 1937 he turned up on the doorstep of Councillor Maurice Brown in North London. Although Brown was a Labour Councillor he also held a Communist Party card, and Ramelson was soon directed to the King Street headquarters of the CPGB in London's Covent Garden.[11] After a searching interview to establish his political commitment, and to ensure that he knew what he was volunteering for, Ramelson was accepted as being suitable for service in the International Brigade. Within days he was in Paris en route to Spain and a fortnight or so later he was making the perilous and exhausting crossing of the Pyrenees on foot and at night, with a hundred or so fellow volunteers from many parts of the world.

In the battle for Spanish democracy against the Franco fascist rebellion, Ramelson served with both the Spanish Fifth Army and the Mackenzie-Papineau Battalion, the Canadian contingent of the 15th International Brigade. He rarely later talked about his experiences in Spain, and in our researches we unearthed no written articles in his name on the issue. He was extremely modest about his activities, and always deferred to Bill Alexander, who was in Spain for longer and rose to a much higher rank.[12] (Alexander, who became a close friend, was of course attached to the British Battalion, which saw more action than the units to which Ramelson was attached).[13] Ramelson fought on the Aragon Front as a Company Commander of an Artillery Battalion, and in the Ebro Offensive. In both operations he was wounded and taken to hospital, with bullet and shrapnel wounds. Franco's troops were vastly superior both in numbers and equipment, and were backed to the hilt by Mussolini and Hitler – unlike the democratic government they were seeking to overthrow, who were abandoned by other western governments. During one headlong retreat with the Republican forces, Ramelson, who could not swim, and had been nervous about water ever since the drowning of his brother some twenty years earlier, was forced to float across the Ebro on a door that he came across on the river bank.

Like many Brigaders, Ramelson's war was an heroic one, which came to an end in the autumn of 1938, when the Spanish Prime

Minister, in a vain attempt to secure the withdrawal of German and Italian involvement on Franco's side, announced that he was sending the International Brigades back to their homelands, so that they could no longer be used as a pretext for foreign intervention by the fascist powers. This was the Spanish government's last diplomatic card, played a time when military defeat looked very probable, if not inevitable, in face of the continuing refusal of Britain, France and the United States to provide them with the arms and political support they needed. Among the Brigaders there was great disappointment about the Spanish government's decision, however, which was taken while the war was still raging. This was not to be the end of Ramelson's involvement in Spain.

The position of the Canadians was particularly difficult, and they did not leave Spain until May 1939, at which time Madrid was still held by the Republican side. Many of the Canadian Brigaders, like Ramelson, were neither of Canadian birth, nor naturalised Canadians, and because of this they faced difficulties with their own government. It was not clear whether all the Brigaders would be allowed back into Canada, since under Canadian law those of doubtful nationality status and with two years out the country had no guaranteed rights to re-enter the country.[14]

Ramelson, who had joined the Canadian Communist Party on joining the Mackenzie-Papineau Battalion in mid-1938, and was now a member of the Party Committee and its official spokesman, brought his legal and political skills to bear on the situation. With Franco's army less than ten miles away, Ramelson negotiated a right of return for all his comrades on a Canadian Pacific liner from Liverpool. The Brigaders also wanted to make a political point, and demanded the right to stage a demonstration in London while on the way to Liverpool, with the slogan 'Arms for Spain'. Negotiations between Ramelson and a British Foreign Office official dragged on as the Brigaders were hurriedly transported through France to Liverpool. When they arrived at Liverpool the matter remained unresolved, and a number of Brigaders, on the pretext of seeing relatives in London, now demanded the right to visit the capital before returning to Canada. In the end this amenity was granted on the condition that the proposed demonstration was called off, and all Brigaders were given open tickets to return to Canada. A few, including Ramelson, never made the trip. When he arrived in London Ramelson renewed his local contacts and joined the CPGB. Within a few months he had married and started a new life in Yorkshire.

LESSONS FROM SPAIN

The political background to events in Spain tells us much about the anti-fascist struggle in this period. Encouraged by internal forces of reaction, particularly the big landowners and the Church, Franco also received considerable military and political support from Hitler and Mussolini. The elected Republican Government of Spain, which was committed to modest programmes of social and land reforms to benefit working people in the cities and in the countryside, received no such outside support. The west European democracies, France and Britain, refused to supply arms to the Republicans, despite clear evidence that the fascist powers were heavily arming Franco's side. Only the Soviet Union stood by the Republic, supplying arms, mobilising political and diplomatic support, and encouraging the formation of the International Brigades.

The interviews with Ramelson reveal much about his political thinking. He clearly had no reservations about the role of the communist movement or the Soviet Union in Spain, which he saw as making an extremely positive contribution to the anti-fascist struggle. He is insistent that the Soviet Union provided modern and serviceable arms, and would have provided more but for the activities of the German and French navies in blockading Spanish ports, in enforcement of the so-called non-intervention pact.[15] He was sure that the strategy of mobilising the anti-Franco forces in a single-minded struggle to defend the Republic was the correct one. (This is in contrast to critics, who believed that the Soviet Union could have done more to support the Republicans, and that the Communists should have supported moves towards a more revolutionary government in Spain). Had Franco been defeated, new possibilities for social advance would have opened up, but Ramelson's view was that until this was achieved that nothing should have been attempted that divided the forces loyal to the government, or made it more difficult to mobilise international support against the main enemy, international fascism. Furthermore, he was a supporter of a single army uniting all elements of the anti-fascist movement, and of strict discipline, which he saw as necessary to the achievement of a military victory. He was particularly scathing about the indiscipline among some of the anarchistic elements, particularly when their troops were removed from the front against Franco in order to protect the POUM's (Partido Obrero de Unificación Marxista, or United Marxist Workers' Party) political position in Barcelona against the Republican government's attempts to construct an effective national army. Nonetheless, he includes in his praise the efforts of the Spanish troops and the many anarchists who were prepared to bury political differences in order to defeat Franco. His main political conclusion was that this was a war against fascism, and that the overall aim of British and French diplomacy was to avoid confrontation with Hitler and to encourage the Nazi regime to look eastwards towards the military defeat of the Soviet Union.[16] Without foreign intervention from Germany and Italy, Ramelson argued, the Spanish people would have defeated Franco. Ramelson was clear in 1939 that fascism had to be defeated militarily and politically, and that the Soviet Union had a crucial role in bringing about those objectives.

The left in Spain was internally divided. The anarchists and Trotskyists judged that conditions were ripe for a socialist revolution, and that it was possible to conduct simultaneously both the civil war against Franco and the class war against the capitalist and landlord classes in Spain. The Communists, alongside other political elements that made up the Popular Front Republican government, argued that the first and overriding priority was to defeat Franco, and to do this a broad range of democratic forces had to be mobilised in support of the Republic, both internally and externally, including those who were opposed to socialism. The Communists also argued that the conditions were not ripe for a socialist revolution in Spain, and that the views to the contrary of critics such as George Orwell 'were naïve in the extreme'.[17] This was also Ramelson's view, and has since been backed by Britain's leading academic commentator on Spain, Paul Preston. While critical of aspects of Soviet policy and Communist strategy, Preston has this to say in reviewing Ken Loach's 1995 film *Land and Freedom*,

> Ken Loach simplifies massively in the underlying assumption of the second half of his film that it was the Stalinist repression that led to Franco's victory. Hitler, Mussolini, Franco and Chamberlain were responsible for that victory, not Stalin. Indeed, without Russian arms and the International Brigades, Madrid would probably have fallen in November 1936 and Franco been victorious before the

anarchists and Trotskyists of Barcelona became an issue. Like Orwell before him, Loach has produced something that may stay in the memory more as an anti-Stalinist tract than a celebration of those Spanish and foreign men and women who gave their lives fighting Franco and his Axis allies.[18]

THE SECOND WORLD WAR, 1939-1945

Internationally, the actions of Nazi Germany were driving the world inexorably to war. Following the failure of the British and French governments to support it in forming a military pact against Nazi expansionism, the Soviet Union, in order to protect itself, in August 1939 elected to agree a non-aggression treaty with Germany. This greatly perturbed many in the world communist movement, but the majority, including the British Party, accepted that the Soviets were buying time and attempting to neutralise the threat of immediate attack by Hitler's vastly superior military forces.

We have no record of Ramelson's personal reaction to the Hitler-Stalin Pact, but we do know from a later interview that Ramelson had strong reservations about the anti-fascist nature of the war in its initial stages. Speaking about the policies and actions of the British government at this time, he concluded:

> … it became clear to us that there was a mistaken approach, that unless there was a response by Britain and France particularly to the numerous offers of the Soviet Union for collective security, the outcome was bound to be war. Nor did we have any confidence at all that when Neville Chamberlain declared finally war on Hitler that his intention was really to seriously conduct a war against fascism but rather – as a ploy – continuing in all efforts to switch Hitler's strategy to attacking the Soviet Union. And the nature of the Phoney War, an early part of it, confirmed us in that particular view. And so, particularly when weak as the British Army was at that time … when we weren't in a position even to defend ourselves against Hitler, underlined in my view anyhow – that our analysis was the correct one, that Chamberlain never intended to conduct an anti-fascist war but would still manoeuvre in order to change the war from being a war between the Western Allies and the Axis powers into a German attack on the Soviet Union.

Furthermore:

> … there was no chance of conducting a war on two fronts [i.e.
> against both Hitler and the Chamberlain government], that this was
> an imperialist war primarily [and] that the British government would
> not fight Hitler but would encourage Hitler to wage the war against
> the Soviet Union.

From this it is clear that Ramelson supported, as did many other
British Communists, the Soviet view that the failure of the major
European imperialist powers, Britain and France, to join a collective
security pact with the Soviet Union indicated that if war were to break
out it would not be an anti-fascist one. [19]

Ramelson's views changed as events unfolded – rather faster than
those of the Party leadership. Once the Churchill-Attlee coalition was
in place in 1940, clearly determined to defeat Hitler, Ramelson felt
that the phoney war stage had finished and that the line should have
changed to reflect this. In the event it was to take Hitler's attack on the
Soviet Union to convince the CPGB as a whole that the war was an
anti-fascist one, to be fought unreservedly, and with full support given
to the British government's efforts to cement the alliance between the
UK, the USA, and the USSR. [20]

By 1941 Ramelson, then thirty-one, was eligible for military
service, having spent two years in Britain. He was called up in May
1941, trained as a tank driver and mechanic for a few months, made
a lance-corporal, and then posted to Cairo in October 1941. After a
disastrous desert campaign near Tobruk, Ramelson, with thousands
of other British troops, was captured by the German Army in
September 1941, and spent the next six months in an Italian-run
desert prison camp, where he almost starved and hundreds of his
fellow prisoners died of dysentery. In these appalling conditions
Ramelson, on his own initiative, organised political education classes
for the prisoners. He gave a lecture on Marxism every morning, and
his captive audience grew from a handful to over two thousand in a
matter of weeks. Ramelson later described this as a 'very inspiring
period' of his life. But it did not stop there. After a short while other
groups were set up – Salvation Army, religious cranks and so on, such
that at their peak there were some dozen different meetings going on
all the time. Out of this Ramelson built a Communist Party branch

of some dozen comrades, and the collective was able to develop a number of projects, encouraging the prisoners themselves to participate by giving talks on 'My Town' or 'My Job'. Ramelson recalls in particular a week's series on 'Britain after the War', where prisoners were asked to express their views on the sort of country they would like to return to and rebuild. He described this as 'the most fascinating series I have ever heard'. He was also able to call a meeting to which the whole camp turned out, to mark 7 November, the anniversary of the Russian Revolution.[21]

Writing some years later, Marian Ramelson introduced her groundbreaking work on the history of women's struggle for equal rights, *Petticoat Rebellion*, with a few paragraphs that described aspects of women's experience. The passage quoted below shows that the battle for equality had a long way to go, but is also a vivid testament to the democratic sprit of camp debates:

> There were thousands of Allied prisoners in a PoW [prisoner of war] camp in North Africa after the fall of Tobruk. The camp was a large fenced-in area of desert without amenities. Food and water were in famine supply. Three hundred men died. Demoralisation began to spread more infectiously than any plague.
>
> Two men discussed what could be done to counteract this, the most menacing thing to the very survival of life. The only help that could be summoned to aid were those in the human body and mind. It was agreed to put these to organising lectures, debates, discussions, anything which could be devised that could stretch men's minds beyond the miseries of the day and thereby build up hope again.
>
> Within a short time, thousands and thousands were attending these events which lasted hours and hours at a time. Every subject under the sun was discussed. India gained her freedom, racial intolerance was condemned, a brave new world was projected for after the war, but one subject was resolutely thumbed down: 'That woman was equal to man and could enjoy the same rights'.
>
> This contributor to discussion got vociferous support from all sides for his view that 'he was going to have his wife at home when he came in from a hard day's work, with his slippers warming by the fire, his meal ready and on the table, and his children bathed, fresh as paint and ready for a good-night kiss'.[22]

One of the two men organising these morale-raising and life-saving discussions was, of course, Marian's husband Bert.

From these experiences Ramelson learnt many lessons – that some British troops were receptive to socialist ideas and wanted radical change after the war. More importantly he learnt that participation developed skills, confidence and morale, and that working-class people, given the opportunity, had unlimited capacities for personal development. He summed it up like this: 'One of the periods that led to my own development as well as a real appreciation of the potentialities of humanity was developed during that period in the prisoner of war camp'.[23]

As Montgomery's Army began to turn the tide in North Africa, following the victory at El Alamein, so the Italians became increasingly nervous and began preparations to evacuate thousands of prisoners from the desert to Italy. The trip from Tripoli to Palermo was sheer hell. Packed in cargo ships, and deprived of adequate food and clothing, the men also suffered the taunts of the Italian ratings who used food to exchange for the few possessions, including clothes, that the prisoners had. Once they disembarked at Palermo, the ordinary Sicilian people lined the streets and rushed towards the prisoners to give them bread, tomatoes and fruit.

In Southern Italy the camp conditions were far better than Ramelson had experienced in the African desert. Again he was in the forefront in organising education and other activities, helping to raise morale and solve any problems or disputes in a socially disciplined way. With British troops crossing into Sicily the prison camp at Torhuna was broken up, and the prisoners taken north to Ancona on the Adriatic Coast. There Ramelson found an active Communist Party Branch in the prison camp, a well as a left group, leading the same kind of activity he himself had started in the desert. By this time, in early 1943, the Italian Army was being driven north, and the mainly communist-led partisans were increasingly active fighting for their country's liberation from fascism. Ramelson, whose Italian was now at least serviceable, found out in discussion with the guards that mass desertions were taking place throughout the Italian Army, including amongst the guards themselves. It soon became clear that the camp was inadequately policed, and after a Party Branch discussion it was decided that the time was ripe for a mass breakout. This was put to an open meeting of the prisoners, and it was agreed to carry out the attempt the next morning. The senior officer, a lieutenant colonel, then broadcast over the tannoy system an instruction to the men not to breakout, on the threat of a court martial. The broadcast was widely ignored, and Ramelson and thousands of his fellow prisoners walked out of the camp. Of the two thousand that escaped, most were rounded up by the German troops within forty-eight hours of the break out.

Ramelson was one of a small group determined to walk south to join up with the British Army, which was fighting its way north from Sicily. However, both the British Army and the escapees made slow progress, and it took over three months and 400 miles of walking from village to village, often at night, to link up with British forces. During this time Ramelson and his small group relied heavily on Italian peasants to feed and shelter them. Eventually, and accidentally, Ramelson made contact with the Italian partisans and the Communist Party, and was reunited with the British Army at Foggio. He was then sent back to England by ship, via Tripoli and Greenock.

In reflecting on his experience as a prisoner of war Ramelson later said:

> I sometimes – thinking over my experiences in the camp and what I did there – think that I owe the greatest debt of all to my feeling for the party, because if I didn't feel that as a communist I could face the Communist Party if I behaved in the way which I was tempted to more than once – driven by hunger, to participate in the fiddles that were going on in the camp in order to get some extra food – if it hadn't been for this powerful feeling within me that I belonged to a party that I couldn't face if I had acted in such an unprincipled way, and if I didn't feel as a communist it was my duty to do all I could in order to help my fellow prisoners of war to understand what it is that makes people misbehave. It's not because of their nature. But it's the circumstances that force them into behaving as they do. If they were capable they would withstand the temptation. And the temptations were very strong – particularly the temptations of hunger – to overcome. And you must feel some very strong powerful allegiance to a concept and to an idea to be able to withstand these temptations.
>
> And for me it was membership of the party. And for that I'm eternally grateful to the party, that my feelings as a communist helped me to overcome the temptations that I had more than once.
>
> I think it changed me primarily in strengthening my communist

philosophy in a sense, not that I learnt more Marxism, except you learn from all experiences to underline a philosophy or reject it. To me it underlined everything, the behaviour of people and how market conditions can change people's attitudes and so on, how a market can arise even, and so on.

But above all what it did for me was it developed me in the sense of ... making me more confident and being able to express my ideas. I had a lot of experience, and I was forced into it so to speak. But most of all it enhanced my appreciation of the limitless capacities ordinary people have, that can flourish given the opportunities. And that is really the basis of confidence in the future. Once the people are given the opportunity ... and to have seen in the camp ordinary lads who wouldn't normally ... would be afraid to say five words in public ... who didn't have any confidence in themselves, but encouraged and given the opportunity there, flourishing out and able to use language to describe their love of their town in that series, or the intricacies of the job and the joy of a job well done of a craftsman, whatever the skill happened to be ... [that] was a tremendous experience which gives one confidence in the future of mankind.[24]

Ramelson's lectures clearly made a lasting impression on at least one 'student'. Writing to a local newspaper over twenty years later, when Ramelson's name appeared on every front page of the national press in connection with the 1966 seafarers' strike, a correspondent had this to say:

The Prime Minister and others seem to be all against the Communist Bert Ramelson. Allow me to say something in his favour. Ramelson was a PoW in the same camp as myself and many other Tees-siders. They can all verify that his lively political debates were the only thing we had to pass our time away and if we had all had half his 'guts' we would have followed his lead and broken out of the camp by over-powering the guards, as Bert was always wanting the prisoners to do.

He couldn't possibly remember me, but I most certainly remember him in his Tank Corps beret and old pair of faded shorts talking to whole crowds of PoWs where our duty lay and that was to overpower the lot and take over the camp. I refer to the Tarhuna camp.

'Long Memory', Middlesbrough [25]

BACK IN THE ARMY, 1945-6

After two months leave Ramelson was sent to Catterick to be trained as an artillery officer. He stayed there for a year and graduated as a Second Lieutenant (Royal Artillery). He was then sent to Bishop Auckland training centre, and during this period spoke on several general election platforms in support of local Labour candidates. In August 1945 he was sent to India, where he was posted to Deolali as a legal officer, and soon after was appointed Acting Staff Captain (Legal), where his role was mainly to defend troops charged by the Army with disciplinary offences.

Deolali was in essence a large transit camp dealing with both new troops assigned to Asia and the Far East and demobilised troops who had finished their tours of duty in these theatres. It also had a Forces Parliament in which not surprisingly, Ramelson soon became a leading force. In this Parliament the government was a left coalition (Communist and Labour) and around a thousand troops attended the twice-weekly open-air sessions. Ramelson recalled an incident involving John Saville, who later became an influential Marxist history professor and for a while was a member of the Yorkshire District CP at the same time as Ramelson was the District Secretary (see chapter two). Saville passed through Deolali on his way back to Britain having been demobilised from Karachi. At the time a small number of British service people, including some CP members, were being court-martialled for mutiny after pressing for demobilisation now that the war was over.[26] The question of Indian independence was also high on the political agenda and it was widely felt that demobilisation was being delayed in case of civil unrest erupting in support of claims made by Indian political leaders which the British ruling class was not yet prepared to concede. The two questions – demobilisation of British service people and Indian independence – were intertwined and the impatient Saville wanted to know from his fellow communist (Ramelson) what action he was going to propose to the troops at Deolali in support of the Indian people and the Karachi 'mutineers'. This seemed to Ramelson to be an adventurist position to take and he pressed Saville for ideas as to how such a campaign could be launched and sustained with the prospect of success without exposing rank-and-file service people to the threat of reprisals from the authorities. When Ramelson, as Minister Without Portfolio in the Forces Parliament and therefore responsible for the business agenda of that body, suggested a debate in support of immediate and full independence for the Indian people, Saville pooh-poohed the proposal as idle talk when action was required. The pity is that the impatient young Regimental Sergeant Major who could have had little inkling of the political level of the troops in Deolali had no proposals to make of his own and they parted soon after with Saville returning to England. The Parliament duly carried the independence motion by an overwhelming majority but within days and as a direct result of this resolution it was closed down by the British authorities.[27]

While in India Ramelson took the opportunity to get to know the Communist Party leadership. The Communist Party of India (CPI) leadership lived in a commune in what was then Bombay and most weekends Ramelson would use his leave to visit the Indian comrades for discussions on contemporary political issues particularly that of independence and self-government for the Indian people. He was in regular correspondence with D.N. Pritt MP, the well-known lawyer who specialised in colonial liberation issues and Willie Gallacher the Communist MP who by then was an experienced Parliamentarian. He raised with the MPs questions concerning independence and asked them to intercede to support his campaign to re-open the Deolali Parliament.

He was also in correspondence with Palme Dutt, the British Party's leading authority on India and all colonial issues. Dutt was highly regarded both by the Indian Party and by Ramelson himself, who was an avid reader of Dutt's monthly journal, *Labour Monthly*, during his formative years in Canada. In discussion with the Indian comrades, particularly General Secretary Joshi, Ramelson found that a big difference had arisen between the Indian and British parties on the future of India as an independent, self-governed country. Dutt supported the position adopted by Nehru and the Congress Party, which was for a strong centralised administration. Joshi and his comrades were convinced that the best way forward was to recognize the great diversities of language, history and culture, particularly religion, within the Indian people and to reflect this in a confederal constitution with extensive powers devolved to regional assemblies. This was particularly necessary to accommodate Moslem aspirations and the fear that this sizeable minority could be dominated by the Hindu majority. These arguments convinced Ramelson at the time and he entered into a long correspondence with Dutt, acting as a direct voice for the Indian comrades. His and their arguments fell on stony ground and less than two years later the tragic bloodshed which accompanied partition, followed by establishing a separate Muslim state, Pakistan, had occurred.[28]

It was during his discussions with Joshi that the question of Ramelson's plans for his future life in England came up. At this time Ramelson received a letter from the Yorkshire CP District Secretary, Mick Bennett, offering him full-time Party position as Leeds Area Secretary. Ramelson had his doubts about the wisdom of accepting such a position. His wife Marian was a Party full-time worker in Yorkshire and by this time they had been married for seven years. So he had a good idea of what the job involved. It is not clear what his doubts included. It could have been money (Party wages were way below average industrial earnings), or more likely it was the strains that such an arrangement might put on his marriage, with both partners working in the same pressurised environment. Joshi quickly made up Ramelson's mind for him. He asked a rhetorical question. 'You are being asked to become a professional revolutionary, to work full-time for the Communist movement in its efforts to emancipate the whole of humanity – and you hesitate?'[29]

In India, as at every other stage of his adult life, Ramelson immersed himself in the political struggles of the people around him. In every situation he offered leadership and steadfast solidarity without making adventurist gestures. He always sought out his fellow-communists for advice and support knowing that it was collective strength and discussion which produced the best guide to action and the best available decisions.

In any event, the British military authorities had become pretty fed up with the articulate lawyer who had the contacts and skills to raise difficult questions about their conduct with British MPs. So a few months after the Deolali Parliament closure Ramelson was back in Britain, demobilised on 6 May 1946.

NOTES

1. A counter-revolutionary force drawn from dissident sections of the Tsarist Imperial Army and supported with military supplies and finance by the governments of Britain and France.
2. Imperial War Museum tapes.
3. Bickerstaffe tapes.
4. The best single account of this period remains Carr, E. *The Bolshevik Revolution,* Penguin 1973.

5. Imperial War Museum tapes.

6. *Edmonton Journal*, 29/6/66; and correspondence with the Edmonton archivist.

7. At this time Palestine was administered by British authorities under a mandate issued by the UN.

8. Imperial War Museum tapes.

9. Palme Dutt was the CPGB's leading theoretician from the 1920s to the 1960s. He is the subject of an ungenerous biography, Callaghan, J. *Rajani Palme Dutt, a Study in British Stalinism*, Lawrence & Wishart, London 1993.

10. Imperial War Museum tapes.

11. Branson, N. *History of the Communist Party of Great Britain 1927–1941*, Lawrence & Wishart, London 1985, p. 157 for an explanation of the dual membership phenomenon, a policy which was abandoned at the outbreak of war in 1939.

12. This period of Ramelson's life is recorded in extensive interviews carried out both by Rodney Bickerstaffe and by archivists at the Imperial War museum.

13. Bill Alexander was Commander of the British Battalion and author of *British Volunteers for Liberty – Spain 1936–1939*, Lawrence & Wishart, London 1982. He later became Assistant General Secretary to the CPGB and did much to keep the memory of the British Battalion's contribution to the anti-fascist struggle alive, particularly through the International Brigade Memorial Trust.

14. Jim McCrorie, a Canadian academic, recalls how Ramelson warned his comrades against assuming that they would be welcomed back to Canada by the authorities. See Beeching, C. *Canadian Volunteers – Spain 1936-1939*, Canadian Plains Research Centre 1989. In his e-mail to us of 10/10/2009, Jim McCrorie quotes from the book, 'Many volunteers believed that Ottawa was sympathetic to their predicament but Bert Ramelson argued, 'The Canadian Government is not our friend … You who came to Spain should know and understand that' (p. 190).

15. Graham, H. *The Spanish Civil War*, Oxford University Press, Oxford 2005.

16. In Ramelson's view, the civil war in Spain was in fact the opening of the war in Europe, and that victory for the Republic would have decisively changed the political and military balance of forces against Hitlerism (Imperial War Museum tapes).

17. Alexander, W. 'George Orwell and Spain' in Norris, C. *Inside the Myth: Orwell: Views from the Left*, Lawrence & Wishart, London 1984, p. 100.

18. 'Spanish Civil War' by Paul Preston, *New Statesman*: 16/2/1996. There is a voluminous bibliography on the Spanish Civil War. The Communist perspective is outlined by Bill Alexander 1982 op.cit., and in Agosti, A. *Palmiro Togliatti, a Biography*, I. B. Taurus, London, 2008. Togliatti was the Comintern's representative in Spain for most of the Civil War period. The

best non-Communist but not anti-Communist account is probably Preston, P. *A Concise History of the Spanish Civil War,* Fontana, London 1996.

19. This and the Comintern-encouraged change of line by the British Party about the nature of the war is still highly contested in the Communist movement. Monty Johnstone, a strong critic of the British party's position, nonetheless accepts the case of the Soviet Union in signing the German-Soviet Non-Aggression Pact. At a conference organised by the Communist Party History group in April 1979, he argued, 'The Soviet Union felt itself obliged, in my opinion correctly, to conclude with Nazi Germany a Non-Aggression Pact on 23 August 1939, because it did not want to find itself in a position where it was left by the western powers to fight on its own against Nazi Germany when it was not sufficiently prepared militarily to do so. Therefore the German-Soviet Non-Aggression Pact of August 1939 was essentially a diplomatic agreement designed to gain time for the Soviet Union to prevent itself from being put in that kind of position'. At the same conference Dave Priscott presented a paper which strongly supported Ramelson's position that during the phoney-war period (from September 1939 - May 1940) the war was in essence an inter-imperialist war. Monty Johnstone came to a different conclusion and argued that from the start of the war the only guarantee of defeating Hitler was an allied victory. Many comrades, including Ramelson, having seen the betrayal of the Spanish Republic as recently as 1938 by the British and French governments, were not at the time convinced by this argument. For inner-Party debate consult Attfield, J. and Williams, S. (eds) *1939 The Communist Party and the War,* Lawrence & Wishart, London 1984. See also Branson 1985 op.cit. chapters 18-24 and Morgan, K. *Against Fascism and War,* Manchester University Press, 1989.

20. Imperial War Museum tapes.

21. Imperial War Museum and Bickerstaffe tapes.

22. Ramelson, M. *The Petticoat Rebellion: a Century of Struggle for Women's Rights.* Lawrence & Wishart, London 1976, p. 15.

23. Imperial War Museum tapes.

24. Ibid.

25. An unsigned letter to the *Middlesborough Gazette,* July 1966. Ramelson family papers.

26. Duncan, D. *Mutiny in the RAF: The Air Force Strikes of 1946.* Social History Society Occasional Paper No.8, 1998.

27. Imperial War Museum tapes. Saville recalls the same incident with fewer details and no mention of his own role. See Saville, J. *Memoirs from the Left,* Merlin 2003, p. 72.

28. Beckett tapes and Ramelson family papers. Interview by Francis Beckett with Bert Ramelson, 1992, and Kisch 1985 op.cit. pp. 121-122.

29. Beckett tapes.

2. Life in Yorkshire, 1946-1965

STARTING OUT

Ramelson met Marian Jessop soon after he arrived in Britain, and within months they had married. Marian was the daughter of a Leeds Labour councillor and a leading CP activist in the town. Before Bert had joined up in the Second World War the Ramelsons had settled in Yorkshire, and it was to Yorkshire that Bert returned after the war.

Ramelson had also been introduced to a Marks & Spencer director shortly after arriving in Britain in 1939, at a time when the company was recruiting International Brigaders (mainly British of course), which it saw as 'good-for-business anti-Nazi politics'. Ramelson, who was penniless, took up the offer, starting on the shop floor at their Huddersfield store, before being rapidly promoted to become under-manager at a Bradford store. He had quickly made his mark in retail management, but had also joined the Shop Assistants Union, and tried to build a union branch, a task made more difficult by the company's paternalist anti-union attitude towards staff relationships.

The Ramelsons had soon become great friends with Colin Siddons and his wife, having met when Siddons, a newly married young physics teacher and active CP member, had been sacked from his job after being jailed for making allegedly subversive statements at an open air public meeting in June 1940. On his release from jail Bert had appointed Colin Siddons to the grand position of under-porter at the Bradford store, and there the two men had spent many happy hours, discussing politics and Marxist theory in the store's storage cellar, from where they organised distribution of the *Daily Worker* for the Bradford and Leeds area.[1] Ramelson therefore had had some political experience in Yorkshire before he joined up, both as a trade unionist and a Party member.

Post-war Britain was full of political optimism, with a Labour government carrying through a generally progressive programme (apart from foreign policy matters, where the old Foreign Office imperialist policies – including anti-semitism – were faithfully carried out by Labour's Ernest Bevin). The Communist Party had also had a good war, at least from the time that the Soviet Union became an ally in June 1941. From then until the beginnings of the Cold War in 1947-8, links with the Soviet Union had become an attractive recruitment aid. So when Ramelson returned to civvy street, prospects for the left looked good – better in fact than at any time since the Party's founding in 1920. It is not surprising therefore that when the Party offered him a full-time position as Leeds Area Secretary Ramelson accepted it. Now he was a fully-fledged professional revolutionary, and the new role suited him very nicely. This was of course largely new territory for him, and in the beginning he relied very much on the political and organisational support of Marian.[2]

Here he was rubbing shoulders with experienced trade unionists from important industries such as engineering and textiles. Ramelson was a good listener and a quick learner, with bags of confidence in his own abilities and judgement. So he quickly found his feet, both in the Party and in the Shop Workers' Union, where he soon became a delegate to national conferences. It was in Leeds that Ramelson established himself as an outstanding outdoor orator, with a regular weekly pitch on the Town Hall steps. Older comrades still mention these meetings, the crowds they attracted and the audience participation, including the heckling that Ramelson elicited and encouraged. Indeed Bert's stepson, Richard Craven, recalls that, when he was a youngster, groups of secondary school children used to go along and wonder at the power of the oratory and the theatre of the occasion.[3]

At this time the Party's main efforts were directed toward the peace campaign. This became doubly urgent as the Cold War deepened and the race to further develop nuclear weapons accelerated. Any illusions that the Party leadership had previously entertained concerning the continuing viability of the war-time pact between the three allies were quickly shattered, as British Labour ministers now presented the Soviet Union as the main threat to world peace, and world communism as the biggest single danger to British imperialist interests across the globe. During the early years of the Cold War, launched by US President Truman in 1947, anti-communism became the dominant ideology in both the United States and Britain.[4] The imperialist powers strove to hold back the national liberation movement in colonial countries and the left in the advanced capitalist countries – which was in many places led by the Communist Party, with considerable mass backing, particularly in the trade unions. Anti-communism was a set of ideas and values that was backed by all arms of the state and supported by wider sections of the media and organised religion, and was used to attack and demonise the Communist movement and its allies on the left. In a statement recommending to affiliated unions that they ban Communists from holding office, the British Trade Union Congress (TUC) General Council justified limitation on members' rights by describing communists as foreign agents who worked to enslave England.[5] The *Daily Herald*, then the organ of the Labour Party, used more lurid language the communist 'wants to make all his countrymen into the helpless and blindly obedient vassals of a foreign power … [the communist] is a "dangerous microbe"'.[6] This may be risible stuff, but such was the intensity of the ruling-class offensive, backed and sometimes led by the official labour movement, and it was bound to make the job of a Communist organiser much more complicated than it might have been. For Ramelson, within a period of less than three years, the promise of 1945 had turned into an anti-communist offensive designed to isolate and marginalise the Party he was trying to build as an integral part of the labour movement.

The increased tension was of course greatly exacerbated by the outbreak of the Korean War in 1950. The British political establishment, backed by a compliant mass media, made the civil war in Korea a pretext for beefing up its anti-Communist, anti-Soviet campaign. The United States and Britain intervened militarily with land, sea and air forces in support of the American-sponsored government of South Korea. On 9 July 1950 the CPGB issued the following statement. 'The Executive Committee of the Communist Party condemns the American invasion of Korea carried out with British armed support and assistance, and sends its warm greetings to the Korean people in their heroic fight for independence'.[7] This strongly anti-imperialist policy was not widely supported by the British people, but this did not deter Ramelson from taking the issue to the people of Yorkshire in a series of open-air and factory gate meetings, where he explained that the Soviet Union was proposing an immediate ceasefire in Korea and universal nuclear disarmament, while the US administration was waging war on foreign territory. In these meetings Ramelson faced strong heckling and some threats of violence. He stood his ground in order to get the peace message across, and to counter the anti-communism spread by Labour politicians and the press.[8]

THE RAMELSON TEAM AND UNION POLITICS

Marian Ramelson was a formidable political figure. She was an outstanding organiser who had trained at the Lenin School in Moscow during the 1930s, and had grown up in the Leeds labour movement, as the daughter of Tom Jessop, an Amalgamated Engineering Union (AEU) stalwart and Labour councillor. With her experience, her steadfast attention to detail, and her leading position as a member of the Party's National Executive Committee, Marian was able to provide Ramelson with both guidance and support, particularly in his early years as a Party full-time worker.[9] She also remained an important political figure in her own right, particularly in campaigns for women's rights.

Both Ramelsons were leading rank-and-file trade union activists in the shop workers' union, the National Union of Distributive and Allied Workers (NUDAW) which became USDAW in 1947, during the late 1940s and most of the 1950s. Each was regularly elected by their branch to attend the union's annual policy-making conference, at which Bert, in particular, was a regular speaker, putting the left's views on a range of issues, from the wages struggle, to peace and disarmament, and share ownership of the *Daily Worker*. Many of his speeches to conference are reproduced in full in the union's journal, *New Dawn*.[10] Without exception they are powerful, no-holds-barred presentations of the Party line, challenging any attempts by the union's leadership to support wage restraint, or British foreign policy when it was used to pursue colonialist and imperialist objectives. What is striking in these reports is Ramelson's ability to link the wages issue with attempts to build union membership – in Ramelson's experience in Leeds, wage restraint and acceptance of Wages Council rates as maximums rather than minimums was responsible for creating difficulties in recruiting new members and retaining existing ones.

Not surprisingly the Ramelsons were also prominent in conference debates on anti-communism, a topic which featured regularly both at conference and in the correspondence columns of *New Dawn*. This was a direct consequence of the TUC General Council's campaign, encouraged by the Labour Party leadership, to isolate the Communists by introducing bans and proscriptions, preventing them from holding union positions. In these debates Bert was not at his diplomatic best. Clearly annoyed at the underlying assumptions of the campaign (that in some way communists were anti-union and anti-British), he gave the delegates the full force of his views. He told them: 'Every time you move something progressive they [the leadership] wave the red hand-kerchief and immediately the lot of you are sticking your hands up and betraying your real interests'.[11] This would have been delivered, as all Ramelson's speeches were, in a loud voice and with assertive body language to accompany it. It was no doubt in the same rhetorical style that Ramelson opposed the TUC General Council's splitting activities – for reasons of Cold War realpolitik – within what was at the time a united international trade union movement, the World Federation of Trade Unions (WFTU). According to Ramelson:

> The reason we have left the WFTU is not because we have suddenly discovered we cannot work with the Russians, and not because the Russians are dominating the WFTU. The reason we have withdrawn is because they [the TUC leadership] get their orders from America.

One of Ramelson's shrewdest contemporaries, Beryl Huffingley, recalls that Bert's forceful presentation often failed to win the middle ground in debates. In union conferences Marian was a more effective speaker, and between them they were a very formidable political presence.[12]

Ramelson lost the vote on all the issues opposing TUC and Labour Party policy that he spoke on – usually by around 3:1. That is until the 1950 conference, when he successfully moved a motion to condemn the Executive Committee for having voted for the TUC General Council position at a Special Conference of Union Executives, even though their policy stance contradicted USDAW Conference policy, which opposed further wage restraint. Clearly this was a substantial victory for the left on the central issue for the bulk of members, and was of the utmost political importance for the whole of the labour movement. Indeed it was on wages policy that Ramelson carried most influence with USDAW conference delegates.

In 1947 he spoke in favour of a motion supporting a National Wage Policy, which included demands for equal pay for women, controls on prices and profits and increased wages – an embryonic alternative economic strategy. By 1948 the fog of Cold War obscurantism had descended. The USDAW General Secretary, Walter Padley, spelt it out at the 1949 Annual General Meeting (AGM):

> many of the rank and file Communists are innocent of evil intent but the leaders of Cominform know that in an expanding socialist democracy the doctrine of the police state will make no headway … it is my profound hope that when the second majority Labour Government comes in 1950 we shall witness the decisive changeover from capitalism to socialism.[13]

The implications were clear enough to delegates – the evil forces of international communism were out to destroy Labour's attempts to build socialism in Britain, and good comrades like Ramelson were merely dupes in a wider struggle they simply did not understand. It is perhaps no wonder that someone of Ramelson's intellect should have felt insulted in being patronised by Padley's assertions. The reality was that Padley's 'expanding' socialist democracy was going nowhere, and the Attlee government was instead creating the conditions for thirteen years of Tory rule.

Ramelson was able to work within the union structures to create a good base for trade union and political activity in West Yorkshire. In the early 1950s he was elected Second Vice President of Leeds Trades Council, which he represented on the West Yorkshire County Association of Trades Councils; and he quickly won an elected position to the County Associations Executive Committee, a development which did not escape the TUC Head Office anti-communist dragnet operation. Vic Feather, later to become TUC General Secretary, was an enthusiastic and effective witch-hunter. He set about trying to persuade the County Association to throw Ramelson off its Executive Committee.[14] In so doing he was fighting above his weight. Ramelson used his political and legal skills to outmanoeuvre the TUC, and remained as an EC member of the County Association until he chose to stand down several years later.

DEVELOPING INDUSTRIAL WORK

Confident that it was moving into a new and much more favourable political environment, characterised by the UN's ethos of co-operation not conflict, the Party saw prospects for significant electoral advance and a new relationship with Labour in the early post-war years. During this time the Party failed to prioritise industrial work, concentrating instead on building its electoral base in the towns and cities, rather than in building new factory branches and strengthening existing ones.[15] By the late 1940s this error had been rectified, and Ramelson was quick to recognise that the big workplaces could become the centres of political struggles that were much wider than those traditionally engaged in by trade unionists. So he welcomed the turn to industry as he served his political apprenticeship in Leeds.

By 1953 Ramelson was a well known figure in most areas of the Yorkshire labour movement, and it was in this year, at the age of forty-three, that he was appointed as the Secretary of the Yorkshire District Committee of the Communist Party, a position which more or less guaranteed him an elected position on the Party's Executive Committee and its inner cabinet, the Political Committee. Ramelson's contemporaries recall that the Yorkshire District Office was a busy centre of political activity, with the energetic Ramelson at its heart.[16] There was a full-time staff of eight, and the political leadership was immersed in the struggles of the time, in particular in the efforts to build both the peace and trade union movements. Bill Moore, the Party's West Yorkshire District Secretary in the 1950s, recalled that one of his main jobs was to build a union in the woollen industry, commenting: 'This was Bert's strength – working with the unions'.[17]

Ramelson often referred to Yorkshire as a centre of Britain's main industries during the post-war years.[18] With the largest coalfield in the UK, the metals and general engineering industries in Sheffield and Leeds, and textiles in Bradford, Yorkshire certainly was the base for large and well organised workplaces. The potential here for Communist activity and left advance was apparent to Ramelson from the day he became District Secretary.

Ramelson readily acknowledged his debt to the many experienced communist industrial cadres with whom he had worked. Such comrades in Yorkshire had developed their skills in the harsh industrial climate of the 1920s and 1930s, and then in the special conditions pertaining in wartime, and were able to guide and assist Ramelson, particularly in his early years as District Secretary. One comrade in particular stands out as a key influence – Jock Kane, who was the outstanding miners' rank-and-file leader of his generation. Kane had taken part in the successful campaign against the breakaway Spencer union during the 1930s, and would go on to become leader of the 1969 coalfield-wide unofficial strike in Yorkshire, which in many ways was the precursor of the national strike of 1972. Throughout his time in Yorkshire Ramelson relied on Kane's advice and judgement.[19]

During his early years as District Secretary, Ramelson constantly called for the elevation of the political struggle, arguing that by boldly campaigning on issues such as peace, disarmament and women's rights, as well as on economic issues, the left, far from being isolated, would become more rooted in the movement. This is an early instance of Ramelson's long-running campaign to end the dominance of economism, which limited the movement's ambitions to the day-to-day concerns of wages and conditions. In 1955, for example, he highlighted a glaring weakness in the Party's industrial work, telling District Congress delegates: 'we must use our influences to turn the attention of the labour movement as a whole to start paying serious attention to the special problems affecting women'.[20] The central political message was twofold –eschew economism by campaigning on political as well as economic issues, and build the revolutionary party: 'the class struggle cannot destroy capitalism to build socialism – a revolutionary party is needed to co-ordinate and guide the class struggle with the sole aim of enabling the working class to seize power'. He argued that in Britain a united working-class party based on Marxism would only come about if there was a strong CP capable of fundamentally influencing the broader labour and trade union movement. These political tenets were the basis of Ramelson's politics until he died – the relevance of an influential Marxist political party, the necessity of revolution, the need to tackle economism and reformism, and the vital importance of unity and struggle. On left unity he had this to say at the Congress:

> We must dispel the illusion that a great expansion of left forces is possible without a larger CP ... and that with new leadership the Labour Party can be a revolutionary party. Unless we grasp that only a strong CP can lay the basis eventually for a united working class party based on Marxism, we will not help the development of unity.[21]

THE YORKSHIRE MINERS

In the most important areas, the pits and the National Union of Mineworkers (NUM), political progress was being made, although sometimes this was uneven and contradictory. For example, though two new Peace Committees had been established at pit level, the Yorkshire miners voted in favour of German re-armament at their conference. However, an industrial base was eventually laid for future struggles led by the left, and for the emergence of a new and progressive leadership, and Ramelson and Kane were at the centre of all these positive developments.

In 1953, on the initiative of the General Secretary Harry Pollitt, the Party had taken the decision to redouble efforts to strengthen its industrial base, and as part of this decision to appoint additional full-time workers in coalfield areas.[22] This meant that Yorkshire soon benefited from the appointment of Frank Watters, a Scottish miner with considerable political experience under his belt, and Monty Meth, a Young Communist League (YCL) leader in London, who was later to become industrial editor of the *Daily Worker*. These appointments reflected Ramelson's strategic view about the role that the Yorkshire coalfield could play in helping to change the face of British politics. His views had been put to the Party's District Congress in 1953: if the Yorkshire Area of the NUM, a long-standing bastion of right-wing dominance and the largest NUM area in membership terms, could be won for the left, then the political direction of the national union would change, and this in turn would be reflected in the TUC, and in Labour Party Conference decisions. This was a task for the broad left. It could not be carried through by the Party alone.

To carry through this strategy and to implement his general broad left approach, Ramelson could call on the experience of a number of outstanding rank-and-file leaders, and in mining he relied very much on Jock Kane. Soon after nationalisation in January 1947, Kane had been offered a manager's job as National Coal Board (NCB) labour officer for the Doncaster area, the biggest NCB area in Britain with the biggest output. However he had soon become disillusioned with the NCB, realising that the new coal board management were behaving in a very similar way to the previous individual owners. He described his three years there as 'the most disillusioning three years I ever spent in my bloody life'.[23] After his short spell at the NCB Kane returned to his job as a miner, and after years of patient work he became the first Communist to be elected to a full-time position in the Yorkshire NUM. His experience at the Coal Board no doubt influenced

Ramelson's later views about the limitations of worker participation proposals within capitalist society.

Tommy Degnan was another important influence. Like Ramelson he had fought in Spain, where he had served with distinction in the Political Commissariat of the No. 3 Company, British Brigade, and had suffered serious injuries to his lungs. Degnan had joined the Party in 1925 as a working miner, had attended the Lenin School in Moscow between 1931 and 1933, and before going to Spain he had been active in the Unemployed Workers Movement.[24] In 1945 he was elected as Branch Secretary of the Barnsley Party, and as the NUM Branch Secretary. In 1953 Degnan was able to advise Ramelson on his leaflet calling on miners to campaign for higher wages and a shorter working week, as part of his strategy for mobilising Yorkshire miners. Degnan suggested a number of amendments, including correcting some mistakes in the draft about procedure. This is just one example of an experienced comrade who was able and willing to assist the new Party District Secretary: one of Ramelson's strengths was his ability to harness the many talents around him and help put them to work to advance the cause of peace and socialism.

Clashes between the left-led pits in Yorkshire and the region's right-wing NUM leadership sharpened during the 1950s. In her autobiography of Arthur Horner, Nina Fishman attributed much of this renewed militancy to the Yorkshire leadership of the Communist Party, and in particular to Ramelson, Kane and Watters.[25] She goes on to describe how a dispute which began at Kane's Markham Pit spread to cover most pits in South Yorkshire, as they deployed what the local press described as 'flying squads' of pickets conveyed by convoys of cars. Thus the flying picket was born out of the struggles of the 1950s Yorkshire miners, to reappear on the national scene during the 1972 miners' strike, most notably at Saltley South coking depot in Birmingham orchestrated by Watters and Arthur Scargill.[26]

The increased industrial militancy was matched by advances for left political policies in the pits. In 1956, for example, the 140,000-strong Yorkshire Area rejected the strong advice of the union's national leadership, and voted for Aneurin Bevan against George Brown as Labour Party Treasurer. On a CP initiative, pit-based peace organisations spearheaded the campaign against the 'H' Bomb. Membership in the pits grew steadily in this period, as Ramelson, Kane and Watters worked to strengthen Communist organisation at pit and union level.

Mining Advisories (see chapter three) were organised to cover all the main pits, and to include all Communists elected as union council delegates. A Yorkshire District Advisory met monthly, with Ramelson and Watters in attendance and Ramelson ensured that broad political campaigns as well as internal union affairs (including elections to leading positions) featured prominently on the agenda.

The fruits of this work became manifest during the early 1970s. Ably led by Sammy Taylor (then Compensation Agent) and Jock Kane (Financial Secretary), the Yorkshire Miners were in the vanguard of the struggle to improve wages and conditions locally and nationally. It was in these years that Arthur Scargill (ex-communist and still very much on the left) was elected Yorkshire Area Secretary, while Jock Kane and Sammy Taylor served on the National Executive Committee as well as holding leading Area positions. The long years of patient work were paying off and the assessments made by the CP in 1953 proved correct: change Yorkshire and you change the NUM; change the NUM and the balance of political forces means the whole labour movement moves in favour of the left.

In Ramelson's early years as District Secretary, the focus of the Party's work in Yorkshire was very much on peace and industrial questions. The 1955 District Congress, for example, highlighted the threat of war, and called for the banning of all nuclear weapons. As part of this campaign it focused on the questions of German re-armament and banning the bomb. Ramelson linked the political issues of the day to the need to build a labour movement and workplace response, telling the Congress: 'It's in industry that we must lay the ground to take higher forms of action on behalf of peace that will make war impossible if the resolutions, petitions and deputations go unheeded'.[27] In this he was calling for the kind of development that would make it possible to mobilise industrial action on a broad range of political issues normally seen to be outside the compass of trade union concerns. He also reinforced to delegates the strategic vision he had first put forward in 1953 when he told them: 'Without Yorkshire the NUM cannot be won for progress. Without the NUM it is difficult to win the TUC and Labour Party for progressive policies'. This time he was even more specific when he set out the tasks ahead: 'No real and lasting changes can be made until the character of the Barnsley Council of the NUM is changed. The careful and widespread preparation to elect progressive delegates next June is therefore of vital importance'. To achieve this Ramelson argued that it was necessary to recruit hundreds of miners to the Party, and to achieve mass sales of the *Daily Worker*.

RELATIONS WITH LABOUR

By the mid 1950s Ramelson was firmly established as one of Britain's foremost communists. He was acknowledged as a leader in both the industrial field and the peace movement, and also as an authority on the Middle East and the Jewish question. Within the CP his growing influence was recognised when in summer 1956 he was appointed to the three-person British delegation to the Soviet Union for top-level discussions on the implications of the CPSU's Twentieth Congress. He was re-elected to the Executive Committee at the 1957 Special Congress, and subsequently appointed to the Political Committee and the Economic Committee. He was also an important figure in developing Labour/Communist relations.

During the 1950s Ramelson's work in the peace movement brought him into contact with many of the Labour left, and while such relationships were generally fruitful in terms of building support for nuclear disarmament and world peace, they were not without their difficulties. The Labour Party leadership viewed the peace movement as a fifth column directed by Moscow, and some 221 people were expelled from the Labour Party for membership of proscribed peace organisations.[28] This was one of the factors prompting the Yorkshire District to submit an emergency motion to the 1957 national party congress on peace and nuclear weapons. Moving the resolution, Ramelson stressed the poverty of Labour's policies and the need for CP leadership, and called for the ending of tests as a step to the total abolition of nuclear weapons.[29]

Ramelson also used his trade union contacts to promote the adoption of left-wing prospective parliamentary candidates at constituency party level. One such was Joan Maynard, who became a close personal friend. Maynard's biographer records how she used Ramelson as political tutor for constituency party members in North Yorkshire. He was invited to lead discussions on numerous occasions, and one member, John Gascoyne, recalls: 'Between my father and Bert Ramelson we learned our Socialism, our Marxism'. Maynard, a lifelong left-wing socialist, thought that the Labour Party was too much of an electoral party rather than one that educated and campaigned.[30] She was often denigrated by the press as a Communist sympathiser (and sometimes was called 'Stalin's Granny'). Ramelson greatly valued contacts with such Labour Party members: it strengthened his view that in the long term a united Marxist party, based on the unions and with mass support, was an achievable objective.

Ramelson was under few illusions as to the difficulty of the task, and how far the movement stood from its realisation. Writing after the 1958 Labour Party Conference, at which Hugh Gaitskell won a majority to overturn the previous year's vote in support of unilateral nuclear disarmament, Ramelson gave most attention to the failures of the left. He wrote in the CP's fortnightly news sheet, *World News and Views,* that the absence of an effective left input into the Conference could be explained by the following factors:

1. the consolidation of Gaitskell's leadership
2. the capitulation of left leadership in exchange for promises of position in a Labour Government (General Election due within a year or so)
3. Frank Cousin's confusion and vacillation (his panegyric of Gaitskell and Robens in the economic debate in contrast to the Transport & General Workers Union (TGWU) General Secretary's rousing speech in favour of disarmament the year before).[31]

As usual Ramelson was not content simply to criticise and identify shortcomings. He was clear about the way forward. Above all, he argued, what was missing was the injection of socialist ideas: it was necessary both to target the trade unions to win them for a socialist approach, and to rebuild the Communist Party.

1956 – *ANNUS HORRIBILIS*

The great advances made by the international communist movement after 1945 came to a shuddering halt in 1956. In the early part of the year came the revelations of Stalinist crimes, when in a secret speech to delegates Khrushchev laid before the CPSU Twentieth Congress a horrific litany of state-sponsored murder and other forms of barbarity, indicative of a total abandonment of most norms of socialist democracy, and abuse of state power. This was followed by civil and industrial unrest in Poland, and towards the end of the year by the outbreak of civil war in Hungary – and in both these countries the ruling Communist Party was split and discredited. The events in Hungary led to a military intervention by Soviet troops, to put down what Ramelson and the British CP leadership considered to be a counter-revolution, and to maintain Communist rule. Shock waves reverberated around the world communist movement, which lost hundreds of thousands of members in protest about the use of force in Hungary and the realisation of the cruelties of Stalinism.

Although we could find no contemporary comment by Ramelson on these events, he did prepare notes for a CP Education School some years later, in which he compared and contrasted the Soviet interventions in 1956 in Hungary and in 1968 in Czechoslovakia.[32] In Hungary, he argued, there was clear evidence of the insurrectionary role played by extreme right-wing forces, including the Roman Catholic church; and there had been considerable foreign support, particularly from the United States, as well as the targeting of Communist Party leaders at every level for physical attack, including, in hundreds of cases, lynchings. This was a country which had only a decade or so earlier thrown off the yoke of fascist tyranny, and there were clearly powerful elements within Hungarian society determined to overthrow the socialist state and replace it with an anti-Soviet pro-western reactionary government. The British Party leadership did acknowledge at the time that Hungarian workers were in general disenchanted with their government, dismayed that Soviet troops had remained on Hungarian territory for some nine years after the defeat of Hitler, and that the uprising had both popular and counter-revolutionary elements within it. At this juncture it was the latter that Ramelson and his comrades felt to be directing events. The point of Ramelson's later argument was to show that the intervention in Czechoslovakia was of a different character, and should be opposed.

1956 was also a crisis year for Ramelson personally, and was made worse by the revelations following the twentieth congress of savage measures against Jewish intellectuals in the Soviet Union during the period 1948-1953. One of the bedrocks of Ramelson's world view was that it was the Soviet Union which had first tackled anti-semitism in the 1920s, and then protected the Jewish people against Hitlerism in the 1930s and 1940s. This now appeared to have been undermined by Stalin and his secret police chief, Lavrentiy Beria.

As a member of the Executive and Political Committee, Ramelson was privy to all the leadership discussions during the period, and people active at the time recall that he fiercely defended the Party line during the period of political turmoil. As his later notes show, he believed that in Hungary there had been plans to plunge the country into a counter-revolutionary civil war, and that in these circumstances, during a period of Cold War, military intervention by the by the Soviet Union was justifiable.[33] On some of the other questions at issue during 1956 it is clear from Ramelson's later writings that he was beginning to have doubts about the way democratic centralism was practised throughout the international communist movement, including in Britain. Later articles also reveal that Ramelson felt than from the mid-1920s onwards the Soviet authorities had handled religious questions with growing insensitivity, substituting administrative methods for the necessary task of winning heads and hearts for the scientific and moral superiority of socialism.[34]

Some of these questions would have been very much in Ramelson's mind when he visited the Soviet Union in July 1956 as part of the CPGB's delegation – led by General Secretary Harry Pollitt – to discuss the implications of the denunciation of Stalin earlier in the year.[35] During this trip he met his sister Rosa for the first time since 1924. Rosa's life had been scarred by the brutal excesses of Stalinism – her Bolshevik husband had been murdered by the authorities in the 1930s, and Rosa herself had spent many years in a labour camp after the war. This meeting was extraordinary in many respects. As we have seen, more than any other single person in his life Rosa had been Ramelson's political inspiration. So when he was asked by his Soviet hosts if he had anything in particular that he wanted to do whilst in the Soviet Union he asked to be put in touch with his sister. At first the Soviet authorities claimed that Rosa could not be traced, but Ramelson was persistent. He insisted on seeing Rosa, remarking that the British Secret services would have no trouble locating a dissident political activist in London. Thus goaded, the Soviet authorities produced Rosa within twenty-four hours.[36] Ramelson's next shock was to see how much Rosa had changed, and how she now resembled his mother in her late middle age. Bert's memory was of a dashing young Bolshevik ready to change the world. Now he met a woman of mature years who had lived through harrowing times. Yet Ramelson found his sister in good spirits, still proclaiming the virtues of socialism and still loyal to the ideals of the Bolshevik revolution. There is no doubt, however, that what remained of Bert's Ukrainian family was deeply divided by their experiences during Stalin's time. Rosa was able to come to terms politically and emotionally with the terrible events of the previous thirty years, arguing that the crucial achievement had been the defence of the socialist system against Hitlerism and capitalist encirclement. Her daughter was unable to be so understanding of the crimes committed in the name of socialism, particularly since they involved the killing of her father, and the imprisonment of her mother in a labour camp. All this meant that Ramelson had much to think about as he returned to England in July 1956.

To compound his anxieties, a crisis was developing within the Jewish membership of the British Party – a membership which was particularly significant, both numerically and politically in Bert's adopted city Leeds. Following reports in Jewish publications within the United States and Poland, during the second half of 1956 stories were carried that the Soviet authorities had taken brutal action against Jewish intellectuals generally, including those who had continued to argue for zionism and the right to emigrate to the new state of Israel. Such actions, which included disappearances, executions and imprisonments, had been prevalent during the last years of Stalin's rule. At first the accusations were denied by the Soviet authorities, although the substance of the allegations had been confirmed in Khrushchev's secret speech earlier in that year. The British Party joined the call for answers, and a delegation was sent to the Soviet Union, led by J.R. Campbell, a veteran EC member[37] and Pollitt's close ally over some twenty years. Included in the delegation was Manchester academic Hyman Levy, a prominent member of the Party's Jewish Committee and a regular critic of the Party leadership in the columns of *World News and Views*.[38] The delegation was charged with the responsibility of reporting back on all aspects of Soviet life after the 1956 Congress, and Levy was asked by Campbell to investigate the allegations of anti-semitic barbarism. In all essentials Levy found that the reports in the Jewish press were accurate, and this reality was conceded by the Soviet authorities, who laid the blame on Stalin and his secret police chief Beria. Fulsome apologies were made, but these cut little ice with Levy or with the British Party generally. The delegation's report was presented to the Party leadership in December 1956, and published in full in *World News and Views* during January 1957.

This was of course a serious setback for Ramelson, a Ukrainian Jew whose family had been politically emancipated by the Bolsheviks in the early 1920s. Nonetheless, he set about rallying the membership with gusto, seeking to help hold the Party together in face of the multi-faceted challenges of 1956. Above all he argued that the British working class needed a communist party, and that the first responsibility of Yorkshire Communists was to help create the conditions for socialist revolution in Britain. Whatever the reasons for shortcomings and crimes against socialism in the Soviet Union and Eastern Europe, British communists bore no responsibility for them, and neither did such developments fundamentally affect the basic proposition that socialism represented a higher stage of human progress than did capitalism. So while it was important to try to understand what had happened and why, any conclusions to be drawn were not directly relevant to the specific conditions in Britain. Above all it was for the CPSU to sort out the problems in the Soviet system.

Interviewees recall how firm Ramelson was on these difficult issues, particularly with the Jewish comrades.[39] Some argue that in his anxiety to hold the Party together he was abrupt in debate and rather insensitive to criticisms of the Party line and the role played by the Soviet Union.[40] There is no doubt that – probably for the first time in his political experience – Ramelson was shaken by these events. He could readily defend the line on Hungary, but found it more difficult to come to terms with the Stalinist crimes in the Soviet Union, or some of the questions thrown up by the *Reasoner* episode, with the implications they had for inner-party democracy and the need to protect the communist movement from bureaucratic centralism. Whatever doubts he had ultimately proved to be short-lived. While they lasted he was seen to be brushing up his Russian language skills, probably his only non-political and marketable talent, as the prospects for the Party's future became bleaker during the long winter days of 1956/1957.[41]

THE REASONER

The political fall-out from the CPSU's Twentieth Congress was extensive and long lasting. Coupled with the events later in the year in Poland and Hungary, it caused widespread concern and a good deal of dismay right across the ranks of the CPGB's membership. Ramelson was right at the centre of the action from the beginning; and, as it happened, the most important challenge to the unity of the Party and the Party's democratic centralist practices came from his Yorkshire District – in the shape of two academics, Edward Thompson (in Halifax) and John Saville (in Hull).

It would be a serious understatement to say that the CPGB leadership was totally wrong-footed, confused and hurt by the revelations in Khrushchev's speech. It was some weeks later, in the second week of April that the British Party first commented on events. It was this delay, and the way the arguments were presented in explanation both of the Stalinist crimes and the failure of the CPGB to respond to them in a suitably critical manner – particularly those made by the Party's international secretary Palme Dutt – that enraged a sizeable section of the Party's membership.

Prominent among the Party's critics were Thompson and Saville, who were both university lecturers from Yorkshire. Thompson was also a member of the Yorkshire District Committee. The two academics, who at that time were acquaintances rather than friends or close colleagues, came together to launch an independent and unauthorised discussion journal, *The Reasoner*, which was directed at CP members, and argued that the existing arrangement within the Party allowed neither democratic debate nor criticism of leadership positions on matters of vital contemporary interest. Their proclaimed objectives were two-fold – to attack Stalinism in all its forms, and to democratise the practices of the CPGB. Their efforts were not well received in Yorkshire. The District Committee, under Ramelson's leadership, after a lengthy process and two discussions, and with only Thompson's vote against, decided to ask the two dissidents to cease publication of *The Reasoner* immediately, and to argue their positions within the channels provided by the Party.

Ramelson persuaded the District Committee to take two further steps – to call on the national leadership to consider launching a discussion journal under proper editorial control; and to draw to the EC's attention that *The Reasoner* had a broad base of support across Britain, and that the issues arising from its publication and distribution were therefore for the whole Party to consider and not just Yorkshire. The evidence suggests that relationships between Ramelson, Thompson and Saville remained cordial throughout this episode. For example, a letter from Thompson to Ramelson ends: 'I don't need to tell you how grateful we [presumably Thompson and his wife Dorothy] are about the microfilm. I only wish things weren't clouded by present disagreements. Best wishes, Edward'.[42]

Saville's letter agreeing to meet a Yorkshire District Committee delegation to discuss *The Reasoner* is more abrupt but not antagonistic. He ends by declaring: 'I thought the statement following your sessions with Khrushchev was appalling. How tough characters like you can act like political innocents beats me. However, no doubt we can discuss.' Even Saville took time out to pull Ramelson's leg about the material he had passed onto the Thompsons (in the letter above), suggesting that he was trying to win over Dorothy Thompson as part of a charm offensive designed to defuse the sharp political disagreements.

For the majority of Party members the issues were clear enough. For two comrades, with access to funds and distribution networks, to go outside of normal Party channels to attack the leadership offended the basic tenets of communist democracy, which allowed for such criticisms only within the basic Party bodies to which the critics were attached, in official journals over which the leadership had editorial control, or at National Congress. Here, it was felt, were two academic upstarts who thought they knew better than the collective Party leadership elected by the whole of the Party. Of course they had a right to publish, but under Party rules the leadership had the right to take disciplinary action against them if they continued to flout District and Executive Committee instructions.

Arnold Kettle, an EC member and prominent academic, summed up many comrades' views at the Twenty-fifth Party Special Congress:

> one thing that is resented has been an immodest parading of conscience, of moral superiority which some of our middle-class intellectuals have gone in for. It was this which above all was disgusting about *The Reasoner* … the doing of the right thing at each particular moment of struggle is a higher principle that of subjective sincerity.[43]

It is clear from Ramelson's own handwritten notes in preparation for a conference speech some years later that he had tried to keep the matter open, perhaps hoping that a special British Party Congress already called for spring 1957 would find a way, through the Inner Party Democracy Commission, of satisfying aspirations – which he clearly shared – for more open discussion in the Party. Such hopes were to be quickly dashed when the third and last issue of *The Reasoner* (it was replaced by the *New Reasoner* from 1957-9), in response to the Hungarian events, demanded that the EC of the Party 'disassociate itself publicly from the action of the Soviet Union in Hungary';[44] if this demand was not met: 'we urge all those, who like ourselves will disassociate themselves from the Party … to find ways of keeping together'. What had been a gap had become a chasm, and the Party leadership suspended the membership of Thompson and Saville for three months. After a short period of consideration the 'Yorkshire two' decided to resign from CP membership.

Ramelson's notes make it clear that extensive efforts were made to avoid using administrative means against the two dissidents. As Ramelson said in his introduction to an aggregate meeting of Sheffield Comrades, 'it had not occurred to anyone either at District or National level to even suggest that disciplinary action be taken against the comrades for having broken rules'. He went on to argue: 'It's not a question of stopping publication – or a breach of rules – it's a question of one party or 30,000 parties – of collective leadership pooling ideas and arriving at agreed decisions – what's good or not'.[45]

The Sheffield meeting took place before the third issue of *The Reasoner*'s call for CP members to disassociate themselves from the national leadership should it fail to disavow Soviet military intervention in Hungary, and promise to set up a new socialist journal. This was widely and probably correctly interpreted, as an attempt to promote organised factional activity, if not an alternative leadership. Before this stage had been reached it had been clear, even to those who took Ramelson's view, that it was important to reach an understanding following political discussion rather than invoke rule. The die was cast when Saville and Thompson were not prepared to accept the discipline of democratic discourse within the CP.

In 1990 Ramelson was invited to speak at a conference on 1956 organised by the CPGB.[46] He prefaced his remarks by observing that 1956 had been a crucial year, and in many respects was part of the thaw phase in the Cold War which followed Stalin's death in 1953, which affected both international relations and the methods and practices of Communist Parties throughout the world. He cited as examples the much greater openness of the correspondence columns in both the *Daily Worker* and *World News and Views* after 1956, aggregate meetings with recorded votes, and branch and district meetings with much sharper debates and many less unanimous votes. He had hoped to persuade Thompson and Saville to use these new opportunities to argue for their positions: both had had lengthy articles published in *World News and Views* during the *Reasoner* episode, which lasted from April 1956 until October 1956. In conclusion he stated:

> *The Reasoner* played a positive role in expanding a number of key issues … e.g. democratic centralism and Stalinism. Despite the allegations in *The Reasoner* to the contrary, both the District Committee and the Executive Committee were anxious to avoid expulsions. That was the reason for the length of the process. It's my opinion that had their last and third *Reasoner* not contained the leader on the Soviet invasion in Hungary and calling on all Communist to mobilise against the leadership, we may have avoided the expulsions (sic).[47]

Not for the last time in his political career Ramelson's optimism – based partly on his own inner belief that he could through force of argument win the day, and partly in his sometimes sanguine assessment that people generally acted with the best of intentions and said what they meant – was not fully borne out by events. Yet the *Reasoner* episode, or more particularly the de-Stalinization process started by the CPSU Twentieth Congress from which the dissidents drew their inspiration, did promote widespread debate and some change within the CPGB. The discussion columns of the Party's weekly journal were largely taken up with the debate around democratic centralism, de-Stalinisation and events in Eastern and Central Europe right through to the Congress in May 1957. Letters from academics – luminaries such as Eric Hobsbawm, Michael Barratt Brown, Ken Alexander and Hyman Levy – regularly appeared. These were often long letters, as was the fashion in the 1950s, and many of them were extremely critical of the leadership, and the Congress itself, while ruling out factionalism, did agree the launch of a discussion journal, *Marxism Today*, albeit at that time under careful editorial control.[48]

Many of these arguments were reflected in the debate on Inner Party Democracy, which was a central feature of the pre-1957 Congress discussion and at Congress itself. Ramelson was one of four EC members appointed to the Commission to prepare a report on this question, and was a strong supporter of maintaining democratic centralism as the key organisational principle and resisting calls for legitimising factional activity and organisation. In later years, however, he was to become a strong opponent of democratic centralism, in the light of his experience in both the international movement and the British Party.

NORMALITY RETURNS

In the face of the enormity of the problems which the events of 1956 presented to the communist movement, the British Party's resilience was impressive. Some 20 per cent of the membership resigned or did not recard in January 1957, mainly as a result of the events in Hungary, and these included many industrial leaders of standing in the trade union movement, for example, John Horner, the Fire Brigades Union (FBU) General Secretary, Lawrence Daly, the NUM leader and Bert Wynn, NUM Derbyshire Secretary. Yet by the early 1960s membership was back up to pre-1956 levels, and at least in Yorkshire the broad left strategy mapped out by Ramelson and his colleagues was bearing fruit.

This was particularly true within the NUM. Following successful unofficial strikes on wages, the Yorkshire Coalfield had made significant advances in organisation and solidarity. Many of the old right-wing officials were defeated in pit and branch ballots, and the left made some important electoral breakthroughs in the union. Sammy Taylor and Jock Kane became the first Communists in Yorkshire to be elected to Area positions, and Taylor went on to become an NUM National Executive member.

Following the setbacks of 1956, a concerted effort was made by employers and right-wing union officials to challenge the growing strength of the CP, particularly in the vital engineering industry, the centre of Britain's export trade. The Sheffield District Committee of the AEU was one of the targets for right-wing intervention, and the union's national leadership, supported by the local press, launched an all-out attack on the Communists standing for election for union positions, describing them as 'werewolves', and singling out for particular obloquy Herbert Howarth, who was widely recognised as an outstanding trade unionist at shop floor level.[49] The *Sheffield Telegraph* was particularly strident in its attempts to influence trade union elections. On 18 January 1958 it ran an editorial stating that

'Only those who believe in democratic trade unionism should be elected to AEU positions', adding in bold type, 'THAT MEANS NO COMMUNISTS'.

The AEU was not the only target. During this period the TUC, led by Vic Feather in the Organisation Department, was closely monitoring the Trades Council movement and threatening to de-register any local body which was seen to be working with the Communist Party.[50] When Hull Trades Council sent a delegate to Moscow and Bradford Trades Council was represented at an event in Poland, the anti-Communist antennae at Congress House were alerted, and disapproving notes followed. In the event there was no follow-up, but Ramelson, who was Senior Vice President of Leeds Trades Council for much of the 1950s, was acutely aware of the need for caution. There was little point in confronting the General Council on this question – the policy on bans and proscriptions for Trades Council links with the CP was crystal clear. The Party could not meekly accept this attack on the rights of Trades Councils to campaign alongside all organisations seeking to advance working-class interests and world peace. However, though the TUC's approach was tiresomely intrusive, it was for the most part ineffective. Left-led Trades Councils found many ways of working on campaigns that displeased the TUC, knowing that the Congress House bark was worse than its bite when it came to administering undemocratic proscriptions.

The attacks did not only come from the right. In the docks industry, after years of neglect by the Deakinite TGWU leadership, there was a rare breakthrough by Trotskyists, who in some ports were able to promote an alternative union (the National Amalgamated Stevedores and Dockers Union -- NASD or 'blue' union), thereby splitting the workforce. One such area was Hull Docks on Ramelson's patch. With Ramelson's personal intervention and assistance, a small group of Communists, over a period of some three years, was able to overcome division, set up a joint United Port Workers Committee, publish a rank-and-file paper, *The Docker*, and lead two successful unofficial strikes that re-established unity and restored the reputation of the TGWU.[51]

By the mid-1960s most of the problems thrown up by anti-communism had been overcome, and the Party's position was considerably stronger across the trade union movement in Yorkshire. There were exceptions. The ETU ballot-rigging scandal, in which the leading full-time national officials, mainly CP members, were found to have been directly involved, left its mark, though the Party leadership was clear that it had not sanctioned these activities. Stan Davison, a leading rank-and-file activist in the ETU, told us that the General Secretary at the time went out of his way to personally reassure him that the Party knew nothing of these machinations. In a printed statement, 'For Strong Democratic Trade Unionism', the Party Executive stressed its condemnation of ballot-rigging, stating that the Party 'sought to influence but in a democratic way', and that: 'Communists have been more concerned with convincing workers of the need to build up the unions and of the necessity for a socialist transformation than of merely winning trade union posts for communists'.[52]

The Yorkshire CP District Congress in 1961 described the episode as 'impermissible ballot rigging', and referred to 'other crimes against the membership committed by Haxell and Co'.[53] As a result one CP member and Area Official of the ETU resigned from the Party, but leading rank and filers such as Fred Shannon, Paul Watson and Annette Wilton resigned their union lay positions and kept their Party cards. The District Congress records that only two members left the Party as a result of the ETU affair.

The other area where progress was non-existent was in the TGWU – apart from in the Hull Docks. Bans and proscriptions had been imposed on Communists in the TGWU in 1949 under Deakin's baleful leadership, which prevented members from electing or appointing known Communists to positions in the union, whether lay or full-time. The Party's national campaign against these bans was organised by Harry Pollitt's ex-driver and bodyguard, the formidable Sid Easton, with the implicit support of important national figures in the TGWU, including Jack Jones, who was later elected as the union's general secretary. In 1960 and 1961, Easton many times tried to persuade Ramelson to organise a series of meetings on the issue, and sales of a broad left pamphlet. Ramelson always found reasons not to involve Yorkshire, although there can be no doubt that he fully supported the campaign. Easton, who was a man with a short fuse, was scathing in his criticism of this lack of response: 'I have to answer for a National Campaign … over twelve months I have only been to your District area once. One would hardly call that a roaring success. There is nothing we can say. We have not wasted much money on fares for Yorkshire'.[54] Ramelson's knuckles were subsequently rapped by the

Party's then National Industrial Organiser Peter Kerrigan.[55] However, what evidence we have suggests that the Party's base in the Yorkshire Region of the TGWU was extremely weak, and that Ramelson did not want to expose this to close inner-party scrutiny.

The Party's main base in Yorkshire remained in the engineering industry, particularly in Sheffield, where Ramelson was able to work with a group of factory branches, and to take into the labour movement a very broad political agenda. Barry Bracken was the Party Secretary at Shardlows during the 1960s, a factory producing crankshafts, with a workforce of around two thousand. This was a 100 per cent trade union shop, with a long tradition of militant trade unionism and decades of CP activity. Bracken recalls that in the early 1960s the Party branch was a hundred-strong, and that most weeks Ramelson spoke at factory gate lunch-time meetings. He remembered Ramelson as a brilliant speaker who encouraged audience participation, and as a Party leader who was always available to give advice and encouragement. He particularly remembered Bert's role in developing solidarity with weaker groups, and encouraging stray organisations such as the Shop Stewards at Shardlows to support the nurses in their struggles for better wages and conditions:

> I recall there was an issue where the nurses were in conflict and wanted to take some action to improve their wages and conditions, and Ramelson spoke to our Party branch and through the Shop Stewards Committee to seek to win support, industrial support, for the nurses. And as a consequence of that type of initiative the Shop Stewards' Committee took a decision to support the nurses in the one day strike and this was put to the factory. The factory agreed to support it and we in fact held a one-day stoppage in support of the nurses.[56]

Much later, at the time of the 1976/7 Grunwick dispute, it was the by now retired Ramelson who encouraged the Yorkshire miners to send down pickets to North London in support of the mainly female and Asian workforce's campaign for union recognition.[57]

During this period Ramelson attended almost every Executive Committee meeting, and was regularly involved in the weekly meetings of the Political Committee, and he also widened his international experience. In 1961 he joined General Secretary Gollan on an official week-long delegation to Czechoslovakia, and the following year was the British Party's delegate to the Czech Party's Congress. This provided him with some knowledge of the level of economic and social development in one of the few socialist countries which had deep-rooted democratic foundations and a modern industrial economy. This meant that he was better placed than most to assess the events of 1968.

Monty Meth recalls the period of Ramelson's District Secretaryship in Yorkshire as one of considerable achievement. Meth was for some time YCL Secretary in Yorkshire, and later was a regional industrial correspondent for the *Daily Worker*, with an office next door to Bert's. Of Ramelson in his Yorkshire days he recalls:

> He was dynamic … a great talker … even political opponents had a great admiration for Bert. He had a great sense of humour, he loved an argument, but there was never any ill feeling after an argument was over. And he enjoyed life. He enjoyed food, he enjoyed a drink, and he enjoyed talking.[58]

On a personal level Ramelson had some difficult times. Marian's health was beginning to decline, and Ramelson himself was in hospital for two weeks in 1961 following an operation to remove a thrombosis in his right leg.

Ramelson remained in full throttle throughout his Yorkshire years. All the comrades interviewed remember Bert's style – a hard taskmaster, generous in his praise for work well done and optimistic about prospects for the Party and the movement. In Ramelson's time this was a good place to work. The atmosphere was not that of a small isolated political party. Rather, the comrades felt themselves to be at the centre of the progressive movement, as concerned with the development of the peace and trade union movements as they were with building the Party.[59] Through the Party's initiative, campaigns were developed, for example, against low pay, for equal pay for women, and for nuclear disarmament. At the centre of it all, Ramelson was there, leading from the front, always energising, and inspiring greater efforts in the socialist cause. Some found his style to be hectoring, but most commented on a strong sense of shared objectives, and the way in which serious campaigning was interspersed with good humour and an active social life based on the Party. All recognised Ramelson's total integrity and his commitment to the movement.

By the mid-1960s, however, with Ramelson well into his fifties, he was ready for a move. Both his wife and father-in-law were in poor health, and as a leading member of the CP's National Executive he had to be in London on an almost weekly basis, usually for two days, and the constant travel was becoming irksome. So when the London-based National Industrial Organiser's job came up on Peter Kerrigan's retirement in late 1965, Ramelson jumped at the chance of a new challenge.

NOTES

1. The *Daily Worker* was banned in January 1941, but the Party found a way round this by producing a daily duplicated bulletin which was distributed nationally. See Branson 1985 op.cit. pp. 312-326.
2. Beckett tapes. Marian Ramelson had been a full-time Party worker since 1937. She spent two years in the mid-1930s at the Lenin School in Moscow.
3. Richard Craven interview, 2008.
4. The effects of the early Cold War years on the British and international labour movements are described and analysed in Sibley, T. *Anti-Communism: Studies of its Impact on the UK Labour Movement in the Early Years of the Cold War*, PhD dissertation Keele University 2008.
5. Weiler, P. *British Labour and the Cold War*, Stanford University Press 1988, p. 216.
6. Ibid, pp. 215-9.
7. Branson 1985 op.cit., p. 215.
8. Charles Lubelski interview 2009.
9. Joan Bellamy interview 2009, and the Beckett tapes.
10. *New Dawn* was the monthly journal of NUDAW/USDAW: 1947-1950, and can be accessed in the TUC library.
11. 1949 Annual Delegate Meeting.
12. Beryl Huffingley interview 1999.
13. USADW AGM 1949, reported in *New Dawn*.
14. Silver, E. *Victor Feather* Gollantz 1973, p. 102.
15. Communists in Britain have traditionally given great attention to building influence (and membership) at workplace and trade union rank-and-file level, as part of their long-term project of creating a socialist consciousness in wide sections of the working class.
16. Joan Bellamy, Monty Meth, and Bill Moore interviews.
17. Bill Moore interview 2004.
18. Beckett tapes.
19. For more on Kane see Allen, V. *The Militancy of British Miners,* Moor Press 1981, pp. 154-159, Joe Clark, who knew the Kane family well, in

correspondence with the authors stressed the importance of the ground-work done by Kane and other rank-and-file communists before, as well as after, Ramelson became Party District Secretary. Later, as an elected member of the NUM's Executive Committee, Kane led demands to reject the terms proposed by the Wilberforce Report to end the 1972 strike, thereby forcing the concession of further advances in the miners' working conditions.

20. CP Archives, CP/IND/RAM/06/06.
21. Ibid.
22. Westacott, F. *Shaking the Chains: a Personal and Political History*, Joe Clark, Chesterfield 2002; pp. 294-5.
23. Jock Kane's autobiography *No Wonder we were Rebels*, compiled by Frank Watters from interviews in 1978, published in 1994.
24. Much of this information is gleaned from Secret Service files, Public records office, National Archives KV Series See PRO/KV2/1795.
25. Fishman, N. *Arthur Horner: A Political Biography*, Lawrence & Wishart 2010, p. 885.
26. Fishman goes on to argue that there may well have been differences between Pollitt and Ramelson during the 1955 dispute, which was ended when the Yorkshire area ordered the strikers back to work, having received assurances from the NCB that improvements in piece rates would follow. There is no evidence to support Fishman's speculation that Ramelson's militant approach was opposed by Pollitt, and it does appear to be a most unlikely proposition, presented to support Fishman's characterisation of CP leaders as revolutionary pragmatists.
27. CP Archives. CP/IND/RAM/06/01.
28. O'Connor, K. *Passionate Socialist* Politicos, London 2003, pp. 77-80.
29. *World News & Views* July 1957.
30. O'Connor 2003, op.cit.
31. *World News & Views*, October 1958, pp. 603-4.
32. CP Archives. CP/IND/RAM/02/04.
33. Ibid.
34. CP Archives. CP/IND/RAM/02/05.
35. Callaghan op.cit. 2003, p. 41.
36. Joan Ramelson interview.
37. J.R. (Johnny) Campbell was editor of the *Daily Worker* 1949-1959, and was a key supporter of Harry Pollitt.
38. *World News and Views* January 1957.
39. Lubelski and Meth interviews 2009.
40. Ethel Shepherd interview 2009.
41. Joan Bellamy interview 2009.
42. Ramelson's personal papers. The Reasoner file. Letter dated 25 July 1956.
43. *World News and Views*, July 1957.
44. Saville, J. *Memoirs from the Left,* Merlin Press, 2003, p. 112.

45. Ramelson personal papers.

46. 'The CPGB and 1956', *Socialist History Society Bulletin*, 1993.

47. Ramelson personal papers; he made an error here as Saville and Thompson resigned and were not expelled.

48. *World News and Views*, January-April 1957.

49. Callaghan op.cit 2003, p. 239.

50. CP Archives: CP/IND/RAM/11/01.

51. CP/IND/RAM.

52. Stan Davison interview, 2010. For the TUC's view on these events, see *TUC Report to the 1961 Congress*. Hutt, A. *British trade unionism: a short history*, Lawrence & Wishart, London 1975 gives the Party's assessment.

53. CP/IND/RAM.

54. Easton to Ramelson 19/2/1962. CP Archives: CP/IND/RAM/11/01.

55. Peter Kerrigan was an AEU activist from Glasgow who fought in the Spanish Civil War and was CP Industrial Organiser from the early 1950s-1965.

56. Barry Bracken interview 2004.

57. Bill Moore interview 1999.

58. Monty Meth interview 2009.

59. Edna Ashworth interview 2009.

PART II

National Industrial Organiser of the Communist Party of Great Britain, 1965 to 1977

3. Left unity, incomes policy, and industrial advisories

THEMES

When Ramelson arrived in London in 1965 to take up his new job as industrial organiser of the CP he brought with him a good deal of personal and political baggage. Though he felt a great sense of opportunity in being at the centre of a movement he loved and respected, his personal life was overshadowed by his wife Marian's serious and long-standing illness. It was now clear that she had terminal cancer, and she died in 1967. He was also, at the age of fifty-four, leaving his home of nearly twenty years, and moving to the centre stage in British industrial relations and the trade union movement – and the thirteen years in which he held his new post were a time of struggle and intense encounters within and without the communist movement. The main ones discussed here include the relations of the communists with Labour left wingers in the unions and inside the Labour Party; the pivotal role of opposition to all forms of incomes policies through industrial militancy, union programmes and economic debate; and the practical ways in which a small communist party could influence events and ideas through the setting up of industrial advisories and the Liaison Committee for the Defence of Trade Unions (LCDTU).

Ramelson was well able to cope with the daunting tasks ahead, and with the sadness in his personal life. He was a physically strong man with endless energy, and a tremendous ability to focus on the matter in hand while never losing sight of the real purpose of his political convictions. He was also an intellectual with a profound grasp of labour movement issues, from wages and anti-union laws, to piece-work and trade union governance.

His appointment as Head of the Industrial Department and Chair of the Economic Advisory Committee was not significant in political terms. Previously the Industrial Department had been headed by Kerrigan, with the Economic Committee (which had only advisory status) being chaired by Campbell, who worked alongside Kerrigan and contributed major articles on economic and industrial questions. As a longstanding member of the Economics Committee and part of the senior leadership of the Party, it therefore made good sense to give Ramelson stewardship of both bodies on the retirement of Kerrigan and Campbell. The Industrial Department was a relatively autono-mous department, consisting of full-time workers engaged in day-to-day Party work, while the Economic Advisory Committee, chaired by a member of the EC and meeting once every two months, was made up of lay members (mainly academics but including some industrial comrades).

Ramelson's main initial contribution was to give both operations more energy. He quickly re-organised the Industrial Advisories to give proper effect to the Party leadership's position following the ETU debacle (see below), and gave them greater autonomy, and a new orien-tation towards policy issues across industrial sectors, rather than day-to-day administrative and electoral considerations in individual unions. The Economic Committee under his leadership became a lively centre of debate, with a significantly higher level of publications, more seminars and conferences and a greater impact on labour move-ment policy than in previous years.

BRITAIN IN THE 1960s

In 1964, the year before Ramelson took up his new position, the defeat of the Tories under the leadership of Alec Douglas Home had signalled the final decline and eclipse of one-nation Toryism. Attempts were now being made to modernise the old country, seen as a victim of 'external weakness and internal decay'.[1] As obstacles to growth and success became ever more evident, attempts were made to analyse and overcome them, in politics, the arts and popular culture, as well in intellectual life, including new debates in the increasingly popular discipline of sociology. This was the era of Harold Wilson's white heat of technology, and the beginning of many new cultural forms – from the recently launched *Private Eye to The Caretaker, Catch 22, Ken Loach's Cathy Come Home* and the new folk music of Bob Dylan.[2]

It was also a period of significant change and tension internationally, dominated by a space race and technology revolution; wars of national liberation; bitterly contested colonial independence; and a political explosion of rights in all aspects of life including civil rights in the USA, women's rights, and workers' rights. The Cold War was showing no signs of disappearing: nuclear weapons were now the dominant feature of the world's political stage, and the Berlin wall, erected in 1961, quickly became the symbol of European division and bitter hostility, played upon by American fears and bellicose attitudes.

Despite new attitudes, and some economic growth and shared prosperity, the economic situation was still one of limited expansion ranged against balance of payments problems and relatively low productivity. Some of this was fertile ground for a renewed interest in Marxism and forms of communism, and the CP was able to tap into both the frustration and the optimism of current trends in modernity, to develop policy, build influence and launch a series of important initiatives around the transition to socialism. In spite of the Cold War, US foreign policy was becoming unpopular with many people. Substantial numbers of US troops were still deployed in Germany, and the US was criticised by many for its financing of anti-Castro Cubans in the ill-fated Bay of Pigs invasion, as well as its brinkmanship during the Cuban missile crisis of 1962. The Sharpeville massacre in South Africa, the start of the Vietnam war, and the renewed bombing campaigns by the Irish Republican Army (IRA) fuelled fear and confusion as anti-imperialist and anti-American capitalist attitudes were, in some cases, enough to push large numbers of politically active, and newly active, citizens towards the left and partly to the Marxist left.

Thus when Ramelson arrived in London he was in the right place at the right time to use his considerable talents in the cause of revolution. From the race riots in Notting Hill to the scandals of private landlords (Rachmanism), and from the televised assassination of President Kennedy to the emergent nationalism in Wales, Scotland and Ireland the old world order was passing and the new was being forged. At the heart of this was the class struggle, the cause that Ramelson embraced and enhanced.

THE COMMUNIST PARTY, THE LEFT AND THE LABOUR MOVEMENT IN THE 1960s AND 1970s

The CPGB was at that time the best organised and most important element within the left. It was influential, and very effective in helping to move the trade union movement in a significantly militant and progressive direction. During this period the left and CP focused on defeating proposed and actual legislation to rein in union power, and on neutering attempts by successive governments to impose effective wage controls. Successes in these areas were accompanied by radically new approaches to the struggle to protect jobs, as in the work-in in the Upper Clyde Shipyards (UCS), and a genuine widening of traditional trade union political and social agendas. [3] These agendas included, among other things, alternative economic strategies to challenge capitalism's hegemony; international solidarity; and women's and minority groups' rights.[4] The progress achieved in terms of membership growth, the willingness to use industrial action to promote political objectives, and the fight against the threat to trade union rights, was evidence of labour movement achievements that surpassed those of any other period, past or future.[5]

While the objective economic and labour market conditions were in many ways favourable to the development of militant trade unionism, it is widely recognised that the strategy pursued and the arguments advanced by the CP's industrial department under Ramelson's leadership were important in giving direction, political clarity, and confidence to both the rank-and-file movement and to the broad left operating within official union structures.[6] On the labour movement side, it was the CP that pursued a strategic approach to industrial struggle, and it was mainly the communists who were able to link these struggles to realistic political objectives in advocating left advance and socialist change. Rather than counter posing the official and rank-and-file movements as antagonistic antipodes – as other sections of the revolutionary left did reflexively – the CP argued dialectically that a main purpose of militant struggle was to influence and change the policies of the labour movement, while pressure on the government and the state could only be generally effective if it involved the official movement. The election of left trade union officials and the resultant increased possibility of changing Labour Party policies was not an alternative to building workplace struggle and activity: the two developments were mutually reinforcing. The key concept was unity in action of all sections of the movement.

From the mid-1960s to the late 1970s the trade union question was at the top of the establishment's political agenda. Politicians, *Times* leader writers and military and intelligence community figures were by the mid-1970s openly asking whether Britain was governable, given the alleged accretion of trade union power and the chronic crisis of British capitalism. In retrospect – as for many at the time – this seems to have been a hysterical response, deliberately spun to scare the horses. The scenario presented by Labour ministers and senior civil servants to leading labour movement figures such as Jack Jones and Hugh Scanlon, and to selected industrial correspondents such as Geoffrey Goodman – one of dark forces organising some sort of military coup – does appear to have influenced the thinking of some trade union leaders, persuading them towards a position of support for wage restraint and public sector cuts. Sir Conrad Heron, a very senior civil servant, alarmed at the start of the three-day week imposed by the Heath government in response to the miners' strike of 1974, is quoted by Goodman as arguing that 'the country could well be on the brink of revolution'.[7] It is clear that many members of the TUC General Council were also caught up in the whirlwind of conspiracy theories and anti-communist night terrors: 'Nearly every member of the TUC General Council became convinced that Britain's economic situation was so dangerous that there was no alternative but to support the Government's economic policies ... in the main they acted timidly out of pure fear'.[8] Though such concern was overblown, and from the establishment's view motivated more by calculated group interest than by panic and a crisis of confidence in the old order, it is nevertheless true that this was an extraordinary time.

This was a period when for the first time since 1926 trade union powers were used to challenge and subvert policies which were seen by the state as vital to its interests. It was a time when, across industries, genuinely national rank-and-file movements were built that were able to mobilise industrial action that was powerful enough to influence official trade union policy, and as a result to force governments and the judiciary to back down – unheard of before or since. This was a period when hundreds of workplaces were occupied by workers campaigning to prevent job losses or improve wages and conditions. Such activities and developments had no comparable precedents and certainly have not been repeated since.

The rest of this chapter deals with the major economic and industrial questions of the period, giving an introduction to the big issues that unfolded, and to the battle of ideas which was an integral part of the struggles during these years. In all of this there is a common factor – the role of the CP. It was on a CP initiative that the Liaison Committee for the Defence of Trade Unions was built to defend the unions against state-inspired wage cuts and legal attacks;[9] while the CP's *Needs of the Hour* bulletin dominated the policy-making agendas of many unions, and therefore fed into TUC and Labour Party policy during this period. The sit-ins and factory occupations of the period drew much of their inspiration from the UCS work-in – led by CP members and directly influencing a flood of similar activities that played a major role in the union struggle for jobs and industrial democracy in these years.[10] The 'flying pickets' strategy came out of the industrial experience of the late 1950s Yorkshire coalfield, and was popularised by CP members as an example of new demands, new forms of struggle and new structures at rank-and-file level. For nearly all of this period Ramelson was at the heart of these developments

DEBATES WITHIN THE LEFT AND LABOUR MOVEMENT

A central debate that was repeated down the years was the extent to which the Labour Party could be pushed to the left, and how far it could be forced to carry out progressive policies when in government. Most of the New Left and Far Left believed this would never happen, and therefore sought to undermine the Labour Party. They constantly hankered after new political formulations, free from the contamination of Labourism and from Stalinism and Leninism (Communism being seen as damaged goods). They were always stronger on what they did not want than they were on mapping out a serious strategy for Socialist revolution in British conditions.

The communists took a different view, namely that the Labour Party could be won for socialist policies if it contained left-wing activists and was put under pressure from rank-and-file movements, in the union and wider labour movement. The main task, therefore, was to break the political and ideological hold of the right wing (the reform-ists) on the majority of national and local Labour Parties and affiliated trade unions.[11] Eric Hobsbawm summed up the weakness of the Labour right:

> … of all parties the social-democratic ones have been by far the least successful … They have not always been politically impotent; but what they have done, though admirable in its way, is not what they set out to do. The 'welfare state' is not socialism, and indeed its foun-dation does not require a social-democratic party in office or even in existence.[12]

This expressed the wider communist position of both the limitations and the possibilities inherent within such a Party and movement.

The social-democratic programmes of the Labour governments from 1964 to 1970, and from 1974 to 1979 were full of promises, many in accordance with socialist pressures from sections of the trade union and wider labour movement. They were based on a specific view of economic growth, and how such growth could be achieved without inflation. There was much debate on the causes and consequences of inflation and low growth, and Ramelson and his associates in the trade union movement were drawn into the argument over the role of wages in this equation – and therefore of trades unions – challenging the myth that it was the unions that were the causes of inflation and the obstacles to growth.[13]

Writers such as Palme Dutt made devastating assaults on both reformism and revisionism, and developed a convincing account of what a Leninist approach to the Britain of the 1960s would look like.[14] Drawing heavily on Engels, Dutt took on board that the 'heap of tradi-tional inherited rubbish which has to be got rid of by degrees' was still with us; and that there would inevitably intervene in Britain a period of mass parliamentary labour reformist representation and consequent disillusionment before the workers would move to socialism.[15] Such reformism was also analysed by Ralph Miliband, and it was discussed, too, in a series of influential studies on more specific areas, for example John Griffith on the judiciary, Ronnie Frankenberg on communities, and Garry Runciman on social justice and relative deprivation.[16] The CP and its economic committee were fully aware of such developments in the empirical base of contemporary knowledge, both of the consequences of modern capitalism for the working class as a whole, and of some of the methods by which capitalists maintained their grip on power. All served to support the CP line that certain reforms were necessary now, and could be fought for and won through broad left coalitions; but that none of these progressive measures (for example, nationalisation and higher absolute and relative wages) made redundant the objective of socialism.[17] Johnny Campbell, for example, attacked the economic illusions inside the British labour movement, including the illusion of wage restraint (discussed below in relation to Bert's arguments against incomes policies).[18]

The political imperative for the CP and Bert was that when talking with representatives of British workers there was a need to root both theory and practice in the country's own culture, heroes, and sensibilities. Hence the importance of the work of British socialists such as Tawney on the need to reconfigure property relations and the rise of capitalism,[19] Haldane on the inequality of man,[20] and Cole on planned socialist economies.[21] The totality of their work laid the foundations for debates inside the British labour movement, and formed some of the most basic points upon which the great schism in the movement was located. The rival claims on the Britishness of each approach, later fought over when implementing the British Road to Socialism, went far back to the so-called 'English Utopians' from Gulliver to William Morris, and from Luddites to Atlantis.[22] This in turn was made real by the actual life of Keir Hardie,[23] the reformist thoughts of Mrs Fawcett,[24] and events such as the falling out between early socialist groups in the 1890s,[25] and the rise of workers' solidarity, May Day, and the great lock-outs of the end of the nineteenth century.[26] This emphasis on rights resonated with the struggles of the British working-class from John Wilkes in the 1780s[27] and the Tolpuddle martyrs[28], to the Chartists of the 1840s and Taff Vale in 1901.

Of course, much of this was predicated on the experiences and lessons of the Great Depression of the 1930s, which was deeply etched into the minds of those that lived through it. Many agreed with Leo Huberman's assessment that 'something had to be done to bring order out of the chaos created by the breakdown of capitalism. The breakdown was too complete – the credit structure smashed, industry paralysed, millions of unemployed, farmers down and out, poverty in the midst of plenty – yes, of course, something *had* to be done'.[29]

Lenin wrote powerful and highly relevant polemics,[30] but it was Lozovsky,[31] Cole,[32] and Barou[33] who helped to develop a Marxist-Leninist approach to British trade unionism, praising their solidarity and defence of the job while aware of the limitations of their ideological position on the wider and deeper ills of the capitalist system. The selected writings of leading comrades such as Harry Pollitt,[34] Willie Gallacher,[35] and Allen Hutt[36] aided Bert to take forward the Party line into the more complex and more favourable conditions of the 1960s and 1970s. Lenin's own comments on Engels' seminal work, *The Condition of the Working Class in England*, included his view that 'the working class political movement would inevitably make the working class understand that there was no other way out for it except socialism. On the other hand, socialism would become a force only when it became the goal of the *political* struggle of the working class'.[37] Ramelson embodied this analysis of the need to convince and to create the working-class as a class devoted to the struggle for socialism.

This Marxist-Leninist approach permeated all aspects of the CP's work;[38] and Ramelson's strategies for the industrial arm of the movement were no different in principle from those pursued elsewhere by Party activists and leaders. Ramelson's distinctive contribution was to identify lines of advance and forms of organisation which recognised the specific conditions and challenges facing the labour movement in this period. While the weaknesses of the reformists inside the movement were on constant display and easy enough targets, the case for communism itself remained a difficult one to make in British conditions. After 1945 communists had been much more popular, having in every respect in most countries been at the front against fascism in all its forms. As the Cold War gathered momentum, and as doubts increasingly came to be expressed about Stalin's rule in the USSR, the positive case become more subdued.

However there was also an increasingly widespread sense that, internationally, the unpopular Americans were as much to blame as the Soviets for Cold War tensions; old-style colonialism and oppression was as unacceptable as were bad employers, ruthless landlords and callous officials. Here the communists could work and argue for progressive policies across the board, as well as link these to their fundamental positions about the nature of the state, the instability of capitalist economics, and the wider injustices that flowed from such a society. The interest in socialist ideas and the possibilities for revolutionary change was stronger in the 1960s than it has been at any time since the defeat of Hitler.

Thus Ramelson inherited a complex and dynamic situation, full of real possibilities but fraught with old and new problems and obstacles. His tasks in the first few years after taking national office were focused on the need, among other things, to re-elect a Labour government in 1966; to rebut flirtations with wage controls; to develop an alternative economic strategy; to win more union activists and leaders to the Party and its position while keeping those already on the left honest; and make the fight for union and worker rights on a par with civil rights.

Ramelson himself did not often pronounce on questions of Marxist theory and the nature of Leninism, but he did constantly warn against economism and sectionalism. He also stressed the need to unite the movement around left policies, and was therefore against the more militant section divorcing themselves from the main organisation of the labour movement. Thus, though in the conditions of pre-revolutionary Russia Lenin had made the case for communist-led unions, Ramelson, in 1960s-1970s Britain, was arguing for unity of the left in principle and in practice. He argued that to achieve revolution it was necessary to build a strong revolutionary party with deep roots in the organised labour movement. In the conditions of Britain at that time he did not support the notion of the vanguard party, and he also became increasingly sceptical about democratic centralism as an organising principle.

In short Ramelson was a revolutionary who knew that the revolutionary process would be both complex and drawn out. A strong CP was central to the process, but could not and should not attempt to offer exclusive leadership. The key to revolutionary advance was left unity, extra-parliamentary struggle, and a growing understanding of Marxism in all parts of society, particularly within the industrial working class which was the most powerful and best organised section of the people exploited and oppressed by capitalism. This approach had nothing to do with reformism, however, whose advocates, including many in the Parliamentary Labour Party, believed that it was possible to use existing institutions to manage capitalism in such a way as to benefit the vast majority of the British people both materially and culturally. Time and again Ramelson attacked such notions. Only socialism, he argued, could guarantee social advance; and only revolutionary change, including replacing the capitalist state, could guarantee and protect socialism from counter revolution.

The state was also a major subject of analysis for the Marxist left at this time. Almost alone, they were not only interested in the state *per se*, but saw it as part of class struggle and the nature of class society. Ramelson, especially, was drawn to the most powerful analyses of state authority, having been through the Russian revolution, the wars in Spain and North Africa, and the Cold War – all examples of how the state is the central political agency within nations.[39] The state apparatus was analysed as including the monarchy as well as Parliament, the armed forces and the forces of law and order, the senior civil servants and the corporation chiefs, the BBC and public services. They all added up to power structures destined to rule the majority of workers on behalf of the minority of capitalists, and to maintain that rule through both force and the power of ideas: hence the need to overthrow the state, and to convince powerful working-class organisations such as trade unions of the need for revolutionary change.

Rights in capitalist countries had often been won only through the achievements of workers' struggles being enshrined in law and institutions, and they were thereafter often neglected or distorted. The labour movement had fought most of its battles around the need for rights for workers individually and collectively, and for such hard won rights to be operational and meaningful. When the civil rights movement took hold in the USA and followed in Northern Ireland, and then linked in with national liberation movements across the globe, the world's communists saw this as a vindication of their analysis both of state power and of the need for revolution. The CP and its activists were in the forefront of all these struggles. In the UK it was the communists who most actively backed Mandela and Castro, the Vietnamese and the Palestinians, the Chileans and Greeks, the Portuguese and Spanish, and all the African nations and ex-colonies striving for independence. It was the communists who gave substantial support to the civil rights groups in America and trade unionists in Columbia and deplored the slaughter of thousands of progressives in Indonesia.

THE REVOLUTIONARY ROAD

When Ramelson arrived centre stage in 1965 CP policy and strategy were reasonably clear in general terms. They were based on the view that world and British capitalism and imperialism were entering a new phase of state monopoly capitalism, but that nothing fundamental had changed. Both the contradictions and the consequences of capitalism remained, and it was in the interests of the working class to move away from capitalism and towards socialism through a social revolution. Uppermost in the minds of those involved was the desperate impact of the Cold War on all things communist, and this further shaped the presentation and arguments in the *British Road to Socialism*, many of which had been rehearsed in Party literature in the 1940s.[40]

Critical to this analysis was the need for a revolution and an awareness of the role of the state. The state was seen as the main holder of political power, and that its immense authority was used to support the capitalist class in both word and deed. A revolution would have to seize state power and use it to back a working-class regime against its enemies. This is what Lenin both understood and explained.[41] What road was available to the communists that would both play to existing strengths, and assist in the search for new areas of influence, banned and excluded from the Labour Party as they were, and still banned from holding positions in some unions? The first tended to be concentrated amongst workers in unions, and the second to intellectuals within the cultural fields. As far as the unions were concerned, then, the strategy was to simultaneously support militant rank-and-file movements, especially when they were rooted in the shop stewards and workplace organisations, at the same time as seeking to win official union policies and posts, including in the TUC. This would be done through a combination of active co-ordinated campaigning on issues such as wages and jobs throughout the movement, under the umbrella of unity and class consciousness of the powers arrayed against them in the form of employers and the state. This required the construction of organisational forms to maximise the impact of communist activity, and a clear line to put to workers in struggle. This line coalesced around the wages movement, and the fight against state-imposed wage controls. None of this, however, was to reduce or deny the contribution of other progressive movements heavily influenced by communists over the years, such as anti-fascism, anti-racism, women's rights and tenants' rights.[42]

The answer as to which road to take was provided by the CP leadership in a series of debates and articles. For example, General Secretary John Gollan argued that: 'the grip of the right-wing Social Democrats on the labour movement to a large extent paralyses it and prevents its power from being used'.[43] The political need of the moment was to break that grip and to secure state power in a social revolution. It was critical to this position that the role of the CP would be to push the left: 'it is perfectly possible to change the balance of forces within the unions, to establish left progressive and communist majorities. This can have a decisive influence on the future of the Labour Party and on its policies because of the decisive power of the trade union role'.[44]

The task of communists therefore was to win over to a broadly based Marxist approach the left-wingers in the movement at all levels, including MPs, shop stewards, union leaders, and local constituency activists. This required a certain amount of tactical skill and nuance to reach all parts of the movement and overcome union sectionalism. Whether discussing the nature of state monopoly capitalism and its attendant offshoots such as the Common Market, or deliberating about the parliamentary system and the new role of the media, or tackling long-standing worker grievances about exploitation and alienation, the CP and Ramelson could bring to the table a coherent and consistent set of answers, rooted in the theories of historical materialism and the requirements for left advance in Britain.

While Ramelson worked to encourage the development of rank-and-file organisation and struggle, he linked this to the necessity of changing the policies and leaderships of the official movement, including the Labour Party and TUC. The logic was, therefore, that the people to combat were the right-wing social democrats who controlled the Labour Party and the TUC, and dominated many unions. With that view went a positive take on the future of unions that had for some years appeared at best moribund. These years saw a turning point in modern trade union history: 'How different it all looked in the 1950s. It was a worried TUC that debated the stagnation in union recruitment at the 1960 Congress. During the somnolent 1950s the movement had actually gone into decline'.[45] The unions had failed to keep up with developments in the 1950s, and in particular had failed to attract the growing numbers of white-collar workers, for example in education and local government.[46]

Jim Mortimer, who worked at Congress House in the 1940s, commented on how the politics of the movement had changed particularly at General Secretary level, comparing rightwing leaders like Deakin and Tanner with leftwing ones such as Jones and Scanlon.[47]

Membership growth really took off in the unions after 1964, but before then there had several years of wrangling at the TUC and elsewhere over the benefits of union mergers as a way to secure greater strength, attract new members, and act as a more effective pressure group with government. As Taylor showed, the trade union links with the Labour Party in particular gave a very peculiar twist to union activity and influence, especially when Labour was in government.[48] This relationship was an important element in the thinking and strategy of the communist leadership.

Even those critical of Party policy understood the importance of union leadership elections. For example, Ken Coates emphasised the importance of the outcome of the AEU elections: 'the whole course of the next Labour Government may be very considerably affected by the outcome of two trade union elections which are to take place at the beginning of July. The million-strong engineers' union, the AEU, is choosing its two chief officers, secretary and president'.[49] This is exactly why Ramelson believed so strongly in winning elections for the left as well as using rank-and-file power both to help mobilise members to vote for the left, and to sustain pressure on left leaders once in office. The ways in which these general positions became crystallised in the industrial department's work under Ramelson was in part due to the analysis of the role of trade unions themselves. As Ken Gill said at Ramelson's funeral: 'no one did more to avoid ultra-leftism and adventurism on one hand, and right wing opportunism and revisionism on the other, in both the trade union movement and in the Party'.

The question of the role of unions was also rooted in the dialectics of debate and experience. The powerful syndicalist movement led by Tom Mann and James Connolly had grown out of desperation with the limitations of the reformist politics of their day.[50] Both men had moved towards a revolutionary political awareness, and recognised the need to form a separate party of and for the working-class, as debated in the pages of The *Industrial Syndicalist.*[51] In contrast, right-wing thinkers about unionism – such as Allan Flanders (a key author of the Donovan report) and Ben Roberts, alongside the more liberal-minded Hugh Clegg – not only denied the role of unions in class struggle, but actively sought to ensure that the unions, one way or another, would become part of the obstacle to waging that struggle, and would help limit the influence of class politics on the minds and actions of workers.[52] For his part, Ramelson saw the struggle for trade union rights, and for workers to be party to their own pay determination through collective bargaining and strikes, and for the wider working class to control their destiny, as both a revolutionary duty and a communist's desire.

John Kelly[53] examines Lenin's own changing views of trade unionism in response to both ultra-left criticisms[54] and new left versions.[55] In particular he sees Lenin's *What Is To Be Done?* as a timely polemic against economism and showed the tensions within trade unions to form either bourgeois or revolutionary ideologies: hence the requirement to fight this 'contingent' rather than 'inevitable' tendency within the unions. Kelly believes that, 'Lenin argued strongly for Social-Democratic "influence", even control, in the trade unions, thereby indicating his belief in the possibility of a revolutionary trade unionism as distinct from a non-revolutionary or bourgeois trade unionism'.[56] On this account, at least, Ramelson's strategy within the unions and with the Labour Party union links was more Leninist than it was economist, social democratic, or Luxemburgist.[57]

An important reformist hallmark of the time was the re-invention of forms of corporatism or tripartism – an example of the famous Mafia saying to 'hold one's friends close and enemies closer'. This embraced the notion that the best way to secure the national interest, defined in terms of a growing capitalist economy in which the majority would derive some benefit, was for the major players – employers, the government, and the unions – to join together in decision-making bodies aimed at a modernising programme of regeneration and industrial peace. This model, used in some European countries to keep out the communists, maintained the pretence that the unions were equal partners in these arrangements, and that, as they were the representatives of the working class as a whole, this allowed workers a voice at the high table. Not only did this create a further illusion of participation in democratic capitalism; it also led to disillusion with trade unions and their leaders when benefits were not forthcoming. During Ramelson's period of office both Labour and the Conservatives created the institutions of tripartism, as well as some of the policies. In many ways the Social Contract was the final version – before the deluge of what came to be known as Thatcherism. Ramelson therefore had not only to forge a different approach to the issues, but also to overthrow the anti-communist labourism personified in Labour leaders such as Deakin.

Ramelson's view – implicit in every issue of the Party's programme the *British Road to Socialism* – was that revolutionary change would come about in British conditions through the efforts of the labour movement and its allies, and that these efforts would only be given socialist content by building left unity involving communists at every level of struggle. This process would be reflected in a parliamentary majority of Labour and CP members supported by a powerful extra-parliamentary movement, working together to break the capitalist state and begin building a new socialist society. Thus, in making the case for the socialist transformation of society, Ramelson wrote:

> Because our Party is based on Marxism-Leninism – the science of social change – we are better able to understand the world we live in and how to change it. It is not an easy task, nor will it necessarily be achieved in one jump, and certainly not by a handful of dedicated socialists acting on their own. It will require the unity in struggle of the majority of our people with, as the core, the mass organisations of the working class. But to achieve this level of mass activity and socialist understanding, a party of dedicated socialists committed to this objective, basing itself on the creative application of Marxism to British conditions, is needed. This party is the Communist Party, and it plays a key role in the development of the movement.[58]

Similar positions and analysis found their way into the Party's programme in 1977:

> As right-wing ideas and leadership in the labour movement are progressively defeated and replaced by people and policies committed to struggle against the monopolies, as the Communist Party itself grows in strength and influence, so new opportunities will open up for still more developed forms of Labour-Communist unity, including in the electoral field, and with the possibility of future affiliation to the Labour Party.[59]

These CP strategies came under fire from other leftists, partly because of the weakness of the left inside the Labour Party and wider move-ment. Many were disillusioned with the incoming 1964 Labour government right from the start, and argued in various ways that such a government was probably a necessary, but clearly not a sufficient, condition for left advance. Ralph Miliband and John Saville debated these questions in the pages of *New Left Review* and *Socialist Register*.[60]

Their quest was threefold: what kind of policies could the left agree upon; what was wrong with the Labour government; and how could the left respond in terms of working in the unions, in the Labour Party, and/or in forming some other left political grouping. This debate went on apace, especially after the Labour defeat in 1970, and it has continued to echo down the years until today. The problem tended to be posed rather statically as a choice between those who believed that the Labour Party could be won for socialism, and those that did not.[61] This rather stark Manichean fallacy tended to miss the point, as for example with Perry Anderson's limited analysis that 'the most urgent need is to recreate an independent, combative Left, with its own goals and its own timetable'.[62] This was a point taken up by Raymond Williams:

> The Communist Party, since the early 1920s, has worked as a militant wing of the Labour movement: often involved in local struggles against the Labour Party, often influential in particular trade unions, but never looking likely to become a mass party. Labour Government, with the maintenance of a militant Communist minority, has in practice been its normal political aim.[63]

OPPOSITION TO INCOMES POLICIES

The hallmark of much of Ramelson's work was opposition to all forms of incomes policy. This required analysing critically the actual details of the policies – mainly through pamphlets, arguing at meetings with union leaders and activists, helping to frame motions to union conferences, opening up debate through the pages of the *Morning Star (Daily Worker)*, feeding information into education classes, formulating deeper comments around the nature of inflation, and offering an alternative. The fight was effectively against three groups: governmental leaders in favour of wage restraint; those inside the movement who supported incomes policy as a means of protecting lower paid and poorly organised groups; and the ultra-left, whose opposition was based not so much on policy terms but in order to undermine communist union leaders and to build their own organisations.

Ramelson read the broadsheet press carefully, keeping abreast of current debates concerning politicians and economists, and read widely on economics. Ron Bellamy, a lecturer in economics at Leeds University, told us that Ramelson had on his book shelves a well-thumbed hard back copy of Keynes's *General Theory*, commenting that he could think of few politicians with either the desire or the ability to tackle this difficult treatise, which had informed so much of the post-war economic debate. All this helped Ramelson tackle complex economics questions. It was backed by years of participation in Party education programmes, reading Party materials, and a deep understanding of the Marxist classics.

Ramelson had learnt about the nature and function of all and any form of state-sponsored wage controls throughout his time in Yorkshire in the 1950s, and had learnt of the importance to oppose and to be seen to oppose them at every opportunity. In 1956, for example, the White Paper, *The Economic Implications of Full Employment*, called for wage and price restraint,[64] and was followed in 1957 by the Council on Prices, Productivity and Incomes based on the notion that its reports would promote understanding and thus alter attitudes and then behaviour.[65] During Ramelson's period as Industrial organiser the British economy lurched from one economic crisis to the next. While growth in the economy and productivity was historically high for the UK in the mid-1960s, it lagged behind France, Germany and Japan. Thus our market share fell as inflation rose, and this uneven growth meant a severe balance-of-payments crisis, which in turn put pressure on government to reduce demand and slow growth in order to cut back imports. This set of policies was better known as 'stop-go' and fed into the trade cycles of 'boom and bust'.

Trade union membership had grown from 9.5 million in 1951 to 10.1 million by 1964, with union density remaining almost static. Industry-wide collective bargaining was the norm backed by strong central union leadership. By the late 1950s shop stewards had come to the fore in manufacturing, with plant-level collective bargaining, after a chequered history of bitter struggle.[66] By the early 1960s, public concern about industrial relations was growing, due to the increase in strike activity, and there were several public inquiries into various disputes.[67] The dominant political class, including the Labour leadership, were anxious to control the growing strength of the trade union movement, as was a compliant mass media. By the time of the 1964 general election industrial relations was centre stage and reform of collective bargaining was subject to fierce debate within and between the major political parties.

Within a growth economy characterised by relatively low levels of unemployment, the confidence and militancy of the unions grew, and in this milieu the left, including the CP, became more influential. The unions were involved in both political and industrial strategy through their own links with the Labour Party.[68] Ramelson and the CP developed a more open approach to left unity than had been the case in the past, with increased support of non-party candidates for election in unions, and with an emphasis on mobilisation and supporting action. Much of the CP line was based on the reality of industrial militancy. Official and unofficial stoppages and disputes were widespread and growing in intensity, duration, and scope. CP organiser Dennis Goodwin argued that:

> … shop stewards represent one of the most outstanding achievements of British trade unionism. Democratic in form and content, the shop stewards have largely made possible the building of trade union membership and organization … their future role is even more important as elected representatives at the point of production.[69]

The fight against incomes policies from 1960 to 1980 could be seen as having two fronts: political and industrial. Ramelson, through the CP, was in the forefront of working-class and trade union opposition. Incomes policies and the fight against them were seen to be both at the centre of the class struggle, and as crucial for shifting the balance of class forces in favour of the working class. This fight involved some of the most famous disputes in the post-war years, as well as some of the most bitter battles inside the Labour Party.

The two outstanding features of the CP position with regard to any form of wage restraint were: it was located within a traditional socialist critique of modern capitalism and hence was a serious actor; and it addressed the limitations of labourism in ways that allowed Labour supporters to oppose incomes policies without throwing out the rest of the policy mash. Most commentators thought that the evidence was that, in and of themselves, incomes policies did not work in terms of holding back wages for any length of time. In 1980 an ACAS handbook on industrial relations stated that:

Since the end of the Second World War recurrent periods of inflation have led successive governments to intervene in collective bargaining in an attempt to control the levels of wage increases. Since 1965 these efforts have been virtually continuous, and a number of different approaches have been tried, but none has been successful in restraining wage increases for more than relatively short periods.[70]

Ramelson agreed, but felt that incomes policies did tend to confuse and limit the militant struggle amongst trade unionists, especially at times of Labour governments.

How to control inflation became a central concern for every government from the early 1960s onwards. For both Tory and Labour governments tackling what they saw as union power was the solution, and wage controls were seen to be the single most powerful tool in breaking the inflationary spiral. The Labour governments of 1964 to 1970 and the overwhelming majority of the press and other media channels sang from the same hymn sheet on this issue. Inflation, it was argued, was caused by wages (a major cost to most employers) rising faster than improvements in labour productivity. Such wage movements not only raised industrial costs; they also fed into excess demand, leading to both upward pressure on prices as effective demand exceeded the supply of goods and services, and to increased imports as a way of meeting increased demand. The final link in the chain for the incomes policy hawks was that between inflation and unemployment: it was argued that increased costs made British goods uncompetitive on world markets, and in competition with imported goods on the home market. To use a cliché popular at the time, 'British workers were pricing themselves out of jobs'. These arguments were given an academic fig leaf by studies which purported to show that there was an inverse relationship between wage movements and employment levels – the so-called Philips curve, illustrating that as wage levels rose, employment levels fell.[71] Labour politicians argued that if jobs were to be protected inflation had to be controlled, and the key to this was to curb or halt the rise in real wages.

In his pamphlets and articles Ramelson was able to expose various fallacies in the arguments advanced by the dominant section within the labour movement leadership. Whilst acknowledging that wages were a cost for employing and quipping that if we all worked for nothing it would do wonders for keeping down prices, Ramelson was able to show that the fall in the inflation rate during the second half of the 1970s was due primarily to a dramatic reduction in world commodity prices, which had led to reduced costs across the capitalist world, whether or not the various countries had wage controls in place or were experiencing real wage growth. He went on to argue that by depressing demand (reducing consumption power) wage freezes led to lower production, increased unit costs, rising unemployment and lower productivity. If, argued Ramelson, politicians intended to tackle inflation in a pro-worker way they could break the prices-wages spiral by controlling prices, in the expectation that trade unions would reflect this in their bargaining demands.

A major element of policy-making in this area was the need for some kind of tripartite agreement as between government, employers, and unions. This meant that the TUC had to become more important, as the representative of unions to government; and this in turn meant that control over TUC policy became central to the conduct of industrial relations. Ramelson understood this and acted accordingly. As Derek Robinson, an academic labour economist, argued, since no individual union would accept less than it could get: 'it is a necessary condition therefore that the general agreement of the trade union movement be obtained if a voluntary incomes policy is to stand any chance of success'.[72] Robinson went on to explain why incomes policies lead to trade union centralisation, but union opposition may occur because of a narrowing of differentials: 'It is also the case that an incomes policy places a greater strain on the relations between leadership and rank-and-file, and that a point can come where the strain proves intolerable'.[73] He is also clear that 'the importance of trade unions being able to commit their members to the restraint aspect of the policy cannot be over-stressed'; and that within this it had to be remembered that 'the most common objective of incomes policy, or the most often used argument to justify workers' cooperation, is the ending of inflation'.[74] This argument puts the economic case for the later conundrum that:

> over successive incomes policies ... the TUC was persuaded to help rescue Labour governments in economic trouble by agreeing to accept wage restraint or even a wage freeze on behalf of its affiliate members. This often led ... to widespread discontent among ... activists ... which brought about the eventual rejection of incomes policies by many rank-and-file trade unionists.[75]

This sums up the conventional wisdom on the subject, and also confirms Ramelson's analysis and response, based on winning policy at the level of the TUC, winning the argument about the causes of inflation, and encouraging rank-and-file opposition to their own unions' policies and practices. Through an attack on wages and a weakening of union bargaining power, incomes policies, along with other measures, helped shift the power balance in the labour market towards the employer. This was seen as a good thing for the nation – as defined in terms of the interests of the ruling class.

Communists opposed all wage controls under a Labour government on five grounds: first, they did not work, in the sense that they did not reduce inflation, and that through deflation and demand reduction they made the economy worse; second, wage controls were unfair and unjust because only wages as income were being held back, while all forms of rents and profits as income went unregulated; third, they represented an attack on the working class through their main defence organisations, the trade unions; fourth, they encouraged class collaboration and so not only reduced the actual power of the organised working class but also the beliefs (the consciousness) of power and class, and the need for extra-parliamentary struggle to enforce change; and fifth, acceptance of such a policy was a shift in left politics suggesting that a Labour government was both a necessary and now a sufficient condition for left progress, against the general line of the left that it was a necessary but not a sufficient condition, and that struggle, both industrial and political, was required to push forward a left agenda.

In spring 1966 Ramelson began work on a 4000-word article, 'Incomes Policy in Britain: Its Theory and Practice'. This was published in *World Marxist Review* in July 1966, and proved to be a seminal work, setting out the theory of incomes policy and then systematically undermining point by point the justification used by the policy's apologists. It is worth setting out his views on the theory of incomes policy in some detail and remembering their context: an inflation-prone economy with an almost fully employed workforce, and a trade union movement re-invigorated by its increased bargaining strength, particularly at workplace level in the export trades.

Ramelson argued that:

There was a time when the very thought of the State interfering with the free play of the market … was anathema to bourgeois economists. But times have changed and with them bourgeois attitudes to State intervention …

In the past the reserve army of labour – the unemployed – was a built in feature of the capitalist system. The commodity, labour power, was more or less permanently a glut on the market. In these circumstances of supply in excess of demand, the employer … was able to use the conditions of the market to his advantage …

However, for the past two decades … there has existed a situation unique in capitalist history. Since 1946 … far from there being a reserve army of unemployed … the reverse has been the case. There has been a general shortage of labour power and a chronic shortage of skilled labour … This situation provides the best setting for advances on the economic front within the confines of capitalist society. The higher the standard won, the more powerful become the forces for further advance.

The true nature of the State (in this connection it is irrelevant whether there is a Labour or Conservative Government) as the agent of the ruling class now emerges and begins to assert itself. It rushes to the aid of the employers.

He then goes on to vigorously contest the notion that inflation was at that time either out of control or mainly caused by wage increases: 'the argument that says an Incomes Policy is necessary to halt inflation exaggerates the extent of the inflation then ascribes it, without a tittle of evidence, to high wages and proposes the cure: an incomes policy'.[76]

During the 1970s the argument had to change somewhat, since it was evident that inflation was rampant, rather than taking the mild form of the 1960s. This had to be explained if the arguments against wages control were to be convincingly sustained. There is of course a valid argument for leaving wage bargaining to the market in a capitalist society, and to break the prices-wages spiral by acting on prices and profits, thereby changing the environment significantly enough to encourage lower settlement. However it was not difficult to explain how mild inflation had become rampant inflation. In later works Ramelson could, and did, point to the effects of the 1967 devaluation of sterling, the tripling of oil prices following the Yom Kippur war, the general increase in world commodity prices, the further development of monopoly 'pricing', the impact of deflationary budgets on unit costs, and the effect of taxation levels (particularly indirect taxes on goods and services).

The article then examines the alleged trade-off between wages and jobs (the 'workers pricing themselves out of jobs' argument). He shows that the increased demand in the economy resulting from rising real wages saves rather than destroys jobs, and that Britain's chronic balance-of-payments' crisis is explained mainly by huge expenditure on overseas military bases; the needs of the City to keep sterling as an overvalued international currency (making exports dearer and imports cheaper); and deflationary government policies which depress output, thereby raising labour costs as fixed costs rise as a proportion of total costs. The last plank in Ramelson's attack on the justifications for an incomes policy deals with the alleged link between wage controls, planning and egalitarianism, namely the argument that incomes policy is in fact a form of socialist wages policy. As Ramelson says:

> Briefly the argument runs that Socialists believe in planning and this means planning wages too; 'incomes policy' is merely a synonym for planning wages … Of course, the fact of the matter is that the only thing being 'planned' is precisely wages and nothing else. How indeed can it be anything else when the levers of a planned economy – the investment capital, the disposal of surpluses – are not in the hands of, or even remotely controlled by, the would-be planners, the Government.
>
> The argument that incomes policy means closing the gap between lower paid and higher paid is equally false, as seen from the … flat rejection by the National Coal Board recently of the lower paid day-wage miner's claim for higher wages … [and] the cavalier rejection by the Prices and Incomes Board (PIB) also of the railwaymen's claim (also a lower paid section). This is proof enough that 'incomes policy' is aimed at keeping *everyone's* earnings down, whether they be higher or lower paid.[77]

Similar points, refined and developed in the light of experience, are deployed in all of Ramelson's pamphlets from 1966 onwards.

Campbell and Ramelson developed these points in an article in *Marxism Today*. They argued that the Labour government's policies were mainly aimed at modernising British capitalism through the use of state machinery, for example the new ministries of Economic Affairs and Technology and the Industrial Reorganisation Corporation. This strengthening of the role of the state in the interests of big business, as competition from the rest of world intensified, took place as the organised working class became stronger and therefore more able to fight against attacks on its organisations and living standards. As they argue, 'a continuous effort will be exerted to keep under constraint the trade union movement, whose past activities in promoting wage increases have been stigmatised by the Labour Government as one of the sources of Britain's economic difficulties'.[78]

As the crisis refused to go away, it became ever more pressing to produce a radical alternative that would address immediate problems in the interests of the working people and tackle fundamental structural questions, such as the failure to invest in British industry. What is significant in the CP response led by Ramelson is the transformation of the argument from one of what can be called a defensive rejection of incomes policy, with a few shopping-list policy alternatives thrown in almost as an afterthought, to a recognition that the only real answer is a long term one – a fully-fledged socialist economy. By 1977 the long-term aim of socialist revolution remains, but in place of short-term assorted policy demands there is mapped out a strategy for radical change. Now, in answer to the Social Contract and the chronic crisis during which successive Labour governments had shown neither the ability nor the stomach to challenge Treasury policies, or to tackle continuing ills of the British economy in a working-class-friendly fashion, Ramelson produced what amounts to a transitional programme, a genuinely alternative economic strategy. This is dynamic in concept, and based on mobilising the labour movement and its allies to campaign for policies which make inroads into capitalist power. As he put it in replying to discussion at a Party economics seminar in the summer of 1977:

> It must be a programme the implementation of which challenges the ruling class and the only way it can be implemented is to mobilise the people who see the credibility, the practicality and the need for that immediate programme to realise their expectations. It is in the course of that sort of challenge and counter-challenge that the political consciousness and understanding of workers is raised so that they are prepared to take the next step. This is what the first stage of the transitional programme envisaged in the *British Road to Socialism* really is.[79]

This radical development in policy and approach came about because it was clear by the early 1970s that the Labour governments in the 1960s had been failures in managing the British economy. The Labour leadership, in thrall to the Treasury, had no credible answer, and fell back on traditional policies designed to dampen demand and hold back the growth of real wages. Early in the Heath government of 1970-74 it became even clearer that sections of the ruling class, whether under a Tory or Labour government, had determined that a modern capitalist economy could not be managed in the old way. Ramelson picked up on this new mood. It is worth quoting his views at some length, since he clearly identifies the problem facing British capitalism at that time when there had been a discernible change in the balance of class forces in favour of the working class. Ramelson argued:

> In fact the British workers not only refuse to become the sacrificial lambs for British imperialism, they have now got the power to thwart the attempts to place the burden of the crisis on their backs.
>
> Indeed they have the power to take the offensive and go even further. The distribution of wealth between capitalists and workers – wealth which the workers alone produce – has hardly changed in the last 100 years. The growing strength, militancy and political maturity of the working class are putting it in a position to bring about a fundamental redistribution of that wealth in its favour. This is the nature of the problem facing the ruling class. That is why it wants to cripple the unions and do away with collective bargaining.

Ramelson then goes on to quote leading Tory Reginald Maudling, who in September 1972 had published the 'Maudling Memorandum' in *The Times*, arguing that this was a remarkably candid confirmation of this thesis (the italics are Ramelson's):

> The capitalist system ... *has led inevitably to wide disparities in living standards and to the concentration of a large amount of wealth in a fairly limited number of hands* ... We must recognize that this has only *persisted because the majority have not been prepared to use their potential economic and political power against the prosperous minority.*
>
> We have seen in the last two decades *an arising consciousness of the power of organised labour.* Some groups of employees, *organised*

into unions, now possess the power to bring any capitalist economy to a halt.

I do not *think we can now redress the balance by individual measures.* A capitalist economy must be prepared to accept a far greater degree of *systematic control over the level of incomes and prices than we have ever contemplated before.*[80]

In 1972 not only was British capitalism in great difficulty, but, as Ramelson argues, the working class was strong enough to resist attacks on its living standards and trade-union organisations. Ramelson knew that such a situation could not persist. Unless the left advanced policies and campaigns which broke this deadlock on favourable terms for the working class, and mobilised mass support and activity in their support, the state would intervene to limit trade-union rights and powers.

The right wing of the labour movement's answer, both under the Heath government and Wilson's Labour government, was the Social Contract. The left, led by the CP, with Ramelson by far the single biggest individual influence, responded with the Alternative Economic and Political Strategy. Ramelson had no doubts about the need for all-out opposition to the Social Contract, even if the cost was a split with left-wing union leaders such as Jones and Scanlon. Ramelson knew that Wilson, Callaghan and Healey had no intention of introducing radical social change. Their objective was to win a general election and to obtain the co-operation of union leaders for a policy of wage restraint. As Ramelson had predicted, the rest of the Social Contract was ditched, as government cuts resulted in rapidly rising unemployment and reduction in the social wage, and the Social Contract itself morphed into straightforward wage restraint. The consequences were stark. According to Colin Leys, 'estimates of the effects of this restraint vary, but it is generally agreed that over the years 1975-7, manual workers as a whole experienced a cut in real income of between 7% and 8% compared with 1974'.[81]

Some twenty years later, Ron Bellamy graphically analysed the discussions within the Party's Economic Committee, in which some neo-Gramscian academics argued in favour of a social contract. He argued, as did Ramelson, that the post-war capitalist boom, albeit uneven, had petered out by the late 1950s, and that during the 1960s it was very clear that British imperialism was exhibiting 'increasingly potent structural weakness ... in effect with the end of the Special post-war conditions a new phase began – "the party was over". The deep crisis of reformism was marked by sharper class struggle'.[82] These developments had brought with them a renewed interest in Marxism, not least in the field of economic theory, and this in turn had led to a number of young academically-trained economists joining the Party and becoming active, at least at the level of theoretical debate. Here Bellamy is sharply critical of Ramelson's response to such developments as they affected the work of the Economic Committee: 'rightly welcoming this addition to our forces but with over-confidence in his own ability to win them to his views, Bert Ramelson, the Committee's new Chair (from 1965), relaxed the long-standing practice that new members should have some political experience'. One example given by Bellamy of the problems this caused was a meeting at which Ramelson was told that 'he should be more critical of his arguments for he didn't have a degree in economics'.

Bellamy accepts, however, that the broadening of the Committee (in line with Ramelson's instincts) did lead to some useful discussions, which had helped the Party to develop its policies to meet the challenges of imperialist economic decline and the crisis of reformism. Thus, he explains that the term 'Alternative Strategy' was first used in a Ramelson pamphlet in 1967, and following this a 'more narrowly economic version, the AES (elaborated in the book of the newly formed Conference of Socialist Economists) was adopted by the TUC and reflected in Labour's 1973 Programme'. (It should be added that Labour's version was little more than a set of legislative measures, entirely eschewing the dynamic approach of Ramelson, which emphasised the importance of extra-parliamentary struggle in changing the balance of political forces in favour of a new economic programme which would challenge the power and influence of big business).

The divisions in the Economic Committee that were already evident in the early 1970s, widened with the advent of the Social Contract in 1974/1975. According to Bellamy most of the new academic members, argued for a 'socialist incomes policy'. They also claimed that wage militancy was the root cause of chronic inflation during this whole period (from 1964 onwards). Fortunately, Ramelson had rather more success in mobilising the forces in the labour movement that eventually defeated the Social Contract in practice. Within the CP membership Ramelson's line was that of the majority.

Bellamy's criticism of Ramelson highlights aspects of the latter's approach – which had both strengths and weaknesses. Ramelson always expected that well made arguments, put to people with generally good intentions, would win the day. He was open to new ideas, always prepared to have his own views challenged, and when convinced, prepared to change. In the case of the Economic Committee he certainly took risks but in the end his version of Party policy prevailed.[83]

David Purdy, perhaps the most persistent and perceptive of the neo-Gramscian critics, had this to say of Ramelson:

> As chair of the committee, Bert never tried to suppress debate: on the contrary, he encouraged and relished disputation – the fiercer, the better. Like a Jesuit priest, however, he took good care to insulate the rest of the party from heresy – including the Executive Committee.[84]

As we shall see Purdy's allegations of Ramelson's 'hidden debates' were misleading – these questions were openly debated in *Marxism Today* and in the Party's *Economic Bulletin*.

THE ALTERNATIVE ECONOMIC STRATEGY

The Alternative Economic Strategy (AES) was initiated in embryonic form by the CP in the late 1960s, and was quickly taken up by the Labour left and sections of the trade union movement. It was the centre point of the Industrial Department's *Needs of the Hour* in 1974, and was put before the TUC Congress that year in a motion submitted by AEUW-TASS (Amalgamated Union of Engineering Workers and Technical, Administrative and Supervisory Staffs). It contained elements of Keynesianism (state-sponsored expansion to promote growth and create jobs); and argued for indicative planning (agreement with large companies on investment and employment levels linked to government commitments to expand the overall economy); controls (on imports, capital growth and prices), extended public ownership (banks, North Sea Oil); and redistribution (through wealth taxes and reductions in indirect taxes). This is not a socialist programme, but, as Ramelson argued, any such approach would be strongly resisted by big business, the media, and top civil servants. In Ramelson's view, it would only be possible to overcome this resistance 'by the mobilisation of the mass movement resulting in a government which will carry out this policy, and in turn will look for support from the working people'.[85] Ramelson also went out of his way to stress that a government carrying out this policy could expect the support of the trade unions, whose bargaining agenda (including wage levels) would take into account the policies to control inflation and promote investment and jobs.

The AES was constantly refined in the light of experience, and was published in its most developed form in Ramelson's 1977 pamphlet *Bury the Social Contract*. The Party's strategy was based on understanding that, as the struggle for the AES developed, so political consciousness would deepen, while a left government would draw confidence from the growth and increasing militancy of the extra-parliamentary movement. Thus it might take at least two parliaments to adopt the main points of the AES as government policy, and two more parliaments to transform this training programme into what would be recognised as a socialist economy and the basis for a future socialist society. Above all else this depended, argued Ramelson, upon the strength of the extra-parliamentary movement.

The AES was attacked by elements of the left as well as by right-wing social democrats. The ultra-left dismissed it as pie in the sky: such radical change could only be achieved on the day after the revolution, and until that day the capitalist state would fight tooth and nail to preserve the existing order. It was argued that Ramelson and his supporters were building illusions, and that an emphatically socialist programme provided the best basis for mass mobilisation in the struggle for progressive change.[86] Ramelson recognised the problem, and always argued that there is no solution to the security of employment, or meeting the rising expectations of workers, within the confines of capitalist society. The problem to be addressed was how to get from where the movement was in the 1970s, when it was faced by chronic economic problems, to a new stage where socialist policies and values were majority positions. The AES, by addressing immediate concerns in a way which weakened the power of the big international monopolies, provided a bridge from the present towards the socialist future. Mass struggle in the past, Ramelson would argue, had created a National Health Service (NHS) largely outside of the capitalist market, and a welfare state placing considerable burdens on the employers. So, radical advances could be won within capitalism, but such progress could only be secured and guaranteed by a socialist revolution.

Within the CP the neo-Gramscians were critical of the AES's approach to the wages issue. For them, inflation was endemic to the system whenever trade unions were powerful enough to push up wages; and it was the struggle between employers seeking to raise profits, and workers wanting to improve living standards when in a strong bargaining position, which was the basic conflict creating chronic inflation in 1960s and 1970s Britain. The answer for the left, they argued, was a socialist incomes policy (a tripartite agreement between government, unions and employers), which sought to increase real wages when economic conditions allowed, while involving workers, through their unions, in economic planning discussions. In essence this was a souped-up Social Contract, relying on the goodwill of a Labour government. Ramelson was dismissive of such an approach. He argued: 'It is a theory that leads to passivity. I think that if ever there was a misnomer, it is the Conflict Theory (of inflation). It is the exact opposite. It is a theory of non-conflict, that is the logic of that particular theory'.[87]

Later, in his summing up of a discussion at an Economic Committee Seminar on the AES, Ramelson was at his polemical best. Arguing that the basic cause of Britain's economic woes was low investment not high wages, he summed up as follows:

> It is therefore not surprising that the same comrades advocate a social contract and reject measures challenging monopoly capital for fear that the world financial institutions would lose confidence in Britain's ability to cope with its working class, leading to bankruptcy … It is also a theory which condemns, despite the revolutionary phraseology, the working class to the role of being the saviours of capitalism whenever it is in crisis.
>
> This of course is not only the negation of the historic function of the working-class, it is also incapable of being realised. For it could only work – even if the working-class were willing to assume this suicidal role – if the assumption were that the capitalist's inherently basic contradiction between social production and private appropriation, that the basic problem of realisation of surplus value, have somehow been removed and disappeared from the scene of modern capitalism, assumptions which fly in the face of reality.[88]

Ramelson's position on the fraudulent nature of the case made for incomes policies, the bad economics behind this analysis of the causes of inflation, the need for an alternative, and the political fight for free collective bargaining and socialism were mainly derived from these expositions. Here he could draw upon earlier communist pamphlets attacking the Tory incomes policies of the late 1950s and early 1960s, as part of the Party's shift to focus on wages as the central issue in winning over trade union activists, in challenging the authority of the employer, in exposing the use of class power by the state, and, most importantly, in holding the working-class together as a class.[89]

THE COMMUNIST PARTY'S INDUSTRIAL STRATEGY AND ADVISORIES

Ramelson's tasks as national industrial organiser were to keep the EC appraised of developments in the trade union movement, and of industrial trends and developments; to oversee the work of the Party's National Industrial Advisory Committee based on industries and unions; to help develop CP policy for individual industries; and to assist in preparing analysis and propaganda materials on current industrial issues, not least government, Labour Party and TUC policies on these questions. The responsibility for the Party's workplace branches rested with the Organisation Department, whose main function was to encourage branch and membership development. This division of labour – the Industrial Department being responsible for labour movement questions and the Organisation Department for the hundred or so workplace branches – was a constant source of friction. Ramelson saw his main function as promoting Party policy in the labour movement. The job of organising Party building rested, in his view, with the Organisation Department which was in close contact with District leaderships.

When Ramelson came to London, the Party's industrial organisation was in the throes of change. Shaken by the ETU ballot-rigging scandal, the Party leadership was determined to clarify the relationship between Party advisories and individual unions. This was to be carried out in two main ways. Firstly, the advisories were to be organised solely on an industry basis, not a union one. Thus in theory the metals advisory would embrace all the Confederation of Shipbuilding and Engineering Unions (CSEU), while the Railways Advisory would include Party members from the three rail unions – at that time the National Union of Railwaymen (NUR), Associated Society of Locomotive Engineers and Firemen (ASLEF), and the Transport Salaried Staffs' Association (TSSA). Secondly, it was to be re-emphasised that the advisories were quasi-autonomous bodies with their own elected secretariats. Party full-time workers would from time to time attend meetings, usually quarterly. Membership of these bodies was largely determined by rank-and-file activists, often by personal invitation. In addition, there were a number of informal arrangements, particularly in small unions, where groups of leading comrades would consult on conference agendas, and at the time of important elections for full-time official appointments.

The CP's work in the unions was shaken and shaped by the events in the ETU. Unfriendly commentators are quite clear as to what happened. Robert Taylor believes that 'the communists were compelled to resort to ballot-rigging to keep their iron grip until 1963',[90] and Henry Pelling suggests that after the 1956 Hungarian episode many communists left the Party paving the way for a power grab by anti-communists in unions such as the ETU.[91] Rolph gives a detailed account of the trial from a moderately anti-communist position,[92] while Wedderburn explains the legal consequences.[93] Ramelson and the Party leadership were horrified and dismayed by such egotistical foolishness, and vowed to stamp out any corruption through more open and democratic methods of working inside and alongside unions.

Ramelson fully supported the new regime, and added his own ideas and stratagems to the mix. In particular he supported and encouraged the development of formal broad left organisations where this was practicable. He also used his personal links with broad left national union leaders to good advantage, such that the lay structures created by the left and the union leaderships were better aware of each other's positions and thinking. Ramelson was able to use this knowledge to influence the workings of unofficial and official union bodies.

One commentator summed it up as follows:

Ramelson's main contribution was to strengthen the Party's influence and contacts, and to open up new directions within the trade union movement. Many have pointed to his forceful, pro-active style of leadership, his 'dominating personality', and his organisational abilities; all these helped him to win trade unions to communist positions, and his status grew within the Party as he increased the Party's influence in the unions.[94]

In practice the advisories had, in general, good links with the national industrial department staff, and much more often than not looked to Ramelson for advice on difficult policy questions, including the choice of candidates to nominate for leading union positions.

Not that Ramelson's advice was always taken. While Communists were banned from contesting electoral positions in the now right-wing led ETU, they retained important levels of influence and organisation in many parts of Britain. Whoever wanted to challenge the existing strongly anti-Communist leadership of that union in national elections needed the Party's support to have any chance of defeating Frank Chappell's team. So it was no surprise when the former Party members and ETU national official Mark Young approached Ramelson to see if the Party would back him against Chappell for the upcoming election for the General Secretary's position. Since in Ramelson's view the ETU left had no alternative candidate capable of winning such a contest, and Young had at least some national standing in the union, he agreed to sound out the ETU communists about the position. He was in for a shock. Having recommended Young's candidature to a meeting of around a hundred, mainly London-based printers and construction site workers, Ramelson received little support and a fairly frosty reception. In the comrades' eyes Young was a traitor, a former Communist who had given up his Party card in order to keep his union full-time position following the rule change preventing communists from holding union positions. The ETU Advisory went on to back Fred Gore, a rank-and-file convenor from Heathrow Airport who subsequently went down to a substantial defeat.[95]

In practice some Advisories remained one-union outfits whose agenda was very much concerned with elections to full-time and lay positions. Ramelson was realistic enough to know that, even if he had wanted to, in Advisories such as the Metals he could not prevent such discussions from occurring. His task as he saw it was to encourage the debate of broad policy issues, and to emphasise the need for decisions taken to be followed through and implemented, as well as working for the election of broad left supported candidates to all levels of union leadership.

Ramelson's calculations on union elections were based on two criteria – who was best placed to win, and which candidate, if successful, would best help the struggle for left policies and socialist change. Whether or not a candidate held a Party card was very much a secondary consideration. So when in 1967 the post of President of the Amalgamated Union of Engineering Workers (AUEW) came up, Ramelson worked to persuade the left to support Hugh Scanlon, a member of the Labour Party left, rather than Reg Birch, a member of the CP's Executive Committee. He did so in the knowledge that Birch had alienated broad swathes of potential support with his rather arrogant ways and sectarian politics. By contrast Scanlon was a popular member of the broad left leadership, and was younger, more energetic and charismatic, and had wide support in the main centres of British engineering. Furthermore Ramelson knew that he could work with Scanlon, but any co-operation from Birch was improbable.

Anti-communist critics of the Party's industrial and electoral strategies increasingly attacked the strategy as being too interested in helping leading left-wing trade unionists at the expense of both revolution and socialism. Gollan's reply was that 'the role of the British people in decision-making in our class divided society is primarily by conflict and struggle and not by formal participation'.[96] A less extreme version of the electoralism criticism was that the CP's main focus was to secure the elections and appointment of broad left affiliated full-time union officials, and that in the CP's view this was the best way of advancing left policies in the unions and therefore the Labour Party. As a result, the critics continue, the CP both neglected, and downplayed, the importance of rank-and-file work, in order to curry favour with trade union leaders at national level. They argued that when the official movement went wrong, as with the Social Contract – as it was always bound to, given the nature of trade-union bureaucracy and the divergence of interests between full-time officials and rank-and-file members – it meant that the impetus of militant struggle developed over the previous decades was lost.

Darlington and Lyddon imply, with little evidence that the CP had been in thrall to the dispositions of left-wing trade union leaders, to the neglect of building independent rank-and-file organisation. The irony of this is that their book goes on to outline an impressive array of struggles across many industries, most of which were led or heavily influenced by communist militants.[97] Other critics deal with the relationship between the broad left and the CP, and, within this, the particular contribution made by Jones and Scanlon, the two most influential trade union leaders of their generation.[98] Here the suggestion is that the CP tailored its policies and tactics in order to develop mass support for left leaders rather than promote militant, let alone socialist, objectives.

This view, shared by the majority of ultra-left commentators, is clearly erroneous, and is no doubt designed to deny the revolutionary credentials of the CP. There are an overwhelming number of documented examples of Ramelson's leadership style and political practice which show that the Party stuck to its principled positions, and where necessary was sharply critical of left union leaders.

THE BROAD LEFT

The link between organisational forms and political strategies was quite clear in the way in which Ramelson developed the CP's industrial department. The key political idea was that of the 'broad left', a loose grouping of left-minded colleagues within a particular union or part of a union seeking to push through policy issues, agree points on the bargaining agenda, and win positions as shop stewards and regional and national officials. This union-style 'broad left' came out of the wider Party position on 'left unity', and corresponded with both the realities faced by communists and the traditions of the British left; and it also fed into the need to co-ordinate such cadres inside unions through the umbrella of Party policy and industrial strategy: hence the advisory system.

The task of winning the movement for left policies created the need for tactical formulations within individual unions and sections of unions. These tactics would be based around the current situation, in terms of union bargaining position, union activists, and the strength of the CP and other left groups. In addition there would be common goals and common policy initiatives beyond wage campaigns. Two things came together at this time to aid the strategy. First there was the ever-increasing tendency of the state to interfere in wages and unions: a string of incomes policies followed by a wave of anti-union laws allowed the Party and Ramelson to argue forcefully against wage controls, against limits on union actions, and for a higher standard of real and social wage, while supporting both the official and rank-and-file movements. Secondly, the cultural shift in the working class and the waning of post-war anti-communism meant that the Marxist message reached a wider audience than ever before and in many ways a more receptive one.

Ramelson was determined not to attempt to use the Advisories as an adjunct to official union structures. This could be said to be a non-Leninist approach, with Communist trade unionists accountable first and foremost to the trade union bodies from which they came, rather than to the Party line. This appears to be beyond the ken of some commentators. For example, both John McIlroy (the only academic to have contributed a serious, researched article on this issue) and Geoff Andrews have portrayed this apparently non-Leninist approach as a weakness in the Party's industrial work.[99] McIlroy in particular fails to comprehend what Ramelson understood very well. In British conditions with highly developed democratic unions, a serious revolutionary Party cannot simply hand down a line for all its members to fight for, regardless of all other considerations. Of course the Party has to have a line on important issues, and must argue for that line to be followed by its members. In some circumstances this is not possible, and Communist trade unionists, particularly in Ramelson's time, were always encouraged to apply the line with care, taking into account the democratically determined policies of their organisations. Of course there could be no truck with racism, xenophobia, sexism and bigotry, but some other issues were less straightforward, and the comrades in a particular union sometimes took a collective view not to pursue a Party-favoured course of action at a particular time. Such ambiguities could, of course, lead to tensions. In Ramelson's eyes these had to be argued out and settled by debate rather than imposition from the Party centre. Ramelson himself would ensure that the Party's line was understood and where necessary go public to explain to errant comrades 'the errors of their ways'. In this atmosphere and with these flexibilities it was possible to build successful Party-led rank-and-file organisations with substantial degrees of influence on official trade union structures. Organisations like the Trotskyist Workers Revolutionary Party (WRP), the International Socialists (IS, which later became the Socialist Worker Party, SWP) and Militant, with their pseudo-Leninist approach to policy implementation and membership discipline, largely failed to replicate the CP's success either in the 1960s and 1970s (nor have they done so since). While these failures can also be explained by these organisations hostile attitudes towards trade union officialdom, it is not surprising that in general left rank-and-file trade unionists declined to support unofficial bodies dominated by political sects over which they had no influence.

The sometimes difficult relationship between the Party and the CP member trade union activist/leader was brought into high relief at the 1974 TUC Congress. These events have been used by some commentators to illustrate what they see as a serious weakness in the Party's industrial work.[100] At the Congress a CP-led union, TASS, agreed not to push an anti-Social Contract motion to the vote after pressure from its bigger partner (the engineering union) within the AUEW, which was in the process of cementing a four-section amalgamation.[101] McIlroy puts it like this:

> the limits of this approach – [i.e. concentrating on winning leadership positions] was demonstrated by TASS acquiescence in the AUEW delegation's failure to oppose the Social Contract ... this underlined the boundaries of the party control over its members. There were close relations with Ramelson (who even sat in on negotiations over the AUEW merger). But he was perceived as having a voice which would be listened to rather than the purveyor of a line which demanded allegiance.[102]

Later in the piece, referring to the same events he says:

> ... the 1974 TUC demonstrated the magnetic force ran through Hugh Scanlon (President of the engineers) to Ken Gill (general secretary of TASS), not vice versa ... If the CP could not motivate its own leading members, how could it influence those independent of it?[103]

The narrative upon which this analysis is based is inaccurate and partial in both senses of the word. Firstly, there was no AUEW delegation – each section had its own autonomous delegates. Secondly, the motion was withdrawn only after the mover received assurances from the TUC General Council on their talks with the Labour government on the future and developing shape of the Social Contract. Third, the delegates themselves were never consulted – the deal was done between Gill and Scanlon without reference to their delegations. Both men assumed, almost certainly correctly, that the motion would be defeated by Congress, and in these circumstances it made some sense to withdraw. McIlroy also fails to give his readers vital contextual information on both the AUEW amalgamation and on the political balance of forces at the time, with a Labour government facing an imminent general election and defending a wafer-thin parliamentary majority. Neither does he tell us that Ramelson publicly castigated the two trade union leaders closest to his strategic plans in the next day's *Morning Star* (5.9.74). Ramelson did so not so much on political grounds (for he was loath to formally intervene in official union proceedings and decisions) but on the failure of the two leaders to consult their delegations. McIlroy's claim that Ramelson sat in on the AUEW amalgamation negotiations is incorrect. Informally, of course, the main actors were often in the same social environment and it should be assumed that they did not discuss the football results, but that is not the same thing as formal consultation.

McIlroy appears not to understand what the CP was trying to achieve and the methods used to obtain these ends. Under Ramelson's leadership sectarianism was outlawed – what mattered was advancing the interest of working people, which included strengthening the labour movement, which in turn included, most importantly, the CP. Of course he fought to influence leaders at all levels, and for the Party some leaders were more important than others. In these relationships, even with leading communists such as Ken Gill of TASS and Mick McGahey of the NUM, Ramelson did not see himself as a Leninist leader demanding democratic centralist discipline. He understood and respected the democratic constraints placed on trade union leaders and that by and large they knew better than he what was possible within their organisations. As McIlroy recognises, he certainly brought powerful arguments to his discussions with trade union leaders. He was a passionate advocate with strong views. By both temperament and conviction he despised those who used their positions to by-pass democratic norms, and he saw such methods as entirely counterproductive.

Gill later conceded that in hindsight Ramelson had made the correct judgement on the 1974 TASS motion since the TUC General Council went on to totally ignore the eight points in the withdrawn motion. It is likely that, armed with overwhelming Congress support for their own statement on the Social Contract, Len Murray (TUC general secretary) and Jack Jones of the TGWU in particular would have sidelined any successful resolution attempting to restrict their

freedom of movement during discussions with the Labour government. If this incident reveals a weakness in the Party's work during
Ramelson's stewardship, it is not the one identified by leftist critics like
McIlroy: a failure to assert Leninist practice and ensure total obedi-
ence to the Party line. Rather, it shows a tendency to put policy before
politics by overstressing the importance of Congress decisions, which
were not always necessarily backed by mass support among the rank
and file. It is one thing to win TUC Congress and Labour Party
Conference votes, and it is clearly an important objective. Perhaps too
often in the early 1970s such victories were used to overemphasise the
left's advances and misread the actual balance of class forces. For Gill
at the time, the cementing of the AUEW amalgamation, with the left
in a strong position in the leadership, seemed a bigger prize than going
down to almost certain, but principled, defeat on a challenge to the
Social Contract. In retrospect it is clear that Ramelson was on much
stronger ground criticising the failure of Gill and Scanlon to consult
their delegations than he was in taking Gill, in particular, to task for
withdrawing a motion doomed to defeat.

RANK AND FILISM

A central and decisively important plank of Party strategy at this time
was the founding of the Liaison Committee for the Defence of Trade
Unions (LCDTU), under the leadership of communist activist Kevin
Halpin. The LCDTU was set up in 1966 as a loose co-ordinating
body, but it really came into its own with opposition to *In Place of
Strife* in the late 1960s, and to the Industrial Relations Bill and Act in
the early 1970s.

The LCDTU, under communist leadership, was based on workplace trade union organisations, and it set itself the task of mobilising
mass action against anti-union measures (its main strengths were in
engineering, building and print). Among its more important aims was
to influence the official trade union movement, and to move the big
trade union battalions into active struggle.[104]

In a number of industries the Party had established an influential
network of broad left rank-and-file representatives, linked in some
pivotal unions to politically sympathetic full-time officials at district,
regional and national levels. This movement, informed by the clear
analysis of capitalist relations and political possibilities provided by

communists, had the confidence and mobilising power to work for the broadest possible opposition to state policies.

Ramelson's experience in Yorkshire had convinced him of the need to build effective rank-and-file organisation union by union, and with greater emphasis on unions which had significant industrial muscle and strong workplace organisation. The key to transforming the Yorkshire NUM, previously dominated by right-wing officials, had been the emergence and development of organised left opposition based at pit and panel level, with local bargaining units grouping together adjacent pits. CP rank-and-file leaders like Jock Kane and Sammy Taylor, with Ramelson's active support and Party backing, had been able to mobilise growing militancy during the 1950s, and shape it into political opposition to the right-wing area leadership. It is not surprising, therefore, that one of the first tasks Ramelson set himself on taking up the position of National Industrial Organiser was to explore ways in which an effective national rank-and-file movement could be developed alongside stronger organisation across individual unions and industries. The key mobilising event was the 1966 Prices and Incomes legislation (a further attempt by a Labour government to freeze real wages). Ramelson foresaw that the state's likely response, no matter which Party held office, was to intervene to limit union powers, by attacking union rights (particularly the right to strike) and restricting 'normal' collective bargaining (a phrase that Ramelson preferred to 'free' collective bargaining since the latter was always compromised in capitalist markets).

Arising from this analysis, and in response to government policy, Ramelson held discussions with CP rank-and-file members such as Kevin Halpin, Lou Lewis and Jim Hiles to explore what could be done to build effective organisation with the objective of combating state interference in collective bargaining and legal attacks on trade union rights.[105] Out of these discussions – and the lessons of the 1966 seafarers' dispute – the LCDTU was born, in September 1966.

To begin with Ramelson linked together a small number of London-based communist workplace leaders to hammer out a strategy. Two questions dominated initial discussions – what bodies should be eligible to be part of a national Co-ordinating Committee, and what issues it should take up. On the latter question it was decided that the agenda be limited to campaigning against state and legal restrictions on trade union rights, although throughout its existence there were pressures to broaden the Liaison Committee remit. The other main issue provoked more discussion. According to Kevin Halpin, it was Ramelson who insisted that the body be inclusive rather than restricted to workplace organisations only. Halpin recalls that it was Ramelson who argued that it was possible to win official trade union bodies for militant opposition to incomes policy, and therefore necessary to involve such bodies in the Liaison Committee's work. Halpin told us that various types of Trotskyists opposed this approach, arguing that full-time officials representing national or regional trade union bodies would dilute militancy and find reasons for not taking action against Labour government policy. In the event Ramelson's line carried the day. It was based on an optimistic assessment of possibilities, and a realistic judgement that only the power of the official movement, backed and encouraged by strong workplace organisation, could in fact defeat Labour's proposals on wages and industrial relations law.

That Ramelson's strategy was successful is somewhat reluctantly conceded:

> the Party sought consistently to mobilize workers to take industrial action against state policies. It did so, however, on the basis of calculated, limited objectives, with caution and finesse, and through a series of interlocking dialogues between its militants on the ground and the Industrial department which enabled it to select engagements with some prudence ... [but it did make] ... a real contribution to the defeat of *In Place of Strife*.[106]

In an unpublished paper written in 1973 Ramelson set out his views on the role and achievements of the LCDTU.[107] Its achievements were for all to see – it had built a strong enough base of support between 1966 and 1972 to create the political conditions which made it possible to defeat both *In Place of Strife* and the 1971 Industrial Relations Act. Along the road pressure from the Liaison Committee had convinced a reluctant TUC General Council to call a General Strike if five dockers imprisoned under the 1971 Act were not immediately released – as the 'Pentonville Five' quickly were.

In the draft article on 'Rank and Filism', Ramelson had this to say:

> It was the down to earth persistence of the LCDTU series of conferences, representative of the genuine militants in calling for rank and

file industrial actions, unofficial but enough, as a prelude to its pressures on the official movement, to rely on industrial action instead of useless parleying, that led to the decision of the TUC to call a general strike in protest against the imprisonment of the Pentonville Five and eventually to the call for a day of protest and stoppages on May 1st.

This decision would never have been taken if the main enemy had been seen to be the lefts within the trade union movement instead of the ruling class. It was only with the agreement of the AUEW and the T&GWU that the Special Congress took that decision with all its limitations.[108]

These extracts illustrate Ramelson's irritation with ultra-left critics whose rank-and-file politics set workplace trade unionists and trade union officialdom in opposite corners with diametrically opposed interests. For organisations of the ultra-left, trade union officials, because of their objective class positions, could not be trusted to represent workers' interests. Officials were divorced from the workplace, and had positions which demanded that they put organisational stability and the sanctity of national agreements above the immediate interests and demands of their members.

Thus, argued the ultra-leftists, only through self-organisation and activity could the rank-and-file successfully struggle to win its demands; and through such struggle political consciousness in the form of support for a socialist transformation of society would be developed. Ramelson accepted this final point – he had after all been arguing that there was a dialectical link between economic struggle and political change for over thirty years. He strongly opposed every other part of the rank-and-file perspective. His approach was to build a strong rank-and-file movement, but its task was not to replace the official movement but to force it to take up the demands of the workers, and by doing so become more democratically answerable to its members.

The Liaison Committee was the most powerful rank-and-file movements in the history of the British trade union movement. It periodically came under attack for being a creature of the CP, for being undemocratic in its practices, and for not being a genuine rank-and-file organisation with the potential to provide an alternative national leadership to that of the British TUC. It had of course never set out to be an alternative leadership, and it is doubtful whether it could have been as successful as it was if it had degenerated into a bear-pit of political discussion concerning democratic structures. Ramelson replied to some of these criticisms as follows:

> It is an elementary principle of Marxism that the objective and purpose of a movement determines its organizational form, not vice versa. That is why it is so ludicrous for those who claim to be the sole custodian of 'true Marxism' to devote so much space in their periodicals and waste so much time at a conference devoted to encouraging militant action with problems of an organizational and procedural nature as they have done at all conferences of the LCDTU.
>
> The LCDTU, since its coming into existence, has made its objective clear, It was not to form an alternative organization to the TUC – just as Flashlight [the Party-led broad-left organisation in the ETU/EEPTU] and Building Workers' Charter have no intention of creating alternative organizations to the EEPTU [Electrical, Electronic, Telecommunications and Plumbing Union] or UCATT [Union of Construction, Allied Trades and Technicians] and the TGWU Building Section. Their sole purpose is to encourage rank and file activity and bring pressure on the official movement to pursue policies reflecting the thinking of the rank and file.[109]

While the Liaison Committee remained an active force well into the 1980s, its influence began to wane with the introduction of the Social Contract in 1976. Its industrial base shrunk as new technology and lack of investment decimated the activities of the traditional industries from which the LCDTU had drawn its main strengths. Its decline was also brought about by right-wing Tory policies and monetarist economics, which led to mass unemployment and changed the balance of class forces in such a way as to drastically reduce trade union power and organisation. (These factors were also major objective reasons for the decline in the CP in the 1980s).

INDUSTRIAL DEMOCRACY

For a brief period, between the mid-1960s and the mid-1970s, there was a lively debate about industrial democracy both in official labour movement bodies and through the Institute of Workers' Control

(IWC), an initiative which attracted some interest at workplace and local branch levels within the trade union movement. Ideologically the IWC was a somewhat eclectic movement, stretching from the syndicalist approach advocating a socialist revolution to moderate demands for workers' participation in the management structures of private companies as well as the nationalised industries.

This diversity in both theory and practice clashed with the clarity of mind and purpose which Ramelson brought to industrial questions. In an article drafted in the late 1960s Ramelson had this to say:

> The diversity in terminology used to describe the theme – workers' control, workers' participation, joint consultation, involvement, social accountability, self-management, encroachment – is an indication of the diversity in conception as well as motivation of the growing number of participants, at the various levels of discussion on this theme.
>
> It is also a fairly good measure of the confusion and illusions that are being sown – utopian, syndicalist as well as downright class collaborationary and diversionary ideas that surround this subject.[110]

The article goes on to explain the objective and material reasons why the topic of industrial democracy appeared on the labour movement's agenda at this time. Ramelson argued that the new scientific and technological revolution, particularly computer-aided design and production, gave rise to possibilities for employers to increase production with smaller workforces and lower unit costs. For workers this could result in mass unemployment, greater insecurity and increased work intensity. New revolutionary techniques of production would invariably lead to changes in working practices, demanding craft dilution and multi-skilling and increased shift-working (i.e. 24-hours working to maximise the returns on the investment in new technology). For many the world of work was being turned upside down, the rate of expansion was increasing, and the sense of alienation was becoming an even more painful influence. Ramelson sums up the overall impact of these processes as follows: 'These are the objective circumstances which caused the organised workers to demand a say on many aspects of production, including investment policy, which was hitherto, left to management'.[111] This alone, the objective development of production techniques at a much faster rate than previously, was not enough to explain the demands for new forms of industrial democracy. There must, Ramelson explains, be a subjective factor. This he identifies as greatly increased confidence in the ability of trade unions to advance workers' interests. Ramelson summarises thus:

> It is the coincidence in time of technological changes, creating a need to extend the sphere of workers' influence, and the development of a trade union movement capable of demanding the satisfaction of this need, which constitutes the combination of circumstances giving rise to the present day movement for the expansion of industrial democracy.[112]

Throughout the period Ramelson remained suspicious of the motives of those using what he saw as loose talk about workers' control and its weaker form, workers' participation. Forms of workers' participation in management structures were the subject of seemingly endless discussions within the European Commission. These Ramelson saw as diversionary, and as a means of projecting class-collaborationist illusions in order to undermine the struggle for real advances in wages and conditions by extending the collective bargaining agenda. Above all else, Ramelson was anxious to highlight the threat to trade union independence posed by statutory regulation of industrial democracy and the placing of workers on the boards of capitalist companies.

Adapting a war-time slogan, Ramelson argued that in the class war careless talk was a threat to the advancement of workers' rights. The loose talk, particularly by leading members of the IWC, of the possibility of workers' control at workplace level within a capitalist society infuriated him.[113] In many ways, as Ramelson in a later contribution argued, the running was made by sections of the employing class, who in his view were seeking to contain growing trade union militancy by new forms of class collaboration. Ramelson concedes that,

> … we ought to stop and think whether we are not losing the initiative by failing to make constructive proposals so as to meet the workers' aspirations to curb the rights of management in decision-making on production and extend the workers' own rights and influence in this sphere today and not only in the future, not only under socialism. [114]

He goes on to insist that where progress has been made, whether it be through extending the scope of collective bargaining or successfully challenging employer decisions to cut the workforce, it had been due to militant struggle. Workers had made advances in achieving forms of workers' control, but only, Ramelson argues, 'by confronting the employers and insisting that decisions affecting them be made only by mutual agreement'. [115]

Yet, within the broad left, the rather eclectic programme of arguments advanced by the IWC did make some progress. Ramelson supported some of this programme, and was very much in favour of strengthening industrial democracy within the public sector. Requirements on private sector employers to 'open their books' so as to provide trade unions with information relevant to their members' interests were also given Ramelson's strong backing.

This question is probably the only one on which the CP, guided by Ramelson, was unable to establish a clear leadership position within the broad left. So anxious was Ramelson to scotch attempts by Labour governments – sometimes supported by trade union leaders and activists who saw themselves as part of the broad left – to divert growing militancy into collaboration and corporative channels that he often failed to sufficiently 'accentuate the positive' during the discussions which flowed as a consequence of the 1977 Bullock Report.[116] In the end the workers control movement went nowhere. Bullock proved to be a damp squib, and the Wilson government shelved it. Once the trade union militancy of the 1970s started to falter, with the acceleration of de-industrialisation and mass unemployment during the Thatcher years, the debate within the movement virtually ceased.

Ramelson's failure to give positive leadership on the issue should be seen as a rare blemish on his outstanding record. For once he had been too rigid in his approach and presentation. The IWC had captured a mood for progressive change – though it proceeded to misdirect it. A more positive approach by the CP could have helped to build a collective bargaining agenda giving more priority to democratic demands in the workplace. Ramelson trusted neither the leadership nor the politics advanced by the IWC, and it is easy to see why Coates and Topham, the two most prominent members of the Institute, responded in detail to some of the arguments advanced by Ramelson. On many issues there was agreement, but there was an enormous gulf in their perspectives about the transition to socialism. Coates and Topham advance what is essentially a syndicalist line. They see the encroachment on management prerogatives as a process until a point where capitalism cannot rule, and argue that: 'this programme is concerned with the struggle for workers' control here and now – a necessary strategy for achieving and a rehearsal of our socialist goal'.[117] Ramelson was always clear that workers' control, in the sense used here by Coates and Topham, could only be achieved after the working class had taken state control, and that whatever democratic advances were made within capitalism would take a different form in a workers' state, which would represent all workers and their families, not individual workforces.

Writing later, during the 1980s, Ramelson did take on board some of Coates and Topham's approach.[118] After dealing with his reservations, he argued:

> But I do believe that it is important to use the concept of workers' control as an important spur to workers, because in the fight for genuine control over their working lives, working class people will recognise the impossibility of achieving it within the framework of capitalism.[119]

One subjective barrier to relations between the CP and the IWC was the nature of the latter's leadership. Ramelson could debate with and work with Coates and Topham, who though of ultra-leftist provenance were not actively anti-communist. The same could not be said of the IWC's Treasurer, Harry Newton, who was almost pathologically anti-communist. Newton had been active in the CP during Ramelson's Yorkshire years, and the two men at that time had been on good terms. By the mid-1960s Newton was denouncing Ramelson as a Russian agent, and it subsequently turned out that for many years he had been working for MI5; he had been 'their man' inside a number of progressive organisations.[120] Coates and Topham were not to know this, but they must have been aware of Newton's fierce anti-communism, which made him an unsuitable secretary for a labour movement based progressive organisation.

CONCLUSION

When Ramelson arrived in 1965 to take over as national industrial national organiser of the CP he was faced with a set of unique opportunities. Classic Marxist-Leninist principles and practices had been updated and applied with vigour and scope to the situation in the UK across a broad range of policy and theoretical questions, by a group of leading intellectuals and activists on the communist left – of which Ramelson was a leading member. They had sharply distinguished themselves from all forms of reformism and economism, whether militant labour or syndicalist, and now set about developing policies and strategies that were fit for purpose: namely achieving a transition to a socialist Britain. This required a clear assessment of current strengths and possibilities, and Ramelson's role was to focus on the trade union movement. In his work he was able to broaden opposition to wage restraint and mobilise the movement to defend union rights and challenge the dominant conventional wisdom about the causes of inflation and the role of the state. This in turn allowed the debate in the movement to become sharper, more overtly political, and more class-based. The transmission of arguments and policies throughout the movement meant the development of non-intrusive but influential groups, formal and informal, at all levels inside the unions. Here advisories and later the LCDTU played critically important roles in bringing Party policy into the wider movement, and thereby galvanising action, co-ordinating responses and developing socialist consciousness. We will now examine how that played out in the turbulent years that followed.

NOTES

1. Morgan, K. *The People's Peace: British History 1945-1989*, Oxford University Press, Oxford 1990, p. 197.
2. Williams, R. *Culture and Society*, Chatto and Windus, London 1958.
3. Foster, J. and Woolfson, C. *The Politics of the UCS Work-in*, Lawrence & Wishart, London 1986.
4. Aaronovitch, S. *The Road from Thatcherism: the Alternative Economic Strategy*, Lawrence & Wishart, London 1981.
5. See general accounts such as Crouch, C. *The Politics of Industrial Relations*, Fontana, London 1979; and Taylor, R. *The Fifth Estate*, Pan Books, London 1978.
6. Andrews 2004, op.cit.
7. Goodman, G. *From Bevan to Blair*, Pluto Press, London 2003; pp. 145-6.
8. Dorfman, G. *Government versus trade unionism in British politics since 1968*, Macmillan, London 1979; p. 121.
9. McIlroy, J. and Campbell, A. 'Organizing the militants: the Liaison Committee for the Defence of Trade Unions, 1966-79', *British Journal of Industrial Relations* 1999, 37(1): pp. 1-31.

10. Foster and Woolfson 1986 op.cit; and later Foster, J. and Woolfson, C. 'How workers on the Clyde gained the capacity for class struggle: the Upper Clyde Shipbuilders' work-in, 1971-2' in McIlroy, J., Fishman, N. and Campbell. A. (eds.) *British Trade Unions and Industrial Politics: The High Tide of Trade Unionism, 1964-79*, Ashgate, Aldershot 1999, pp. 297-325; see also Thompson, W. and Hart, F. *The UCS Work-In*, Lawrence & Wishart, London 1972, with a foreword by Jimmy Reid. For a useful summary of the literature see Gold, M. 'Worker mobilization in the 1970s: revisiting work-ins, co-operatives, and alternative corporate plans', *Historical Studies in Industrial Relations*, 2004, No.18: 65-106

11. Burns, E. *Right Wing Labour: Its Theory and Practice*, Lawrence & Wishart, London 1961.

12. Hobsbawm, E. 'Parliamentary Cretinism?' *New Left Review* 1961 12: pp. 64-6.

13. Dobb, M. *Economic Growth and Underdeveloped Countries*, Lawrence & Wishart, London 1963; Mennell, W. *The British Economy*, Lawrence & Wishart, London 1964.

14. Palme Dutt, R. *Problems of Contemporary History*, International Publishers 1963.

15. Engels letter to Sorge1890 cited by Dutt, ibid., p. 128.

16. Miliband, R. *The State in Capitalist Society*, Quartet, London 1972; Griffith, J. *The Politics of the Judiciary*, Fontana, London 1977; Frankenberg, R. *Communities in Britain: Social Life in Town and Country*, Penguin 1966; Runciman, W. *Relative Deprivation and Social Justice*, Penguin 1970.

17. Fagan, H. *Nationalisation*, Lawrence & Wishart, London 1960; Brown, A. *Profits, Wages and Wealth*, Lawrence & Wishart, London 1961.

18. Campbell, J. *Some Economic Illusions in the Labour Movement*, Lawrence & Wishart, London 1959.

19. Tawney, R. *The Acquisitive Society*, G. Bell and sons, London 1926; Tawney, R. *Religion and the Rise of Capitalism*, Penguin 1937.

20. Haldane, J. *The Inequality of Man*, Penguin 1937.

21. Cole, G. *Practical Economics*, Penguin 1937.

22. Morton, A. *The English Utopia*, Lawrence & Wishart, London 1969.

23. Fyfe, H. *Keir Hardie*, Duckworth, London 1935.

24. Fawcett, M. *Political Economy for Beginners*, Macmillan and Co., London 1884.

25. Thompson, E. *William Morris: Romantic to Revolutionary*, Merlin Press, London 1977.

26. Hobsbawm, E. (editor) *Labour's Turning Point 1880-1900*, Lawrence & Wishart, London 1948.

27. Rude, G. *Wilkes and Liberty* , Clarendon Press, Oxford 1962.

28. Marlow, J. *The Tolpuddle Martyrs*, Grafton Books, London 1985.

29. Huberman, L. *Man's Worldly Goods*, Victor Gollanz, London 1937, p. 308.
30. Lenin, V. *What is to be Done?*, OUP, Oxford 1902.
31. Lozovsky, A. *Marx and the Trade Unions*, Martin Lawrence, London 1935.
32. Cole, G. *British Trade Unionism To-Day*, Methuen, London 1938; Cole, G. *The World of Labour*, G. Bell & Sons, London 1913.
33. Barou, N. *British Trade Unions*, Victor Gollanz, London 1947.
34. Pollitt, H. *Serving my Time*, Lawrence & Wishart, London 1940; Pollitt, H. *Selected Articles and Speeches*, volume II 1936-9, Lawrence & Wishart, London 1954.
35. Gallacher, W. *The Tyrants' Might is Passing*, Lawrence & Wishart, London 1954.
36. Hutt, A. *The Post-War History of the British Working Class*, Victor Gollanz, London 1937.
37. Lenin, V. (1895) 'Engels and English Socialism' in *British Labour and British Imperialism*, Lawrence & Wishart, London 1969, p. 19; Engels, F. *The Condition of the Working Class in England*, Leipzig 1845.
38. Gallacher, W. *Marxism and the Working Class*, Lawrence & Wishart, London 1943.
39. Miliband, R. 'Lenin's State and Revolution', *Socialist Register* 1970, pp. 309-319; Gramsci, A. *Selections from the Prison Notebooks*, Lawrence & Wishart, London, 1971 edition; Kiernan, V. 'Gramsci and Marxism', *Socialist Register* 1972, pp. 1-33.
40. Childs, D. 'The Cold War and the "British Road", 1946-53', *Journal of Contemporary History, 1988, 23: 551-572;* Piratin, P. *Cut Arms Not Houses - Raise Wages Not Profits*, CP 1949; Piratin, P. *Defend Trade Union Rights*, CP 1949.
41. Lenin, V. *The State and Revolution: The Marxist Theory of the State and the Tasks of the Proletariat in the Revolution*, Lawrence & Wishart, London 1969 edition, original 1917.
42. Piratin, P. *Our Flag Stays Red*, Lawrence & Wishart, London 1948.
43. Gollan, J. 'Which Road?' *Marxism Today* July 1964 pp. 198-216, p. 206.
44. Ibid., p. 211.
45. Taylor 1978, op.cit., p. 23.
46. Lumley, R. *White-Collar Unionism in Britain*, Methuen, London 1973.
47. Jim Mortimer interview, 2009.
48. Taylor, R. *The Trade Union Question in British Politics*, Blackwell, Oxford 1993; Pelling, H. *A History of British Trade Unionism*, Penguin 1976; Harrison, M. *Trade Unions and the Labour Party since 1945*, Allen & Unwin, London 1960; Minkin, L. *The Contentious Alliance: Trade Unions and the Labour Party*, Edinburgh University Press, Edinburgh 1991.
49. Coates, K. 'AEU Elections', *New Left Review* 1964 25, pp. 26-8.
50. Greaves, C. *The Life and Times of James Connolly*, Lawrence & Wishart, London 1961; Torr, D. *Tom Mann and his Times*, Lawrence & Wishart,

London 1956; Mann, T. *Tom Mann's Memoirs*, McGibbon & Kee, London 1923.

51. Brown, G. *The Industrial Syndicalist*; Documents in Socialist History No. 3; Spokesman, London 1974.

52. Flanders, A. *Management and Unions*, Faber & Faber, London 1970; Clegg, H. *Industrial Democracy and Nationalization*, Blackwell, Oxford 1951; Roberts, B. *Trade Union Government and Administration in Great Britain*, G. Bell & sons, London 1956.

53. Kelly, J. *Trade Unions and Socialist Politics*, Verso, London 1988.

54. Hyman, R. *Marxism and the Sociology of Trade Unionism*, Pluto Press, London 1971; Cliff, T. and Gluckstein, D. *Marxism and Trade Union Struggle: the General Strike of 1926*, Bookmarks, London 1986.

55. Anderson, P. 'The Limits and Possibilities of Trade Union Action' in Blackburn, R. and Cockburn, C. (eds) *The Incompatibles: trade union militancy and the consensus*, Penguin 1967, pp. 263-280.

56. Kelly 1988 op.cit., p. 31; Lenin's works cited here include *The Re-organization of the Party* (1905), and *Trade Union Neutrality* (1908).

57. For most of her works see Waters, M. (ed) *Rosa Luxemburg Speaks*, Pathfinder Press, New York 1970.

58. Ramelson, B. *Smash Phase III: the Tory Fraud Exposed*, CP December 1973, p. 20.

59. BRS 1977 edition p. 28.

60. Miliband, R. and Saville, J. 'Labour Policy and The Labour Left', *Socialist Register* 1964, pp. 149-156; Miliband, R. 'What Does The Left Want?' *Socialist Register* 1965, pp. 184-194; Miliband, R. 'The Labour Government and Beyond', *Socialist Register* 1966, pp.11-26.

61. Coates, K. 'Socialists and the Labour Party', *Socialist Register* 1973, pp. 155-178.

62. Anderson, P. 'The Left in the Fifties', *New Left Review* 1965, 29: 3-18, p. 3.

63. Williams, R. 'The British Left', *New Left Review* 1965 30: 18-26; p. 18.

64. Kessler, S. and Bayliss, F. *Contemporary British Industrial Relations*, Macmillan, London 1998, p. 4.

65. In 1957 the government established the Council on Prices, Productivity and Incomes, known as the 'three wise men'.

66. Frow, E. and Frow, R. *Shop Stewards and Workshop Struggles*, Working Class Movement Library, Manchester 1980.

67. Jack Scamp was head of GEC, chaired the Motor Industry Joint Labour Council, and in 1968 helped resolve the famous strike by sewing machinists at Fords that lead to the 1970 Equal Pay Act, and a film made in 2010, *Made In Dagenham*.

68. Thompson, W. *The Good Old Cause: British Communism 1921-1991*, Pluto Press, London 1992.

69. Goodwin, D. 'Shop Stewards – Past, Present, and Future', *Marxism Today*, April 1964, pp. 109-114; p. 109.

70. ACAS *Industrial Relations Handbook*, HMSO, London 1980, p. 35.

71. Phillips, A. 'The Relationship between Unemployment and the Rate of Change of Money Wages in the United Kingdom 1861-1957', *Economica*, 1958, 25(100): 283-299. The general view is that there is an inverse relationship between unemployment and inflation.

72. Robinson, D. *Incomes Policy and Capital Sharing in Europe*, Croom Helm, London 1973, p. 44.

73. Ibid., p. 49..

74. Ibid., pp. 52-4.

75. Taylor, R. *The Future of the Trade Unions*, Andre Deutsch, London 1994, p. 163.

76. Ramelson, B. 'Incomes Policy in Britain: Its Theory and Practice', *World Marxist Review* July 1966 Vol.9 (7): 11-15; p. 11.

77. Op. cit., p. 12.

78. Campbell, J. and Ramelson, B. 'British State Monopoly Capitalism and Its Impact on Trade Unions and Wages', *Marxism Today* January 1968, pp. 7-14, and February 1968 pp. 50-59.

79. CP Economic Bulletin 1977, Vol. 1(new series), p. 36.

80. Ramelson, B. *Heath's War On Your Wage Packet: The Latest Tory Attack on Living Standards and Trade Union Rights*, CP pamphlet February 1973, pp. 5-6.

81. Leys, C. *Politics in Britain from Labour to Thatcherism*, Verso, London 1989, p. 97.

82. Bellamy, R. *Getting the Balance Right – An Assessment of the Achievements of the CPGB*, Socialist History Society, June 1996.

83. Ron Bellamy interview, 2008.

84. Purdy, D. in *Communist History Network Newsletter*, Issue 18, Autumn 2005. See also chapter 8, pp. 28-9.

85. Ramelson, B. *Bury the Social Contract: the case for an alternative policy*, CP, March 1977, p. 34.

86. Kelly 1988 op.cit. pp. 241- 245.

87. CP Economic Bulletin, Autumn 1977, p. 33.

88. Ibid., p. 38.

89. Moffat, A. *Smash the Pay Pause*, CP, 1962; Moss, J. *Wages – The Tory Attack*, CP, 1961.

90. Taylor 1978 op.cit., p. 122.

91. Pelling 1976 op.cit., pp. 250-3.

92. Rolph, C. *All those in favour? The ETU trial*, Andre Deutsch, London 1962.

93. Wedderburn, W. *The Worker and the Law*, Penguin 1986, pp. 749-50.

94. Andrews 2004 op.cit., pp. 75-6. Andrews gets key facts wrong. Ramelson was not chair of the various industrial advisories – these positions were held by lay members of the Party associated through union membership with the relevant industry.

95. Brian Moody interview, Flashlight member, 2009.
96. Gollan, J. *Socialist Democracy – some problems*, CP 1976, p. 21.
97. Darlington, R. and Lyddon, D. *Glorious Summer: Class struggle in Britain 1972*, Bookmarks, London 2001, pp. 28-30.
98. Callaghan 2003, op.cit., pp. 226-267; Callaghan, J. 'Industrial Militancy, 1945-79: The Failure of the British Road to Socialism?', *Twentieth Century British History* 2004, 29: 388-409.
99. McIlroy, J. 'Notes on the Communist Party and Industrial Politics', in McIlroy et al 1999 op.cit., pp. 216-258; Andrews 2004,op.cit., pp. 105-132.
100. 1974 TUC *Conference Report of Proceedings*; Andrews 2004, op cit., p.132.
101. Foley, T. *A Most Formidable Union: the history of DATA and TASS*, TASS 1992, pp. 81-3.
102. McIlroy op. cit., 1999, p. 233.
103. Ibid. p. 246.
104. Kevin Halpin interview, 2008.
105. Ibid.
106. McIlroy 1999 op.cit., p. 243.
107. CP Archive: CP/IND/RAM/02/02.
108. Ramelson personal papers.
109. Ibid.
110. Ramelson, B. 'Workers' Control? Possibilities and Limitations', *Marxism Today* October 1968, pp. 296-303, p. 296.
111. Ibid., p. 297.
112. Ibid., p. 298.
113. Ramelson, B. 'Trade Union Militancy', *Comment*, October 1966, pp. 429-430.
114. Ramelson, B. 'Discussion on workers' control', *World Marxist Review* 1978, p. 92.
115. Ibid., p. 95.
116. The Bullock Report: The *Report of the committee of inquiry on industrial democracy*, HMSO, London1977, Cmnd 6706; and the CP's *Evidence to the Committee of Inquiry on Industrial Democracy*, CPGB February 1976.
117. Topham, T. and Coates, K. 'Workers' Control', *Marxism Today*, January 1969: 24-8; p. 27.
118. Coates, K. and Topham, T. (eds.) *Industrial democracy in Great Britain: a book of readings and witnesses for workers' control*, Spokesman Books, Nottingham 1975.
119. Ramelson op.cit., 1978, p. 95.
120. Bateman, D. 'The Trouble with Harry: A memoir of Harry Newton, MI5 Agent', *Lobster*, Issue 28, 1994.

4. Labour returns (1964-1970): incomes policies and attacks on trade union rights

RAMELSON ARRIVES

Throughout the 1960s and 1970s one of the major themes of public policy and trade union concern was that of incomes policies. As we have seen, these came in a variety of shapes and sizes, but the basic arguments for and against remained the same. What to do strategically and tactically was more of a problem for the left, and especially the CP industrial leadership. Ramelson became a key figure in these debates very soon after he became industrial organiser in 1965, and by 1966 he was known as one of the most powerful figures in the labour movement, mainly because of his intimate involvement in the seafarers' strike of that year.

The political logic applied by Ramelson was clear: incomes policies were designed to control wages in order to boost profits; and, as both were economic representations of the income derived from the use of factors of production – labour and capital – so they also represented classes with different interests and with conflicting political objectives. To control wages meant reforming the main wage determination system – collective bargaining – and that in turn meant weakening the unions, through changes in their ability to influence the short-term supply of labour to any employer (industrial action), and, now that Labour was in office, to keep union leaders friendly to the government and its policies.[1] This meant that he had to counter arguments about both the economics of wages and the politics of the use of state power and authority.

When Harold Wilson formed his first Labour government on 16 October 1964, with an overall majority of four, the dominant mood in the labour movement was muted optimism. At last the Tories had been vanquished after thirteen years of reactionary stagnation, and now a new look Labour leadership with fresh ideas could take over. The image, astutely cultivated by Wilson, was almost ordinary and almost classless, to replace the bumbling grandees of the Tory elite. Indeed in some respects the government started well. For example, Home Secretary Roy Jenkins oversaw the 1965 Race Relations Act, the abolition of hanging in 1966, and the liberalising of legislation on abortion and gay rights in 1967.

It soon became apparent, however, that the new government had no progressive answers to Britain's chronic economic problems, which were characterised by years of low investment, low productivity, a lack of international competitiveness, a constant balance-of-payments deficit, and an over-valued currency. The Labour leadership had no new ideas in this crucial area and took the traditional Treasury brief, seeking to solve the crisis by attacking workers' living standards, through incomes policies and threats to curtail long-established trade-union rights. Ramelson and the communist leadership were at the centre of the political and industrial forces that rallied to thwart Labour's anti-working class policies. Ultimately, the failure of the government by the end of the decade to either manage the economy or to reach a democratic accommodation with the unions culminated in the return of the Conservative Party under Edward Heath in the summer of 1970.

During this period of Labour government many reforms were enacted, from university expansion to higher pensions and better welfare benefits, but much of this was predicated upon planned sustainable economic growth, which the government did not succeed in delivering. The rhetoric and strong belief was that some form of planning would end the stop-go policies of the previous decade, and that, through the efforts of George Brown in the new Department of Economic Affairs (DEA), and the steady hand of James Callaghan as Chancellor, this could be achieved. This was largely idealised nonsense, as the emergency budget in November 1964 was soon to prove. It was to be the hallmark of the next few years that traditional medicine was taken for traditional ills: a massive balance-of-payments deficit, a weak sterling propped up for imperial rather than economic reasons, borrowing with endless strings from the International Monetary Fund (IMF), the USA and other central banks, and eventually panic in the place of strategy.

Though it campaigned on many other issues, the main concerns of the CP leadership during this period were the economy, and industrial relations issues such as wages and union organisation. In the political sphere the emphasis was on left unity – and that included paying increasing attention to the Trotskyist groups on the ultra-left who remained actively opposed to all forms of left unity. There had been a proliferation of Trotskyist groups after the split between those who remained in the Fourth International and those under Gerry Healy who left in 1953 and later formed the Socialist Labour League (SLL) which in turn became the Workers' Revolutionary Party. From the CP's perspective, the calling card of both groups was their anti-Sovietism and anti-communism. Later Betty Reid provided a detailed account of British Trotskyists, in which she noted their tendency to adventurism and disruptive calls for actions that isolated the left – the main concern for Ramelson in the trade union movement.[2] (She also noted their delight in debating the endless myths of Trotskyism itself, their reflexive and strident anti-communism and the strategy by some to secretly enter the Labour Party as organised sects).

LABOUR'S ECONOMIC STRATEGY

By the end of 1964 the government became more clearly focused on the labour market and wages. In December there was the start of a weak movement towards tripartism, with a 'Declaration of Intent' between the government, the TUC and the Confederation of British Industry (CBI).[3] This had three objectives: first, to ensure that the British economy remained dynamic and that its prices stayed competitive; second, to raise productivity and efficiency so that real national output could increase, and increases in wages, salaries and other incomes be kept in line with the increase; and third, to keep the general level of prices stable. As Will Paynter (NUM general secretary 1959-69), among others, noted, such moves towards corporatism raised real dangers for trade unions, especially in terms of keeping a distinctive political philosophy.[4] In contrast John Hughes argued for strengthening the links between 'trade unions and a reforming government' in order to push the union agenda up Labour's list of priorities in government.[5]

There was neither a master plan nor a master stroke on offer. Strongly deflationary budgets in April and July 1965 meant no growth and a growing dependence on the USA government to save sterling.

The government's lack of political direction was illustrated by the ill-fated National Plan, launched in September 1965 but fizzling out by the summer of 1966.[6] Although the plan itself was hopeless from the start, it had three elements of interest: first, much of it was devised by Keynesian economists from the major universities; secondly, it raised the issue of planning, which provided the left in general with something to bite on; and, thirdly (and less propitiously), it contained as a central plank a commitment to incomes policies. At this stage it was deemed essential by government ministers that the TUC accepted the need for voluntary wage controls and restrictions on industrial action. As we will see later, as things got more difficult, statutory wage control became the preferred policy.

For the CP, development of left unity in the face of these attacks was paramount, as demonstrated, for example, in Arnold Kettle's open letter on the future of the left to a 'non-communist left winger', in which he argued that fundamental social change was still relevant and necessary, and that anti-communism in all its forms held back all left movements.[7] One purpose of left unity was to support the move in the unions to a more progressive and widespread set of leaders, actions and policies; another was to combat the trend towards a tougher incomes policy and more strident attacks on the unions, as well as the role of right-wing union leaders in delivering their unions and members up to the sacrificial altar of wage controls.

Soon after the 1966 general election (which Labour won with an increased majority), a major currency crisis developed which helped to create the political conditions for the imposition of a total wage freeze, through the prism of tripartite agreement. By autumn 1966 a whole panoply of right-wing labourist policies was in operation, with backing from unions such as the NUR; and there were ferocious attacks on shopfloor bargaining and 'wage drift'. All this alerted the comrades to the urgency of defending the unions, and to the possibility that a more permanent system of wage controls might be imposed in the near future. Ramelson demanded to know when the right to collective bargaining was going to be restored, and made a powerful attack on the government's position, repeating the Party's view that:

> there was never a shortage of evidence that the incomes policy and its latest form – the wage freeze – were totally irrelevant to the problem of the payments deficit … [there is a] total absence of any connection

between our wages level with its effects on the competitiveness of our exports and the most recent run on the pound, leading to the panic measures of July 20 with its vicious attack on earnings and the sovereignty of the trades unions.[8]

By 1967 the government was in disarray and leaderless. Its weak attempts at planning had failed. Ministers were divided, economic policy was panic driven, and the flight from the pound denied, while devaluation, first postponed at great cost, in November was carried through at even greater cost. All of this was to be addressed by a shocking dose of deflation: taxes were put up and public spending was cut, and, at the beating heart of this policy misdirection, there was a wages' standstill.

As Labour's policies lurched to the right and the attacks on working-class organisations grew apace, so the debate as to the nature of the Labour Party itself and the relations any left group could have with such a reformist institution became sharper and more relevant. John Saville, for example, provided a hostile summary of the failures of Labour governments since 1945.[9] He explained that leading labour movement figures understood political power in the narrow sense of parliamentary majorities, with no real notion of the state and class. Sharing Ralph Miliband's analysis, Saville also delved into the hopelessness of Labour in office, and its failure to deal with inequality or capitalist institutions, as well as its degrading national ideology of Empire. He underestimated, however, the importance of nationalisation and public service expansion, especially in the areas of health, education and social services, and failed to come up with a realistic and sustainable political way forward.

Monty Johnstone, a leading communist intellectual, penned a classic defence of the CP's long-standing position,[10] concluding:

> the working class cannot act as a class except by constituting itself into a political party distinct from, and opposed to, all old parties formed from the propertied classes, [this was] indispensable in order to ensure the triumph of the social revolution.
>
> [Marx and Engels] did … see the proletariat as the leading force for social emancipation; they were to base themselves on existing organizations created by advanced sections of that class and to condemn as sectarianism any attempt to impose pre-conceived organizational forms on the working class movement from outside.[11]

Such a clear statement of the need for a non-dogmatic approach to the politics of the day was also reflected in Ramelson's principled pragmatism.

INCOMES POLICIES AND PRODUCTIVITY BARGAINING

In February 1965 the government put forward an agreement on Machinery of Prices and Incomes Policy, using both the National Economic Development Council (NEDC, founded in 1962) and the newly set up National Board for Prices and Incomes (NBPI). As these 'voluntary' measures failed, so in April came the Prices and Incomes Policy, based on a 3.5 per cent norm for wage increases, to which there were four exceptions: higher productivity, national interest to shift manpower around, redressing low pay, and redressing falling behind comparatively.[12] The NBPI favoured productivity cases above the other causes for exception, for example, supporting payment by results schemes for manual workers in the NHS and local government, for gas and electricity workers, and busmen.[13] Its solution to low pay was to automate and raise productivity.[14] As inflation became worse, so government brought in an early warning system, and after the 1966 currency crisis it brought in a statutory pay standstill. The historic logic of wage restraint, from exhortation through voluntarism to compulsion, was once again enacted, despite the denials of the revisionists and reformists. Only the communists under Ramelson's direction stood firm from start to finish in opposing all and any version of state-regulated wage controls.

The CP's Economic Committee made it quite clear that the roots of the economic problem were in Britain's imperialist past and present: excessive export of capital instead of home investment, arms expenditure to keep up with the American, Russian and especially French Joneses, and a low growth rate, especially in sectors such as chemicals, machine tools, and electronics. The Labour government's response had been in part institutional, with the creation of the DEA and the NBPI; in part a simple panic in the face of the balance-of-payments crisis; and in part a shovelling of the burden of costs onto the working class through wage controls.[15]

The economy was an endless source of comment and analysis especially by the CP's Economic Committee whose line remained unchanged throughout this period. In May 1964 it issued a statement on the Tory policy 1951-63, and firmly concluded that all incomes policies were a fraud, that they did not work, and that continued trade union struggle against wage controls was necessary.[16] Much centred on the causes of inflation. As has been noted if wages did not cause inflation, then obviously control over wages *per se* was irrelevant, but if wages did contribute to inflation, what then? These points exercised the comrades who debated the details and the principles in great depth. Emile Burns, a leading economist, remained unsure of the impact of money and real wages on demand in the economy and his less than decisive comments later drew the wrath of Bert.[17]

The CP's focus in 1965 was very much on the labour movement. The essence of the work remained the same: fight to keep the Labour government true to election promises on progressive changes such as pension increases despite the economic crisis.[18] It was incomes policies that kept the comrades busiest. The tasks were numerous: first it was necessary to explain that by any other name an incomes policy was wage controls whether it be George Brown's 'guiding light' or whatever; secondly the theoretical and historical models needed to be clear to show that inflation was related to Marx's law of value and prices;[19] thirdly to illustrate that from the late 1950s onwards first the Organisation for Economic Co-operation and Development (OECD) and then 'academic economists and Fabian theorists generally began … to advocate a national wages policy' which linked pay rises to productivity gains[20]; and fourthly to expose the fact that the government was trying to present the policy, 'Joint Statement of Intent', in such a way that allowed the TUC and some union leaders to support it. This last was particularly aimed at the then leaders of the engineering union who were seen as in the forefront of class collaboration.

Many of the CP's bullets were aimed at specific unions, for example, the National Union of General and Municipal Workers (NUGMW), which was pushing the highly revisionist line that those workers able to push up their wages through struggle should restrain themselves in order to help their weaker brothers and sisters. The TUC General Council also continued to be caught up in this muddle over the Labour government's policy ambiguities especially on the issues of public ownership, new technology, and the nature of the whole crisis and its remedies. At its 1966 Congress, for example, the TUC General Council gave strong support to the NEDC, NBPI and incomes polices, as it accepted the government's economic analysis and polices. It defended itself from left attacks by declaring that, 'an incomes policy of the sort the TUC has in mind needs time to grow and mature'.[21] TUC General Secretary George Woodcock was pleased because he saw the role of the TUC as being enhanced as it was sucked into government policy and committees. Campbell, with Ramelson's approval, was as usual scathing about the TUC leaders' capitulation to the Labour government's incomes policies and anti-union reforms: 'the majority in the British unions are [willing to acknowledge guilt for the economic crisis]; and in doing so they are preparing the way for a more rigid state control over all forms of union activity'.[22]

The importance of resisting the idea that unions were in any way to blame for inflation was heightened as all the main political parties gathered together to publicise and propagandise the link between wages and inflation, and union power and economic crisis. In particular Labour's early abandonment of its National Plan was no surprise: it had never been a plan but only a hope. The 'non-plan' was characterised by the communists as a tool to convince workers and union leaders that by making sacrifices now there would be prosperity ahead. The sacrifice was of course to adhere to the incomes policy, and the growth was a political chimera inspired by President Kennedy's 1961 Paris speech to the OECD – even though both the OECD and the National Institute for Economic Research (NIER) opposed the notion that lower wages now could lead to higher growth tomorrow.

Ramelson now launched a new pamphlet taking his cue from Robert Tressell's famous book and the section on the wages' trick, referring to the proposed incomes policy as 'the great wage freeze trick'.[23] He calculated that six million workers would be 'robbed of rises they [were] entitled to under agreements freely entered into with the employers':

> Thus interference with our wages and earnings is seen by the employers and the Government not as something transient, a temporary, unpleasant experience, but as something permanent.[24]

He also argued that the dominant conventional wisdom, that the state should not interfere in markets, had been jettisoned in favour of state controls over the labour market to hold wages down, and that this had happened because of relative full employment after years of post-war economic growth. The notion that wages were the main cause of inflation was dismissed, because the real causes were huge arms expenditure; the growth of non-productive labour; the development of monopoly power; and government policies that had deliberately increased the cost of living, thus forcing workers to chase price rises.

Once the analysis had been laid out, the argument within the labour movement began. Ramelson demolished the case that there was a trade-off between inflation and unemployment, and denounced the suggestion that any incomes policy could be a socialist wages policy. He went beyond negative criticism by providing an alternative, based on cuts to military spending, an end to private investment abroad, opposition to all and any wage controls in order to maintain high levels of demand, a price freeze, more nationalisation, and controls over foreign trade and the deficit. He concluded:

> incomes policy would not only fail to solve our economic problems; it would aggravate them – The Prices and Incomes Act is aimed at foisting the policy on the movement, and the first step towards state regulated wages and working conditions and the destruction of trade union independence. The trade union and labour movement can defeat the incomes policy … [but] it must put forward an alternative policy.[25]

Writing at the end of 1966, the Party tone was set by Sam Aaronovitch: 'we enter 1967 with this large Labour majority being used not only to repeat Tory policies but to magnify them'.[26] Aaronovitch also argued that, though the Party supported Labour because of its trade union links, it also needed to expose the right-wing leadership as pro-capitalist. He restated the Party's recognition of the need to develop an Alternative Economic Strategy (AES) to combat the negativity within the ranks of union leaders.

The organs, arguments and consequences of incomes policies continued to dominate Party thinking. Ramelson described the NBPI thus: 'this body, composed of one super-egoist, Mr Aubrey Jones, and a tiny group of mediocrities, has been allowed to assume the power of commentary on every wage rate in the country'; furthermore, the NBPI's notion that wage increases might follow on after proved rises in productivity was 'an unbelievable insult to trade unionists and will be widely resented'.[27] It was clear that a Labour government was using the state to benefit capitalists at the expense of workers. The 'national interest' might have allowed some TUC leaders to go along with the policy, but Marxists, armed with their analysis of the state as an instrument of class rule, could not.

A paper by Ramelson and Campbell on incomes policy used the wider debate amongst Marxist economists to explain the fundamental flaws in the policy and support for it, and to put forward the argument that an important corollary of holding wages down was the spread of poverty.[28] Margaret Woddis, in a piece that has disturbingly contemporary resonances, suggested that 'in practice, the Labour Government has proved itself unable and unwilling to either "seek out" or "alleviate" poverty'.[29]

The Party steadfastly continued its opposition to all forms of incomes policies and associated anti-union laws, and busied itself in attacking ideas that were being put forward by the Tories on binding collective agreements. In particular it targeted its arguments on the TUC leadership and its centenary conference in 1968. By the time of this conference the TUC's support for voluntary incomes policy, although still publicly strong, was being counter-posed by a clear opposition to any form of compulsion, and antagonism to all legal restraints: it issued an early warning to the government that prices had to be controlled as well as workers' wages if the next election was to be won.[30]

In 1970 Ramelson turned his attention to productivity bargaining, which he saw as a key part of the government's strategy on pay. Once again he used the pen as his weapon of choice to dismantle his opponents' case – in January 1970 the CP published *Productivity Agreements: an Exposure of the Latest and Greatest Swindle on the Wages Front.* His starting point is the government's White Paper, *Productivity, Prices and Incomes Policy in 1968 and 1969,* and the accompanying mass propaganda in its favour from the media and academic studies, as well as generous time off given for stewards to study such agreements.[31] Cabinet ministers, the TUC, and the ETU at its Esher training college, were all involved in selling productivity as a great benefit. The NBPI plugged it with a Special Report (no 123), which then formed part of the White Paper itself.[32] Employers were full of enthusiasm and praise, and ended up paying out millions of pounds to management consultants in the field. Barbara Castle claimed that over six million workers had been involved in over 3,500 productivity agreements. Yet, as Ramelson complained:

there is more confusion in the Labour movement on this subject than on probably any other aspect of the wages' struggle. Yet in my opinion, 'productivity bargaining', as projected by the Government and employers, is the greatest threat to the workers' living standards and fighting capacity since the attempt was made to saddle the movement with an 'incomes policy' and its stable companion anti-trade union legislation.[33]

The pamphlet, aimed at the 'shop floor', outlined the dangers of productivity bargaining, and the threat it posed 'to the workers' ability to achieve, in struggle, a bigger share of the wealth they produce, without undermining their working conditions, or losing the rights they have won in over a century of bitter struggle'. Ramelson saw productivity bargaining as the practical expression of the 'class biased philosophy of incomes policy', because all its agreements were based on the assumption that workers did not have the right to demand and fight for higher wages for other reasons, such as rising prices, rising profits, fair comparisons and redistribution. Productivity deals denied collective bargaining, and asked workers to pay for their own pay rises through 'extra effort and redundancy'. They shifted the whole basis of collective bargaining from 'how much to increase wages, to how to reduce the wage cost per unit of output'.[34] Ramelson linked these arguments to incomes polices: 'the productivity agreement is the latest and most sophisticated technique devised by the ruling class to implement its main objective on the wages front – "incomes policy"'. The whole idea was to replace traditional collective bargaining, and therefore to stop workers fighting for pay rises and challenging profits; the employers sought to 'destroy the shop steward movement and workshop organisation. The aim is to convert the shop stewards from being the key lay trade union officials leading the daily class struggle at the place of work'.[35]

THE 1966 SEAFARERS' STRIKE – 'THIS TIGHTLY KNIT GROUP OF POLITICALLY MOTIVATED MEN'

As we have seen Labour had won the March 1966 general election easily enough. The Tories under Edward Heath had looked bereft of ideas and policies, shabby and outmoded in image, and not in the right mind to fight an election. The larger majority in parliament brought with it no change in the wider economy and in the deteriorating international situation. These familiar problems were soon compounded by the seafarers' strike, which began in May and lasted six weeks.[36]

By the end of June, after a forty-five day strike, the seafarers had won what their general secretary Bill Hogarth called a 'definite victory': a move from a 56-hour to a 40-hour working week, and agreement to increase annual holidays from thirty-nine to forty-eight days.[37] The strike was seen by the government as responsible for economic chaos. The dispute captured the nature of class struggle at the time, and the confusion sown by incomes policies as the 'epitome of right-wing social democratic use of the labour movement to carry out reforms and restructurings on behalf of the class enemy, the capitalists'. It 'helped create the myths and legends about communist influence in the unions, both exaggerated and demeaned, and showed the importance to a Labour government of having the TUC and other union leaders on board'. [38] As Communist organiser Dennis Goodwin explained, it also raised the importance of exposing the secretive employers, and the need for far-reaching reform of the industry and the ways in which major industrialists carried out their business.[39]

The impact of the dispute on the union and the left was clear – it enhanced the reputation and influence of the CP inside the union, inside the wider union movement, and of Ramelson himself. The impact on the Labour government and various ministers was less beneficial and less clear cut. It is possible that the success of this strike, and the support that it attracted in the wider labour movement, served to alter the balance of argument within Cabinet with regard to union reform and wage controls, and weaken Wilson's authority. It is certainly true that the strike was followed by compulsory wage restraint, as the government lost any confidence in the TUC as a credible partner; and soon after Frank Cousins resigned from the government. Equally, the strike was herald to a period of intense struggle over wages, trade union rights and jobs, in which Ramelson and the CP were key protagonists.

It was during this dispute that Ramelson became, if not a household name, at least a national figure, when he was singled out by Harold Wilson and sectors of the press as the man who was fermenting activities designed to undermine Britain's economy – no doubt to his delight, for it helped no end in establishing his national standing on the trade union left. He even made headline news in Canada, when on 29 June 1966 the *Edmonton Journal* (Ramelson's hometown paper) carried a front-page story about his involvement in the strike.

Wilson was right in at least one respect. Ramelson's role in the dispute was critically important in securing a positive outcome for the union. He helped to bring together a group of rank-and-file seafarers in order that they might better organise a national dispute for a substantial improvement in wages and conditions of work – one that had already been officially approved by their union's annual conference – in spite of a Prices and Incomes policy that attempted to restrict wage increases to around 3.5 per cent per annum. The success of the rank and file in strengthening the union's hand subsequently led to an important breakthrough within the National Union of Seamen (NUS), opening the way for the election of a significant number of left and progressive EC members, and thereby transforming a traditional right-wing moribund union. It was clear that Ramelson played a major role in sustaining the action and broadening the base of solidarity support, particularly after the Labour and TUC leaderships had turned against the strikers. Indeed Wilson's red plot story and the TUC's rebuff to the NUS executive served to strengthen the hand of the communists inside the union, and of the ability of Ramelson to influence events.

Through the Party's rather flimsy network in this difficult-to-organise occupational group, Ramelson was able to help put together an effective national steering group, and to encourage similar groupings at port level, at the same time stressing the importance of building links with other transport unions as well as trades councils, well-organised factories, and district committees. Through this network Ramelson was able to offer a relatively poorly organised group of workers day-to-day help in running the strike, thus raising morale and giving militant seafarers the confidence needed to take on the employers and the government.[40] This task had been made doubly difficult since the majority of the union's elected officials had little stomach for the battle, and the TUC General Council had opposed it, on the grounds that the claim broke the voluntary incomes policy it had signed up to.

During the dispute Ramelson worked mainly through the Party, having little if any contact with the strike committee itself. An especially established Party committee, drawing on London-based militants in strategically key industries who were in a position to argue and work for solidarity action in support of the seafarers, met regularly throughout the dispute and Ramelson was present at every meeting. Party member Gordon Norris, who was on the NUS strike committee, was the key link person between the Party committee and the strike committee. This was not a formal arrangement, but it worked well enough to reassure strike leaders on the non-CP left that there were practical possibilities for developing industrial solidarity despite the approach of the TUC General Council and the reluctance of many of the union's top officials to prosecute the strike. Later, when the union leadership decided to accept the employer's terms following the Pearson Committee Report, communists argued for a return to work in unity, rather than as some on the ultra-left favoured, to continue with unofficial action which was bound to split the union.

THE ANTI-COMMUNIST WITCH-HUNT

It was clear even before the strike started that members of the Labour Cabinet were convinced, rightly or wrongly, that communists were behind every strike and strike threat. On 10 February 1966, for example, when the NUR called a railway strike, Dick Crossman wrote:

> Certainly when the Cabinet met at ten o'clock its mind was fixed on the railway strike. George Brown told us the news that a vote had been taken by twelve to eleven to keep to starting the strike on Monday, and that this had been achieved by the Communists, who suddenly decided they wanted to break the incomes policy.[41]

Clearly the Secret Services, on Wilson's instructions, were already actively monitoring the meetings of both the CP and key unions. The official historian of MI5 describes intelligence gathering on the seafarers' dispute:

> F1A (counter-subversion) later recalled that the Security Service initially regarded the seamen's strike as 'a straightforward industrial dispute – nothing to do with us'. Then two NUS militants were overheard by A2A transcribers visiting the CPGB's King Street headquarters to ask the Party's chief industrial organiser, Bert

Ramelson, for advice on how to run the strike … A4 began surveillance of several NUS leaders to obtain evidence of their contacts with Communist 'trouble makers'. The Security Service provided both the Prime Minister and the Home Secretary with regular reports on the seamen's strike, which convinced Wilson that the NUS was controlled by an inner core of Communist militants who were manipulating the strike for their own subversive purposes … on 26 May, following Wilson's decision to declare a state of emergency, eavesdropping in King Street revealed that the CPGB Political Committee had set up a secret committee, headed by Ramelson, to co-ordinate Party activities in support of the strike.[42]

The bugging of CP headquarters and the committee showed that the Party wanted the strike to be run by the union's strike committee, of which Gordon Norris was an elected member, rather than a subcommittee of its EC, on which there were no communists. Ramelson was apparently heard plotting with Norris to widen the dispute and to reject any agreement that did not breach the government's pay policy. It should at this point be noted that, as Wedderburn points out, the strike was totally lawful: 'in the big seamen's strike of 1966, which ended with 26,000 on strike from 800 ships in its sixth week, seamen terminated their contracts by the appropriate contractual notice as ships docked'.[43] It was the government spies that were outside the law.

In Andrew's view this was the most active the Security Services had ever been in an industrial dispute; though the Home Secretary was not involved, they had the very active support of George Wigg, the Paymaster General. For example, it was Wigg who wanted to discredit the strikers through the media, and to feed leading questions to television journalist John Freeman when Norris and Ramelson were to be interviewed on 11 June 1966. (Wigg was persuaded against this course of action by senior MI5 officers on the grounds that Norris was a charismatic character who might well benefit from being on TV).

Wilson had already broadcast on the day the strike began, claiming that it was against the state, the national interest, and – worst of all – the incomes policy.[44] On 20 June he decided to denounce the strike leaders in the Commons. The MI5 brief had been that it was Ramelson who was the central figure, and Wilson now made a point of stressing this in his speech. He went to great lengths to spell out what the government and he personally had done to secure an agreement, and how angry he was that, despite the personal intervention of the PM, the NUS leadership had refused to cave in. This could only be explained by communist pressure:

> It is difficult for us to appreciate the pressures which are being put on men I know to be realistic and reasonable, not only in their executive capacity but in the highly organised strike committees in the individual ports, by this tightly knit group of politically motivated men.[45]

A week later he had this to say to the Commons about the influence of communists and in particular that of Ramelson:

> The House will be aware that the Communist Party, unlike the major political parties, has at its disposal an efficient and disciplined industrial apparatus controlled from Communist Party headquarters. No major strike occurs anywhere in this country in any sector of industry in which that apparatus fails to concern itself … No other political party is organised on these lines.
>
> In particular Gordon Norris and some well-known Communists on the North-East coast are going round all ports to ensure that the Communist Party keeps a firm grip on the movement … The Communist Party's industrial organiser is Mr. Bert Ramelson … He has three full-time officials on his staff and in the London area, where the docks provide his hunting ground, his principal lieutenant is Mr. Dennis Goodwin.
>
> I have referred to the numerical weakness of the Communists in the N.U.S. Yet, despite this, as soon as the strike began, they were successful in ensuring that the chairmanships of the strike committees in the country's two major ports, London and Liverpool, were taken by two Communists, Mr. Jack Coward and Mr. Roger Woods. Again, in the union's negotiating machinery, a leading member of the negotiating committee, not himself a member of the executive council, who was elected from the floor at the annual general conference, was also a highly articulate and effective Communist, Mr. Gordon Norris.
>
> The objectives of the Communist Party in this dispute were, first, to influence the day-to-day policy of the executive council; secondly, to extend the area of the stoppage; and, thirdly, to use the strike not only to improve the conditions of seamen – in which I believe them

to be genuine – but also to secure the destruction of the Government's prices and incomes policy.

Time and again the Communist Party's objectives have rapidly become the policy of the executive. This is particularly true in relation to the determination of the party to spread the strike ... The policy of extending the dispute was, however, conducted by Mr. Ramelson, Mr. Goodwin and a number of other influential Communists whose influence extended to unions beyond the NUS.[46]

This account by Wilson is quoted at length to illustrate the profound impact of the strike and the Party's position on government leaders, the press, and wider trade union and public opinion. Wilson is careful to recognise that ordinary workers are not to blame, but the frontal attack on Ramelson and the CP is intended to warn trade union leaders of the need to keep faith with the Labour government's definition of the national interest. It is ironic that Wilson's red scare tactics in themselves gave weight to the conventional view that Ramelson and the CP had an important and effective say during the strike and over many other industrial disputes through to the late 1970s.[47]

In an unpublished paper Gordon Norris records:

Harold Wilson announced to the House of Commons on June 28th (Hansard pages 1603-1734) the names of the 'Politically motivated men', beginning with Bert Ramelson as National Industrial organiser of the CPGB, Dennis Goodwin, London Industrial Organiser of the CPGB, Jack Coward NUS, Roger Woods NUS, Gordon Norris NUS, along with James Slater NUS, Joseph Kenny NUS, (the last two not attending the meetings) Jack Dash, TGWU docker, Harry Watson, President of the Watermen, Lightermen, Tugmen and Bargemen's Union. ... Such was the interest shown by the state machine that the meeting places were continually changed, starting with Marx House in Clerkenwell Green and Danny Lyons flat in Globe Road, Bethnal Green. I regularly reported back to Joe Kenny and Bill Brankley from Dover, the outcome of the meetings and our strategy was adjusted accordingly.[48]

Wilson did what he could to give such meetings a sinister resonance. In essence, he was accusing Ramelson of plotting to help the NUS win its official claim, of attempting to make this more likely by broadening the dispute to include other waterfront and transport unions, and of using the dispute to attack the government's incomes policy agreed with the TUC General Council (he did have the good grace to concede that all these activities and motives were entirely constitutional and within Britain's democratic traditions). Ramelson gladly pleaded 'guilty' on all three fronts.

Richard Crossman, then Minister of Housing, was one of many of those involved at the time who sought to explain and justify what happened in this historic dispute. He described the situation in Cabinet on 21 June 1966:

> the interesting question was how, individually and collectively, we would react to Harold's cool and deliberate Statement to the House yesterday that he knew the names of the active communists who had been responsible for starting the seaman's strike. This had caused consternation on the Labour back benches, but Harold showed no kind of repentance. Instead, he went round the table and forced each of us to define our position. Frank Cousins, Barbara Castle and I were pretty critical of him, and on this occasion we had rather more support from people like Fred Lee. The Cabinet in fact was fairly balanced and his position is not too strong.[49]

The point was that Wilson wanted to attack the communists, irrespective of the strike, throughout the union movement, in order to weaken their grip on the anti-incomes policy forces.

REPORTING THE DISPUTE

As in many long drawn-out national disputes, there was considerable debate after the event concerning the wisdom of the tactics employed and the balance of forces that determined the outcome.

The left's response, *Not Wanted on Voyage: the Seaman's Reply, to the First Report of the Court of Inquiry into Certain Matters Concerning the Shipping Industry Cmnd. 3025*, was partly organised by John Prescott – later to become Deputy Prime Minister – and written by academics at Hull University. It starts with an introduction by Charlie Hodgins and John Prescott as a riposte to the bias of the Pearson report. They argue:

… from the beginning our strike, though essentially industrial, has been overshadowed by political implications and attacks. The publication of the Pearson report has provided the final proof that our struggle is not just against the ship-owners, but also against mounting political pressure being built up by the Government – no doubt in the interests of its 'Incomes Policy'.[50]

Furthermore:

… we had to be beaten, because our claim was 'a breach in the dyke of the Incomes Policy'. Hence the special Emergency Powers, hence the Labour Prime Minister invoking the sacred nature of the 'state', and hence above all, the state's total failure to do any other with the owners than grant them total support.[51]

Perhaps the best known account of the dispute from the left is that by the then relatively young journalist Paul Foot, a member of the International Socialist group, on the whole favourably reviewed by Ramelson.[52] However, Ramelson did castigate Foot for not checking out the facts concerning his involvement, and accused Foot of reproducing rumour and presenting it as reality. The rumour in question was that Ramelson had given direct advice to the militant strike leaders to call off the strike. As Ramelson pointed out, this rumour merely added weight to Wilson's accusations about the role of a 'politically motivated group of men', as well as being baseless in fact. He also called into question Foot's analytical skills: 'when it comes to analysis Paul Foot grossly oversimplifies'; and: 'he doesn't seem to be aware of the complexities of some of the problems'. The complexities referred to were difficulties faced by rank-and-file leaders in other unions in developing effective solidarity action against the background of total opposition from the whole of the official trade union movement, including both the TUC General Council and the NUS leadership.

Ramelson could also have pointed out that part of Foot's objective in presenting his account in this way was to portray the CP as an industrial paper tiger, timid in its actions and unable through lack of vision or poverty of organisation to offer effective leadership. This was an argument implicitly put forward in the final essay of the book in which Foot's piece appeared, by Perry Anderson, which Ramelson describes as being 'in ways the most interesting'. Anderson asserted the need for a revolutionary party with roots at workplace and trade union levels, but without actually mentioning the existence of the CP, let alone its characteristics and shortcomings.[53] As Ramelson says, 'if Anderson believes that the Communist Party cannot play such a role he should argue the case', going on to point out the contrast between the sharpness of the analysis and the vagueness and confusion of the conclusions. He could also have concluded that Anderson and Foot shared a common mission – to downplay or distort the role of the CP in the 1960s and that such analysis helped to consolidate rather than challenge the right wing's domination of the labour movement.

All sections of the press gave great prominence to Wilson's pronouncements on the strike, and many focused on Ramelson's personal role. For example the *Daily Mirror*, then much closer to the Labour Party than it is now, and the biggest circulation tabloid newspaper in Britain, with sales of around five million, on 29 June devoted its front page and much of the back page to the dispute. The front page was dominated by a photograph of Ramelson. The story centred on Ramelson's leadership role, and noted that he was 'a fluent speaker of Russian … and seen by top British Communists as their best link with the Soviet Union'. This was a blatant attempt to suggest that Ramelson was acting on behalf of the Soviet Union in order to undermine the British government and economy.

Television coverage was no less partisan than the written press. Ramelson later recalled how Robin Day and BBC producers edited a *Tonight* programme on the strike to prevent the seafarers from having the last word.[54] The programme was designed to put the men named by Harold Wilson in the House of Commons on the spot. Knowing this, Jack Coward, chairman of the strike committee in London, had sought to establish some terms of reference for the programme, and an agreement had been reached that Bert Ramelson would be given time at the end of the programme to sum up the seafarers' case. When the programme went out some hours later, however, Ramelson's contribution was edited out. (This was not to be the last time Ramelson would fall foul of TV journalism. In the 1970s Lord Chalfont, a man of changeable political beliefs and with an arrogant and ignorant view of the left, hosted a series of programmes on Marxism, in which he sneeringly recalled 'the *Morning Star*, *Tass*, and the splendid Mr. Bert Ramelson, Industrial Organiser of the Communist Party (not, one might guess, a full-time job), lambasted me on the grounds that we had actually cut interviews'.[55])

THE DOCKERS' STRIKE

In October 1967 the dockers' strike sent out the same signals as the seafarers' dispute a year earlier: the government was not governing. This dispute triggered the run on the pound that brought about the inevitable sterling devaluation on 18 November 1967.

The strike was part of the battle for implementation of the long-fought over decasualisation of dock work. As David Wilson says:

> on D-Day, men at London, Liverpool, Manchester and Hull struck. Most drifted back within the first week, but Liverpool dockers stayed out solid, totally rejecting the new working conditions … the strike lasted six weeks and was settled after a government inquiry, headed by Sir Jack Scamp, went some way towards meeting the men's case.[56]

All in all over 12,000 Liverpool dockers were involved, and later some 8,000 from London, nearly a third of the workforce there. Wilson concludes: 'more than 500,000 working days were lost, morale in the TGWU was severely dented and the Government had launched a new "red scare" and devalued the pound before the ports were back to normal'.[57]

Harold Wilson, in his attempt to explain the botched devaluation, argued that the unease in the foreign exchange markets 'had been touched off by bad trade figures … very much affected by the dock strikes … In Liverpool and the areas of the London docks affected, £100 millions of exports were held up'.[58] As was his habit, he blamed the left for fanning the flames: 'The fact that the local strike leadership was in the hands of an unholy and rare alliance of communists, near-communists and Trotskyites'.[59] This was underlined by a strong condemnation of industrial militancy in a speech by the Minister for Labour, Ray Gunter, on the next day. Gunter claimed that the strike was a 'red plot' designed to undermine social democracy.[60] Jack Jones in particular felt that there were real grievances, and went to Liverpool to meet with the unofficial strike committee, something that had not happened with the local union officials. The Liverpool strike was ended by Jones's intervention, but the London dockers under Jack Dash carried on their dispute.

Jack Dash described the ways in which the London dock strike spread through the various areas, and tells of his meeting with Frank Cousins: 'my task was to discuss the issue and inform him of our objections'.[61] The London dockers organised a mass meeting, alongside press from all over Europe. As Dash expressed it:

> standing shoulder to shoulder, six weeks without wages or strike pay, stood dockers, stevedores, clerks, young, middle-aged and on the threshold of retirement, one solid mass of 7000 men, united as a single whole in defence of the protective practices of their trade – torn from the employers in a century of struggle and privation.[62]

He asked the men on behalf of the Liaison Committee to reject the offer, and they did.

This was not the only strike of importance in 1967. There were many more, for example, engineering workers at the American-owned Roberts-Arundel factory in Stockport started an action that lasted over a year, and which at one time involved thousands of other workers in solidarity events.[63]

DONOVAN AND *IN PLACE OF STRIFE*

In 1965 there had been a flurry of activity around the reform of industrial relations. This, as usual, was a mixed bag. On the positive side there was the 1965 Trades Disputes Act, which was brought in to reverse the judges' rulings in the landmark case of Rookes v. Barnard.[64] But this was also the period in which the government began to marshal its arguments about the trade union movement being too powerful, and the threat to the economy posed by rank-and-file action to increase wages. To gather evidence for these arguments they set up the Donovan Commission, which would be dominated by Hugh Clegg and Allan Flanders.[65] General Secretary George Woodcock embodied the TUC position in all this: although he was a well worn right-winger with strong anti-communist credentials, he was also deeply resistant to change and a staunch believer that the state should keep out of industrial relations.

As the trade union question in British politics[66] took off so a series of articles appeared explaining the structure and purpose of unions, and focussing on the need for mergers to reflect the growing concentration of capital, for growth especially among the unorganised, and for policy changes often based on a more open and democratic leadership.[67] These were supplemented by further debate as the issue of reform from government became more urgent.[68] Hughes in particular focussed on the ways in which trade union structures responded to the changing landscape of occupational and industrial sectors with the rapid growth of white-collar professionals in the state sector and the general movement towards larger units of activity (Fordism). He lists the main responses of a more dynamic movement to such changes: organizational with union mergers and rationalization, bargaining in terms of long-term agreements linked with more use of the strike weapon, more judge-made restrictions on striking and picketing, and a policy response in terms of the role of the TUC in national economic bodies associated mainly with control over wages in some form.[69]

The CP favoured mergers and wanted the TUC to lead a faster rate of change in terms of structures fit for the purpose of fighting the employer and creating organisations capable of shifting Labour to the left.[70] This resonated with early studies and analysis of the growth of white-collar and professional worker unions.[71] These were seen by the CP as a great potential source of working-class strength and development. Max Egelnick, following on from debates in *World Marxist Review,* argued that such groups were proletarians and could and should be unionised.[72]

The Donovan report itself was finally published in 1968, with the main authors once more opting for the traditional voluntary system of regulation: they neither assuaged growing calls for tighter controls over unions nor provided government with a coherent set of alternative actions.[73] (Vic Feather had by now succeeded George Woodcock at the TUC but this made no difference to the Commission's outlook as a conservative vehicle for the status quo.) What was to be done? Both voters and investors wanted reform, yet the long awaited report had little new to say. It was the Tories with their *Fair Deal at Work* in April 1968 that now opened up the debate.[74] Their mooted 'cooling off' period was attractive to Labour, who were still furious over the seafarers' and dockers' strikes; and this was reinforced by a run on the pound ('Mad Friday', 6 December 1968), partly based on rumours of further union action.

Donovan's main focus was on fairly recent changes to collective bargaining structures and practices.[75] The heart of its case was that there was chaos and anarchy in shop floor relations, caused by the clash between inadequate managers hounded by the need to maintain productivity and powerful shop stewards able to use labour market conditions and hard-won solidarity to fight for what their members wanted. The result was an informal system that, according to the report, caused three damaging (for employers) outcomes: wage drift (the difference between earnings and agreed wage rates); unofficial and unconstitutional strikes (allowing shop stewards to act outside both union executives and agreed procedures); and restrictive practices (allowing low productivity to be constantly bought out through forms of extra payments). Together these were seen as hampering British managers' ability to solve the labour problem and encouraging shop floor union militancy. To change such behaviour it was deemed necessary to incorporate the shop stewards into the union decision-making process, and to bring formal agreements down the line to the factory. This pluralist take on labour-management relations reflected a dominant reformist approach to class conflict at the workplace. On one vital issue however, the report was explicit. It opposed further statutory regulation of collective bargaining, to the surprise and annoyance both of the Tories and Labour Ministers. As we shall see, Labour ministers subsequently totally rejected Donovan's voluntarist approach when in 1969 it introduced *In Place of Strife*, with its proposals for legal sanctions against strikes and state powers to enforce compulsory arbitration (the 'cooling-off' period) before national strikes.

The CP soon got to work denouncing both the theoretical assumptions and policy implications of the report. Campbell wrote a scathing critique of the Donovan report, its conclusions, its recommendations, and its entire political approach.[76] He did so in line with the CP's original evidence to the Commission. Taking up the Party's emphasis on false consciousness, he refers to the 'delusions of Donovan' much as Bert did with his 'con-tricks'.

Ramelson was keen to put the Party case, as he recognised the potential damage to the trade union movement from both the analysis inherent in the report and the probable outcomes in terms of policies and politics. His pamphlet on the report develops the case that: 'this is a most dangerous report, basically acceding to reactionary demands, but couched in subtle language, coupled with recommendations for some minor concessions'.[77] The Commission members and researchers had made it crystal clear that the Government had been determined that the Report should basically reflect its views. Ramelson took the strong line that Labour ministers had wanted the report to create both confusion and illusion, in order to provide a fig leaf to push through anti-union measures with the support of some unions. This was essential for the success of any incomes policy. As he stresses: 'so far we have shown that all the demands made by the Tories save one have been conceded by the Commission … the exception was legally binding collective agreements'. The Report's 'smooth liberal tone' concealed its efforts to rid the system of struggle as a means of resolving conflict; the bait being offered was a tribunal against unfair dismissal, but it would have no power to reinstate.[78]

The whole policy, Ramelson argued, was aimed at controlling wages in line with the general economic squeeze, itself a reaction to the crisis and demands of foreign bankers. This would stop workers being able to claw back wages cut in real terms by price increases caused by government devaluation. The report was aimed at creating a successful incomes policy, as Donovan makes clear in its statement that: '"incomes policy can make a contribution of outstanding importance to the economic growth of this country and a more ordered system of industrial relations and that any proposals which we make for the reform of industrial relations should assist an incomes policy to work effectively"'.[79] Ramelson concludes that the essence of the report is to replace struggle with peaceful incorporation and institutionalisation of activists. This is achieved through anti-union laws, the use of incomes policy, the rise of productivity bargaining, the extension of state intervention in union affairs, the restriction of rank-and-file and lay officials in determining take home pay; 'above all the whole weight of the report is aimed at eliminating struggle from the industrial field'.[80] Unions will be thus transformed to become partners with governments and employers with common interests.

In the period towards the end of the Wilson government, the Labour leadership's policies to deal with inflation and slow growth increasingly focused on reform of the labour market, and by implication therefore on the reform of pay determination, collective bargaining and the unions. Much of this was based on the final Donovan report, which came to dominate industrial relations thinking and academic studies, but which was also taken apart from various perspectives. One telling repudiation insisted that in the report problems had been defined in purely class terms, and therefore were problems for the employers and government but not for the workers and their unions.[81] There were also countless attacks on Donovan from left-wing union leaders, including for example George Doughty (general secretary of Draughtsmen and Allied Technicians union, DATA), who called it 'a sugar coated pill with a bitter centre'.[82]

The CP had an anxious time of it during this period, because just as their industrial policy and attacks on incomes polices were paying off, the Soviet intervention in Czechoslovakia renewed the anti-Soviet and by default anti-communist rhetoric.

ANTI-UNION LAWS: CASTLES BUILT ON SAND

The real start of the brave new world for labour relations came when Barbara Castle was made Secretary of State for Employment and Productivity in April 1968. Castle brought renewed energy to the role, and, backed by Bill McCarthy, she started on a road aimed at bringing some order to the 'chaos' of industrial relations.[83] With the support of Wilson and Jenkins, she unveiled *In Place of Strife*, which sought to use anti-union laws to shift the balance towards greater state intervention including secret ballots before every strike; a cooling off period of twenty-eight days before major strikes; to make collective agreements legally binding; and to create a new Industrial Relations Court with the right to apply penal sanctions to force unions to comply.[84]

All this seemed plausible at a time when disputes in the steel industry and at Ford motor company had allowed the media to create the false impression of powerful unions out of control. In taking this line the government headed into dispute with the TUC, and in particular with its two most high profile union leaders, Jack Jones and Hugh Scanlon. Within the Labour Party opposition to these proposals included both the traditional left and right-wing trade unionists. Michael Foot, for example, thought that Castle had got it badly wrong with her approach to the unions. Scanlon, while careful to avoid any head-on collision with the predominantly right-wing Labour government, saw both the attacks on unions and the use of incomes polices as aimed at a weakening of working-class organisation, and a likely fuel to flame the fire of rank-and-file militancy.[85]

Even before this the CP leadership had been in despair at the Labour Government's performance, along with much of the labour movement. Its warnings came replete with historical references: the

1931 betrayal was contrasted with the heroic struggles of the Coventry shop stewards in 1917, the cotton worker struggles of 1929-33, and even the victims of the 1819 Peterloo massacre.[86] The purpose of CP historical studies was to provide evidence that only through struggle could workers ever achieve progress, and that therefore historical materialism provided the best basis for analysing events in class terms. The focus remained on the current struggles of workers through strikes – official and unofficial, constitutional and unconstitutional – and the attacks upon them by the rightwing aided and abetted by some trade unionists. Ramelson, for example, made the following point on the question of unofficial strikes:

> The Labour Party believes that some electoral kudos would be gained by the suppression of unofficial strikes. So it hands this over to the Commission for Industrial Relations to deal with it in its own sweet devious way. Say a body of workers see their shop stewards arbitrarily dismissed and strike on the spot, rather than go through a long drawn out time wasting procedure. The shop stewards violate a procedure which may take from three to six months to come to a conclusion … Mrs Castle and her henchmen decide that this is an unconstitutional strike.[87]

Ramelson was also concerned that at the very moment that the government was seeking to restrict trade unions, it intended to deregulate monopolies. He had condemned Donovan for seeking to incorporate trade union decision-making into a corporatist model of industrial relations, without class and therefore without class struggle, and for its acceptance of the class nature of the state; and he railed equally against the proposed use of the law to reach similar ends.

As was his habit, Ramelson penned another CP pamphlet in February 1969, *Keep the Unions Free,* as a direct response to *In Place of Strife.* His claim was that the government's proposals were an all-out offensive against the trade union movement at a time when workers faced the treble threat of unemployment due to company mergers; more powerful employers; and government control over wages at a time of inflation. The policy may have been based on Donovan, but 'it out-Donovans Donovan'. It represented 'the ending of the era of free collective bargaining'. He argued that the whole basis of the White Paper, including its title, indicated its right-wing philosophy and misplaced view of the causes of strife: 'strife within this society is not due to a scarcity of institutions, faults in the trade union structure or to bloody-mindedness of shop stewards. This capitalist society is a class divided society which necessarily generates a permanent state of class struggle'. [88] He cogently argued that Labour went further than the Tories and the employers in seeking to control struggle and unions through notions of corporate statism.

Ramelson characterised the position of the government as: first, the state has always intervened in worker rights; secondly, it was necessary to limit disruption, especially in essential services; and third, that everyone now agrees that it is acceptable to interfere in collective bargaining despite both the TUC and Labour Party taking the opposite view. He explained that in reality both Donovan and the White Paper aimed to prevent unions resisting incomes policies: 'It cannot be stressed too often that once national agreements are given up and replaced by productivity agreements, the principle of incomes policy is conceded ... Tenacious and militant shop stewards', who had played a major role in stopping incomes policies, were now under attack. [89]

Further, the White Paper aimed to 'convert the stewards from trade union officials elected and responsible only to their fellow workers, into a body whose role and function would be the subject of negotiations with the employers. This is an employer's dream'. As another part of that dream, 'the real purpose of the ballot is to weaken the trade union negotiators and disarm them in their confrontation with the employers'. [90]

Warming to the theme of the 'sugar coated pill' Ramelson explained that to sell all of this to the public and the movement the government had a stick and a carrot: the few goodies on offer included trade union recognition, unfair dismissal appeals, more information, and some financial aid. This had to be taken with the 'poison' of trade union registration; certain rules having to be in rule books; delay over solidarity strikes; ballots; enforceable agreements; registration of procedure agreements; setting up of the Commission on Industrial Relations (CIR); and powers to fine unions in breach of legislation.

Ramelson was rightly convinced that 'the fate of the unions is in the balance'. So: 'the fight is on to keep an independent trade union movement in the face of attacks by the Labour Government. The counter-offensive must firstly break the incomes policy with its Donovan Report and White Paper, its PIB's and CIR's and so on'. [91]

On May Day 1969 there were tens of thousands of workers on unofficial strike against the government's proposals. As Morgan reports, the defining meeting of this period was that between Wilson and union leaders: 'on 1 June 1969 the Prime Minister ... urged Scanlon and his trade-union troops to "get his tanks off my lawn"'.[92] This reference to the events in Prague in the previous year was typical of the view of the right-wing core of the Labour government that in some sense they were the democrats despite ignoring party policy, while left-wing union leaders following democratic decisions were the real villains, the 'Stalinists' at the centre of the left opposition to government. Such an easy and slick view was commonplace in the press and amongst lazy academics and opinion-formers. Harold Wilson's own detailed account of these negotiations with union leaders through the TUC shows clearly enough that, while the Cabinet was concerned about unofficial strikes, union leaders were anxious about government proposals to legislate in this area, thus creating the basis for more unrest.[93]

The special TUC congress at Croydon on 5 June voted overwhelmingly to oppose the Bill. The TUC General Council welcomed any provision that defended and extended collective bargaining, but unequivocally opposed what it called the Bill's 'penal clauses', including 'the proposals ... that would empower a Minister to impose a 28-day "conciliation pause"'.[94] By now most labour movement bodies, including the Labour Party NEC and many Labour MPs and some ministers, were formally opposed to Labour's plans. In the end the government lost the day and shelved the reform, and by the meeting of 18 June Wilson needed to save face.[95] The TUC obliged with a promise to monitor disputes itself, with a 'solemn and binding' agreement; – later ridiculed as Soloman Binding, the well known useless hypocrite. The episode became known as 'In Place of Government'! This was a misreading of the TUC position, which remained ambivalent with regard to the proposed legislation as a whole, although it had moved away somewhat from its reluctant acquiescence in the earlier incomes standstill.[96] It was individual unions that carried on regardless, for example, with strikes of 1300 blast furnacemen at Port Talbot steel, and 11,000 at Pilkington glass. Indeed from January to June 1970 strike days lost went over the six million mark.

The TUC was becoming increasingly important as the voice and face of the movement to government and the wider world. Its political role as a broker of controls over both wages and unions made it a target for immense government pressure. It was through counter-pressure that Ramelson could try to influence TUC outcomes at this critical time. The TUC report, *Programme for Action*, to the 5 June 1969 special TUC in Croydon spoke of a guarded welcome to those elements of the White Paper that backed collective bargaining, but: 'the general council therefore still hope that the Government will reconsider its decision to press forward with legislation involving the use of penal clauses on unions and workpeople'.[97] This line was expressed more fully by John Hughes in his Fabian tract on the future of the TUC itself. He showed how incomes policies in particular had altered the role of the TUC as successive governments understood the need to take the TUC with them rather than just impose pay norms. In this sense the TUC had become the guardian of trade union members' say in national pay determination, but at the same time its pragmatism allowed ministers to use and abuse this role. Hughes, with the tacit support of the TUC leadership, effectively provides the rules by which the TUC would support a voluntary incomes policy, and thus helped to prepare the way for the Social Contract.[98]

PROGRESS AND REACTION: COMMUNIST GAINS AND LOSSES

As the decade passed the mood had shifted, with an unpopular Labour government in depressed disarray, the more or less feeble Tory Party bitterly divided, and the wider labour movement seeking to defend gains and push forward for new victories through an increasingly broad left approach. Left unity around issues identified as of critical importance to the working class became the main game in town.

> the aims of such a [national] convention [of the leftwing May Day Manifesto Group] , it was suggested, would be to bring together, without exclusions, members of different left organisations and groups to discuss their common problems; to try to reach agreement on a minimum statement of common policy; and to find ways of promoting left co-operation, especially on a local basis, in ways that did not supplant members' commitments to their existing organisa-tions, but offered an opportunity for talking and working together on the many issues where united left action was urgently needed.[99]

Left unity therefore addressed the central concern for the trade union movement, which was to counter TUC backing for incomes policy and productivity bargaining, and to bring inside the tent the forces of the so-called new movements. The Party was leading the way in an understanding of the failures of incomes policies in their own terms, but also in terms of the way they confused activists and leaders into the false belief that wage controls also meant profit controls so that productivity increases could be used to help the country rather than big business.

At this stage the CP leadership was clearly encouraged by the development of the mass movement against Labour's plans. As noted above the Special TUC Conference on 5 June 1969 (called by the LCDTU to protest against In Place of Strife) was an excellent example of what could be achieved by mass action and protest (such as had taken place on 27 February and 1 May); and, along with several major regional conferences against the proposed legislation, forced the right-wing TUC leadership to finally oppose the Labour government. As the hallmark of the right wing is an avoidance of struggle, causing it to act like a dead hand over the movement, so the TUC and the special conference only changed because of mass action: 'there can be no doubt that no Special Congress would have been held, nor would the report prepared for this Congress have contained in it so many positive ideas were it not for the build-up of mass agitation and activity by the more militant sections of the movement, in which the CP played a key role'.[100]

At the full TUC Congress in September in Portsmouth, the mood was clear as it marked the consolidation of the left trend within the trade union movement due to the forging of a united left. At the Labour Conference a few weeks later there was further left success as the unbridgeable gap between the policies demanded by the movement and those pursued by a Labour government was exposed. As 1969 ended the catalogue of industrial action was laid out from Standard-Triumph in Merseyside to London Underground with miners, dustmen and fire fighters. These strikes were seen as a vindication of Ramelson's strategy as increasingly the militant rank-and-file action was supported by union leaders.

Glyn and Sutcliffe noted this process:

Britain's fifth Labour government came to power in October 1964 at a time of rapidly maturing economic crisis for the capitalist system.

The political existence of the Labour Party, as of all reformist social democratic parties, rests on its ability to gain reforms for the working class within the capitalist system. A crisis, therefore, which can only be deepened by the granting of reforms, magnifies the contradictions of reformism. It was inevitable that Labour, given its working-class base, would attempt to introduce some reforms. But it was equally inevitable that it would be driven more and more towards policies designed to restore the level of profitability necessary for capitalist accumulation. The commitment to capitalism led to the failure of the reforms; the strength of the organised working class within the party paralysed the social democratic leadership in its efforts to solve the crisis on behalf of the bourgeoisie.[101]

While the focus of the industrial department was on left unity in the unions, the CP as a whole sought to forge new links with the growing group of citizens involved in fighting for their rights. The anti-imperialist struggles of the national liberation movements featured high on the agenda, and the Party was active across a range of issues concerning democratic rights and solidarity with national liberation movements. Ramelson's task was to encourage the trade union movement to put its considerable weight behind such campaigns, and in this he had some success. The link was made between such struggles and the civil rights movement in the USA, and the fight against racism in the UK with the founding of the National Front in 1967.[102] Such reforms were also closely associated with student unrest, the struggle for women's rights, the national question especially in Ireland, and issues of media freedom.[103]

THE PRAGUE SPRING

In January 1968, Alexander Dubcek, a longstanding Communist with a distinguished record in the wartime resistance movement and the subsequent liberation of Czechoslovakia from Nazi occupation, was appointed General Secretary of the Communist Party of his country. There followed at breathtaking speed a process of democratisation now known as the Prague Spring. In April the Czech Party published an Action Programme which included strongly critical sections on past abrogations of socialist democracy, degeneration and stifling bureaucracy, all of which had combined to result in profound social crisis and a lack of popular support for the existing system and government. It promised to sweep all this away, and went on to champion a new broad democracy, giving new rights to individuals and collective organisation to directly influence state policy and to end the monopolisation of state power by the Communist Party. At the time this statement of intent was widely welcomed in many parts of the international communist and labour movement, not least in Britain.

The Soviet Party, however, began in May to express serious concerns about Prague's proposed reforms, labelling them as a threat to socialist society, and it accused the new leadership of being 'anti-Soviet'. On the night of 20/21 August, Warsaw Pact troops (overwhelmingly Russian) entered Czechoslovakia. The Soviet government claimed that this action was at the request of a group of Czech government ministers in order to defend socialism against counter-revolutionary imperialist-backed forces.

The first British communist to hear of this was Ramelson: General Secretary John Gollan was on holiday (when he had left the week before it had appeared that Dubcek had reached some sort of accommodation with Brezhnev, the Soviet leader). At 3am on the morning of 21 August, Ramelson, a Russian speaker, was phoned by the Soviet Embassy and urgently summoned to see the Ambassador. According to CPGB Assistant General Secretary Falber, Ramelson asked for the names of Czech leaders who had requested military intervention, but this information was refused. Falber says:

> In the heated exchange which followed, Bert challenged the truth of the claim that the Czechoslovak Party leadership had invited the Warsaw Pact troops in, and warned that the British Communist Party would not accept so blatant an intrusion into the affairs of a fraternal party and another Socialist country.[104]

In Ramelson's judgment these developments were a serious setback for the communist movement and to all those struggling to advance the interests of working people and their allies. The renewed activity of the Czech people, most of it a positive expression of democratic aspirations, as well as the events in Vietnam where US imperialist invaders were facing imminent defeat, and the student revolts in Paris, at first encouraged progressive forces to believe that the people in action could make a positive difference.

At this time the Prague events led to sharp differences within the CP, but it was soon evident that majority opinion stood behind the sentiments expressed by Ramelson at the Soviet Embassy and subsequently endorsed by the Party's Executive Committee. In the run-up to the 1969 Party Congress there was sharp debate in the Party's press on the issue, which revealed deep divisions. This culminated in a fierce exchange between two old adversaries – Rajani Palme Dutt and Bert Ramelson. In October 1969 Palme Dutt – for many years seen to be the British Party's leading Marxist theoretician, not least by the CPSU – challenged the Executive Committee's position, which Ramelson had done so much to frame. The EC's resolution, to be debated at a Party congress the following month, condemned in forthright terms the military intervention, called for solidarity with the Czech communists and people, and confirmed the Party's opposition to such a blatant intrusion in the affairs of a fraternal party. Dutt called on the Executive to withdraw its resolution, or failing that for Congress to decisively reject it on the grounds that it would split the Party and that the 'revolution's success is the highest law' – implying that the events in Czechoslovakia preceding the military intervention had indeed been a threat to socialism worldwide.

Ramelson was asked to reply. He recalled Palme Dutt's 'spots on the sun' reference to the 1956 revelations of Stalin's horrendous crimes;[105] and went on to remark: 'what I find odd is that apparently Comrade Dutt's criterion for the permissibility of criticizing brother parties is whether he agrees with them or not and which party it is'.[106] This public division among leading communists was picked up by sections of the national press. *The Guardian* ran the 'story' front page, with banner headlines and photographs of the two main protagonists. The Party meanwhile moved quickly to reassure its members and the wider public that it was only a grown-up difference of opinion, and that in the lead-up to a policy-making congress it was not indicative of an imminent split. Gordon McLennan (later CP General Secretary) issued a statement to this effect, and Palme Dutt was persuaded to add his support, in saying 'this is a particular question on which there are two opinions. It has nothing to do with the question of leadership'.[107] The exchange appeared to have gone Ramelson's way. This was confirmed at the 1969 Party Congress, where delegates voted by over two to one in support of the EC's position of opposition to the Soviet military intervention. Before this, at the Polish Party Congress, Ramelson had once again shown his independence of mind and fighting spirit. There as the fraternal delegate representing the British Party, he had included in his speech a passage condemning the Soviet intervention. When pressed to remove this section of his speech under pressure from both the Polish and German Democratic Republic leaderships, Ramelson had refused. He left the Congress the next day in protest.[108]

Nearly twenty years later the question was re-opened by the Soviet leadership on the initiative of President Mikhail Gorbachev. One of the vehicles used for this was *World Marxist Review;* a monthly theoretical and discussion journal based in Prague, on whose editorial board Ramelson represented the British Party. The Soviets were now ready to back the position taken by the British Party in 1968, and to recognise, with suitable apologies, that a serious mistake, amounting to a violation of communist principles, had been made. Ramelson was pleased to add a personal statement which subsequently appeared in *World Marxist Review.* His letter to the editor was as usual forthright and uncompromising. It pointed out that the invasion was:

> an act which was wrong in principle and was bound to have serious consequences for the invading countries in particular, and the world Communist Movement in general. I never did believe that the invasion was a response to requests by 'leaders' of the Czech Government or Communist Party. All our requests for the names of the Czech 'leaders' who requested military help were refused.

Ramelson went on to spell out how these events impacted on the communist movement:

> it led to considerable disillusionment amongst both communists and sympathisers. Many left our party as a consequence … I am certain, if the invasion had not taken place the developments then in Czechoslovakia, would have had a great impact on the speeding up of the movement for renovation, *glasnost* and economic reform we now witness.[109]

THE END OF WILSON'S GOVERNMENT

By 1969 Ramelson was at the heart of the left unity strategy inside the unions fighting for public sector wage increases alongside the strikers at Fords.[110] The linkages between the industrial and political role of the CP were never in doubt, and both fed off each other, as Andrews notes: 'the party leadership was convinced that the strategy adopted under Ramelson since 1965 was correct, and was crucial to its overall political strategy'.[111]

Nothing, however, could knock the British left off its collision course with the Labour government and its reformist supporters. An assessment of the Labour years was made in 1968 by John Mahon, who argued that after the 1966 election victory the government's policy of freezing earnings, increasing unemployment and raising the cost of living had brought it into conflict with the labour movement. With devaluation in November 1967 had come further tax and price increases, and compulsory restraint on earnings. As the government had moved to the right to appease big business, there had been a mass movement against this trend, and a coming together in a positive development of the left among organised workers, elements in the Labour Party, and socialist and communist forces. This left shift was based on union militancy on the job, and exemplified by the 1966 seafarers' strike, the dockers' strike in 1967, and even the resignation from Cabinet of Frank Cousins in July 1966. Crucially, by 1967 the TUC conference was voting against the Labour government's policies, despite the leadership, and the left voice was being heard more stridently on issues such as the Vietnam war, nuclear disarmament, racism, the European Economic Community (EEC), public service cuts, and of course incomes policies.

According to Mahon:

> Up to 100 Labour MPs now openly backed the socialist left and all had links with the left in the unions. All of this Parliamentary voice was rooted in the resurgence of the unions with mergers aimed at strengthening their bargaining position and the rise of powerful shop steward groups, and of the left, with the lifting of bans on communists in unions such as the TGWU, the organization of the unorganized, and the power of union committees.

Crucially: 'the most committed, constructive and far seeing in the struggle against right-wing domination has long been the Communist Party with its campaign for an alternative, socialist policy for the labour movement'.[112]

James Klugmann brought this together in an article dealing with student revolts, trade union anger, and civil rights more widely understood. His focus was on a critique of reformism: its rejection of class analysis and struggle; its support for a foreign policy based around imperialism's interests; its view that the state was neutral in politics; its Fabian-style belief in gradual progress; and finally its denial of the relevance and need for socialism.[113]

By the late 1960s the pressure was building politically, as the Labour government committed itself to a low level revival of the economy, and to righting the imbalances in the economy through loans and re-assertion of conservative and traditional monetary and fiscal policies. The results were low growth, rising prices and unemployment. Throughout the period the government had engaged in fruitless and damaging efforts to control wages – never prices and profits – through a variety of hotchpotch notions about voluntary and compulsory methods of limiting pay rises, reducing the impact of free collective bargaining, minimising the scope within which unions could negotiate, launching a series of propaganda offensives against the left at home and abroad, and focusing on attacking militant trade union action to defend and improve wages. The need for a socialist alternative remained paramount, and this could only be achieved in the UK through a leftward shift in both arms of the labour movement: the Labour Party itself and the trade unions, including the TUC. Such a shift would allow a national debate on real issues of concern to working people across the board, and would create a policy base from which to start the mass pressure required to turn policy into practice. To achieve this required broad left leadership promoting militant action, left policies and securing backing for left candidates in union elections.

The CP line remained that capitalism in all its varieties was at core the same, and that under state monopoly capitalism most things were worse. This system could only be kept going by a reduction in democratic rights and accountabilities, as well as by pushing down on working-class organisations such as unions, in terms of their freedom to act and to act decisively to break the incomes policy and to fight off attempts to shackle the movement. *In Place of Strife*, the child of reformist ideals and Barbara Castle's anti-union prejudices had proved to be a disaster. Intellectually incoherent, economically foolhardy, and politically an own goal, the whole programme, in intent and direction, was a recipe for electoral defeat and political division.

By 1969, in conference after conference and in meetings and strikes all over the country, workers and their leaders were rejecting the policy, the wage controls, and increasingly what lay beneath. Even the TUC and Labour Party conferences moved resolutions to the left, despite the blackmail from government ministers about the impending election. This vindicated the Party line on left unity, and Ramelson's push against incomes policies and against industrial relations and anti-union laws.

While left unity was the watchword of the time, its application to the industrial relations arena was of vital interest and importance:

> 1969 was a year of extending mass struggles and the development and advance of the left in the Labour and Trade Union movement. Looking back over 1968, and especially 1969, we get a picture of the involvement of practically every section of working people, wage and salary earners, women, young people and students, in important struggles. Engineers, dockers, railwaymen, miners, London underground men, postmen, busmen, dustmen, TV and university lab technicians, now teachers and nurses – all have been in battle. The significant thing has been not only the militancy of industrial workers, experienced in strike stoppages, but also that of the new contingents of professional workers.[114]

Left unity was rooted in the fight against monopolies, as the 31st CP Congress noted:

> the adoption by the Labour Government of policies which sacrifice the needs of the people on the altar of monopoly profits has brought about the crisis within the labour movement ... the militant and left progressive forces have stiffened their resistance to the right-wing leadership ... through mass pressure and struggle important victories have been gained. The incomes policy has been breached with many sections winning.[115]

Throughout this period the Party put forward its basic Marxist position. This can be summarised as follows. Capitalism is a system of contradictions that make it unstable and dangerous; it is inherently a system of gross inequality in all aspects of life; and it is created by and exists for the benefit of a relatively small minority of the world's population. The only known reasonable and possible alternative is a form of socialism that allows a better life for the vast majority. Capitalism is a stage in the development of human history, and can be replaced but will not necessarily collapse by itself. Therefore human agency is required to end capitalism and bring in socialism. The debate is not about the need for the change, but about the manner. Revolution is required, and revolution itself requires a revolutionary party based in the working class and based in the need to further the interests of the working class. In both *State and Revolution* and in *What is to be done?* Lenin explained the political power of the state as an instrument of class rule. What separates out revolutionary Marxists from others is an understanding of the nature of class society and the class nature of the state. This allows a strategic programme of change to be formulated and pursued on the basis of the centrality of class struggle and the balance of class forces. That is what guided Ramelson in all of his work.

LABOUR'S ELECTION DEFEAT

The early months of 1970 saw more strikes, as tension mounted in the battle against wage controls, against a background of poor economic growth and unequal distribution, allied with resurgence in the declaration of citizen rights throughout the world. In the run-up to the June election little was said by either main party about the real issues of economic and social crisis; but there was some, *sotto voce*, cross-party agreements on union reform, wage controls, the denial of civil rights, condemnation of militancy and strikes, and on a wholesale anti-socialist and anti-progressive line. The communist left was meanwhile busy with debates about the nature of class, the state, the Party, and democracy. All impinged intimately upon both the internal strife of comrades, the fight against reformism, and the wider struggle with the capitalists.

One critically important reworking of Marx makes the significant theoretical point that exploitation is not logically or empirically linked with the creation and extraction of surplus value, and therefore those workers not involved directly in such work are also workers in the classic sense. This is because their proletarian nature stems literally from being propertyless: they own nothing of economic worth to generate income except their own ability to labour and sell that labour in the market for whatever deal they can strike. So all such persons, those forced to sell their labour power for income, are part of the working-class whatever happens after they are employed.[116]

Labour lost the general election in June 1970, with the government in much the same state as when it had started out in office. It was split on many issues of social and economic reform, and despite some genuinely social-democratic credentials on inequality and public ownership, it had remained wedded to a policy of growing the economy and then redistributing some of the benefits among the masses. Its failure of economic management, partly due to world forces and partly because of the pro-capitalist nature of the Labour leadership's beliefs, had meant a failure elsewhere in terms of much needed social reform. As the government and its advisors sought remedies, they had reached out to dominate those sections of economic life most under their control and deemed to be the weakest. They had decided that both absolute and relative levels of wages needed to be restrained by state intervention, and to succeed in that policy it was necessary to weaken union organisation and activity through incomes policies and legislative intervention in union rules and rights. This had put the government on course to clash with much of the organised movement, and to eventually side with the employers in the struggle for profitability based on lower relative working-class incomes.

Ramelson had stood out against these challenges at all levels and in all ways. As a result he had taken on a leading role in the struggle and enhanced his own reputation as a class warrior and socialist revolutionary.

NOTES

1. Minkin op.cit., 1991.
2. Reid, B. 'Trotskyism in Britain Today', *Marxism Today*, August 1964, pp. 274-284.
3. For more on George Brown's 'Declaration of Intent' see Broadway, F. *State Intervention in British Industry 1964-8*, chapter six 'New agencies of intervention', pp. 60-7; Associated University Press, New Jersey 1970.
4. Paynter, W. *British Trade Unions and the Problem of Change*, George Allen & Unwin, London 1970, pp. 160-3; Paynter, W. *My Generation*, Allen & Unwin, London 1972.
5. Hughes, J. 'British trade unionism in the sixties', *Socialist Register* 1966, pp. 86-113, p. 101.
6. National Plan 1965, see Thorpe, A. 'The Labour Party and the Trade Unions' in McIlroy et al op.cit., 1999, pp.135-6.

7. Kettle, A. 'The Future of the Left: an Open Letter to a Non-Communist Left Winger', *Marxism Today*, January 1966, pp. 5-10.

8. Ramelson, B. 'Truth about that deficit', *Labour Monthly*, October 1966, p. 469.

9. Saville, J. 'Labourism and the Labour Government', *Socialist Register* 1967, pp. 43-71.

10. Klugmann, J. *The History of the Communist Party of Great Britain, Formation and early years 1919-1924*, Lawrence & Wishart, London 1969; Klugmann, J. *The History of the Communist Party of Great Britain, The General Strike 1925-1926*, Lawrence & Wishart, London 1969.

11. Johnstone, M. 'Marx and Engels and the Concept of the Party', *Socialist Register* 1967, pp. 121-158, p. 121.

12. Kessler and Bayliss 1998 op.cit., p. 9.

13. NBPI Report No 29 *The Pay and Conditions of Manual Workers in Local Authorities, the National Health Service, Gas and Water Supply*, Cmnd 3230, HMSO, London 1967; NBPI Report No 16, *Pay and conditions of busmen*, Cmnd 3012, HMSO, London 1966.

14. McKersie, R. 'The British Board for Prices and Incomes', *Industrial Relations* 1967, 6(3): 267-284.

15. Report of the CP's Economic Committee, *Marxism Today*, May 1965, pp. 134-148.

16. Report of the CP's Economic Committee *Marxism Today*, May 1964, pp. 134-144.

17. Burns, E. 'Problems of Inflation', *Marxism Today*, December 1964, pp. 370-4.

18. Wainwright, W. 'Labour What Next?', *Marxism Today*, September 1965, pp. 4-9.

19. Dobb, M. 'Inflation and All-That', *Marxism Today*, March 1965, pp. 84-87; Marx, K. *Capital: A Critical Analysis of Capitalist Production*, Vol.1, Swan Sonnenschein, Lowrey & Co., London 1887, pp. 1-55.

20. Campbell, J. 'The Development of Incomes Policy in Britain', *Marxism Today*, March 1965, pp. 69-75, p. 69.

21. *TUC 1966 Annual Report*, TUC, London, p. 76.

22. Campbell, J. *Hands off the Trade Unions*, CP 1965, p. 10.

23. Ramelson, B. *Incomes Policy: the Great Wage Freeze Trick*, CP 1966; Tressell, R. *The Ragged Trousered Philanthropists* Monthly Review Press, New York 1962; first published 1914.

24. Ibid., pp 3-4.

25. Ibid., p. 21.

26. Aaronovitch, S. 'Forward or Back? Prospects for the Movement', *Marxism Today*, January 1967 pp. 6-12, p. 6.

27. Bert Ramelson editorial in *Marxism Today* May 1967, p. 129; most editorials on industrial matters in these years were written by Ramelson.

28. Campbell, J. and Ramelson, B. 'British State Monopoly Capitalism and

Its Impact on Trade Unions and Wages', *Marxism Today* January 1968, pp. 7-14, and February 1968, pp. 50-59; this was a reworking of their paper in *World Marxist Review*, 25 October 1967.

29. Woddis, M. 'Some Problems of Poverty In Britain Today', *Marxism Today*, December 1967, pp. 357-363.
30. *TUC 1968 Annual Report*, TUC London, pp. 94-5.
31. *Productivity, Prices and Incomes Policy in 1968 and 1969* (1968) HMSO: London; Cmnd 3590.
32. NBPI Report 123, *Productivity Agreements*, HMSO, London 1969, Cmnd. 4136.
33. Ramelson, January 1970, op.cit., pp. 3-4.
34. Ibid., p. 4.
35. Ibid., p. 16.
36. Morgan 1990 op.cit., p. 254; and also see Morgan, K. 'The Wilson Years 1964-1970' in Tiratsoo, N. (ed.) *From Blitz to Blair*, Phoenix, London 1997, p. 139. Note in both cases he makes the mistake that there were communists on the union executive.
37. *Morning Star* 30/6/66.
38. Thorpe, K. 'The 'Juggernaut Method': The 1966 State of Emergency and the Wilson Government's Response to the Seamen's Strike', *Twentieth Century British History*, 2001 12(4): 461-485.
39. Goodwin, D. 'Profits from the seamen', *Comment*, June 1966.
40. Gordon Norris interview, 2009.
41. Crossman, R. *The Diaries of a Cabinet Minister 1964-1966*, Book Club Associates, London 1975, p. 451.
42. Andrew, C. *The Defence of the Realm: the Authorized History of MI5*, Allen Lane, London 2009, pp. 527-8.
43. Wedderburn 1986 op.cit., p. 657.
44. Coward, Jack *We Want 40*, CP 1966.
45. *House of Commons Debates, Hansard 20/6/66, vol. 730, cc38-54.*
46. House of Commons Debates, Hansard *28/6/66, vol. 730, cc1603-733.*
47. Taylor 1978 op.cit., pp. 120-1.
48. Kenny and Brankley were members of the union's Strike Committee. Kenny, who later joined the CPGB, was at the time of the strike, like Jim Slater, a Labour party member.
49. Crossman op.cit., 1975, p. 544.
50. *Not Wanted on Voyage: the Seaman's Reply*, Hull NUS Branch, 1966, p. 1.
51. Ibid., p. 17.
52. Foot, P. 'The Seaman's Struggle' in Blackburn, R. and Cockburn, A. (eds.) *The Incompatibles: Trade Union Militancy and the Consensus*, Penguin 1967; for Ramelson's review see *Morning Star* 25/5/66.
53. Anderson, P. 'The Limits and Possibilities of Trade Union Action', in Blackburn and Cockburn 1967 op.cit., pp. 263-80.
54. Beckett tapes.

55. Chalfont, A. *The Shadow of My Hand: a Memoir*, Weidenfeld & Nicholson, London 2000, p. 161. This is the ineffable Chalfont's pathetic attempt at irony.
56. Wilson, D. *Dockers*, Fontana, London 1972, p. 187.
57. Ibid., p. 189.
58. Wilson, H. *The Labour Government 1964-1970: A Personal Record*, Weidenfeld and Nicolson, London 1971, p. 440.
59. Ibid., p. 441.
60. Jones, J. *Jack Jones: Union Man*, Collins, London 1986, pp. 186-190.
61. Dash, J. *Good Morning Brothers!*, Lawrence & Wishart, London 1969, p. 157.
62. Ibid., p. 159.
63. Arnison, J. *The Million Pound Strike*, with foreword by Hugh Scanlon, Lawrence & Wishart, London 1970; for a account of other strikes see Hyman, R. 'Industrial Conflict and the Political Economy: Trends of the Sixties And Prospects for the Seventies', *Socialist Register* 1973, pp. 101-153.
64. Wedderburn 1986 op.cit., pp.40-7.
65. Kelly, J. *Ethical Socialism and the Trade Unions: Allan Flanders and British Industrial Relations Reform*, Routledge, London 2010. Clegg in particular was a strong advocate of incomes policies, see his Clegg, H. *How to run an incomes policy, and why we made such a mess of the last one*, Heinemann, London 1971.
66. Taylor, R. *The Trade Union Question in British Politics: Government and the Unions Since 1945*, Wiley, London 1993.
67. Allen, V. 'Trade Unions in Contemporary Capitalism', *Socialist Register*, 1964, pp. 157-174; Mortimer, J. 'The Structure of the Trade Union Movement', *Socialist Register*, 1964, pp. 175-191.
68. Allen, V. 'The Centenary of the British Trades Union Congress,1868-1968', *Socialist Register* 1968, pp. 231-252.
69. Hughes, J. 'Trade union structure and government', Donovan, op.cit 1968, Research paper 5.
70. Kerrigan, P. 'Trade Unions and Amalgamations', *Marxism Today*, June 1964, pp. 166-170.
71. Bain, G. *The Growth of White-Collar Unionism*, OUP, Oxford 1970.
72. Egelnick, M. 'Non-manual Workers in the Sixties', *Marxism Today*, August 1964, pp. 239-245.
73. Report of the *Royal Commission on trade unions and Employers' Associations 1965-8* (Chairman: Lord Donovan), HMSO, London 1968, Cmnd 3623.
74. Conservative Party, *Fair Deal at Work*, London 1968.
75. Kilroy-Silk, R. 'Donovan research papers', *Parliamentary Affairs* 1968, Vol. 22, 82-7; and in particular McCarthy, W. 'Shop stewards in British industrial relations', Donovan, op.cit, Research Paper 1, 1966; and Stieber,

J., McCarthy, W., Marsh, A. and Staples, J. 'Three studies in collective bargaining', Donovan op.cit., Research Paper 8, 1967.

76. Campbell, J. 'The Movement and the Commission: Delusions About Donovan', *Marxism Today*, September 1968, pp. 264-272.

77. Ramelson, B. *Donovan Exposed: A Critical Analysis Of The Report Of The Royal Commission On Trade Unions*, CP 1968.

78. Ibid., pp.12-13.

79. Ibid., p. 5.

80. Ibid., p. 14.

81. Goldthorpe, J. 'Industrial Relations in Great Britain: A Critique of Reformism', 1974, in Clarke, T. and Clements, L. (eds) *Trade Unions under Capitalism*, Fontana, London 1977.

82. Doughty, G. 'The Donovan report', *The Trade Union Register*, Coates, K., Topham, T. and Barratt Brown, M. (eds), Merlin Press, London 1969, p. 41.

83. Bill McCarthy was the Director of Research to the Donovan Committee and later became a junior Labour Minister based in the House of Lords.

84. *In Place of Strife*, HMSO, London 1969, Cmnd 3888.

85. Scanlon, H. 'The Role of Militancy', *New Left Review*, 1967 No. 46: 3-15.

86. Biggs, K. 'Coventry and the shop stewards' movement 1917', *Marxism Today*, January 1969, pp. 14-23.

87. Editorial in *Marxism Today*, February 1969 p. 33.

88. Ramelson, B. *Keep the Unions Free*, CP, February 1969, p. 3.

89. Ibid., pp. 6-7.

90. Ibid., pp. 8-9.

91. Ibid., pp. 15-16.

92. Morgan 1990 op.cit., p. 302.

93. Wilson 1971, op.cit., pp. 650-4.

94. TUC *Programme for Action*, Report of the 5 June 1969 special congress at Croydon. p. 3.

95. Wilson 1971, op.cit., pp. 655-661.

96. *TUC 1967 Annual Report*, TUC, London, p. 319; *TUC 1969 Annual Report*, TUC, London, p. 437.

97. *TUC 1969 Programme for Action*, op.cit., p. 5.

98. Hughes, J. *The TUC: a Plan for the 1970s*, Fabian tract 397, London 1969.

99. Editorial in *Marxism Today*, June 1969, p. 161. The May Day Manifesto Group, led by academics such as Raymond Williams, was short-lived. The Socialist Society was its heir (see chapter 7, Footnote 3).

100. Editorial in *Marxism Today* July 1969, p. 193.

101. Glyn, A. and Sutcliffe, B. 'Labour and the Economy', *New Left Review* 1972. No.76: 91-6.

102. Bellamy, J. 'Politics and Race', *Marxism Today*, October 1969, pp. 311-318; Walker, M. *The National Front*, Fontana, London 1977.

103. Nicholson, F. 'Student Perspectives', *Marxism Today*, October 1969, pp. 295-301.

104. Falber, R. 'The 1968 Czechoslovakia crisis: inside the British CP', Socialist History Society Occasional Paper No. 5 1995, p. 51.
105. Implying that Stalin's crimes were insignificant when placed in the context of the Soviet Union's dazzling successes.
106. Bert Ramelson's letter to *Comment* 19/10/69.
107. *Morning Star*, 24/10/69.
108. Joan Ramelson interview.
109. Draft version in personal paper.
110. Mathews, J. *Ford Strike: The Workers' Story*, Panther, London 1972.
111. Andrews 2004 op.cit., p120.
112. Mahon, J. 'The record of the labour government 1964-1968', *Marxism Today*, August 1968, pp. 231-245, 231.
113. Klugmann, J. 'The Revolutionary Ideas of Marx and the Current Revolt', *Marxism Today*, June 1969, pp.165-175.
114. Editorial in *Marxism Today*, February 1970, p. 33.
115. Falber, R. 'The 31st CP Congress and the Fight Against Monopolies', *Marxism Today*, February 1970, pp. 40-49, p. 41.
116. Cohen, G. *Karl Marx's Theory of History: A Defence*, OUP, Oxford 1978; Cohen, G. *History Labour and Freedom*, Clarendon, Oxford 1988.

5. Edward Heath's Conservative Government and heightened class conflict, 1970-1974

INTRODUCTION

The years of the Heath government proved to be among the most turbulent in the history of the British working class. The Tories were determined to deal with the trade union question, which in their minds meant weakening the unions in order to change the balance of class forces decisively in favour of the employers. Building on Labour's *In Place of Strife* and the Donovan Report, the Tories now embarked on a strategy to constrain union power through legislation (the 1971 Industrial Relations Act); through wage controls, beginning in the public sector; and through withdrawing, withholding or reducing state assistance to so-called 'lame duck' industries (such as shipbuilding and coal mining), where unions were often strongly organised.

The working-class response was powerful and effective. Political strikes, mass demonstrations, and a wave of workplace occupations and sit-ins stopped the Tories in their tracks, and created the conditions for the return of Labour government in 1974. As we shall see, there were casualties along the way, but this period of the class war was one of progress for the unions. In this the CP played an important role, and that Bert Ramelson provided clear leadership and strategic analysis.[1] The trade unions and the left in the Labour Party emerged stronger at the end of this period, but the CP, though proving itself to be an effective force in influencing trade union policies and linking rank-and-file struggles, was unable to make the political breakthrough its revolutionary strategy demanded.

In many ways the Heath government was doomed from the start; there were just too many major problems beyond its reach. Although

Heath's own instincts were sympathetic with the one-nation Toryism of Macmillan, the government started out with the intention of reducing state intervention in all aspects of society and economy. In the 1970 dock strike, for example, Robert Carr, the relevant minister, refused to intervene at all, and Anthony Barber as Chancellor abolished the NBPI, cut public expenditure and taxes, and in general behaved like 'Selsdon Man', a rightwing and anti-collectivist precursor to Thatcherism.[2] This did not last for long, and once again it was the fundamental weaknesses in the economy that drove the political agenda.

From 1971 the era of stagflation began, with 14 per cent inflation and no increase in production or productivity. At this point the 'lame duck' policy was jettisoned, for example with the nationalisation, of Rolls Royce. Meanwhile the strength of left-led opposition had forced a u-turn on wage control, and by 1972 the Tories were seeking accommodation with the unions in the form of talks about a voluntary incomes policy and a Social Contract.

This was a period of unprecedented industrial action over a range of issues, including incomes policy, anti-union legislation, the protection of trade union rights and the imprisonment of activists; and there were sit-ins and strikes in a range of industries for better wages and against job losses. There were strikes by workers at Pilkington Glass,[3] steel workers at Corby, dockers in July, car workers at Cowley, engineering workers at Fine Tubes in Plymouth,[4] and manual workers in local government in the late autumn. These years saw some of the most famous moments of post-war working-class history, from mass demonstrations against the Industrial Relations Act and its consequences, through workplace occupations at the Upper Clyde Shipyards (UCS) for investment and jobs, to national wage claims for miners (twice), and a TUC General Council call for a General Strike. Despite momentous events elsewhere – with the military coup in Chile, the start of the world economic recession with oil price increases following war in the Middle East, and the arms race – it was industrial relations, class struggle that focused the minds of most politically aware and active citizens most of the time.

At the heart of these struggles were communist and left-leaning political and industrial activists. As the last chapter showed, Ramelson, the CP and the Liaison Committee for the Defence of Trade Unions (LCDTU) were by 1970 established as important influences in the leadership and conduct of such struggles. In his writings and analysis throughout this period, Ramelson brought together the political and industrial struggles; the official and unofficial movement; and the experience of industrial struggle and political campaigning and the know-how of organisation. From the moment the Conservatives were returned to government until their defeat by the miners and the wider labour movement, Ramelson attacked them, organised against their policies, and consistently fought for socialist alternatives.

THE 1971 INDUSTRIAL RELATIONS ACT

The Tory strategy depended on drastically reducing union power, and their legislation to curb strikes and weaken collective bargaining was at the centre of all that was to follow. They soon began drafting the 1970 Industrial Relations Bill, at a speed that was at odds with its complexity and the controversy it was bound to provoke. The proposals in the Bill aimed to put the unions into a legislative straitjacket and destroy normal collective bargaining. Measures proposed included: compulsory strike ballots and a sixty-day cooling-off period; outlawing the closed shop; legal protection for non-unionism; making collective agreements legally binding; proscribing a list of 'unfair' practices for which union and members could be legally penalised (for example giving solidarity support to fellow workers through any form of industrial action); and depriving unions of some immunities (which had previously protected unions taking strike action) against some common law actions.[5]

Heath's attacks on trade unions created conditions which allowed communists to exercise significant and effective influence in the broad labour movement, the aim of which was both to defeat the Tory measures and to turn the TUC and Labour Party towards more progressive policies across the board, starting with union and worker rights. Ramelson pointed out that:

> this year's TUC and Labour Party conferences [1970] marked a key advance of the left in the labour movement – especially in the trade unions … as a result of unremitting united activity between comrades, Labour party members and other militants, many trade unions – above all the two largest and most powerful ones, the TGWU and the AEF [Amalgamated Union of Engineering and Foundry Workers] – have now militant, progressive leaderships, and

these dominated both conferences both in the speeches made by Jack Jones, Hugh Scanlon and others, and in the weight of their massive votes behind progressive resolutions or in opposition to reactionary ones.[6]

The 1970 TUC Congress reported the General Council's rejection of all legislation concerning collective bargaining and trade union organisation and activity. Its opposition to Barbara Castle's proposals had drawn a line in the sand which made it quite clear that the TUC would not tolerate any additional legal interference in union affairs; and this was to be tested soon after, when the TUC was called upon to support all-out attacks on the Industrial Relations Bill.[7] The industrial arm of the labour movement was clearly on the move, but it required political direction and class-based analysis to guide and influence events.

Ramelson responded with another pamphlet, arguing:

> The Industrial Relations Bill 1970 is the most vicious piece of politically motivated class legislation since the Combination Acts of the early 1800s. It has been framed by big business for big business. The threat to trade unionists and their rights is also an attack on other democratic rights … the new Bill replaces all existing legislation wrenched out of the ruling class in thousands of class battles over the past centuries.[8]

Furthermore:

> The Tories – the henchmen of the boss class – have thought of most of the circumstances when trade unions are likely to have to take industrial action, declared them 'unfair industrial practices', and therefore illegal … the Bill even deprives the trade unions of the right to remain voluntary organisations framing their own rules … most of the ideas underlying the Bill owe more to the British Imperialist Colonial Office, responsible for setting up stooge trade unions in the colonies, than to labour laws operating in America or any other capitalist country.[9]

The Bill itself is condemned as an attack on the working class as a whole in order to weaken it as the crisis deepens. Ramelson goes on to explain that the plan to cut wages through inflation and unemployment could only be stopped by the organised working class, and this Bill aimed to prevent that. Various recent strikes would be illegal under the Bill, such as those by Post Office workers, airport workers, and the Clydeside strike, as would any actions against the Vietnam war, the Common Market, Apartheid, and of course the Act itself. The LCDTU action on 8 December would be illegal under the Act against which people were demonstrating. There was an urgent need to oppose the class war of the Tories, despite the defeatism from the TUC and other union leaders: 'To be effective the counter-strategy must work for the mobilisation of the whole movement – a mobilisation for determined action of every variety, and in particular, industrial action'.[10]

As Ramelson also pointed out:

> What is required now is to involve the whole labour movement, with the organised unions as its core, in a relentless mounting campaign culminating in actions of General Strike dimensions. Rank-and-file action is vital in the development of such a campaign, but it must be made clear that it is infantile 'day dreaming' to imagine that its objectives can be achieved by rank and file alone, no matter how militant the rank-and-file leadership thrown up by the struggle may be … the December 8th action reached such a size and breadth precisely because it wasn't only or even mainly a rank-and-file action. A number of trade union Executives – SOGAT [Society of Graphical and Allied Trades] Div. A, CEU [Construction Engineering Union], The Watermen & Lightermen, ACTT [Association of Cinematograph Television and Allied Technicians] and DATA – called for support for the National Strike … The task now is to involve more unions and the TUC itself. It won't be done by irresponsible 'ultra-revolutionary slogan mongering' and blanket attacks on all trade union officials which create the impression that the rank and file can do it all on their own without the official trade union machine.[11]

He recognised that the TUC's pamphlet attacking the Bill, *Reason*, was helpful, but argued that it was mass action that mattered: there had to be more than a propaganda exercise. The TUC's efforts to sabotage the 8 December day of action had been feeble and wrong.[12]

1971 was truly a year of monumental class struggle. While the British government was concentrating on taking the UK into the

Common Market, and while there were progressive stirrings in South America and parts of Africa, the absolute centre of class struggle in the UK remained in industrial relations. The Party urged the movement to capitalise on the mass day of action of 8 December 1970, and work towards other demonstrations for 12 January and 21 February 1971.

The Times reported:

> more than 20,000 trade unionists stayed away from work in Wolverhampton yesterday in protest against the Government's proposed Industrial Relations Bill. Between 5,000 and 7,000 took part in a march through the city centre. Many factories were closed and production was affected at dozens of others.[13]

This was just one example of massive demonstrations and shut-downs throughout the country. In another example, 'strikes at five British Leyland plants in Oxford forced the management to lay off other workers, so that 12,000 employees were idle and no production was possible'.[14] 'The great national demonstration against the Industrial Relations Bill organised by the TUC on 21 February was claimed by Vic Feather to have been the biggest London had seen this century'.[15] Over 100,000 marched on that day. *The Times* reported trade unionists marching 'in their thousands', but its editorial noted in the same issue that 'mass demonstrations such as yesterday's in London, marches, and even strikes are not going to prevent the Government from getting their Industrial Relations Bill through'.[16]

That day allowed the momentum to carry on to the strikes and demonstrations on the 1 and 18 of March. Again The Times reported: 'engineers used their day off yesterday to demonstrate their implacable opposition to the Industrial Relations Bill with shuffle of marching feet and fiery oratory in the centre of London'.[17] A few weeks later it reported:

> the TUC special congress at Croydon yesterday decided that there should be no more official strikes against the Industrial Relations Bill. It ruled that affiliated unions should be advised not to register when the Bill becomes law. There may be calls for further stoppages when the communist-dominated Liaison Committee for the defence of trade unions meets in London on April 24. About 1,500,000 workers took part in yesterday's one-day strike.[18]

In all this action Ramelson focused on the link between government policy, struggle, and workers' rights and living standards. In such an atmosphere there were renewed arguments about the nature of the state in a class society. Now was the time to educate the movement's activists:

> We have often argued in these columns that one of the most serious weaknesses of the British labour movement, affecting even its most militant wing, is the lack of understanding of the class nature of the state. The traditionalist reformist theory that our British state is neutral, non-political, above classes, still weighs heavy on the minds of millions of working people.[19]

This reinforced the line taken by CP General Secretary John Gollan:

> we have got to realise the limits of militancy in the economic struggle, and even on the wider social and foreign policy issues … as society remains capitalist society, new dangers, new social problems arise … Increasingly the issue of wages, trade union freedom, racialism, war and peace, the defence of the social services, is bound up with the general political struggle, the nature of government policy at home and abroad, state intervention and the like. Increasingly it is the capitalist system that must be challenged.[20]

The Labour Party had swung to the left in terms of conference resolutions and constituency activity, but the leadership, under a quietly depressed Wilson, remained largely unreconstructed. It was therefore increasingly the under-fire communists who set up organisational structures to meet the needs of the movement, who created the mainstream debates on class and struggle, and who ultimately stood out as the movers and shakers of the movement. The times appeared to vindicate both the *British Road to Socialism* strategy and Ramelson's behind-the-scenes work with the unions. By the autumn of 1971 the CP noted:

> this year's conferences of the Labour Party and the TUC resulted in decisions which could mean that when the Party next faces the electorate it will have a more socialist programme than ever before … the influence of the leftward movement within the trade unions is beginning to be felt strongly in decisions at the party conference. These

called for extensive nationalisation, to include banking and insurance, with a say for workers in running industry. The TUC debated unemployment, pensions, and Tory attacks on social services and trade union rights, therefore the CP line was correct and exposed the shallowness of the super-left militants who discuss the unions as 'bureaucracies' increasingly incorporated into the imperialist state machine.[21]

This position was borne out by events at the 1971 TUC Congress, which endorsed the decision of the special conference on 18 March not to register as was required under the new law, and gave full support for the days of action earlier in the year. Left progress can be seen in statements such as: 'it should not be assumed that rising wages were the sole cause of inflation';[22] and that legislation was 'class-conceived';[23] while the fraternal speech from Labour MP Ian Mikardo urged that there should be 'total and unconditional repeal of the infamous IR Act'.[24] This was also a time of expanding union growth, and of the development of unions and traditional forms of union organisation and action in relatively new areas such as among white-collar and professional staff, especially in public services and new technology industries.

By the end of 1971 inflation was nearing 20 per cent and the government's position of non-intervention was impossible to maintain. The National Industrial Relations Court (NIRC) set up under the Industrial Relations Act, and the now statutory based CIR were showing themselves to be ineffective, especially as most unions did not register under the Act, on pain of expulsion from the TUC. Disciplinary actions taken against trade unionists were beginning to founder, most famously with the release of the 'Pentonville Five'. When the CBI supported the TUC line that the law should be kept at bay, the government effectively shelved the use of the legislation.

Meanwhile the Labour Party, stagnant in the polls and still jaded and divided, sought an accord of sorts with the TUC and began to hammer out the ill-fated Social Contract. As Taylor later wrote: 'During the 1970s the TUC appeared to many outsiders to grow much too close to the Labour Party through the development of the ambitious Social Contract, although it was Edward Heath's Conservative government that went the furthest in offering the TUC a direct role in the management of the economy in the autumn of 1972'.[25]

In these years Ramelson sought to influence and direct the actions and arguments of the trade union movement. This was neither through set piece speeches at union conferences, nor indeed through any platform accorded him by the mass media and BBC. He worked, as always, through endless meetings, pamphlets and articles. Ken Gill, for example, gave us a number of instances of Ramelson's direct influence on day-to-day struggles.[26] Ramelson's influence was probably at its zenith during the Heath government years and the struggle against the 1971 Industrial Relations Act. The London dockers' action against aspects of containerisation and the use of non-registered labour was a highlight in this campaign, as we shall now see.

THE 'PENTONVILLE FIVE'

In spring 1972 a dockers' dispute was looming and the Industrial Relations Act soon kicked in. Jack Jones of the TGWU sought support and assurances from the TUC leadership that if legal problems arose they would back the union. By late April the 'blacking' of ports over containerisation measures was growing, and the NIRC sought to respond to employers' requests to ban the action. In Hull, Liverpool and London the dispute carried on without official support. As part of moves to stave off a national strike an inquiry into job security was set up, headed by Lord Adlington and Jack Jones. At this point the London Docks joint union stewards committee, of which Bernie Steer and Vic Turner were leaders, decided to picket firms at Chobham Farm, and the NIRC took action against Steer, Turner and Alan Williams, threatening them with prison for contempt if they refused to appear before the court. As noted by Darlington and Lyddon: 'On the previous Saturday, 10 June, an LCDTU conference, attended by over 1,200 delegates from 500 union branches and shop stewards' committees, had already called for strike action if any trade unionist was imprisoned by the NIRC'.[27] At this stage of the dispute, the government, through the Courts, backed off.

A re-run then took place at Midland Cold Storage in early July, with dockers picketing the depot while drivers from the same union wanted to carry on delivering. This time seven named dockers were ordered by the Court to stop their activities – and refused. On 21 July five of the seven were ordered to be arrested, and were placed in Pentonville prison (Turner, Steer, Derek Watkins, Con Clancy and

Tony Merrick). There was an immediate rank-and-file response at workplace level. Beginning in the print industry demands mush-roomed for industrial action, linked to calls for the dockers' immediate release.

Ramelson took the first opportunity to give this solidarity move-ment political direction. He called an emergency industrial aggregate meeting for London communists with General Secretary Gollan in the chair, and urged the one hundred or so leading militants present to go into their shop stewards committees and union branches to make the case for a TUC General Council-led General Strike unless the dockers were released.

Martin Gould, then a young shop steward in the Sheet Metal Workers Union, recalls the meeting well. He told us that for security reasons it was held in the bleak basement area of CP headquarters in King Street, and that following a forceful opening from Ramelson a lively discussion ensued. According to Gould, Ramelson was in masterful and inspirational form. He commanded respect and total support for a carefully crafted strategy designed to put the maximum possible pressure on the TUC General Council.[28] The solidarity strike wave was continuing to spread, with support from Kevin Halpin, the CP leader of the LCDTU; and with the TUC calling for a one day general strike, the dockers were released on 26 July.[29]

As Darlington and Lyddon state:

> the wave of solidarity action reflected the influence of socialists, particularly CP members, and the activity of the dockers centred around Pentonville. The LCDTU, which had played a crucial role in leading opposition to the anti-union legislation, sent a formal letter to affiliated bodies calling for the implementation of the 10 June conference decision to organise industrial action.[30]

It was clear to all but the most prejudiced observer that the action against the Industrial Relations Act by the dockers and other workers was a great example of extra-Parliamentary rank-and-file agitation against employers and the government's anti-union laws. A commu-nist-led movement was able to make the vital links between the everyday understanding and demands of everyone involved the destructive and undemocratic tendencies of the capitalist system, and the class nature of the exercise of state power. Ramelson's edito-

rial for *Marxism Today* expressed the mood: 'the last days of July saw
mass action which forced the release of the Pentonville Five and the
declaration of the national strike of the dockers following the rejection of the Jones-Aldington Report'. It was the solidarity of groups
such as the bus workers, dockers, miners, print workers, building
workers, engineers and transport workers that had forced Sir John
Donaldson 'to eat his own words and to open the prison doors, and
the TUC to come out in favour of a One Day General Strike'. He
continued:

> it is the rank and file and their shop steward committees, which are
> increasingly dictating the course of events. They are the real focal
> point of powerful and consistent struggle against the Industrial
> Relations Act and the Donaldson Court which it has spawned to try
> to use the full power of the law to smash trade unionism ... this is
> the power that can force a change in the policy of a number of unions
> and in that of the TUC and compel an all-out struggle to repeal the
> Hated Act ... never was the contrast between the mood and readi-
> ness for struggle of the mass of the workers, and the outlook and
> activities of many of the leaders of the TUC so striking. The latter
> are still engaging in discussions with the Government on economic
> and other questions. [31]

The actions of 1971-3 built upon years of struggle against incomes
policies and anti-union laws, and owed much to the CP's industrial
organisation and its industrial organiser. Even *The Times* noted the
importance of a national dock strike thus, 'the dock strike was called
by the National Docks Delegate Conference of the Transport and
General Workers' Union by 38 votes to 28 with 18 abstentions after
the rejection of the Jones-Aldington plan to help the industry', it
continued:

> more than 500 dockers danced and sang in London yesterday to
> celebrate a 'major victory' after the national dock delegates had
> rejected the Aldington-Jones report on the future of their industry.
> Later, after a three-mile march to Tower Hill, their shop stewards
> said: 'this is only the beginning. We have won an unparalleled
> victory, but there is a long hard struggle in front of us which will not
> end until we have got all our jobs back'. The scenes outside Transport

House were wilder even than the celebration outside Pentonville prison when the five dockers were released on Wednesday.[32]

The day before, the *Morning Star*'s dramatic headline had declared 'They're Free!' and the day after, in the same paper, Mick Costello and Bernie Steer explained the issues, and described the international as well national level of solidarity, including the crucial support of lorry drivers. The message was clear for all to hear. This was a major triumph for co-ordinated and disciplined working-class trade union action backed by widespread solidarity and organised through the good offices of the Party's industrial department, with Ramelson as the leading comrade. As Mike Seifert told us:

> his greatest moment was the Industrial Relations Act under Heath, where he coordinated all the struggle against the Industrial Relations Act on the basis of not going to court; and when they imprisoned the five dockers, Bernie Steer and others, and they were put into Pentonville, Bert orchestrated a fantastic fight back. He was the chief, even though he wasn't anything to do with the TUC officially or anything like that. But, working tirelessly behind the scenes, he forced a position where the TUC, against all their better judgements, were going to call a General Strike. And there were all these demonstrations outside Pentonville with all the TU leaders and bus drivers and dockers, and everybody, and they released the Dockers.[33]

Jack Dash provided a vivid account of the release of his comrades in his typically colourful style:

> the impact of the arrest was immediate; a wind of fury rose to a storm of anger and brought about a spontaneity of united action from all trades and professions never experienced in the post-war years, so fierce that the Knights of the TUC Round Table were forced to stop shadow-boxing and reluctantly threaten a 24-hour general strike unless the five men were released. But the Pentonville Five did not have to spend another weekend away from their families. The grass-roots rank-and-file had forced the Government to release the five, and the most tremendous victory of the post-war industrial struggles was achieved.[34]

In an article for the Party journal *Comment*, Ramelson explained the basic causes of the original dock strike, the issues surrounding the imprisonment and release of the dockers, and the overall context of the class struggle. He argued that the Aldington-Jones report was rejected because it failed to deal with the basic demands of the dockers – for job security based on work done by registered dockers; and for the growing small ports to come under the scheme. As he makes clear, 'the real reason the five dockers were released was because of the mounting industrial action which was quickly escalating to a general strike and the decision of the General Council to actually call a one-day general strike'. This point is linked by Ramelson to the wider issue of Tory anti-union legislation and the absolute need to defy it. He ends optimistically as ever:

> this shows the tremendous possibilities that exist as a result of the struggles that are now taking place for the development of a confrontation on a whole number of important policies, which could lead to forcing the Tory Government to resign, face a general election and be replaced by a Labour government which elected in such circumstances could be pledged to carry out policies radically different than those which Wilson carried out when he was Prime Minister.[35]

FURTHER DEFIANCE

There were several other major disputes, and the Con-Mech dispute in particular was a classic example of Ramelson's all round work. Here an AUEW (Engineering Section) District Committee launched a boycott of a non-union firm in order to win union recognition. The company then went to court, and in late 1973 the union was ordered to end its action. It refused to obey the Court Order, however, and was subsequently fined £15,000, which the union refused to pay. The fine was in fact later paid off by a group of employers in order to head off the possibility of a national engineering strike, and the Court then stopped its proceedings against the union.

Ken Gill recalled how Ramelson covered all the angles. Firstly, he convinced Gill of the necessity of attending the AUEW Executive meeting called to discuss the issue, which had the potential of either bankrupting the union or fatally weakening the anti-union laws and the Tory government. The stakes were high, and Ramelson urged Gill to use his position to urge defiance of the law. According to Gill, Ramelson also phoned Scanlon, the AUEW President and most influential member of the EC, assuring him that the CP would pull out all the stops to build a solidarity movement behind the country's most powerful industrial union. Both men knew that Scanlon's election as AUEW President owed much to Ramelson's work, particularly in ensuring that he became the left's candidate despite the ambitions of Reg Birch, a member of the Party's EC. At this stage Scanlon had good reason to believe that Ramelson could deliver, and this was a powerful factor in persuading him to use his casting vote in the previously deadlocked EC to call a national strike of AUEW workers, and not to pay the fines imposed by the NIRC.[36]

Ramelson also knew that it was essential to maintain rank-and-file pressure on the full-time officers, both to 'keep them honest' and to strengthen the left's case for defiance of, rather than compliance with, the anti-union law. Working with Kevin Halpin, who was both a leading rank-and-file member of the AUEW and chair of the LCDTU, Ramelson ensured that a mass lobby of the AUEW Executive meeting was organised on the day the decision was due to be taken. The lobby, several hundred strong, was both boisterous and disciplined. Scanlon was impressed enough to meet a small delegation, including Halpin, and encouraged enough to go into the Executive meeting to call for strike action.[37]

Thus the union stand was vindicated and the authority of the NIRC was fatally damaged. Within weeks it was wound up. Here, as with the release of the Pentonville Five, we see Ramelson at his most effective. Able to work with both the left at national trade union leadership level and with rank-and-file leaders, he was in a position to co-ordinate militant policies and actions. He recognised that only by uniting the actions of the official and rank-and-file movements could strong and effective pressure be mounted against anti-union laws and the Tory government. Ramelson summed it up thus:

> the determination and unity to use industrial action is an irresistible force and can overcome all the barriers, legal and otherwise, erected by the ruling class to exploit workers and undermine their organisations of struggle.[38]

VICTORIES AND DEFEATS

The Upper Clyde Shipbuilders

The struggle to save the Upper Clyde shipyards from closure with the loss of 6,000 jobs started in June 1971. The management, supported by the government, determined to close the business, having failed to make it profitable. The workforce, led by their shop stewards, including a number of communists, refused to accept the liquidation of the ship-yards and the sell-off of assets and sites for redevelopment. They decided on a work-in, keeping the workforce together and machinery intact, working on current contracts while campaigning to force the company and the government to withdraw the closure threat.

The campaign lasted several months. In this period workers were made redundant but they were not sacked, as the Shop Stewards' Solidarity Fund, which raised over £485,000, mainly from the trade union movement, was used to pay their wages and keep them employed.[39] On 28 February 1972 – the day the victorious miners returned to work having broken through the government's incomes policy limits (see below) – the Tories caved in. The threatened yards would become part of the Govan Shipbuilders Ltd, and £35 million of government investment would pay off inherited losses and provide for significant capital investment. A great victory had been won. The UCS workforce had shown that workers could indeed run industrial enterprises, and this reinforced the message that struggle and the building of powerful alliances could force the hands of governments.

The work-in had had limited objectives, namely to stop closures and save jobs. It was not planned as the first stage in the battle to establish workers control on a permanent basis. If it had been it would have been defeated, since no government, even a Labour government, would have financially underwritten such a project. The action did promote a new level of consciousness and the idea of the right to work became stronger in workers' minds. As a result of the UCS example there were fifty-seven sit-ins in the first six months of 1973 and a subsequent report concluded:

> many of the redundancy sit-ins were successful in achieving part or all of their main objectives, the prevention of threatened closures and redundancies taking place. The workers involved in the sit-ins are

convinced that the factories would have been closed if they had not sat in, and most companies confirm that there would have been total shutdown.[40]

Throughout the UCS campaign Ramelson and Jimmy Reid, the UCS workers' main spokesperson, were in contact.[41] Both men served on the CP's Executive. The Party and the *Morning Star* gave great prominence to the campaign, always stressing that it was rank-and-file led and that the key to its success was broad left leadership and widespread solidarity, based on tapping into both industrial and community support. CP involvement was critical in giving political guidance but it was always discrete. Ramelson was content to leave the day-to-day leadership to the Scottish Communists, and to concentrate his efforts in ensuring that every CP Industrial Advisory was mobilising effective solidarity support, and that the *Morning Star* was giving clear political guidelines in its daily columns. However he did offer advice to the work-in leaders. In a three-page handwritten note dated 17 September 1971, Ramelson suggested that an emergency resolution be prepared for the forthcoming Labour Party Conference, that a UCS shop steward should speak at the Tribune Rally on the Sunday night before the start of Conference, and that a Scottish convention 'embracing sections outside of the Labour Movement' be organised. He urged that solidarity support, in the form of industrial stoppages, should be sought from shipbuilding yards throughout Britain. He also advised that it 'may be necessary to introduce greater flexibility in the overall practices in conducting the dispute and to give consideration to a "stay-in" and stoppages as well as the work-in'.[42] Here again we see Ramelson the shrewd tactician suggesting ways of broadening the struggle and seeking the widest possible solidarity support, both inside and outside of the labour movement. Here was the broad democratic alliance in action years before the latter-day neo-Gramscians championed it.

Foster and Woolfson have provided a detailed and sympathetic account of the action. In a compliment to the communist leadership they argue:

> the process of unlocking the narrow sectionalism of the shipbuilding crafts, and politically harnessing the growing homogenisation of the labour force, depended on the skill of those who understood, in a

scientific sense, the character of class struggle … [because] it required
an overall knowledge of the contradictions within the development
of the capitalist system, of the nature of the specific bargaining
perspectives required to hold together the unity of the work-force
and sustain its support from outside. Such perspectives were totally
alien to the 'right wing' who, by definition, did not seek to introduce
questions of state power.[43]

This echoes the conclusion reached in Thompson and Hart's account:
'UCS demonstrated with an exceptional forcefulness that in the
endless contest between the working people on the one hand and
capital and its governments on the other, what counts in the last analysis is not persuasion, or eloquence, or even skilled negotiations, but
power'.[44]

The Shrewsbury pickets

The 1970s is often presented by right-wing politicians and commentators as one of overweening trade union power, which, whenever
exercised, threatened the very fabric of parliamentary democracy. In
fact there were many setbacks for the trade union movement in this
period. For example, after a nine-week national strike in defiance of
the government's wages policy, the postal workers were forced back to
work in March 1971 without achieving their main objectives. During
this strike Tom Jackson, the union's general secretary, who knew
Ramelson from their Leeds days, accused Ramelson of interfering in
union affairs and encouraging workers who were short of money to
continue a strike which could not be won. Ramelson rejected the accu-
sation of interference and criticised the union leadership for not
seeking solidarity support from the rest of the movement. Meanwhile
the government maintained its short-lived and ill-conceived policy of
non-intervention in industrial disputes.[45]

The biggest setback during Heath's government, however, concerned
the Shrewsbury pickets, a number of whom were jailed under nine-
teenth-century conspiracy laws, including Des Warren, a leading
communist rank-and-file trade union leader from the North West of
England.[46] Their picketing was part of a militant pursuit of a national
building workers' union claim for significant improvements in wages
and conditions, a claim that was based on the twelve points of the

Building Workers Charter. This had been formulated by a rank-and-file movement which spanned Britain and was greatly influenced by communist activists like Warren.

The rank-and-file organisation had grown out of frustration with the official union (mainly UCATT but including the building workers section of the TGWU). There was considerable resentment among activists over the 1970 agreement between the unions and employers, which was viewed by rank-and-file activists as giving concessions to the employers over bonus schemes and the expanding use of casual labour (lump labour – workers categorised as self-employed and therefore exempt from employers national insurance contributions). By 1972 the Building Workers Charter movement, with communists very much in the vanguard including Lou Lewis, who worked closely with Ramelson, was strong enough to win official union support for its demands. These were wide-ranging and included a call for greater democracy in union organisations within the industry. Most of the Charter's twelve points had become UCATT policy at its national conference in the summer of 1972, and most importantly the delegates had agreed to back the wages and conditions claim with strike action. All this was against the background of considerable militant action by workers across a number of industries against Tory wage restraint and anti-union laws, and in defence of jobs at a time of growing unemployment.

The strike began on 28 June 1972, with regional committees of the unions calling out selected sites. Not surprisingly, these were the big well-organised trade union jobs. This quickly escalated into an all-out national strike, and by mid-August local action committees were co-ordinating mass picketing activities, and were now targeting poorly-unionised sites. Once more the flying pickets' strategy first developed in the Yorkshire coalfield became widely adopted.

The clashes that followed between the pickets – who were often inexperienced – and the so-called self-employed lumpers, often threatened to break out into violence, and on a number of occasions did so. This was the background to the Charter's, with the North Wales Action Committee, call to picket sites in Shrewsbury on 6 September. Coaches from all over the North West carried over 200 pickets to the Shropshire town that day. It was a rough day, with some fist fights breaking out, and many examples of threatening behaviour on both sides. There was a substantial police presence throughout the day, but there was not one arrest on the day itself. Early on in the dispute the *Morning Star* announced that most small and medium-sized building firms were cracking under the pressure, and had called for more talks at national level. By 14 September it reported that 'builders step up the pay drive', and lobbied for talks between the unions and the bosses.

The strike ended on 15 September. Not all the union demands were met but the settlement reached was the biggest pay increase ever recorded for organised workers in the building industry. It was a significant victory, brought about mainly by the strength and determination of the rank-and-file activists, who in the end were reluctantly backed by the official union. This was difficult for the Tory government to accept. Not only was their wage restraint policy in tatters; the anti-union Industrial Relations Act was also proving increasingly difficult to enforce in the face of militant trade union actions. Tory MPs and some big employers wanted action to be taken to restrict the power of pickets. Government ministers made it clear that powers already existed to restrict mass picketing, and that the law states that sheer numbers attending can constitute intimidation.

Home Secretary Robert Carr stated that he intended to write to Chief Constables, drawing their attention to the law governing picketing and asking them to draw up strategies to make enforcement the order of the day. Within weeks over eight hundred people had been interviewed by the police in connection with incidents occurring in the North Wales and West Mercia police area. Five months after the end of the strike, arrests began. In July 1973 twenty-four strikers were sent to trial on charges of intimidation under Section 7 of the Conspiracy and Protection of Property Act 1875, and five of their number, including Des Warren, faced the added charges of unlawful assembly, affray and conspiracy to intimidate. This was the use of capitalist law to end the use of flying pickets in successfully waging industrial struggle against the employers. Des Warren was found guilty and given a three year jail sentence.

The case became a touchstone of state oppression of unions and union activists, and eventually went down in history as the 'Shrewsbury Three'. Ricky Tomlinson, Des Warren and McKinsie Jones were all sent to prison (at the time of writing there are still moves to get justice for the original Shrewsbury 24 through an admission that none should have been found guilty, let alone sent to prison). Ramelson wrote the foreword to Jim Arnison's account of the dispute, making it clear that

Ramelson's father, in Edmonton, Canada (undated)

*Ramelson in the
British army during
the second world war*

Ramelson with British army comrades in the second world war

*Marian Ramelson in
the early 1950s*

Leading from the front: Leeds Trades Council demonstration, circa 1954

*Speaking outside a Leeds factory during the Leeds South
by-election, June 1963*

Explaining the law to the constabulary, 1954

*Among those gathered at a party social in the mid-1950s are Tommy Degnam
(front row, seated) and Jock Kane (top right-hand corner)*

Making the headlines, Daily Mirror, June 1966

Ramelson with his sister Rosa

Bert Ramelson tribute night, April 1988. Left to right: Ken Gill, Arthur Scargill, Joan Ramelson, Bert Ramelson, Bill Alexander

Bert with Joan and his extended family in the 1980s, early 1990s

since the industrial relations legislation had failed to stem the tide of strike action, the state had resorted to traditional charges of conspiracy and affray.[47]

Des Warren wrote to Ramelson from prison on 9 February 1974:

> through their attack on the trade union movement and workers' reaction to it, in the form of 'Free the Three' campaign, new links, contacts and friendships have been made and unity is being formed as with the miners' fight, which will last long after we are out of prison and which will stand the movement in good stead in the continuing struggle.[48]

These sentiments echo his speech at the end of the original trial: 'it has been said in this court that this trial had nothing to do with politics. Among the ten million trade unionists in this country I doubt if you will find one who would agree with that statement'.[49]

There was widespread anger in the trade union ranks, and there began a drawn-out campaign to secure Warren's release from prison. Ramelson played a leading role in this campaign, and was in regular contact by letter and through prison visits with Warren throughout his prison term. It is clear that Warren looked to Ramelson for advice and support. This was given unstintingly, and both the CP and the *Morning Star* reflected this in their campaigns and coverage. Throughout 1973 and 1974 reportage of activities in the 'Free the Shrewsbury Pickets' campaign was seldom off the front page of the *Morning Star*, which reported meetings and lobbies, mainly organised by rank-and-file committees, in many parts of Britain.

During 1974 Warren's health deteriorated, and the harsh prison regime was taking its toll. He had responded to the indignities of his treatment, and the failure to secure justice through the legal system, by adopting a stance of non-co-operation with the prison authorities. Working-class struggle takes its toll on individuals as well as movements, and this grim example shows the personal price many are prepared to pay for the cause.

By the beginning of 1975 it was clear that the political campaign was not getting the desired results. Hopes that the recently elected Labour government would review the case were quickly dashed by Home Secretary Roy Jenkins, and the TUC leadership was not prepared to lead a determined political campaign to force a change in government policy. The official movement remained hung up on the sanctity of the law, even where it had been used to attack trade union rights and working-class interests through vindictive sentences, and where its charges – which were never and could never be proved – had been based on an 1875 Act. UCATT leaders had actually condemned the pickets for 'committing acts which are obviously of a criminal nature and which are contrary to the union's instructions'.[50]

Against this background Ramelson, in a letter dated 24 March 1975, advised Warren to end the non-cooperation campaign in order that the TUC and sympathetic Labour MPs could pursue demands for early release on humanitarian grounds. There were serious worries about Warren's health and his ability to serve the rest of his sentence without irreparable damage to his physical and mental well-being should he continue with his non-co-operation regime. At the time Warren accepted Ramelson's advice and acted accordingly. Later however, in his book, *The Key to my Cell,* he attacked Ramelson personally, and the CPGB generally, for abandoning him, and for publicising his alleged change of mind on non-cooperation without his agreement, in order to advance the Party's strategy of courting trade union leaderships.

By this time Warren had joined the Trotskyist Workers' Revolutionary Party. In a letter to a friend, written some twelve years later, Ramelson explained at length what actually happened. The key paragraph reads as follows:

> The simple fact is, of course, that as he [Warren] points out, he accepted my advice and that made me very happy. He writes that he did so reluctantly, but doesn't deny that he did. He implies that I didn't visit him in Lincoln jail, and that the *Star* news item came to him as a shock. I refer you to my letter to him dated Nov 4, and reprinted on p.277 [of *The Key to my Cell*) where reference is made of my visit to him in Lincoln jail. He implies that I couldn't have visited him before he started cooperating. I never claimed I did nor did the *Star* news item say so. Indeed, I had argued with the Prison Governor to allow me to visit him in his cell and was refused. But then there is no mystery about it. Des, as he admits, accepted my advice and decided to cooperate. That enabled me to visit him in Lincoln and it was during this visit that we discussed and agreed that I inform via the *Morning Star,* of his decision and reasons for that decision.

Later in the letter he says this:

> When Des was finally released, I saw quite a bit of him. At no time
> did he raise it with me. Long after I retired I heard that he joined
> the WRP and that he started complaining about the Party and
> myself. I did nothing about it nor do I intend to now. I'm satisfied
> that I did all I could to help develop one of the most difficult and
> longest campaigns for class justice. It failed, but then the history of
> the working class is a history of many failures – but they are never
> in vain. It just isn't true that we concentrated on resolutions to the
> Gen. Council, or relied on influencing MPs. The facts are that the
> main emphasis was at grass root level, with the objective of compel-
> ling the official movement to respond. Indeed the mass campaigning
> through Des's imprisonment, which was probably the longest
> campaign in the Party's history, laid the foundations for the
> campaign which led to the demand for and declaration of a 1 day
> General Strike by the General Council compelling the release of the
> Pentonville Five.[51]

We have quoted this letter at length, because these extracts tell us much
about the Party's strategy and approach during this period. They also
remind us that, far from being too powerful, in the 1970s the trade
union movement was not always strong enough to protect activists
against class laws employed to undermine effective picketing.

AN INCOMES POLICY FOR ALL SEASONS, AND THE FIGHT FOR THE PARTY LINE

As a result of its evident failure and weakness in the face of opposition,
the Heath administration now began to take cover in a kind of corporatism. The TUC and CBI were approached within the NEDC to
forge some form of voluntary wage restraint system. By the beginning
of November 1972 talks to this end had failed in the face of TUC
opposition, and the government announced a unilateral statutory
incomes policy. By the end of the year Phase I of the policy, which
imposed a six month freeze on prices and wages, had gone through
Parliament. Most trade union leaders, including Jones and Scanlon,
were utterly opposed to the scheme and the arguments behind it. It
raised important issues about the role of the state and the reach of law

into civil society, especially in relation to freedom of association, organisation and strikes by workers, and fed into some important theoretical debates about the class nature of the state, and some more detailed aspects of the law. In particular, the notions of a voluntary system of industrial relations seemed to go against the idea of statutory regulation of unions and the labour market.

The Counter Inflation Act 1972 started with a freeze on pay, prices, rents and dividends; Phase II from April to November 1973, allowed for rises of £1+4 per cent, up to a maximum of £250 per year for any worker (unless it was part of a move to equal pay for women); and Phase III, from November 1973 to July 1974, allowed for 7 per cent increases, with a maximum of £350. Machinery set up to implement these stages included a Pay Board and Price Commission. [52]

Meanwhile the debate among the left was gathering pace, both because the lacklustre Labour opposition was being pushed leftward in some areas, and because across Europe and the rest of the world generational change was taking place among those active in various left movements. In the UK, where the left was weakest but also the most agonisingly introspective, neo-Gramscians appeared to debate the role of the revolutionary party and the nature of the dictatorship of the proletariat; and elsewhere entryists (Trotskyists inside the Labour Party) became more vocal but also more exposed. The CP's criticisms were particularly focused on Tariq Ali and his assorted International Marxist Group (IMG) followers: 'the utter irresponsibility and real anti-working class face of "ultra-leftism" behind all the "revolutionary" phraseology, is revealed in the constantly repeated calls for the destruction of the Labour Party by helping to separate the trade unions from it'.[53]

In light of this, Reuben Falber again restated the position of the CP from its 1972 Congress. His report repeated the clear and agreed strategy to fight the Tory government:

> at the heart of this fight is the need to work for and develop the central strategy of winning the Labour Movement for militant left progressive policies, and rallying around it the numerous and varied anti-monopoly forces whose demands can be satisfied only by a programme of far reaching change. The key to this strategy is the aim of turning the trade unions into militant fighting organisations of the working class campaigning for socialist policies, with a leader-

ship reflecting the aspirations of the most progressive sections of the movement.[54]

A core part of this was to build the Party, the YCL, and increase the *Morning Star* circulation, through further agitation and activity. The frustration was palpable: a clear and unifying line, a reactionary government, a dithering right-wing leadership in the Labour Party, uplifting struggles and victories abroad, some outstanding fights by the British trade unions, and an upsurge in progressive ideas and actions throughout the country – yet the CP, a key mover in much of this, was unable to make the necessary political breakthrough, either in terms of mass membership growth, or electorally. Why this should happen and what could be done eluded the leadership, despite some forcefully brutal self-analysis and the willingness to change with the times, new and old. The strategic analysis revolved around Gollan's interpretation of Marx's work that capitalism creates an ever-larger working class with common interests.[55] This in turn fed into debates about the changing composition of the working-class[56], and therefore, the need to develop a strategy to mirror that in both the unions and the Labour Party.[57]

It was once again the fight against incomes policy that allowed both the widest possible left unity within the union movement and the chance to raise issues of class struggle and the class nature of the state with a larger audience. The effort put in by the comrades to persuade the TUC leadership that all of this was huge, and well directed at what as that time a key decision-making body as well as a platform for widely reported debate. At the 1972 TUC Congress further signs of leftward movement were evident, with strong support for workers in struggle, from miners and the Pentonville Five, to disputes at C.A. Parsons involving AUEW (TASS) members, and at Heaton's (TGWU) over containerisation. However one decision in particular of the General Council infuriated the left and that was to continue talks with the Tory government. Scanlon and Doughty were trenchant in their attacks on the leadership, and Tony Benn (the fraternal Labour Party delegate) called for wider solidarity across the movement as well as in defence of collective bargaining.[58]

Andrews acknowledges that 'the Communist Party played an important organisational role in the industrial struggles of the period' – which included defence of collective bargaining; and furthermore:

'the party leadership derived much confidence from its role in this unprecedented period of militancy. For Ramelson, the influence of the Party in trade union affairs had never been greater'.[59] In 1972 the TUC ended its twenty-two year ban on communists attending trades councils as elected delegates from their branches; and by 1974 10 per cent of union full-time officials were estimated to be in the CP, while it was also well represented on the executives of the NUM, NUR, Union of Post Office Workers (UPW), UCATT and TGWU, as well as AEUW, National Union of Teachers (NUT), TASS, and ASLEF: 'Figures alone probably do not explain the extent of communist influence, given their behind the scenes organising abilities, the role of advisories in influencing candidate selection and promoting policy, and the tendency for communists to be trusted with key roles'. In particular, Andrews notes the influence on trade union activists of Ramelson's 'Needs of the Hour' bulletin. [60]

Two debates – on the changing nature of the working class and on the central role of union militancy in the fight against the Tories and capitalism – reflected how the industrial relations anti-union laws reforms had become the focus of class struggle. As we have seen, part and parcel of Ramelson's tactics was to knit together all those involved on the left within the trade unions. Ramelson was also able to bring into his circle academics and intellectuals, journalists and political advisors, and some MPs and local councillors. Thus left unity meant something tangible, and did influence the labour movement as a whole through the central role of his department.

1973 was a further year of government dithering, limitations in Labour opposition, and industrial unrest, in which there emerged a possible way forward for the movement in the shape of an ill-considered 'social contract'.[61] Ramelson was totally opposed to such deals, and sought both to undermine the economic case made by the Tories and warn off any incoming Labour government when it came to wage controls. The Middle East crisis was also now beginning to have an effect on the economy. Itself a subset of a wider crisis of British and American foreign policy, as well as of regional political ambitions, the crisis was propelling fuel prices ever upwards, and with that had come a genuine exogenous shock to the energy markets, and therefore to the price and demand for alternatives to oil, such as gas and coal.

The economy again took centre stage, both in terms of the mainstream political debate, but also among the left and the communists. The key issues of inflation, unemployment, economic growth and investment focused attention.[62] The CP was concerned that recent gains made in the thinking of left trade union leaders would melt away in the desperate search for a Labour election strategy. The need to convince all those interested in the nature of the crisis, and the causes of the problems facing working people, was paramount. Ron Bellamy restated the Marxist case:

> the slogan 'militancy is not enough' welcomes, on the one hand, as a tremendous positive advance, the growing boldness and initiative of the working class and wider sections of the people on economic and social issues which state intervention increasingly convert into issues of political struggle. But at the same time it recognises the need to deepen the struggle against effects into struggle against causes. The cause of the monopoly-capitalist state's offensive against the advance of the left forces is the need to increase the profits and power of British imperialism in the face of increasing difficulties.[63]

Bellamy makes the important link between British imperialism in all its forms and the rise of finance capital and the power of the City of London. These are the main movers in creating crises and breeding inflationary pressures.[64]

It was the government's income policy Phase II's six month freeze that created an opportunity for Labour under Wilson to come back into the debate, with a concordat with the disaffected and angry union leadership. This was the moment of conception of the Social Contract. It was Phase III in autumn 1973 that really riled the unions, and especially the NUM. The line-up of unions taking on and defeating the government was growing, with miners, power workers, electricians and dockers leading the way. There was nothing left in Heath's tank: no powers, no institutions, no policies, and no support for his brand of pay control and industrial relations reform. Critically for him and the country, the next miners' strike, in early 1974, came after the massive oil price jump and the associated crisis in the Middle East.

In February 1973 Ramelson published another CP pamphlet, *Heath's War On Your Wage Packet: The Latest Tory Attack on Living Standards and Trade Union Rights*. He opens by noting that:

the Phase II clamp-down on wages is the latest in a whole series of efforts by the ruling class to do away with collective bargaining and replace it by state-regulated wages. Since the end of World War II, eight different attempts have been made by a succession of Governments, Labour as well as Tory, to impose an 'incomes policy' in a bid to solve the chronic crisis of capitalism at the expense of the working people.[65]

Ramelson was also quick to publish an attack on Phase III of the government's policy in his December 1973 pamphlet. Here he starts to develop the argument that it is all a big swindle, a 'con trick' to be exposed, and in particular he aims to persuade the TUC leadership to actively oppose and expose the government's case:

> for nearly ten years … successive governments have been issuing a stream of White Papers, Codes and Statutes, in efforts to con working people into accepting drastic cuts in real earnings. But it is doubtful whether any previous legislation could match Phase 3 for its brazen dishonesty, double talk and outright lies.[66]

Towards the end of the pamphlet Ramelson makes his political points aimed at union activists and leaders, and provides a case to put pressure on the TUC leadership. The real purpose of Phase III was 'not to hold back inflation but to reduce real wages and earnings, to ensure that increases in take home pay are kept well below the rapidly rising cost of living'. He also picked up the argument about breaking the law: when the minority imposed laws on the majority against their will this was undemocratic, and the workers had the right to oppose through any means the class bias of the legislation. [67]

The 1973 TUC Congress represented both a turning point and an illustration of the tensions and muddles at the heart of the organised labour movement. On the one hand Ken Gill and Alan Sapper (ACTT general secretary) pushed the motion that 'Congress opposes wage restraint imposed by any government', on the grounds that 'inflation was never caused by workers' wages'. [68] On the other hand, although the TUC leadership opposed the current wage freeze it kept talking with the government, even though such talks were useless.[69] Talks with the Labour leadership were more productive. The TUC-Labour Party Liaison Committee produced a wide-ranging draft document addressing trade union concerns about anti-union laws and economic policy.[70] The committee's report *Economic Policy and The Cost of Living* argued along the lines of the CP position that 'wages and salaries are very far indeed from being the only factor affecting prices'. It then spelled out an alternative strategy, again heavily reliant on CP thinking, which included price controls, a major house-building project, more public transport, a redistributive tax system and investment in growth and jobs. However, as we shall see in chapter six, this document also contained the nucleus of what was to become the Social Contract – a rather less propitious development.

THE 1972 AND 1974 MINERS' STRIKES

The real nemesis of Tory policy was the clash with the miners and the NUM. The scene was well set: miners' pay had been falling behind comparable groups for some time; world energy prices were volatile and the supply of coal to power stations was still the mainstay of electricity generation in the UK; the miners as a group remained popular among ordinary people; and the left was the strongest political force in the union, which was led by two major figures – the former communist and leftwing sympathiser, Lawrence Daly, who had been general secretary since 1968, and Mick McGahey, a longstanding communist, who was Vice President.

In the mining industry the patient work which Ramelson had done so much to encourage in the 1950s in the Yorkshire coalfields was now paying dividends. By the early 1970s the left was in a powerful position within the NUM leadership nationally, as well as in Yorkshire, Scotland, Wales and Kent – and for the first time in the Nottinghamshire coalfield, where the communist Joe Whelan won the NEC seat. This move to the left corresponded to a growing tide of unrest in the coalfields, particularly on the question of wages, aggravated by the effects of successive income policies.

In 1971 there had been a partial and unofficial strike. This had been followed by an NUM conference decision to back a call from the communist-led Scottish area for a substantial wage increase, if necessary using industrial action to achieve it. The claim included a minimum wage of £26 for surface workers, £28 for underground workers and £35 for those under the National Power Loading Agreement.[71] The 1971 miners' claim had been rejected by the Coal

Board, acting on instructions from the Heath Government, which was then operating an informal incomes policy in the public sector, as part of an attempt to progressively force down the level of settlements for all major groups of workers.

The 1972 strike itself formally started when the NUM rejected an 8 per cent pay offer from the NCB. While union president Joe Gormley, as always, sought and believed in a negotiated settlement, Heath and Carr put huge pressure on Coal Board chairman Derek Ezra not to give an inch. Mick Costello reported that Gormley wanted a negotiated settlement and was prepared to make concessions to achieve such an aim, but that the government's representatives had been unable and unwilling to agree to the deal on the table.[72] As a result, on 9 January 1972 a national coal strike started, the first since 1926. Bad weather and poor management meant that the strike cut deep and quick: power was cut, homes were in the dark, and the notorious three-day week was introduced. The NUM was well organised, had mass support in all coalfields, was mobile with picketing, and was tactically responsive to what was happening around them. In contrast the police and their political leaders in government were heavy-handed as well as leaden-footed.

A key moment in the strike, and in modern British history, was the closure of the massive Saltley coke depot in Birmingham. When over 2000 'flying pickets', orchestrated by Yorkshire miners' leader Arthur Scargill, were deployed, backed up by 15,000 engineering workers, the battle was won.[73] Subsequently the government's reputation for sound economic management was in tatters, in the media, politically and industrially. With the closure of fourteen power stations, and having imposed a state of emergency, the government needed a way out. On 11 February Heath reverted to a very British solution by setting up a Committee of Inquiry under Lord Wilberforce, and very soon afterwards Wilberforce recommended large pay rises, based on the contrived notion that the miners indeed had a special case.[74] In spite of this offer the NUM NEC voted twenty-three to two against the settlement. However, after a few more concessions on holidays, pensions and shift working, the NEC voted by eighteen to seven to settle.[75] On 21 February the strike ended, and a week later the *Morning Star* headline ran: 'miners show the way to oust Heath'; and it proclaimed the call by communists 'to follow up this great victory'. Malcolm Pitt from the Kent NUM explained in detail what had happened in his area, and what it meant in terms of action and politics:

> In this epic class battle, the Kent Area of the National Union of Mineworkers was made responsible for picketing south-east England from the Thames estuary to Brighton, and – jointly with the Midlands area – Greater London. There were only 3,500 miners in the Kent Coalfield, and they had to cover 150 miles of coastline, and the biggest concentration of power stations, coal wharves, and depots in Britain. It was a mammoth task to which the Kent miners responded with a massive mobilisation of the union rank and file.[76]

As Darlington and Lyddon write: 'the miners had won a historic victory. The settlement completely shook the confidence of the government'.[77] They also recognised that the CP had played an important role, through people such as George Wake of the Power Workers Combine, and CP Birmingham Area Secretary Frank Watters, in particular in organising solidarity: 'they [Scargill and Watters] decided to win the support of leading shop stewards for a one-day strike and mass picket. Of vital importance was the network of industrial contacts around the CP, which had about 800 members in Birmingham, including leading stewards and convenors in factories across the city, particularly in engineering'.[78] NUM General Secretary Lawrence Daly also recognised the importance of the flying picket faction, attesting in an interview that 'suggestions for flying pickets came from E.C. member Jock Kane'. Both Kane and his fellow communist Sammy Taylor pressed for a way of using the energies of miners who were on strike, and for them in Daly's words to 'go and ensure that supplies were not getting to power stations … it was surprising how effective it was'.[79]

The CP saw the battle as 'part of a great new development of working class struggle' against inflation and incomes policies, with 'new levels of strike militancy, of working class solidarity, exemplified above all by the action of the Birmingham Engineering workers at the Saltley Gas Depot'. As a direct result of the strike and its impact on the political and trade union consciousness, Scargill became President of the Yorkshire miners in 1973, and the whole NUM Executive moved to the left.

After the strike Prime Minister Heath asked the Secret Service to look into the role of 'subversive' organisations in bringing about the government's defeat.[80] By this he meant the Communist Party. Not surprisingly, MI5 officers reported that the Party had supported the strike to advance its chief political aim, the defeat of the Conservative government. This was of course not entirely correct, and represented rather a partial view. The Party had been determined above all – and with Ramelson overseeing industrial activities – to convince workers of the need to break the state-imposed incomes policy as part of a wider argument for alternative economic policies which opened the road to socialist advance.

The intelligence officers also noted that Mick McGahey kept in regular contact with Ramelson. They found that there had been close contact between communists in the leadership, and between communists in the union at area level and with local CP officials. All this was overseen and sometimes co-ordinated by Ramelson, who had a keen eye for detail and highly developed political antennae; this helped him to assess when it was necessary to intervene, and when it was better – as it usually was – to leave it to the comrades on the ground to interpret the messages coming out in the columns of the *Morning Star* and the Party's weekly letter (which went to all Party district leaderships). Ramelson saw the strike's outcome as a great victory and as part of an emerging pattern. He wrote, 'the magnificent struggle of the miners, followed by that of the railwaymen, shattered this incomes policy'.[81]

The ruling class took a similar view, as was expressed by one of their able representatives, senior Department of Employment civil servant Sir Dennis Barnes: 'generally I regard the course of the strike as one further example of the greatly increased militancy of the minority of workers which has developed over the last years and the much greater effectiveness of the weapons they are using'.[82] While Ramelson could be pleased with the outcome of the dispute and the role the Party had played in helping to bring it about, he knew that his task was that of turning Sir Dennis Barnes 'minority' into an increasingly powerful majority.

The year after the miners' victory, the Yom Kippur war in October 1973 triggered a tripling of oil prices while reducing supply. This meant that coal was better placed in the international energy markets, and that workers who provided coal would be in an even stronger bargaining position. This meant that the 1974 miners strike was somewhat different in origin from the 1972 strike. Although both were against restraints placed on miners' pay by incomes policies, the 1972 strike reflected the need to 'catch-up' after a long period of relatively low pay settlements, while the 1974 strike was grounded both in the relative rising price of coal itself and of course the negative impact of inflation on real wages.

As the strike threat loomed, Heath called another state of emergency, on 13 November 1973. On 28 November talks between the NUM and government broke down, and once more a three-day week commenced, on 13 December. By now Wilson and the establishment's anti-communist paranoia had reached Heath's government: 'Heath was convinced (erroneously) that Communists like Mick McGahey on the NUM executive were trying to overthrow the elected government of the day for purely political purposes'.[83]

At its July 1973 conference the NUM had decided to push ahead with pay claims ranging from £8 to £13 rises, along with demands over shift pay, sick pay and holiday pay. This was lodged on 12 September, coinciding with the published details of Phase III of the incomes policy; on 23 October the NUM leadership met with the Prime Minister (although there had already been secret meetings between Gormley and Heath's representative in July), but Heath failed to understand the nature of the bargaining process, which meant that deadlock and recriminations quickly ensued. On 12 November an overtime ban came into force, and by 22 November Heath and Carr embarked on their disastrous 'who rules Britain' campaign. On 9 January 1974 the NUM leaders met with Willie Whitelaw [Employment Secretary], and on 17 January Lord Carrington [Defence Secretary] announced the three-day week. This inconsistent and incompetent approach by government ministers made it easier for the NUM to secure an 81 per cent majority in favour of strike action in the ballot of 31 January. Again it was the *Morning Star* that spelt out the implications in straightforward terms, with headlines on 2 February proclaiming 'miners hit Heath with huge vote', and 'pit ballot blow to Tory Phase III hopes'. Three days later the *Star* quoted Mick McGahey as saying that the miners' 'response was quite clear': '4 out of 5 say: cash or we strike'.

The strike was called for 9 February 1974, and on 7 February the government called a General Election for 28 February. After the election had been called the NUM leadership pursued the strike with soft feet and hands: it became a low-key event, partly because this time the

NUM were sure to win, and partly because they wanted to help Labour secure a parliamentary majority. In the event Labour just won the General Election with 301 seats to the Tories 296, with the Liberals securing 13 and the rest 23 (mainly nationalists).

During the election campaign the government introduced the 'red scare' tactic, centring mainly on the leadership role played by Mick McGahey in the dispute. In the Conservative Party political broadcast of 7 February 1974, some three weeks before the election, both McGahey and Ramelson were singled out for attack. Ramelson's famous quote – 'the Party can float an idea early in the year and it can become official Labour Party policy by the autumn' – was again trotted out, with sinister overtones. Ramelson had never denied saying this – it had in fact been reproduced in a *New Society* interview – but he always insisted that it had been quoted out of context, though it did pithily but accurately describe an aspect of policy-making progress in the labour movement at the time. In the same broadcast Chancellor of the Exchequer Anthony Barber had this to tell the nation:

> You see, when Mr McGahey, the Communist Vice President of the Mineworkers' union, when he said that only a massive industrial action can defeat the Tory government, when he said that he knew that in order to succeed he and his communist friends had to achieve two things. They first had to force a general election – and the fact is, you know, and it may as well be admitted, that the action which they advocated has forced a general election – but the second thing they had to do to succeed in their communist aims – as they frankly stated – was to replace the Conservative government with a Labour government – a Labour government that would be putty in their hands.

In reply Ramelson accused Barber of distortions and lies, pointing out that 'Barber was unable to answer some of the progressive left policies in Labour's manifesto, or the question of why the Tories decided on an election in the middle of a miners' strike'. He continued:

> communists are proud of the role they play alongside many others in alerting the movement to the threat to democracy, living standards and jobs of the continued Tory rule. Far from being conspiratorial, we have been tireless in our public efforts to advocate this need and

called for the next Labour government to be committed to, and to implement, radically different policies from those they pursued when last in office.[84]

As Ramelson made clear in his report to the Party Executive in January:

> Faced with the gravest economic, social and political crisis for years the government and mass media have launched a massive 'cover up' campaign. Its aim is to disguise the depth and the causes of crisis, to find scapegoats, be they miners, locomen, trade unions or communists, for the attacks the government is making on the entire working class. By such means, they hope to halt the development of a mass movement capable of imposing a real programme for taking us out of crisis at the expense of big business.[85]

In the end the Tories' efforts came to nought. They narrowly lost the election, and the Labour government's first act was to free the Coal Board from the restrictions of Phase III of the Prices and Incomes Act. Increases of some 30 per cent (inflation was over 20 per cent at the time) were then negotiated by the union, and a victory was achieved. Even *The Times* editorial appreciated the situation: 'this has been a historic dispute. It is the first time that an industrial stoppage has provoked a general election and indirectly brought down a government'.[86]

The miners had won an historic victory, which owed much to the work of the CP over two decades. Ramelson, first in Yorkshire then nationally, had been the key political figure in bringing about the transformation of the NUM over these years. The once right-wing led union, which in the 1950s was more like a loose-knit collection of area organisations than a national body, was by the late 1960s operating nationally, and on the left of the TUC's political spectrum. Furthermore, it had an effective broad left operating at national level as well as in the great majority of the regions. There were still problems associated with inter-area rivalries, but in the overall environment of greatly increased workers' militancy and trade union struggle that characterised the 1960s and 1970s, the miners were able to overcome longstanding obstacles to effective national industrial struggles. Ramelson's role had been to promote left unity, encouraging the development of broad left structures across the union, and intervening where necessary. He, alongside Jock Kane and Mick McGahey, was the key figure in bringing the left together, and in working out new forms of industrial struggle (the flying pickets). In the 1972 dispute it had been Frank Watters and Arthur Scargill – both protégées of Ramelson, who had learnt their industrial politics in Yorkshire – who had worked out the strategy for the Saltley Gates siege, when Birmingham engineering workers in their thousands had come together with Yorkshire miners to close the largest coke depot in Britain. Only the CP in 1970s Britain could have provided the strategic guidance and the solidarity links so necessary to winning the dispute.

GLOBAL ECONOMIC CRISES AND THE END OF THE HEATH GOVERNMENT

In 1973-4 the capitalist world experienced the second of the three great economic crises of the modern period. The other two – 1929-36 and 2008-2012 – took place within the context of unregulated free market dominance, and hence created catastrophic consequences for the working class across the globe. The crisis of 1973-7 was equally great in terms of economic indicators, but because its context was a more regulated Keynesian-style world economy, the impact on unemployment and living standards was generally less appalling. It did, however, as with all such crises of the system, change both the nature of the economic policy debate – in terms of the use of domestic monetary and fiscal devices, and of the world trade and currency order.

Meanwhile the CP kept its focus on the need to develop left unity in practice through class struggle and alliances. As the Conservatives fell apart and as Labour was feeling its way towards a consensus-based policy programme incorporating some of the demands of the left, the communists were concerned to broaden and deepen the struggle, to encompass demands which if conceded would present real challenges to the ruling class, for example extensive public ownership and substantial redistribution of wealth and income.

Further debate around and refinement of the *British Road to Socialism* was also taking place, as the failings of the Tories created an increase in anti-capitalist opinion, while the manoeuvres of the right-wing Labour leadership sought to channel such feelings into their re-election. The dilemma, as seen by the CP ideologues, was that anti-capitalism was not the same as pro-socialism:

> the militant struggle is growing on economic and social issues, on issues of democracy, anti-racialism and peace. A great question arises, and shouts aloud for an answer. How is it possible to develop in the British working-class and progressive movement, as the struggle develops, a socialist consciousness, an understanding both of the need for socialism and how in Britain it can be achieved.[87]

As part of its defence of Marxism-Leninism and its basic tenet that the working class form the major element in both the revolutionary movement and in the post-revolutionary socialist society, the CP leadership launched a series of attacks[88] on the 'new' breed of ultra-leftist revolutionary vanguardists such as Herbert Marcuse, Frantz Fanon and their English apostles.[89] Their efforts to substitute an underclass (lumpens) and intellectuals for the core working class in the revolutionary process, borrowing without much reflection from C. Wright Mills,[90] seemed both opportunistic and harmful to the main focus of struggle. As the 1973 conference season approached, the CP again watched with interest as more and more left-wing resolutions at labour movement meetings were approved. Phase II of the incomes policy had already been rejected by the miners and engineers, and the Party through Ramelson put its efforts into winning the TUC to a stronger position: 'Thus the TUC will be the battleground where all ideas of Incomes Policies – voluntary or statutory – can be soundly defeated. Such an outcome will be of tremendous importance for the period ahead, shifting the emphasis of struggle towards political solutions'.[91]

Strengthening the left in the Labour Party was also important:

> Hard on the heels of the militant resolutions being debated at this month's TUC come resolutions framed in similar spirit for next month's 72nd annual Labour Party conference. They reveal the enormous difference in outlook between the rank-and-file activists and the right-wing Labour leadership entrenched in both Parliamentary Labour Party and the Shadow Cabinet. On all the outstanding issues facing the British people, prices, incomes policy, control of the giant monopolies through more extensive and effective nationalization … the Industrial Relations Act, housing, transport,

regional development etc etc resolutions express the desire for clear, militant, class policies.[92]

In the end both conferences did reflect a shift to the left, on pensions, wages and other matters, but the TUC also agreed to keep talking with the Tory government. While the Labour conference – which was neither as Marxist as *The Times* stated nor as statically right-wing as the *New Statesman* believed – did move on public ownership, comprehensive education and some foreign policy matters, it still refused to acknowledge the power of big business and the class base of the state, and the overall impression given was that the illusions of reformism still dominated the thinking of most delegates. In many ways, then, the labour movement was inching to the left on some issues, but it remained firmly reformist, with victories coming only after hard work and mass protests. There was no sense of a shift to class politics to go along with class attitudes to unions and wages, and there was little evidence that an incoming Labour government would be forced into a new way of working.

Yet, in spite of this lack of fully developed class politics, a strike by workers had effectively brought down an elected government (albeit partly through a Tory own goal), and the CP was clear that the miners' strike had been a major class confrontation; part of its role now was to support the mass mobilisation of the trade union movement against Phase III of the incomes policy, and in support of the miners. Their fight was everyone's fight. It seemed that an important section of popular sentiment – forged by the miners' strike and the government response – was moving to link justice and equality with worth and value to society. Such industrial clashes raise and change opinion and debate about fundamentals, and Ramelson was always there fighting against the narrowness of economism, the limitations of labourism and the falsehoods of reformism.

The left was once more entering into a pre-election period of analysis about the true nature of the Labour Party, and the realistic propositions of it being captured for the left. In this the communist leadership were actively concerned to show that from the very start the Labour Party and the wider movement had been split between the left and the right, but that it remained the mass organisation of the working class. The task of the CP, therefore, was to determine its relationship to the mass party based on current concrete analysis.

The CP leadership viewed the rightwing of the Labour Party as reformist, and so the Party line was to support the left and to base a challenge to right-wing dominance from the twin two pillars of trade union action and Marxist theory. To achieve this, 'it needs the left, needs unity with the non-communist left in the labour and trade union movement'.[93] What remains a puzzle is that anyone who has been involved in the movement in the UK must know that isolated leftist demands receive little support and do not last long. All experience shows that broadly based left unity on a range of issues and interventions are more likely to secure success, more likely to hold on to the spoils of victory, and more likely to build a base from which to move forward.

The gains made by the left during this period were reflected in the Labour government's initial programme. Both the Industrial Relations Act and the Prices and Incomes Act were to be repealed, collective bargaining was to be restored for now, public ownership was to be extended, and there was a promise to bring about 'a massive redistribution in the balance of wealth and power in favour of working people'. Ramelson had lived through Labour governments before, and he knew that without a big upsurge in class struggle and a substantial deepening of political consciousness in key sectors of the working class and its allies, Labour would eventually turn to the right however progressive its election promises, and in times of crisis would revert to traditional methods of managing a capitalist economy.

NOTES

1. McIlroy 1999, op.cit.; Andrews 2004, op.cit.; Lyddon & Darlington 2001, op.cit.; Taylor, 1978 op. cit.
2. 'Selsdon Man' was the name given to right-wing Tory free marketeers who first met at the Selsdon Park Hotel near Croydon in January 1970 when Heath convened a meeting of the shadow cabinet to develop its new hard line policies.
3. Lane, T. and Roberts, K. *Strike at Pilkingtons*, Fontana, London 1971.
4. Beck, T. *The Fine Tubes Strike*, Stage1, London 1974.
5. Rideout, R. 'The Industrial Relations Act 1971', *The Modern Law Review*, 1971 34(6): 655-675.
6. Ramelson editoriall, *Marxism Today*, November 1970, p. 325.
7. *1970 TUC Annual Report*, TUC, London, p. 45.
8. Ramelson, B. *Carr's Bill and How to Kill It: a class analysis*, CP, November 1970, pp. 3-4.

9. Ibid., pp. 9-10.
10. Ibid., p. 19.
11. Ibid., p. 20
12. *Reason: the case against the Government's proposals on Industrial Relations*, TUC, London 1970.
13. *The Times*, 13/1/71.
14. Ibid.
15. Cited in editorial in *Marxism Today*, April 1971, p. 97.
16. *The Times*, 22/02/71.
17. *The Times*, 2/3/71.
18. *The Times*, 19/3/71.
19. Ramelson editorial in *Marxism Today*, July 1971, p. 193.
20. Gollan, J. *What is the Socialist Way Forward?* CP 1970, cited in Pearce, B. 'The Strategy of Socialist Revolution In Britain', *Marxism Today*, January 1971, pp. 6-18.
21. Editorial in *Marxism Today*, November 1971, pp. 321-2.
22. *1971 TUC Annual Report*, TUC, London, p. 246.
23. Ibid., Lord Cooper (TUC President), p. 382.
24. Ibid., p. 405.
25. Taylor 1994, op.cit., p. 168.
26. Ken Gill interview, 2008.
27. Darlington and Lyddon 2001, op.cit., p. 157. See also Lindop, F. 'The Dockers and the 1971 Industrial Relations Act, Part 1: Shop Stewards and Containerization', *Historical Studies in Industrial Relations*, 1998, 5: 33-72; Lindop, F. 'The Dockers and the 1971 Industrial Relations Act, Part 2: the Arrest and Release of the "Pentonville Five"', *Historical Studies in Industrial Relations*, 1998 6: 65-100.
28. Martin Gould interview, 2009. (Gould is now Chair of the South-East Regional Committee of the TUC).
29. Wedderburn 1986, op.cit., pp. 56-8.
30. Darlington and Lyddon 2001 op.cit., p. 165.
31. Ramelson editorial *Marxism Today*, September 1972, p. 257.
32. The Times, 28/7/72. The conference considered that there were insufficient guarantees on jobs and the scope of the Dock Labour Scheme.
33. Ramelson was very close to the dockers' leader Bernie Steer, and according to Mike Seifert's interview (2009) they met regularly throughout the dispute to plan and co-ordinate action.
34. Dash, J. 'The Pentonville Five', *Labour Monthly*, September 1972, pp. 407-8.
35. Ramelson, B. 'The Industrial Fight: the Docks and the Act', *Comment*, August 1972, pp. 259-261.
36. Ken Gill interview, 2008
37. Kevin Halpin interview, 2008.
38. Ramelson, B. 'The industrial fight, the docks, and the Act' *Comment* August 1972, pp. 259-261

39. Significant donations came from shipyard workers in the Soviet Union, and German Democratic Republic (GDR) unions offered free holidays to hundreds of UCS workers and their families.

40. *An Analysis of 'Sit-Ins'*, Metra Consulting Group, 1973.

41. The three leading stewards were all Communists – Jimmy Airlie, Jimmy Reid and Sammy Barr.

42. Jimmy Reid Papers, Scottish Communist Party, Glasgow Caledonian University archive.

43. Foster, J. and Woolfson, C. *The Politics of the UCS Work-in*, Lawrence & Wishart, London 1986, p. 426; Foster, J. and Woolfson, C. 'How workers on the Clyde gained the capacity for class struggle: the Upper Clyde Shipbuilders' work-in, 1971-2', in McIlroy et al 1999, op. cit., pp. 297-325.

44. Thompson, W. and Hart, F. *The UCS Work-In*, Lawrence & Wishart, London 1972, with a foreword by Jimmy Reid, p. 91.

45. *The Economist*, 6/3/71.

46. For a useful but overly anti-communist view of the dispute see Darlington and Lyddon 2001, op.cit. pp. 179-207.

47. Arnison, J. *The Shrewsbury Three: Strikes, Pickets and 'Conspiracy'*, with foreword by Bert Ramelson, Lawrence & Wishart, London 1974.

48. Ibid., p.10

49. Ibid., p.74.

50. 'UCATT and the Shrewsbury Trials', UCATT, London 1973.

51. Letter from Bert Ramelson to Mike Pentz, Ramelson personal papers, June 1987.

52. Kessler and Bayliss 1998, op.cit., pp. 20-1; *Counter-Inflation Policy Stage Three*, Cmnd 5446; *The Price and Pay Code for Stage Three*, Cmnd 5444.

53. Marxism Today, editorial review of Ali's book, March 1972, p. 68: Tariq Ali, *The Coming British Revolution*, Jonathan Cape, London 1972.

54. Falber, R. 'The 32nd Congress of the CPGB', *Marxism Today*, January 1972, pp. 4-10, p. 4. (Reuben Falber was Assistant General Secretary of the CPGB.)

55. Gollan, J. 'Marxism and the Political Organisation of the Workers', in *Marxism Today*, May 1972, pp. 136-142; for some general comments on this debate see Hyman, R. *Industrial Relations: A Marxist Introduction*, Macmillan, London 1975.

56. Some of this debate was later published in Hunt, A.(ed.) *Class and Class Structure*, Lawrence & Wishart, London 1977.

57. Ramelson, B. 'Strategy of socialist revolution in Britain', in *Marxism Today*, October 1972, pp. 318-320.

58. 1972 TUC Annual Report, pp.401-2. George Doughty was General Secretary of TASS, and was succeeded by Ken Gill in 1974.

59. Andrews 2004, op. cit., pp. 114-6.

60. Ibid.

61. Barnett, A. 'Class Struggle and the Heath Government', *New Left Review*, 1973 No. 77, pp. 3-41.
62. Turner, H. *Do Unions Cause Inflation?*, Cambridge University Press 1972.
63. Bellamy, R. 'Trends in British Capitalism in the 1970s', *Marxism Today*, January 1973, pp. 22-30; p. 24.
64. Glyn, A. and Sutcliffe, R. *British Capitalism, Workers, and the Profit Squeeze*, Penguin 1972.
65. Ramelson, B. *Heath's War On Your Wage Packet: The Latest Tory Attack on Living Standards and Trade Union Rights*, CP February 1973, p. 3.
66. Ramelson, B. *Smash Phase III: the Tory fraud exposed*, CP December 1973, p.2.
67. Ibid., pp. 12-13.
68. *1973 TUC Annual Report*, TUC, London, pp. 512-3.
69. Ibid., p. 277.
70. Ibid., p. 488.
71. McCormick, B. *Industrial Relations in the Coal Industry*, Macmillan, London 1979, pp. 197-209 for a detailed account of the negotiations and strike.
72. *Morning Star*, 4/1/72.
73. On the 'battle for Saltley Gates' see McCormick 1979 op.cit., p. 206; and Bunyan, A. 'From Saltley to Orgreave via Brixton', *Journal of Law and Society*, 1985, 12(3): 293-303.
74. Report of a Court of Inquiry into a Dispute Between the National Coal Board and the National Union of Mineworkers, under the chairmanship of Lord Wilberforce, HMSO, London 1972.
75. For details see Hughes, J. and Moore, R. (eds), *A Special Case? Social Justice and the Miners*, Penguin 1972.
76. Pitt, M. *The World on our Backs: the Kent Miners and the 1972 Miners' Strike*, Lawrence & Wishart, London 1979, p. 19.
77. Darlington and Lyddon 2001 op. cit., p. 72.
78. Ibid., p. 58.
79. Whitehead, P. *The Writing on the Wall – Britain in the 1970s*, Michael Joseph, London 1985, p. 92.
80. Phillips, J. 'The miners' strike: popular agency and industrial politics in Britain', *Contemporary British History*, 2006 20 (2): 187-207.
81. Ramelson February 1973 op. cit., p. 3.
82. Cited in Phillips 2006, op. cit., p. 24.
83. Morgan 1990, op. cit., p. 347.
84. *Morning Star*, 21/2/74.
85. Ramelson, B. 'The crisis, the government attacks, and the way to fight back' *Comment* 26/1/74 pp. 18-21; p. 18
86. *The Times* 29/2/74.
87. Editorial in *Marxism Today*, April 1973, p. 97.

88. Woddis, J. *New Theories of Revolution*, Lawrence & Wishart, London 1972.
89. One such was Peter Worsley, see his 'Frantz Fanon and the "lumpen proletariat"', *Socialist Register* 1972, pp. 193-230.
90. Wright Mills, C. *The Sociological Imagination*, Oxford University Press, Oxford 1959.
91. Editorial in *Marxism Today*, August 1973, p. 225.
92. Editorial in *Marxism Today*, September 1973, p. 257.
93. Priscott, D. 'The Communist Party and the Labour Party', *Marxism Today*, January 1974, pp. 5-15; p. 9.

6. Bert Ramelson and the Social Contract, 1974-7

LABOUR RETURNS

The general election of February 1974 resulted in a narrow Labour victory, and the new government set about preparing the ground for electoral consolidation in a second election by replacing the Tories' statutory restrictions on wage bargaining with a new voluntary incomes policy, agreed with union leaders. This became the Social Contract, the development and subsequent failure of which are the single most important events in the history of the 1974-9 Labour government – which eventually ended in the strike wave known as 'the winter of discontent' and ignominious defeat at the polls for Labour in May 1979.[1]

Ramelson and the CP warned the movement that another tranche of incomes restraint, particularly if linked with deflationary macro-economic policies, was bound to end in industrial as well as electoral disaster. Ramelson's particular contribution was to produce a series of pamphlets providing analysis and promoting struggle by detailing the fallacies in the TUC's case for supporting wage restraint, while exposing the duplicity of the Labour government as it reneged on its side of the Social Contract agreement (for example on its pledge to control prices). His role became increasingly Cassandra-like – accurately predicting disaster while being unable to prevent it.

With the victory of the miners and the election of a Labour government, Ramelson had reason to look forward to further progress for the left in the labour movement and the socialist cause. He also knew that the right wing was still the dominant force within the labour movement, and that until its grip was broken the prospects for progressive advance remained precarious. He recognised that the ideological attractions of the government's Social Contract for many trade union

216

leaders and activists were powerful. In essence the Contract was a trade off, with union leaders agreeing to voluntary wage restraint in exchange for progressive government policies, including economic measures to promote economic growth, industrial innovation and repeal of the Tory anti-union laws. Its language was appealing to many, with its references to social justice and economic planning.

By the time Ramelson retired as industrial organiser in November 1977 the Social Contract was on its last legs. His analysis that Labour's wages policy was a 'con-trick' had proved to be correct, as wage settlements had continued to trail behind the rate of inflation, unemployment had grown, and public spending had been seriously cut. It was inevitable that attempts to prolong wage restraint against this background would provoke a response from well-organised sections of the workforce. And so it proved. During late 1978 and early 1979 'the winter of discontent' shattered any remaining illusions that Labour's special relationship with the unions could be used to hold down wages for any length of time. As a result, the Social Contract ushered in nearly two decades of Tory rule (1979-1997), years characterised by mass unemployment and attacks on worker rights.[2] The Social Contract was an electoral disaster for right-wing Labour, as well as a major setback for the left. It succeeded, however, in its aim of heading off the industrial militancy of the late 1960s and early 1970s. The promise of left advance in the spring of 1974 was thereby stopped in its tracks, as the costs of the crisis of capitalism were placed on the shoulders of working people with the acquiescence of the reformist leadership of the wider labour movement.

THE SOCIAL CONTRACT BEGINS

When faced with the possibility of mass unemployment and economic meltdown, many trade unionists bought into the deal on the table from the government: some friendly laws and social policies in exchange for wage restraint. Nevertheless, Ramelson renewed his attacks on all things related to incomes policy and anti-union reform, whether through legislation or by means of a Social Contract. He fought against the thinking behind the Contract, and waged a war of words and deeds against both the immediate and long-term damage it would wreak on the lives of workers and their families. He struggled in particular to keep both the TUC and the Labour Party true to their own conference resolutions and electoral manifestos. In all of this he had to combat the growing threats from the ultra-left in the form of Trotskyite impossibilism, from inside the CP from the increasingly influential Eurocommunists, and from resurgent reformists behind the Wilson-Callaghan governments. What is more, all the while the CP was failing to build its own organisation, or to meet internal targets on *Morning Star* circulation and electoral support. His main response was in writing a series of Party pamphlets, in efforts to re-invigorate the LCDTU and the industrial advisories, and to renew Party policy with a new revised version of the BRS.

One of the new Labour government's first acts was to quickly settle the miners' strike on favourable terms for the NUM, thus allowing the country to return to normal working.[3] From the beginning the government was weak on many issues; there were divisions and uncertainties in policy, and the spectre of more economic crises loomed. Its first response to the economic climate – as seen in its first budgets – was a return to policies to reduce real wages and weaken working-class living standards, as noted by the Cambridge Political Economy Group, which, in presenting substantial evidence that the economic crisis was the worst since 1929, concluded:

the current economic crisis is a manifestation of a long-run deep rooted situation … the need to end this situation and halt the steady relative decline of British living standards has been recognised … a planned economy would be feasible only on condition that the working class was mobilised and involved in attaining its economic and social objectives … the capitalist solution to the crisis is … to cut real wages. This can only be done by smashing the organised working-class movement.[4]

Healey as Chancellor did, however, move towards a cautious Keynesianism in his two budgets in March and July that year. His March budget reflected the strength of the left with rent freezes, higher pensions and promises to repeal the 1971 Industrial Relations Act; but the dominance of the right wing was also seen in its higher rail and fuel bills. Much of this approach reflected the new 'bible' of the right, Tony Crosland's Socialism Now, with its claims of a classless society with no poverty, based on economic growth driven forward by the dynamism of the private sector.[5] The real weaknesses of social democracy were being exposed, and, as we shall see, this appeared at first to present the left in the unions and the CP itself with real chances to move the socialist agenda forward.

Healey's July budget went further, with efforts to maintain public spending, increase overall demand, and stabilise the balance-of-payments through early returns from North Sea oil. Inflation remained high but was not increasing, and for a brief period a certain calm surety fell over government actions. Wilson saw this as the right time to bid for an improved electoral mandate, and called a second election In October 1974. Labour was then returned with a much strengthened majority. Unfortunately they did not use their victory to continue a demand-led Keynesian strategy, but sought to resolve the economic crisis through monetarist policies of spending cuts and wage freezes.

In the central arena of industrial relations, Labour ministers were believed by the dominant conventional wisdom of the time to be better than the Conservatives in dealing with the unions and indus-trial unrest, and with Jones and Scanlon now sitting alongside Michael Foot on TUC/Labour Party joint bodies, something positive was expected to emerge. Instead Labour used its better relationship to promote the 'social contract' that had begun to be developed by the newly created Labour Party-TUC Liaison Committee between 1972 and 1973. Ramelson was not a fan of the new arrangement. He saw it as:

> … an undertaking by the TUC to restrain workers from using their bargaining strength to achieve wage and salary increases which they feel necessary, justified and attainable. Instead, affiliated unions in national claims and workers at the enterprise level are expected to restrict claims, both with regard to amounts and frequency, to norms and defined guidelines laid down by the General Council of the TUC in its document *Collective Bargaining and the Social Contract*.[6]

We have seen how in 1972/3 the Labour Party leadership sought a way back from their own disillusion and unpopularity through a compro-mise arrangement with trade union leaders about the future of wage policy, economic growth, and relevant social and legal issues. By 1974 with Labour back in government this concordat, the social contract, was at first based on a deal with the TUC committing itself to annual wage rises only founded on cost-of-living arguments in exchange for government action to control prices, increase public expenditure, reduce unemployment, and remove anti-union laws. By 1975 as we will see inflation was out of control and the TUC consented to a more formal deal with the government (Social Contract Phase I) with agreed limits on increases in wages, which was followed in 1976 by Phase II. There was some reduction in inflation until 1977, but nonetheless by then the TUC had given up on the arrangement thus allowing the government to go it alone leading to the disastrous Healey-Callaghan pay policy of 1978 that created the conditions for both the 'winter of discontent' and the election of the Conservatives in May 1979.[7]

The term itself originated from the debates about constitutional democracy in the seventeenth and eighteenth centuries with Thomas Hobbes, John Locke and later Jean Jacques Rousseau all suggesting that there had been or should be a kind of contract between ruled and rulers that provided rights, duties and obligations on both parties in exchange for a form of contingent stability. Hobbes famously noted that without the security afforded by the authority of the state, 'the life of man [is] solitary, poore, nasty, brutish, and short'.[8] This modern variant tried, at least on the surface, to provide economic stability and growth in exchange for the trade unions handing over to government an array of rights associated with their own decision-making with regard to the pursuit of wage claims and industrial action. It was the rights, rather than the obligations, that Bert felt were at risk and which had been fought for over many decades, and that the current leadership had no mandate to bargain away.

The key element in both elections and the Labour Party conference after the second 1974 general election was a clear sharpening of the conflict between left and right inside the Labour Party and the wider movement. The left won important ground on South Africa and Chile, but the right won more importantly on support for Chancellor Healey's budget proposals and decisively over the Social Contract with Wilson and Callaghan pitting unemployment against wage increases in a dogmatic adherence to the Phillips curve thesis (see p96). Leftwing leaders made the point time and again that there was an urgent need to defend the most progressive elements in the Labour manifesto[9], and to push hard for the most pro-union aspects of the social contract itself.[10]

No real advance had been made in Labour-union relations and most senior ministers still distrusted the unions, and continued to be convinced that communist influence was a major factor in the rumbling discontent. MI5 kept tabs on Jones and Scanlon as well as on communist leaders such as Gill and McGahey.[11] Secret reports about the left in the unions were sent to Wilson and Jenkins without telling Foot and Benn.[12] Despite all of that the real problem remained that none of the policy solutions really worked. The hasty and somewhat botched compromise on incomes policy that Jack Jones had brokered was neither rooted in labour market realities nor indeed in the real world of international economic crisis, but just a device to get both the Labour and TUC leadership off various hooks. Ramelson knew from experience that such an arrangement, though still 'voluntary', would be open to abuse by Labour ministers, as well as acting as a demobilising force among rank-and-file trade unionists who would be deprived of some of the means to organise struggle for improved living standards.

DIFFERENCES ON THE LEFT

Ramelson was particularly concerned with two aspects of the Social Contract and its possible supporters amongst the left. First there were those who felt that it could be used to push the Labour government into a series of concessions on a range of issues, from the Clay Cross Councillors and the Shrewsbury pickets to reform of collective bargaining.[13] Secondly, the CP leadership was aware of the dangers of sections of the union movement accepting some form of wage restraint dressed up as a more coherent planned approach to the nation's ills, as well as being more convinced that the economic crisis would inevitably mean fewer jobs, higher inflation and lower wages. The Social Contract was seen by some on the left as a worthwhile trade off between some voluntary wage restraint in exchange for helpful legislation and progressive social policies. Ramelson saw this as a terrible error of judgement, as he believed that a Labour government would only be held to its left-leaning policies if there was pressure from below in the form of union militancy around wages and other issues. The resurgent reformism of the movement threatened not only the CP strategy but the entire basis of independent working-class organisation and action.

Within the CP Dave Purdy argued that the social-democratic attraction of incomes policies was based on the fear of social disintegration if inflation persisted; that it could form part of some kind of indicative economic planning; and that strong union bargaining, which pushed up wages, also pushed up prices. He summarised Ramelson's communist critique of the policy: that wages did not cause inflation anyway; that wage restraint allowed profits to rise at the expense of working-class living standards; that its aim was to cut real wages; and that state regulation threatened 'free' collective bargaining and the union movement itself. Purdy believed that the communist critique was only partly correct: it exaggerated its case and ignored the relative pay issue, whereby stronger workers could push up their wages while leaving their weaker brothers and sisters behind. In contrast to Ramelson, Purdy wanted a framed wage control set of policies under the cloak of a transitional programme.[14] This view was shared by others on the CP economic committee, in particular Pat Devine, but it was very much a minority position within the CP, and was strongly refuted by Ramelson. In contrast the SWP leadership overstated the position with regard to seeing a rejection of the Social Contract in and of itself as a sign of a shift towards a socialist consciousness amongst British workers.[15]

One key defender of collective bargaining and all its associated attributes was Ken Gill. He argued that, for example, the 1974 miners' strike, while an industrial dispute between 250,000 miners and their employer, created an ideological and class battle against the Tory government, the capitalist state, and the reformists in the labour movement.[16] It was the Marxism of the leadership that had enabled them to take the fight of workers with one employer in one industry to a national and class level. It was the political and the economic coming together that mattered, and it was that which exposed the role of the state as the friend of monopoly capital and the foe of the working class. This general position was supported by Ron Bellamy in a series of trenchant polemical attacks on the Devine-Purdy axis, in which he argued that the real and main causes of inflation remained rooted in the imperialist legacies of militarism, currency destabilisation, credit creation, commodity price fixing, and competition between multinational corporations, all fuelled by USA borrowing to pay for the Vietnam War and the oil price hike. In this the role of wages remained relatively small, so that wage controls would not in and of themselves be capable of bringing down prices.[17]

Gill, Ramelson and others were acutely aware of the problems of relations with the Labour Party and the wider union movement. The strategy was to encourage left unity in practice wherever it was possible, but to maintain a clear communist identity in analysis and line. This was seen as all the more urgent when it began to emerge that, in its efforts to win maximum support in the October election, the government was moving to the so-called middle ground, in an attempt to align itself with progressive liberalism and thereby win votes from the Liberal Party – while taking for granted the core working-class vote. John Gollan made this clear in his report to the July meeting of the Party's EC.[18] In fact, when the Labour government was re-elected in October, instead of its larger majority leading to a more independent economic policy, it simply disintegrated into the shared mainstream conventional wisdom – egged on by the Tories and Tory press – that what was needed was to cut wages, cut public expenditure and blame the unions. The CP was at the forefront of attacking the weaknesses and fallacies in both the economic analysis and remedies of this consensus, and of providing the left with a real alternative set of proposals.

Then as now some elements within the movement argued that the Social Contract had been, in some limited way, beneficial, because it did deliver supportive legal reforms: though the government failed to deliver on much of its side of the bargain, it did repeal the Tory legislation and protect some basic worker rights. As Wedderburn notes:

> the Labour Government envisaged three phases: first, repeal of the 1971 Act and restoration of the 'immunities'; secondly, modernization of trade union rights in an extended and improved collective bargaining structure, with an extension of the 'floor of rights' for workers; thirdly, further democratization of the political economy with extensions of 'industrial democracy'.[19]

Wedderburn goes on to argue that little of this had anything to do with the Social Contract, but simply reflected the dominant view of the Donovan report concerning the need to extend collective bargaining. The main legislation was the 1974 (amended 1976) Trade Union and Labour Relations Act, the 1975 Employment Protection Act, which set up ACAS and its consolidated version in 1978, with unfair dismissal and redundancy provisions; and the 1974 Health and Safety etc at Work Act. In addition there were important if slightly disappointing improvements to both Sex Discrimination (1975) and Race relations (1976) laws.[20]

There was also a group of left Labour MPs who, basing themselves on the election manifesto, argued that the priority was to push hard for the pro-union aspects of the Social Contract, rather than to oppose the Social Contract as was the Communist Party's line. By 1976 it was clear that this position, 'a progressive' Social Contract, was all but finished, as Labour ministers turned their backs on price controls, full employment strategies, and investment to promote industrial growth.

THE LEFT/RIGHT STRUGGLE

The key element in both elections, and at the 1974 Labour Party conference, was a clear sharpening of the conflict between left and right inside the Labour Party and the wider movement. The right won support for Healey's budget proposals, and decisively for the Social Contract, with Wilson and Callaghan successfully pitting wage increases against unemployment.

Once again it was industrial relations and the unions that formed the central concern of government. Incomes policy this time round was to be negotiated with the unions through the Social Contract, but once more it was seen as the only means of reducing inflation, paying back debts, and therefore saving public services. All of this was much sound and fury but in essence signified very little. On the economic front the orthodox Treasury line easily carried the day, with the support of the overwhelming majority of ministers. Efforts to boost manufacturing investment through state-led intervention, in line with Labour's election manifesto, came to nought once Tony Benn had been moved from the Department of Industry in 1975 (which followed the left's substantial defeat at the EEC referendum that summer). Yet there had been no further evidence that wage controls of any type would work. Meanwhile the unions were growing rapidly, especially in the public sector and among white-collar workers, partly because of the general economic ills of inflation, and partly because of the state's involvement in labour market matters.[21]

The lines of cleavage were clear. Cabinet members supported an incomes policy plus tight controls on public expenditure, and Prime Minister Wilson wanted to protect the Social Contract at all costs, in order to bind trade union leaders to government policy. He recognised, however, that a voluntary policy based on union approval and involvement had more chance of success than the state-imposed wage controls for which the Treasury mandarins were lobbying.

On industrial policy, the full-scale intervention pioneered by Tony Benn had proved to be ineffective because the government had not been prepared to invest significant state money. Thus instead of becoming a powerhouse of modernising industrial investment (as envisaged in the manifesto), the National Enterprise Board (NEB) quickly became a cross between a hospice for dying companies (such as International Computers Limited, ICL) and a hospital for long-term lame ducks (such as British Leyland). Companies were kept alive in the short term to protect jobs, but no effort was made to create a thriving manufacturing sector stimulated by state funds. Similarly, the manifesto pledge to develop government-sponsored Planning Agreements with the major private sector oligopolies was a miserable failure. Only one such agreement was negotiated, and that was used by the private sector company involved, the US motor giant Chrysler, to dupe the British taxpayer by selling off to Peugeot. The best that can be said for Labour's interventionist policies is that, in a few cases, they bought some time and saved some plants in the short term. The measures that were adopted were under-resourced both financially and politically, even though they had initially been put forward as an important part of the government's side of the Social Contract. The hopes of the Labour left, in and out of Parliament, were very quickly dashed, and before long few could raise their sights above the need to maintain a Labour government in power.

The Social Contract was seen by government ministers as the magic solution to all ills. Even though it directly addressed none of the underlying problems, as Ramelson demonstrated time and again in his highly effective pamphlets. As Ramelson showed, inflation fell in every major industrial country during this period, whether or not there were wage controls in place: the major element at play here was falling international commodity prices. From Ramelson's perspective the main stumbling block to left advance and social progress was the Social Contract itself.

Some important trade union leaders of the left, with distinguished records of progressive leadership, were now enthusiastic advocates of wage restraint. In particular Jack Jones, Hugh Scanlon and Lawrence Daly argued that the Social Contract was in fact a socialist incomes policy, linked to socialist measures of economic planning. Others on the left argued for normal collective bargaining and radical measures – such as those contained in the 1974 Congress motion in the name of AUEW-TASS (see chapter 3) – to deal with the root problems of the economy. This second group consisted mainly of leaders from smaller unions, and therefore with less political clout. The trade union left, which had been so united in the struggle against *In Place of Strife* and the Industrial Relations Act, was now divided. So, to a lesser extent and in a less fundamental way, was the government. The main quarrel among government ministers, once the Department of Industry was defenestrated following the EEC referendum, was between those who favoured statutory incomes policy and those who for pragmatic reasons stuck to the voluntary Social Contract formula. In the Labour Party generally there were few in leadership positions either at constituency party or parliamentary level who opposed incomes policy in the first years of the 1974 Labour governments.

Ramelson saw that the Social Contract was much more than a temporary expediency to put a cap on the growth of real wages. It was in essence a long-term approach to the management of the British economy in the interests of monopoly capital. The justification given – that it helped to protect the low paid and the unorganised, and that it was part of a socialist approach to economic planning – were entirely specious. Ramelson demonstrated these points over and over again in his pamphlets. Indeed within three short years the Social Contract was on its last legs – organised workers rejected it and Labour ministers stopped pretending that it had anything to do with social justice. By 1976 ministers were more concerned to reassure international creditors, particularly the IMF, that they had effective control on wages and levels of public expenditure. The concern by the late 1970s was to protect the pound, not to curry favour with trade union leaders ahead of an imminent general election.

It was clear to Ramelson that the first priority for a revolutionary party in this environment was to challenge the theory and practice of the Social Contract. Do this, he argued, and you not only hastened its defeat, but you could also put socialism at the centre of the labour movement's political agenda. Ramelson saw that while the Social Contract lasted it fostered illusions about the nature of right-wing social democracy and reformist approaches to deep-seated class contradictions. He also knew that in the short term Labour's Social Contract would be the harbinger of yet another Tory government that was likely to be more reactionary than previous administrations. To prevent this required unity of the left around clear anti-capitalist policies, including support for trade union rights and freedoms. The defence of the rights of trade union members to frame their own wage claims and take action where necessary was central to the battle to extend democratic rights generally, and was therefore a highly political demand rather than an economistic one.

RAMELSON'S RESPONSE

In December 1974 the CP produced another pamphlet by Ramelson, *Social Contract: Cure-all or Con-trick?* This followed on from his previous critiques of wage restraint, productivity bargaining, and the thinking and reality of Donovan. His previous pamphlets on incomes policies had been produced under the Labour governments of 1964 to 1970 and the Tory government of 1970-4, but now Labour and Wilson were back in office and the line had to shift, given that the audience was trade union activists largely supporting the Labour government. Both this 1974 pamphlet and a further one written in March 1977 – *Bury the Social Contract: the Case for an Alternative Policy* – are part of the same summary arguments that had been forged from the debate with left-wing union leaders and Party economists. As Gill said in his review of the pamphlet: 'Bert Ramelson's pamphlet will help that struggle, and is essential reading for the whole movement'.[22]

The 1974 pamphlet states that its purpose is to show that 'the Social Contract, far from solving the problems facing the British people, would make them worse'; and to provide an alternative set of policies to fight inflation and unemployment; and it also sought to demonstrate that the alternative policy would 'at the same time weaken the grip which the big monopolists have on Britain and create conditions for achieving the aim set out in the Labour Party election manifesto – "a fundamental and irreversible shift in the balance of wealth and power in favour of the working people and their families"'.[23]

Healey's budget, with its wage cuts and public expenditure reductions, was seen as a typically conservative Treasury response to the crisis. It was the Social Contract that George Matthews hammered,

> the social contract is not merely irrelevant to the main problems which face the British people, but will make them worse. It also

diverts the labour and trade union movement from the fight against the real causes of inflation and growing unemployment ... Labour's emphasis on the social contract, which boils down to wage restraint, plays right into the hands of the Tories, the City and big business.[24]

Ramelson also argued that the ruling class was worried about the crisis in capitalism, and that it knew that an incomes policy would divert the labour movement away from the central issues; thus its biggest fear was that working-class struggle would defeat incomes policy. This struggle was therefore at the centre of the class struggle, and the balance of class forces could be tipped in favour of the working class. Ramelson saw the crisis at the end of 1974 as the worst in living memory: all indicators pointed to an 'all embracing economic, political and social crisis'. Inflation was at 18 per cent and rising, unemployment was surging towards one million, investment was at an all-time low, output was falling, there was a huge balance-of-payments deficit, and sterling was losing value. When faced with all of this the Labour leadership called for faith in the 'simple cure-all, the newly-discovered wonder drug – the Social Contract'.[25]

The problem for Ramelson and others was that the Social Contract, in its name and nature, contained several elements, of which wage controls were only one. As we have seen, these other parts of the bargain included reform of labour laws and some social progress measures. In addition to this there was also an aspect of economic justice built into the model and the debate, which camouflaged the central core of wage restraint and union conformity. The idea of justice, and models of economic justice, are a major part of the left/right debate, and of the argument between reformists and revolutionaries. Amartya Sen has recently set out the antecedents of this major debate – which embraced both Marx and Mill;[26] and in the early 1970s the debate included a range of progressive economists who were concerned with the role of income tax, public expenditure, and inequality.[27] These writers fed policy programmes and helped to strengthen the social democratic version of an 'affluent society' in the making.[28] All this helped some confused labour movement opinion-formers to open the door to the Social Contract. So when Ramelson attacked the policy as a 'con' intended to buy over trade union leaders to the cause of panic-driven social democracy, he had to contend with an increasing body of debate that was moving away from a socialist perspective towards a USA-style Democratic ticket.

By the end of 1975 there was no sign that wages and the labour market were responding to any form of regulation. Slowly the arguments that wage increases caused inflation, and that inflation was threatening the entire economic well-being of the country, and thus of the majority of workers, took hold at the TUC and among some union leaders and activists. As Morgan notes, 'it was at least the clearest indication to date that the unions were aware that excessive wages led to rising inflation and diminishing employment, and that their monopolistic control over the job market was proving self-defeating, most of all for the ill-organized and low-paid'.[29] This economic account of the crisis, while sounding like a Keynesian analysis, was increasingly clouded by the fog of emerging neo-liberalism and supply-side monetarism.

This was the pivotal debate. Jack Jones took the lead in a proactive manner within the TUC and his own union, the TGWU, helping to push through a policy of voluntary restraint based on a flat rate of no more than £6 per week at the TGWU conference in March 1975. By June the TUC General Council had agreed this policy on a vote of nineteen to thirteen. On 3 September 1975 the TUC conference voted by two to one to back Jones (supported by Geoffrey Drain, general secretary of National Association of Local Government Officers, NALGO), when he moved composite motion eight in favour of a voluntary agreement on wage controls.[30] It was Ken Gill once again who led the left opposition. Heavily influenced by Ramelson, he argued that free collective bargaining was under attack and explained:

> … last year our union withdrew a motion opposing the social contract. We did it to help win a General Election and because of guarantees given by the platform that certain objectives would be pressed on to that Labour Government … not only have our demands been ignored; they are being turned into their opposites. They are: massive and rocketing unemployment … we are seeing cuts in real wages.

He urged the delegates to adopt a set of alternative economic policies, including selective import controls, a public investment programme, price controls, lower interest rates, controls over the export of capital, and increases in pensions, benefits and public spending.[31]

By the time of the April 1976 budget inflation was still high, and Healey now imposed a three per cent maximum wage increase along the lines agreed by Jack Jones and Michael Foot. Barbara Castle makes quite clear in her diaries the strength of the Cabinet view that incomes policies were essential, and the TUC's compliance in accepting the government version of both the causes and the solutions to the economic crisis. She makes the point that they feared a public sector wage struggle against their norm; and that Healey, and even more so Shirley Williams and Roy Jenkins, wanted to cut public expenditure and hold down wages. Even Castle noted, 'how these people come out in their true colours!'[32]

Eric Hobsbawm argued that the economic crisis was the worst since the 1930s, but 'the capitalists have no readymade solution'.[33] His view was that, though 'we have a Labour Government based on a weakened Labour Party', the left, through the trades unions, could be 'increasingly and maybe decisively influential'.[34] His main point was that, despite this leftward swing, the union leadership was trying to keep pace with grass roots militancy that was not itself co-ordinated with politics. This was a movement lacking discipline, and aimed exclusively at protecting working-class wages; and things were made more difficult by the weakness of the Marxist left, with the CP and other groups divided and with no mass base. Hobsbawm ended with a plea for support for some form of alternative left economic strategy based on the militancy of the labour movement.

In a last desperate bid to save jobs and itself, the government nationalised parts of shipbuilding and aircraft, before turning to British Leyland in 1976. Unemployment and inflation both rose again, and the government was buffeted by winds from all directions. In April 1976 Wilson resigned, and Callaghan won the subsequent leadership election.[35]

THE SOCIAL CONTRACT ENDS

Once more an economic crisis changed everything: in July there was another budget in which Healey capped the money supply. Callaghan told the 1976 Labour Party conference about his monetarist conversion on the road to Downing Street:

> We used to think that you could spend your way out of a recession and increase employment by cutting taxes and boosting government

spending. I tell you in all candour that that option no longer exists, and in so far as it ever did exist, it only worked on each occasion since the war by injecting a bigger dose of inflation into the economy, followed by a higher level of unemployment as the next step … we must ask ourselves unflinchingly what is the cause of high unemployment. Quite simply and unequivocally, it is caused by paying ourselves more than the value of what we produce.[36]

It looked bad and was in reality worse. The government's parliamentary majority was dwindling as by-election losses mounted up, and just as the seafarers called a strike so Bank Rate went up to 15 per cent as the pound slumped. Again the government went cap in hand to the IMF, and, despite endless Cabinet meetings to discuss terms, Healey came back with the requirement to cut and cut again. This was the real start of monetarism and the demise of traditional Keynesian policies, thus, as Miliband foretold, paving the way for a more strident right-wing government.[37] The immediate impact was that intended, however: a short period of market and currency calm, and with it a sanguine optimism that all would now be well – especially with a UK friend in the White House (Jimmy Carter) and North Sea oil revenues reversing the balance-of-payments deficit.

The left remained small but at times influential; there was a socialist resurgence of a kind around strikes throughout the 1970s, linked to a radical shop stewards movement and leaders such as Derek Robinson, as well as the left shift in the NUM.[38] Demands for industrial action also grew from the newly radicalised groups such as teachers, nurses, civil servants and other technical and white-collar workers, many of whom were women, as they sought to inject left politics into their industrial activities. A typical dispute of the time was by 400 women members of the AUEW at Trico in Brentford over equal pay, led by Sally Groves, a prominent member of the CP.[39]

Stage Two of the pay policy ran from August 1976 to July 1977, and limited rises to 5 per cent, with a £2.50 minimum and a £4 maximum. As Healey told the House of Commons, this policy provided no loopholes for perceived anomalies as had occurred before – and it was this that sealed its fate, as union after union rebelled against what they saw as both arbitrary and careless guidelines.[40] In practical terms some of this was illustrated by the TUC annual conference where the General Council won the vote to support the Social Contract, but lost the argument. Twenty-seven CP members spoke lead by Ken Gill and had a sustained impact on the conference and eventually on what happened when the Social Contract fell apart in 1977.[41]

The CP executive argued strongly for a wages struggle and against an incomes policy, backed by Ramelson's vigorous analysis attacking those who would link wages with inflation and thus give succour to the government's policies. As Ramelson argued again and again:

> … only by retaining free collective bargaining … can the trade union movement responsibly take into consideration all factors in the situation, including government policy, in framing its wages policies without throwing away its means of exerting pressure on the government.[42]

The TUC proved unable to deliver its membership into the hands of the increasingly desperate Callaghan-Healey axis. At its 1976 congress the TUC reported on the new pay deal that had been struck at the 16 June special TUC, but the worm was already turning, as the President made clear in his speech: 'in the last twelve months the TUC and the entire trade union movement has proved its loyalty not only to the Government but to the Nation. But we cannot stand by and tolerate these levels of unemployment'.[43] The debate on the Social Contract signalled its downfall. Moving the end to the deal, Furniture, Timber, and Allied Trades Union (FTAT) General Secretary Ben Rubner argued that 'events have now shown that this policy has led to a deterioration in minimum wage rates, effectively lowered living standards, and failed to prevent the numbers of unemployed reaching an unacceptable level'.[44] This line was supported by Alan Sapper: 'it makes economic nonsense to maintain low wages in this economic situation. It brings about an economic disaster'.[45] By the following year's 1977 Congress the Social Contract was no more – and agreement was replaced by Government dictat.

Leading CP economists analysed the nature of the economic crisis and the government's response. Then as now the starting point was that this was a crisis of capitalist production in general, whether or not it started in the money and currency markets, and that the only strategy that could both strengthen the economy and help working-class people was that of the socialist and communist left, based on alternative ways of stabilising confidence, reducing debts and allowing for planned growth.[46] Gordon McLennan publicly and frequently called for mass struggle against the government.[47] This position was emphasised by Ramelson in a piece arguing for the relevance of general strikes and the role of industrial action generally:

> ... to reject syndicalism as an ideology does not mean to reduce industrial action to purely economic struggle, drained of political and social content or even objective, and to embrace parliamentarianism as the sole means of achieving socialist objectives.[48]

In the constituencies Labour Party membership fell away. They were also subject to 'entryism' by some Trotskyist groups, such as the Militant Tendency.[49] As the Labour government moved to the right so local Labour and some of the unions moved left, exemplified to some extent by Ken Livingstone at the Greater London Council (GLC); Tony Benn was becoming the focus for much of the coalition of leftist forces and ideas now circulating freely in the wider labour movement.[50]

The political scene was dominated by the massive crisis in the economy, and the debates and struggles over which way the Labour government would eventually turn to remedy the economic and social ills of the nation. At the centre of much of this was a proxy debate about wages, the role of wages in causing inflation, and the cuts in wages proposed by the IMF and pursued by the government. This was a shadow fight over the nature of class conflict, the class nature of the state, and the extent to which workers would and should carry the burden of the crisis over which they had no say and no responsibility. At this stage the Party stepped up its campaign to win support for an Alternative Economic Strategy.

As Ramelson wrote:

> since the Labour Government mortgaged the country's future to the bankers of the International Monetary Fund, Bank of International Settlement and the Euromarket ... for massive loans, the £ has stopped falling ... the stock market has risen, and hot money has started flowing into instead of out of Britain. But while this may bring joy to the tycoons and speculators, it is of less relevance to the working man or woman. What wage and salary earners are concerned about is the high level of unemployment, the higher rate at which the

cost of living is rising … and whether cuts in the social services will continue.[51]

The alternative strategy was given more prominence and coherence in this pamphlet:

> We believe that the resistance of the working class to the effects of capitalism on their lives – and in the course of it the deepening of their political consciousness through struggle and a growing aware-ness that there is no permanent solution within the framework of capitalism – will lead many millions into the struggle to replace capi-talism by a socialist planned society, using its resources to satisfy the growing material and cultural needs of the people. In the new draft of our programme *The British Road to Socialism*, now being widely discussed, we indicate how we see this being achieved.[52]

In the debates about the 1977 version of the *BRS*, Ramelson called for mobilisation of the mass movement to force the government to change policy, and argued for the benefits of a decentralised trade union movement opposed to the centralising tripartite tendencies encour-aged by the Social Contract. The fight for a democratic and independent trade union movement which could champion their members' case whatever government wanted required the CP to play a leading role in the struggle because 'this helps to illustrate the key and indispensable role which the Communist Party, basing itself on scientific socialism – Marxism – occupies in the labour movement'.[53]

The debate about the causes of inflation was of vital importance both to the immediate union response to the Labour government's incomes policies, and to the development of the Alternative Economic Strategy. In addition, it became a proxy argument about the wider direction of the CP in terms of the *BRS*, the nature of British capi-talism and the revolutionary potential of the British working class. We have discussed some of these issues earlier, but in 1976/7 the battle lines hardened. Dave Purdy, for example, in a series of papers on British capitalism since the war, attacked the short-term unplanned use of incomes policies as a form of 'wage repression', but wanted it to be replaced with a long-term planned incomes policy which would allow for wage growth in line with economic progress, and therefore not inflationary.[54]

Ramelson was totally convinced that the Social Contract needed to be jettisoned before more harm was done, and as more and more workers were opposing it. In his pamphlet he argued: 'It is doubtful whether the TUC ever took a more disastrous decision than it did in September 1975 in endorsing the Social Contract … the TUC agreed, for the first time in its history, to collaborate with the Government and employers to cut real wages, and to police the implementation of the cuts'.[55] Despite the failure of the government to meet its side of the contract, the TUC had promised to keep its side for another year, until 1977 at least.

The union position had shifted: most of the left trade union leaders who had played a key role in convincing the TUC to reject unconditionally all forms of incomes policy were now amongst 'the foremost champions of the Social Contract'. While Ramelson did not question the sincerity of these left leaders – as was typical for him – and understood that they were motivated by solidarity with the Labour government, he nevertheless took them to task for failing to protect their members. Here he was referring to Jack Jones, Hugh Scanlon and Lawrence Daly in particular. He argued that both the 1972 and 1974 miners' strikes had been won because the NUM had remained in control and used the solidarity of others as part of their struggle; it had never allowed the TUC General Council into the decision-making process. Interestingly he made the point that the 1974 strike was about wages, and that although the employer wanted to settle, it was the government that refused to make concessions, thereby making the strike more political. It had challenged the incomes policies of the day, and so challenged the use of state power to drive down public sector wages. This was part of the era of 'confrontation', whereby the increased power of the working class was matched by greater state intervention in all aspects of industrial relations and economic life in general. As he reminds us: 'this confrontation between trade unionists and the state reached its peak with the arrest of the Pentonville Five … and the AUEW's call for an unlimited national strike'.[56] The lessons from all of this at a time when the government was attacking working-class living standards were that a general strike was not the weapon for seizing state power, and was no substitute for the role of a revolutionary communist party. The real role for such action is to create the ideological disposition among workers that political change can come out of prolonged struggle, and to defend real gains from non-democratic attempts to reverse the momentum of a growing progressive movement.

He makes two more important points here. First:

> incomes policy is now recognised as having distorted wage structures and created anomalies, storing up troubles for the future … causing friction between worker and worker and a spate of strikes to restore differentials … voluntary wage restraint always has been the thin edge of the wedge of compulsory wage restraint.[57]

Secondly, having noted in 1974 that 'loyalty to Labour, instead of correct policies, has been the primary cause of the failure of previous Labour governments, and it is a major factor in the present crisis',[58] he repeated this point in 1977: 'when all their other arguments are answered, the only one left to protagonists of the Social Contract is that it is essential to sustain a Labour government at any price'.[59] That they were wrong in this view was argued at the time by a number of leading left-wing trade unionists and Labour MPs, in a series of articles and speeches – and was re-affirmed throughout 1977/8 by the CP leadership. [60]

By 1977 government policy was again in disarray. The TUC conference moved back to support free collective bargaining, and the media once again turned on the union leaders, pushing the myth of the over mighty subjects, the barons, and the men of chaos. In the 1977-8 pay round the average wage rise had been about 15 per cent. In a long-winded and somewhat mealy-mouthed about-turn, the TUC leadership reported to Congress that:

> for the past two years the trade union movement has operated an effective voluntary policy of restraint on wage settlements. Trade unionists accepted and sustained the policy as the major contribution to the struggle to beat back the inflation … but the pride of trade unionists in their unprecedented and unrivalled contribution … is damped by their disappointment that the policy has fallen short of its objectives of containing inflation and reducing unemployment.[61]

Ramelson had been proved right and the CP line was vindicated. James Callaghan used all his skills and authority to sway the delegates:

'but the gain you made then has not been lost forever. It was delayed'; this was followed by 'you decided, and it is your right, to return to a system of free collective bargaining', but there was a subsequent rambling threat that wage restraint had to continue in one form or another – with or without the TUC.[62] Critically, Hugh Scanlon noted that 'the grass roots of our movement have made perfectly plain their revolt against any question of a Phase 3 and therefore there must be a return to free collective bargaining'.[63] In keeping with the new mood, in 1977 the firefighters went on national strike for the first time, under their left-wing national FBU leaders, and after nine bitter weeks settled for a pay formula indexed with male skilled manual earnings.[64]

By the time of the 1978 TUC Congress the line was established: 'the 1977 Congress was clear on the need for an orderly return to collective bargaining'.[65] What this exactly meant was debated in full, with Lawrence Daly and Ken Gill making the case for genuinely voluntary collective bargaining as the real remedy for reducing unemployment and increasing investment.[66] As Phase Two of the pay policy ended in July 1977, there could be no formal Phase Three as the TUC would not agree to one. The Labour Research Department *Guide to Pay Bargaining 1977/8* shows that, taking 1974 as 100 in terms of real take-home pay, it had stood at 94 in 1970 and was again 94 in early 1978. In other words, despite all the efforts of the movement and the policies of successive governments, there had been no change in workers' standards of living between 1970 and 1978, and a substantial fall between 1974 and 1978 (the Social Contract years). This failure, allied with the TUC's too little too late withdrawal from the Social Contract, created the conditions by which Callaghan and Healey could devise the disastrous pay policy later in 1978 that led directly to the strike wave known as the 'Winter of Discontent' – and to the election of the Thatcher government in May 1979.[67]

THE GRUNWICK STRIKE

In stark contrast to the previous ten years, strike activity during the Social Contract years had been at a low ebb. Now, out of the blue, there erupted a dispute involving a group of low paid mainly Asian women workers that told us much about the values and priorities of the Labour government.

The strike began on 23 August 1976, and escalated when in

September the company sacked 137 of the strikers for joining the union (Association of Professional, Executive, Clerical and Computer Staffs, APEX).[68] It was a vivid case of exploitation of mainly Asian women by an extravagant and ruthless entrepreneur, George Ward – aided and abetted by his friends in the Conservative Party. The solidarity that the dispute attracted raised all the old issues of policing, picketing and secondary action, and helped the Conservatives to regroup around a root-and-branch anti-union platform.

The Brent Trades Council, with its Communist Chair Tom Durkin very much in the van, took up the struggle, and in solidarity with this group of low paid and inexperienced trade unionists organised mass picketing in an attempt to force the employer to agree a negotiated settlement. The employer refused to budge, and the labour movement responded by stepping up solidarity activities. The impasse went on into 1977 and by that summer the dispute was grabbing national headlines. The response from the wider trade union movement was impressive. Ramelson was content to leave the day-to-day running of the strike to Durkin and the Brent Trades Council leadership, but Bill Moore recalled that it was Ramelson who first raised with Arthur Scargill the possibility of sending down a strong contingent of Yorkshire miners to the Grunwick picket line, in support of the 8 August 'Day of Action' called by the Strike Committee.[69] Just before the planned action however, the government had asked Lord Scarman to intervene, and his first action had been to call for calm and to request that the mass picket be called off. The union at national level – much to Ramelson's chagrin – gladly acceded to Scarman's request. Yorkshire miners did from time to time support the Grunwick picket but Scargill, reluctantly, respected the APEX decision to call off the 8 August mobilization.

The Security Service was very much on the case, at the request of Prime Minister Callaghan, who appeared to be much more concerned about the growing and successful use of flying pickets than he was about workers' rights and the struggle against racial discrimination. The surveillance of CP HQ in King Street using electronic bugs was stepped up, and Ramelson was reported to have muttered a curse when the planned 8 August Day of Action was called off, and to have expressed extreme disappointment when the Yorkshire miners failed to support the hastily called mass picket on 7 November 1977.[70] Ramelson felt that momentum was being lost and would be difficult to regain. He was unfortunately proved correct in this assessment.

Although both ACAS and the government-appointed Court of Inquiry headed by Lord Scarman recommended that the strikers be reinstated and their union be recognised for collective bargaining purposes, the company refused at any stage to accept the validity of such findings, and this stance was supported by the law lords, the final court of appeal.[71] The action carried on well into 1978, but in the end it proved impossible to sustain the necessary levels of solidarity and pressure on the employer or the Labour government. So a courageous struggle failed. It had shown that a group of previously unorganised Asian women workers had taken inspiration from the militant trade union struggles that had characterised much of the late 1960s and early to mid-1970s. However, it had also shown once again that the Labour government of that time was not prepared to support extra-parliamentary struggle to achieve fundamental human rights. Durkin's later assessment concluded that: 'the key lessons in our view are, first, the difference between left and right within our movement, second, the dangers of over-reliance upon procedures laid down by law and, third, the lessons for the movement on the relationship of the immigrant community to the Trade Union movement'.[72] Even in 2011 there were moves by the Communications Workers Union (CWU) to honour the postal workers who had put their jobs at risk on behalf of the courageous strikers and Jayaben Desai, the charismatic leader of the 'strikers in saris'. It was Desai's picture, confronting alone the serried ranks of police officers that created one of the most expressive photographs of modern working-class struggle.[73]

The strike formally ended on 14 July 1978. Andy Forbes was one of many commentators who agreed that this dispute had showed the power of the movement and its ability to mobilise ordinary workers, and the shocking nature of the injustices, but had also pointed to the limitations when official bodies such as the TUC and union general councils refused to give real support – for fear of breaking the law, embarrassing a Labour government, or deserting their reformist principles.[74] It also exposed the limitations of the Social Contract. When it came to the crunch, Labour politicians were not prepared to take on the legal establishment in order to support workers' rights.

As 1977 went on it become clear that the Labour government was in thrall to IMF monetarists as well as to their own narrow electoral miscalculations. Callaghan and Healey dominated the party and the government, and were in no mood to listen to their supporters, take notice of the TUC and the unions, and alter course. Ramelson could see what was happening, and warned time and again about disastrous TUC policies and the need to fight at every level for the Alternative Economic Strategy. He predicted the fall of Labour and the emergence of an anti-union and anti-worker government. Not even he could foretell the extent of the strike wave to come, the total failure of the Labour leadership to deal with it, and the way in which sections of the working class were subsequently seduced into backing an anti-union right-wing Tory regime.

In September 1977 Ramelson attended his last TUC as industrial organiser. He reported back, as he had done for last twelve years, to the Party's EC, as follows:

> the basic feature of this TUC was that the rapidly mounting grass roots revolt against the consequences of the social contract on jobs and living standards in the branches and district committees, as well as in the factories, mines and offices, which forced National Conferences against their own leaders' advice to reject the social contract with its central core of wage restraint, and found expression on the agenda and in the composition of lay delegates, was frustrated by manipulation to provide a fig leaf of majority support for government policy.[75]

He went on to criticise Scanlon and Murray for thwarting the clear wishes of the majority, and gave examples of unions breaking through the pay policy at Lucas and in the bakers' strike. He was particularly frustrated by the fact the 'real ideological case against wage restraint and for free collective bargaining didn't come through' – though Callaghan had made the dual assertions that the government had to stick with its incomes policies whatever the TUC decided, and that it required TUC co-operation to stay in office. Ramelson was particularly disappointed that the argument had been lost among public sector workers, who had felt that the issues made no difference to them since their pay was effectively controlled by government policy anyway. On the other hand opposition to the Social Contract, both official and unofficial, had grown since 1976, and the LCDTU's mass lobby and the industrial action in Sheffield had shown that the left was regaining lost ground, as with the TUC's endorsement of the Alternative

Economic Strategy.[76] Despite the existence of some form of alternative since the mid-1960s, the articulation of such a strategy had been slow to take centre stage. For example, in the early signs of crisis at British Leyland in 1975 little had been said, but by 1978 the trade unions were producing their version of an 'alternative'.[77]

THE *BRITISH ROAD TO SOCIALISM* AND RAMELSON'S FIGHT FOR THE PARTY LINE

As all this was taking place, the CP was preparing for its National Congress, at which the Party's revolutionary strategy, the *British Road to Socialism*, was up for debate and revision. As the Party's opposition to the direction of the Labour government had grown, and as its disappointment with some left-leaning union leaders was becoming more apparent, so the search was on to broaden the Party's base and to refashion its image and message in line with changes in the working class itself. Ramelson himself was very interested by the developments inside the working class, with the rise of new technical and white-collar jobs, and the relative change in the proportion of skilled manual workers amongst men. He understood how this might impact on the arguments needed to persuade this generation of workers about exploitation and unionism, but also that different ways of working mattered.[78]

Early in 1976 the CP leadership had recognised the need to update the *BRS* and to refashion both its style and substance to take account of new forces. It had started with a reappraisal of socialist democracy, through the prism of the occasion of the twentieth anniversary of the CPSU's revelations in 1956 of Stalin's awful crimes. Gollan, through the pages of *Marxism Today* and other Party organs, developed the main themes: that Stalinism was a distortion of communism and that his misuse of the Party apparatus had been a terrible corruption of the role of the state; that, despite those desperate years, socialism in the Soviet Union had survived and developed, showing its ability to overcome mistakes and misdirections; that the lessons included the need to be democratic not only inside the Party but also in the wider movement; and that 'the cult of the individual' could never be allowed to emerge again, with the best safeguard against this being socialist democracy.[79]

The CP was losing ground, but still maintained a sufficient presence in the unions, amongst certain groups of intellectuals, and with some emerging protest movements such as women,[80] blacks, gays, and greens to allow its voice to be heard, its activists followed by MI5, its leaders attacked in the media, and its policies contested from lecture theatres to production plants, and from civil service offices to building sites. The CP's General Secretary summed up the position as he saw it,

> The logical outcome of the fight to extend democracy and under-mine monopoly capitalism is the winning of political power by the working class and its allies. This requires a social revolution without which socialism cannot be built. Political power, won by the working class, supported by a broad alliance, must establish a new socialist state. The Communist Party has a decisive part to play in all this and it stands to reason that a much stronger Communist Party is needed. This whole process can only arise out of struggle in which important inroads will be made into monopoly power. Our aim must be to isolate the monopolies and the Tories, to break the right wing domi-nation of the labour movement. Working class unity, necessary for the immediate struggle, is even more vital for winning political power. It is at the heart of the wider anti-monopoly alliance which is necessary. Political co-operation between a left majority in the Labour Party when it is won and the Communist Party will be indispensable.[81]

Over the next few years the debate inside the CP turned to an accom-modation of the views of Lenin and Gramsci, a restatement of relations with the Labour Party, and the development of ideas about the 'Broad Democratic Alliance'. There were a series of reports to the CP's national executive on the crisis in the left, and these began to reflect growing splits inside the Party, which started as strategic differences but ended disastrously as irreconcilable conflicts of principle.[82] Among some there was increasing interest in the Italian communist electoral success and the formulation of 'a historic compromise', which was echoed by some of what Carrillo was saying in Spain. As Labour, divided and confused, changed its leader, so the rest of the left contemplated the best way of moving the left show forward. The debate about alliances and allies become sharper and more central.

Jack Woddis was one of many communist thinkers to consider the works of Gramsci as part of a tradition of writing about political power from Machiavelli and Lenin to Mao and Mandela. The central questions revolved around the nature of the state, and the tensions within it as the ruling class sought to secure its domination through consent (hegemony) as well as coercion, and the struggle for democracy through working-class alliances with other groups. This allowed the developing view that it was not necessary to 'smash' parliaments themselves in a revolution, since the parliamentary struggle was part of class struggle and not separate from it.[83] Some Party intellectuals sought to develop Gramsci's 'war of position' (contrasted to a 'war of manoeuvre') alongside the new BRS as explained by the new CP General Secretary Gordon McLennan, who stressed the importance of left unity.[84] Woddis debated the question of alliances through the works of Marx and Engels under the title 'a single gigantic flood'; and these arguments were developed by Yorkshire District Secretary Dave Priscott in a further analysis of the relationship between the Labour and Communist Parties.[85] Priscott argued that the *BRS* steered a correct middle course between those left-wingers who believed the Labour Party to be beyond reach – both the ultra-left and Miliband's more thoughtful new left – and those that saw the Labour Party as the only organisation capable of delivering change, and thus felt that the CP should be disbanded. Some of this debate was summarised in a range of obituaries for James Klugmann, who died in 1977, having edited *Marxism Today* since its foundation in 1957, and had fought for democracy and socialism all his life. [86]

None of the deeper and wider questions about the role of the unions within a Labour government's industrial strategy were being answered. Benn's support for the genuine efforts by the left to move forward, the Alternative Economic Strategy, had been thwarted by Wilson, Healey and Callaghan. His backing for a variety of worker co-operatives had been contemptuously dismissed in Cabinet by Denis Healey: a moving rightward show in one person, he argued that the state should intervene less, that government should be friendlier to the private sector, and that public expenditure should be reduced.[87] All of this gave impetus to the new Tory leadership under Mrs Thatcher (who had become Tory leader in 1975) and its right-wing think tanks, which proposed the monetarist solution to all industrial and economic problems. The new neoliberal mantra was being established: let the market sort it out; the freer the market the better will be the outcome, and all things collectivist must be opposed, traduced and reduced.[88]

The major effort of the Party to renew itself and its cadres at this time centred on the new version of the *BRS*. Throughout 1977 CP members debated amongst themselves at meetings and conferences, and in the pages of the *Morning Star* and *Comment*. The starting point for much of the debate was an analysis of the nature of the capitalist crisis and of capitalism itself. Here most Party members were in agreement with the basic Marxist-Leninist line espoused most forcefully by Ramelson. This included classic interpretations of Marx and Engels, and their views on the contradictions of capital that create instability and inequality, alongside attempts to define the current phase as one dominated by international monopolies, and with an ever-active state being used to bolster the influence of big business.[89]

The CP officially restated its commitment to public ownership and nationalisation, to democratically accountable services, and to a planned economy within a more just world order. The ramifications of the emphasis on principles became more apparent in the debates on policies. The immediate focus was on the crisis and its burden on working people. Here problems arose over muddles between the here and now, the medium-term alternatives and the long-run aims. While all agreed on the objective of socialism, the real fights and bitter divisions became apparent on the short and medium term strategies. Centre stage – both in its own right and as a proxy argument for differing analyses of class and the possibilities of the working class acting as a class – were incomes policies. These were debated in terms of the knock-on effects to trade union activity, Labour's electoral strategy, the causes of inflation, the incorporation of rank-and-file militancy into a vague policy commitment to fairer wages for all, the AES, and, vitally, Communist-Labour relations.

The main task of the 1977 CP Congress (the 35th) was to revise the *British Road to Socialism* by taking into account developments since the last revision, published in 1968, and it promised to be one of the more significant ones. In Britain it was clear by 1977 that the Labour governments from 1964 onwards had been to a considerable extent failures. They had set back the course of socialism and prepared the ground for the return of a neo-liberal Tory government. The International Communist Movement was still deeply split by the 1968 events in Czechoslovakia, and the continuing Sino-Soviet split. Furthermore, new approaches to social revolution were emerging, particularly among intellectuals supporting what became known as neo-Gramscism or

Eurocommunism, with its emphasis on the importance of the new social forces (e.g. the students' movement, women's liberation, the dispossessed), which some saw as more dynamic agents of radical change than the working class. While this position was very much a minority taste in Britain, as we shall see, it did command important and growing support in the upper echelons of the Party leadership.

Ramelson was to play a major part in the debates at the Congress. He was strongly placed to do so, having played a leading role in applying the Party's strategy to the industrial struggle during the preceding twelve years. It was undoubtedly the case that as a result of this work and the struggles it encouraged, the CP was by the mid-1970s more influential within the trade union movement than it had been at any other time in its history. Not that Ramelson was under any illusions about the balance of political forces at that time. He recognised that the right wing was still in control, but on the other hand it was no longer as dominant as it had been since at least the period after the 1926 General Strike. Ramelson knew that many on the left, particularly those in leadership positions, had been seduced by the rhetoric of the Social Contract, thus abandoning their previous support (particularly during the years of the Heath government) for normal collective bargaining and trade union independence from government. Thus, while acclaiming the growing rank-and-file opposition to the Social Contract as exemplified by the NUM and TGWU National Conferences' rejection of the concept earlier in the year, Ramelson also called for more attention to be placed on winning the battle of ideas. In his final report to the Party EC as National Industrial Organiser he underlined the need to 'eradicate the confusion that exists on pay as the lynchpin of the Alternative Economic Strategy'. In other words, he said, 'more emphasis should be placed on ideological struggle in the highly complex period we live in'.[90]

Ramelson also knew that the advances made in the unions were not reflected in the Party itself. In the few years running up to the Congress, membership had declined by some 2000 (around 7 per cent) of which only 500 or so could be attributed to the split led by the Party's Surrey district to form the New Communist Party (NCP), as a delayed reaction to the CP's criticism of the Soviet invasion of Czechoslovakia in 1968.

It was also a matter of some concern that the parliamentary left and the left in the Constituency Labour Parties were as far away from the

CP's concept of left unity as at any time since the Second World War. In the Constituency section it was the Militant Tendency which was gaining ground, while the Tribunites and others at Westminster remained hopelessly in thrall to electoral politics and their own (and parliament's) self-importance. For Ramelson, who put great emphasis in all he did on building influence right across the labour movement, this was disappointing. He always argued, however, that it was in the power of the unions, if convinced by the need for socialist policies and their implementation, to change this, given their role in the selection of the MPs and their representation on Constituency Labour Parties' General Management Committees right up to the National Executive Committee.

Ramelson's report to the EC called for greater efforts to be made in building the Party, particularly within the organised working class. To do this he recognised that the Party needed to broaden its appeal and the range of its activities. In this respect he always welcomed new thinking and the youth and intellectual energy which sometimes came with it. What he could not accept were notions which effectively side-lined the need for revolution, based on the working class and its allies taking state power.

By 1977 Martin Jacques had emerged as an effective representative of the minority neo-Gramscian position. He had been appointed as editor of *Marxism Today* following James Klugmann's death and was a member of the Executive's drafting committee for the revised version of the *BRS* to be debated and amended by the Congress. When it came to appointing a chair for the Congress Committee which was to guide the discussion at Congress – the *BRS* Committee – the Executive Committee turned to Ramelson rather than Jacques. The latter was on the Committee but was very much overshadowed by Ramelson, who used his position as Chair to identify key issues for debate and to head off any attempts to refer back the whole draft to the incoming EC.

In the event, much heat was generated around what appear now to be rather esoteric questions. The main points at issue were expressed in challenges made by leading intellectuals on the more traditional wing of the Party, who felt that the draft's definition of the working class was too broad, and that the 1968 *British Road to Socialism* more correctly identified the class nature of the alliances needed to overthrow capitalism. This latter point represented to some the crux of the differences which had emerged between the small minority neo-Gramscians and traditional Party approaches to the class struggle and the revolutionary process. The draft sought to replace what the 1968 *BRS* identified as the agent of revolutionary change – the anti-monopoly alliance – with a new concept, the Broad Democratic Alliance. The latter expressed, in clearer terms, the notion that class oppression resulted in a denial of democratic rights, across society, from the workplace to the family, from the political to the personal.

Congress rallied behind the new draft and decisively rejected attempts to amend its new approach. There is no doubt that as the Chair of the *British Road to Socialism* Committee, Ramelson assisted the Party in finding a synthesis between the position of the traditionalists and the neo-Gramscians, who favoured placing social movements at the heart of the revolutionary process (the broad democratic alliance) rather than one unequivocally based on the leading role of the working class (at the head of an anti-monopoly alliance). Ramelson argued that without the leadership of the organised working class and its mass organisations, meaningful and effective alliances could not be built, and that therefore only by putting the labour movement at the heart of the broad democratic alliance could it be given revolutionary content.

On this basis the Congress overwhelmingly voted to accept the new formulation. In later years the neo-Gramscians were able to exploit what some (but not Ramelson) have described as ambiguities in the 1977 *British Road to Socialism* to elevate the role of non-class based social movements above that of the working class and the trade unions in the struggle for social change. *Marxism Today* was of course the main vehicle for such arguments. It was the militant solidarity and organisational stability provided by the unions which gave the whole progressive movement its inspiration and political power. The high-point of the peace, women's and anti-racist movements coincided with the decade of militant industrial struggle, and it was no accident that it should have been so. It was on this basis that during the 1980s Ramelson consistently argued that the editor of *Marxism Today* had abandoned the *British Road to Socialism*, and that the *Morning Star* much better reflected the revolutionary strategy outlined in the 1977 programme.

Of course all of this was part of a wider and deeper set of Marxist analysis of the changing world from the emergence of China and decline of old imperial certainties, and from the advance of new technologies to the development of a post-Keynes neo-liberalism. As Sassoon reminds us the crisis of capitalism was not '*the* crisis, but only one of its crises'.[91] The managed corporatist solution imposed by some European governments could only work when the trade unions in some sense 'trusted' the government to deliver a something-for-something deal if real wages were to be held down on a voluntary basis. Hobsbawm states this more grandly, 'the history of the twenty years after 1973 is that of a world which lost its bearings and slid into instability and crisis'.[92] One immediate result was to convince labour movement leaders in many countries to 'co-operate' with the state in stabilising capitalism, and therefore another consequence was sharp questions about the relevance of communism to solve these problems. Hence the CP's need to restate its alternative economic and political strategy for the new order and for the new times.

The *British Road to Socialism* process itself became the subject of an acclaimed three-part television documentary, *Decision*, directed by Roger Graef and broadcast in July and August 1978 by Granada. The three hours of film made engrossing viewing for many television critics, particularly when the programmes went from the Congress floor to look at the work of the various Congress Committees. Not surprisingly, particularly in a TV programme, it is the personalities rather than the complexities of the issues under discussion which grab the reviewers' attention. Many of the reviews captured Ramelson's qualities. For Elkan Allen, in the *Sunday Times*, the film 'is full of incident, intensely dramatic … The man to watch is Bert Ramelson. Born in the Ukraine, educated in Canada, a veteran of the Spanish Civil War and now a full-time CP official'.

The *Daily Mail's* reviewer found it 'fascinating to watch at least three "stars" emerge in committee: an ex-nun named Irene – cool, sunny, and tough as a rope – her colleague behind the top desk, Bert, whose menacing spectacles and jowly grin dominate the proceedings and a little lady from the floor who faces up to these giants with true grit'. Ramelson's political style said much to *New Statesman* reviewer Geoffrey Hodgson as well:

> We are given an unforgettable vignette of Bert Ramelson crushing a revolt in committee … in unmistakably Stalinist style. He interrupts, he wags his fingers in the dissidents' faces, he bullies and he

manipulates procedure until even one of his opponents says with a bitter smile, 'As a chairman you're magnificent in dominating the place'.

The *Daily Express* also spotted Ramelson's qualities. Reviewer James Murray felt: 'He may well become a television personality. Like a bear with a sore head he listens in frustrated patience while quarrelsome members exercise their democratic right to be heard. Then he stentoriously cajoles them into seeing sense'. In a later review he wrote: 'Mr Ramelson and Mrs Simpson fought one of the great, no-holds-barred television battles in last night's programme … Simpson badgered Ramelson mercilessly … while the great bear of a man waggled his head in despair'.[93]

THE END OF AN ERA

Ramelson retired as Industrial Organizer at the CP Congress in November 1977, and was replaced by Mick Costello. Costello shared Ramelson's views, and – as Ramelson had been – was attacked both as being economistic and as using the Industrial Department as an autonomous Party within the Party. The new national organiser, Dave Cook, wanted Party union activists to be more up front about the Party, under the umbrella of the Broad Democratic Alliance. By the late 1970s the old guard was certainly passing away in the CP, and the policies and personnel within the CP leadership were changing, splitting, and leading to fatal divisions.

Notwithstanding these internal disputes, Ramelson continued to oppose the Social Contract and any variant of incomes policies, through his usual mixture of public and private debate. There is no doubt that Ramelson and the CP were influential players in the collapse of pay restraint, and in opposition to the IMF-inspired economic policy. As Robert Taylor put it:

> The role of the industrial department of the Communist Party cannot be denied … Ramelson was a key influence on the deliberations of the TUC General Council broad left … certainly the TUC leaders believed that the Communist Party had been very important in the collapse of the Social Contract.[94]

We can assess the period from 1965 to 1977 – the time of Ramelson's tenure as industrial organiser – through several accounts. Union membership, for example, was 10.3 million in 1965 and rose to 12.8 million by 1977. In terms of union density this represented a shift from 44 per cent to 53 per cent (it was about 27 per cent in 2010). All the strikes and controversies had added to the unions' positive image as organisations that could and did represent the working-class interest. This was an image which Ramelson helped to create, with his pamphlets and articles giving left activists confidence in their arguments, and the conviction that struggle could win benefits for members.

The evidence is that during this period unions, union activity and union policies developed into a more formidable left-looking fighting force than at any previous time since the 1920s. Despite the tendency to sectionalism and associated economism, the union movement as a whole could be – and was – mobilised in defence of union rights; in support of collective bargaining; and in efforts to maintain and raise the living standards of their members and the wider working class. At the centre of this were Ramelson and the CP: they were not the sole left voice, and were never the only element in this complex equation, but they were sufficiently powerful and important to influence effectively the direction of policy, the nature of action and the end purpose of struggle.

Ramelson left a legacy that maintained the dual strategy within the unions of winning official positions and policies and keeping up rank-and-file action and pressure. These two elements reinforced each other – though it was above all rank-and-file activity which created the conditions for progressive change in the official movement. The wages' struggle, the most unifying type of struggle for workers within unions, was intensely bound up with state policy and so with state power. Costello, Gill and others followed this line, and fought for the restoration of collective bargaining rights as an issue that could unify the industrial and political issues.

Throughout this period the left debated with itself about the familiar issues of the day, including the true nature of European social democracy and therefore of the Labour Party. Once again it was being suggested by some ultra-left academics and leaders that the Labour Party, due to its origins, structure, organisation and parliamentary focus, could never be won for genuinely left policies and practices; and that when it formed the government there were always too many powerful vested interests at work that prevented it enacting socialist measures. This argument implied that the CP position was of no real use, as well as downgrading and therefore weakening the revolt from below of the rank and file. These arguments were endlessly reconstructed through discussion in the pages of the *Socialist Register, New Left Review, Capital and Class* (from 1977) and *Tribune*. In 1977 a whole edition of *Socialist Register* was given over to contemplate 'the future of the left'. SWP leader Duncan Hallas opened his argument with efforts to support Miliband's critique of the limitations of the Labour Party:

> Politically, the Party must firmly reject the view that the Labour Party can ever be won to 'socialist policies'; hence it must reject the Communist Party's *British Road to Socialism,* for this view is central to that strategy. It must also take a critical attitude to the USSR and similar regimes.[95]

George Bridges provides some counter to Hallas and Miliband from a CP perspective:

> Ralph Miliband undoubtedly speaks for many socialists who feel there is no natural or comfortable political home for them in the presently existing organisations of the left. Distaste for the negative aspects of various organisations, or lack of confidence in a left alternative, often leads to a political limbo … The ability of the left to project itself as a potential alternative national leadership depends on … firstly … elaborating a strategy … secondly … that the concept of 'left unity' *is* meaningful in terms of how the left can work for a strategy. Thirdly … [to dispute] that the CP cannot be transformed into a useful vehicle of left politics.[96]

As these debates unfolded, the CP, and Ramelson as a leading comrade, now had increasingly to debate not only with the right-wing social democrats (the main foe) and the familiar ultra-left sectarians, but also with a renewed assault on Party strategy from the so-called Eurocommunists (this was the name by which the neo-Gramscians were widely known). This debate was the more crippling as it depleted the already diminishing resources of the Party. While much of the substantive international debate in this area was carried out by left intellectuals in a whirl of conceptualised linguistics, yet part of the core was about democracy under socialism, under capitalism, and in the USSR. These questions mattered, since the repressive nature and imagery of the Soviet Union and its sister states in Eastern Europe were a stumbling block to the development of popular support for socialist ideas and policies in the UK and Western Europe.

Panitch provides a generally clear summary of the comings and goings of these arguments. First, the case for the left staying inside the Labour Party:

> In the 1973 *Socialist Register,* Ken Coates produced a timely and brilliant defence of socialists working within the Labour Party. The argument was largely cast in terms of the absence of any alternative agency capable of maintaining a full scale political presence outside the Labour Party. But at the same time Ken Coates provided a positive case for working within the Party, stressing the critical role it plays in defensive struggles, the importance of parliamentary activity, and the possibilities for change in the Party contained in the radicalisation of the unions in the late sixties and early seventies.[97]

Panitch goes on to suggest that the reason that 'this militancy was indeed dissipated from 1975 to 1977 has a great deal to do with the inability of the Labour left, *no less than the various socialist groupings outside* of *it*, to capture the political imagination of rank and file activists'.[98]

As Ramelson's time as industrial organiser was drawing to a close, the CP's decline was escalating, with bitter splits and falling membership. There have been, of course, several accounts of why this happened and when it happened. Raphael Samuels (an influential Marxist historian opposed to the CP) sought to convey the substance of the beginning of the end in the late 1970s (with the end really coming in the mid-1980s) in terms of deep-seated and long-standing differences of analysis and approach. Others have attributed the decline to personalities and policy failures, anti-communist pressures, wider (European) influences, and above all changes in the nature of British society, class, and state. Samuels wrote three long pieces between 1985-7 for New Left Review, in which he tried to explain what went wrong, as far as the CP and the wider labour movement was concerned. He suggested that the CP split was part of a wider set of splits in the Labour Party and the trade unions because: 'the division in British Communism had been simmering since 1968, and therefore covers a whole epoch of the rise and fall of trade union militancy – and there has been an open split in the Communist Party's ranks ever since'.[99] Samuels argued that it was not being too close to the militant tide of unionism that had weakened the communists; much more important had been the deep damage that had been inflicted by the ruling political class's use of the Cold War – as had reoccurred with Harold Wilson in the 1966 seafarers' strike, and with later Labour leaders in other major disputes. After a long and rather muddled homily on Party organisation and cadres' Party discipline, Samuels returns to his main theme of schism.[100] He suggests that:

> The debate on the 'British way' – the major issue at the 1977 congress when the present schism first emerged – echoes the never-resolved debate on 'parliamentarianism' which nearly paralysed the CPGB at birth; while the argument for the 'broad democratic alliance' mirrors the turn from the 'class against class' politics … to those of the Popular Front.[101]

These years from 1974 to 1977 saw the defeat and decline of the reformist leadership of the Labour Party and the trade union movement, and exposure of their ideological failings. The reformists had been challenged by the communist left under Ramelson's relentless waging of class struggle around the triptych of the wages' movement, union militancy, and direct confrontation with the state. They were also in the end undone by the Social Contract, which allowed the right wing back into the wages' game, distracted left-wing union leaders, and dissipated the political and class nature of the struggle. The fallout from all this was felt quickly and deeply across the left, including the communists. By 1977 Ramelson had been proved right. The Social Contract had fallen apart and electoral disaster lay ahead. His formal retirement coincided with the collapse of incomes policy, the rise of anti-union sentiment in the Labour Party, and the turn of old Labour away from Keynes, Beveridge and Bevan into the arms of the monetarists, social engineers and anti-collectivists, as they reformed under Neil Kinnock (after the 1983 election defeat) to pave the way for New Labour proper.

NOTES

1. Taylor 1993, op.cit.; Fryer, R 'The politics of industrial relations in the public sector' in Mailly, R.; Dimmock, S. and Sethi, A. (eds.) *Industrial Relations in the Public Services*; Routledge, London 1989, pp. 17-67.
2. See, for example, LRD's *New Tory Attack on Union Rights*, London 1981.
3. McCormick 1979, op. cit., pp. 211-217.
4. Ellman, M., Rowthorn, B., Smith, R. and Wilkinson, F. *Britain's Economic Crisis*, Cambridge Political Economy Group, Spokesman Pamphlet, No.44, Nottingham 1974, p. 38.
5. Crosland, A. *Socialism Now*, Jonathan Cape, London 1975.
6. Ramelson, B. *Social Contract: Cure-all or Con-trick?* CP December 1974, p. 6.
7. In July 1975 the White Paper (*The Attack on Inflation*, Cmnd 6151) had TUC support for a policy of £6 flat rate increase with direct control over public sector wages, and indirect pressure on private sector wages through contract compliance. By August 1976 another policy started with the White Paper (*The Attack on Inflation – the second year*, Cmnd 6507) providing for a 5% limit up to a maximum of £4 per week. In September 1976 the TUC called for a return to free collective bargaining from August 1977. So there was no TUC support for another year as outlined in the White Paper (*The Attack on Inflation after 31 July 1977*, Cmnd 6882), which wanted deals of 10% or less. In July 1978 another White Paper (*Winning the battle against inflation*, Cmnd 7293) set out a fourth year of restraint with a 5% limit except for the low paid, self-financing productivity agreements, and serious anomalies. The TUC rejected this, and after the major strike wave 1978/9 (Winter of Discontent) the government set up Clegg Commission in March 1979 (*The Economy, the Government and Trade Union Responsibilities* HMSO 1979) aimed at reducing inflation. See ACAS 1980 op.cit, pp. 35-8.
8. Hobbes, Thomas *The Leviathan*. First published 1651, this edition, Everyman, London 1914, p. 65; also see Locke, John *Two Treatises of Government*, first published 1689 – only the second treatise is relevant here; Rousseau, Jean Jacques, *The Social Contract*, first published 1762.
9. Renee Short MP 'Dilution the road to disaster', *Labour Monthly* 1974 7(56): 300-4.
10. Ray Buckton (general secretary of ASLEF) 'The sort of social contract we really want', *Labour Monthly* 1974 7(56): 349-52.
11. Andrew 2009 op.cit.; Callaghan, J. and Phythian, M. 'State Surveillance of the CPGB Leadership', *Labour History Review*, 2004 69(1): 19-33.
12. Morgan 1990, op.cit., p. 379.
13. For more on this see Dennis Skinner MP, 'Clay Cross and the Social Contract', *Labour Monthly*, November 1974; and Bert Smith (chair of UCATT), 'Thoughts on Shrewsbury', *Labour Monthly*, July 1974.

14. Purdy, D. 'Some Thoughts on the Party's Policy Towards Prices, Wages and Incomes', *Marxism Today*, August 1974, pp. 246-252,

15. Cliff, T. *The Crisis: Social Contract or Socialism*, Pluto Press, London 1975.

16. Gill, K. 'Marxism and the Trade Unions', *Marxism Today*, June 1974. pp. 163-174, p. 166.

17. Bellamy, R. 'More on inflation', *Marxism Today*, November 1974, pp. 340-349.

18. *Comment*, 27/7/74.

19. Wedderburn 1986, op.cit., p. 61.

20. Ibid., pp. 458-472.

21. *Benn, T. Against the Tide: Diaries 1973-1976* Hutchinson, London 1989.

22. Gill, K. 'Review of "Social contract" by Bert Ramelson', *Comment*, 8/2/75, p. 47.

23. Ramelson, December 1974 op.cit., p. 3,

24. Matthews, G. 'The Wilson Government and Britain's Crisis', *Marxism Today*, February 1975, pp. 35-46, p.39.

25. Ramelson, December 1974 op.cit., pp. 4-5.

26. Sen, A. *The Idea of Justice*, Harvard University Press, Harvard 2009.

27. Atkinson, A. 'How progressive should income tax be?' in M. Parkin (ed.) *Essays on Modern Economics*, Longman, London 1972; Arrow, K. 'The utilitarian approach to the concept of equality in public expenditure', *Quarterly Journal of Economics*, 1971 85(3): 409-415; Tobin, J. 'On limiting the domain of inequality', *Journal of Law and Economics*, 1970 13(2): 263-277.

28. Galbraith, J.K. *The Affluent Society*, Penguin 1958.

29. Morgan 1990, op.cit., p. 378.

30. 1975 TUC Annual Report, p. 459.

31. Ibid., p. 462.

32. Castle, B. *The Castle Diaries 1974-1976*, Weidenfeld and Nicolson, London 1980, p. 427.

33. Hobsbawm, E. *The Crisis and the Outlook*, London: Birkbeck College Socialist Society and London Central branch of the CP 1975, p. 8.

34. Ibid. p. 13.

35. Morgan, K. *Callaghan: A Life*, Oxford University Press, Oxford 1997.

36. Labour Party Annual Conference Report 1976, p. 188.

37. Miliband 1972, op.cit.

38. Derek Robinson was the powerful Convenor of shop stewards at British Leyland, Longbridge (Birmingham), who was later victimised by the management with the open support of the right-wing AEU leadership.

39. Brasher, J. 'The Trico equal pay dispute', *Labour Monthly*, 1976 58(12): 547-9.

40. *LRD Guide*, 1976.

41. Taylor, R. 'The Rise and Fall of the Social Contract' in A. Seldon and K.

Hickson (eds) *New Labour. Old Labour*, Routledge, London 2004, pp. 87-103.

42. Bert Ramelson, Letter to *Comment*, 10/7/76, p. 221.

43. *TUC 1976 Annual Report*, Cyril Plant, p. 428.

44. Ibid., p. 521.

45. Ibid., p. 522.

46. Harris, L. 'Healey's panic squeeze', *Comment*, 30/10/76, pp. 339-340; Aaronovitch, S. 'Where next for Britain's economy', *Comment*, 11/12/76, pp. 387-8.

47. McLennan, G. 'Report to EC on mass struggle for left policies' *Comment* 18/9/76, pp. 291-5.

48. Ramelson, B. 'The role of general strikes today', *Marxism Today* July1976, pp. 216-220.

49. Militant Tendency was an entryist group within the Labour Party based around the Militant newspaper that was first published in 1964. It described its politics as a Trotskyist form of Marxism-Leninism. In 1983, the five members of the 'Editorial Board' of the Militant newspaper were expelled from the Labour Party.

50. The GLC replaced the London County Council (LCC) in 1965 and remained the governing body for London until its abolition in 1986. Ken Livingstone was a socialist Labour MP who was leader of the GLC 1981-6, and later directly elected Mayor of London, 2000-8.

51. Ramelson March 1977, op. cit., p. 1.

52. Ibid., p. 21.

53. Ibid., p. 35.

54. Purdy, D. 'British capitalism since the war – origin of the crisis', *Marxism Today*, September 1976, pp. 270-277; Purdy, D. 'British capitalism since the war – decline and prospects', *Marxism Today*, October 1976 pp. 310-318.

55. Ramelson, March 1977, op.cit., p. 2.

56. Ramelson July 1976 op.cit., p. 219.

57. Ramelson December 1974 op.cit. pp. 21-2.

58. Ibid., p. 24.

59. Ramelson, March 1977, op.cit., p. 17,

60. Bob Wright (assistant general secretary of the AUEW) 'The lessons Labour governments never learn', *Labour Monthly*, March 1977, pp. 111-3; Derek Robinson (chair of the British Leyland Combine Shop Stewards Committee) 'Leyland workers and the social contract', *Labour Monthly*, April 1977, pp. 156-7; Joan Maynard MP 'No "stage three"', *Labour Monthly*, May 1977, pp. 203-4; For the official CP line on the Social Contract see *Comment*, 23/7/77, pp. 259-260.

61. *TUC 1977 Annual Report*, p. 227.

62. Ibid., pp. 432-3.

63. Ibid., p. 467.

64. Bailey, V. *Forged in Fire: the History of the Fire Brigades Union*, Lawrence & Wishart, London 1992.
65. *TUC 1978 Annual Report*, p. 291.
66. Ibid., pp 349-351.
67. For pay policy in 1978 see Callaghan, J. *Time and Chance*, Collins 1987; Morgan, op.cit., 1997.
68. Dromey, J. and Taylor, G. *Grunwick: The Workers' Story*, Lawrence & Wishart, London 1978.
69. Bill Moore interview, 1999.
70. Andrew 2009, op.cit., p. 665.
71. Wedderburn, 1986 op.cit., p. 283.
72. Durkin, T. *Grunwick: Bravery and Betrayal*, Brent Trades Council, London 1978, p. 3.
73. Jack Dromey interview, May 2011.
74. Forbes, A. 'In the Wake of Grunwick', *Marxism Today*, December 1978, pp. 386-391.
75. Ramelson, B. 'Report to EC on the TUC', *Comment*, 17/9/77 p. 339.
76. TUC *Economic Review 1978*.
77. Beynon, H. *What happened at Speke?* TGWU, Liverpool 1978; AUEW-TASS *British Leyland Cars: Collapse or Growth – An Alternative to Edwardes*, TASS, London 1978; Leyland Combine Trade Union Committee *The Edwardes Plan and Your Job*, London 1979.
78. See Braverman 1974, op.cit., for a discussion and analysis of these changes.
79. Gollan, J. 'The 20th congress of the CPSU in retrospect', *Marxism Today*, January 1976, pp. 4-30; reprinted as *Socialist Democracy – some problems*, CP Pamphlet 1976.
80. Rowbotham, S. *Hidden from History*, Pluto Press, London 1973.
81. Gollan, J. 'Parliament, Anti-Monopoly Alliance and Socialist Revolution', *Marxism Today*, September 1975 pp. 260-264, p. 260.
82. Mathews, G. 'Report to the EC on the crisis and the left', *Comment*, 20/3/76, pp. 83-6.
83. Woddis, J. 'The State – some problems', *Marxism Today*, November 1976. pp. 331-343.
84. Simon, R. 'Gramsci's concept of hegemony', *Marxism Today*, March 1977 pp. 78-86; Hobsbawm, E. 'Gramsci and political theory', *Marxism Today*, July 1977, pp. 205-213.
85. Woddis, J. '"A single gigantic flood": reflections on the democratic alliance', *Marxism Today*, September 1977, pp. 260-269; Priscott, D. 'Problems of Communist Labour relationships', *Marxism Today* October 1977, pp. 294-301.
86. James Klugmann (1912-1977) was a leading communist historian and founding editor of *Marxism Today*. For obituaries see *Marxism Today* November 1977 edition; and, for example, *Bulletin – Society for the Study of Labour History*, Spring 1978, Issue 36, p. 7.

87. Healey, D. *The Time of my Life*, Penguin 1989.
88. Thatcher, M. *The Downing Street Years* , Harper Collins, London 1993; Chomsky, N. *Profit over People: Neo-liberalism and the world order*, Seven Stories Press, New York 1999.
89. Baran, P. and Sweezy, P. *Monopoly Capital*, Penguin 1966.
90. Ramelson, B. 'The TUC Assessed', Report to the CP EC, *Comment* 17/9/77, pp. 339-342, p. 342.
91. Sassoon, D. *One Hundred Years of Socialism*, Fontana, London 1997, p. 445.
92. Hobsbawm, E. *Age of Extremes: the short twentieth century 1914-1991*, Michael Joseph, London 1994, p. 403.
93. All these reviews appeared in early August 1978 in the respective papers.
94. Taylor, R. *The TUC – From the General Strike to New Unionism,* Palgrave, Basingstoke 2000, p. 231.
95. Hallas, D. 'How Can We Move On?', *Socialist Register*, 1977, pp. 1-10, p. 1.
96. Bridges, G. 'The Communist Party and the Struggle for Hegemony', *Socialist Register*, 1977, 14: 27-37, p. 27.
97. Panitch, L. 'Socialists and The Labour Party: a Reappraisal', *Socialist Register* 1979, pp. 51-74, p. 51.
98. Ibid., p. 67.
99. Samuel, R. 'The Lost World of British Communism', *New Left Review*, 1985 No. 154, pp. 3-53; this quote p. 15.
100. Samuel, R. 'Staying Power: The Lost World of British Communism, Part Two', *New Left Review*, 1986 No. 156, pp. 63-113.
101. Samuel, R. 'Class Politics: The Lost World of British Communism, Part Three', *New Left Review*, 1987 No. 165; pp. 52-91, p. 52.

PART III

Class struggle and class warrior

7. Old Bolsheviks never retire from the struggle, 1977-1994

ANOTHER NEW CHAPTER

Ramelson's retirement from the industrial department was announced by Gordon McLennan at the end of the 1977 CP Congress. In a short thank-you speech McLennan referred to Ramelson as a much loved comrade who had given him and other leading communists invaluable advice over the years, based on his long and varied experience in the movement and his unswerving loyalty to the Party and to the international communist movement. He then announced that Ramelson would still be working full-time at the Party's London headquarters, though in an as yet unspecified role.

After a short holiday, Ramelson began to deploy his considerable energies and talents in the international field, and soon started his new life in the Party's international department, then headed by Jack Woddis. He also remained available to give advice on industrial questions, and both the new industrial organiser Mick Costello and General Secretary Gordon McLennan regularly consulted him on a wide range of questions relating to labour movement developments.[1] The *Morning Star* was also able to use his experience and knowledge. Over the Christmas period in 1977 Ramelson penned a series of five feature-length articles on economic issues, the wages question and inflation. These were published in January 1978. Then during 1978, after Idris Cox had retired, Ramelson took over his role as the CPGB's representative on the editorial board of *World Marxist Review*. This was the international communist movement's monthly theoretical journal, published in several languages and with distribution points in every continent, and the role would involve a great deal of travelling to WMR's office in Prague.

Before Ramelson took up his new role there erupted a fierce debate involving communists and others on the left about the state of the British labour movement, given the evident failure of the Callaghan-led Labour government. The debate was stimulated by an Eric Hobsbawm Marx Memorial Library lecture in the late spring of 1978, entitled 'The Forward March of Labour Halted?'. [2]

THE FORWARD MARCH OF LABOUR HALTED?

Shortly after Ramelson's retirement Hobsbawm, a longstanding CP member and internationally respected Marxist historian, gave a lecture at Marx House in Clerkenwell Green, London. The lecture highlighted changes in the structure of Britain's productive capacity: not only was the computer replacing much routine clerical labour, it was now being used to usher in a new age of computer-aided information technology, manufacturing, design and process; labour units were getting smaller and the white-collar, female and immigrant labour force was getting larger, while traditional bastions of working-class organisation such as the miners, railway workers and engineers were declining quite rapidly, sometimes in actual terms (e.g. coal mining) but always in relative terms (i.e. manufacturing in comparison to the fast-growing services and commercial sectors). These developments could not but affect the organisation and outlook of the labour movement. The growth of plant and company-wide bargaining within companies at the expense of industry or sector-wide bargaining, encouraged the development of sectionalist attitudes to wage bargaining. All this, Hobsbawm argued, undermined solidarity and potentially weakened the political and industrial coherence of the labour movement.

None of this was particularly new, and some of it was extremely contentious. Furthermore, Hobsbawm's analysis, at least in 1978, was not strongly supported by conclusive evidence. For this was a time when trade union membership was still growing and expanding into new areas, reaching an historical high-water mark. This growth was particularly noteworthy among white-collar and women workers. It was also the case that the trade union agenda was becoming broader, to increasingly encompass political and social questions as well as purely economic and other traditional trade union demands; and the movement was increasingly looking outwards to embrace international solidarity issues. [3]

In conversation with what was by now his rather limited circle, Ramelson expressed his disagreements with Hobsbawm's approach. To Ramelson, Hobsbawm's analysis of industrial and social change in post-war Britain was unexceptional and broke no new ground. He accepted that sectionalism and economism were features of trade union practice which had to be constantly guarded against and challenged by the left. He had after all spent the last thirty years of his life working to strengthen the movement by promoting solidarity based on common class interest, and opposing economism as an approach which elevated the wages struggle above the need to work for political change.[4] Ramelson saw no need on the part of the broad left in the labour movement to take much notice of Hobsbawm's position about the perils of sectionalist trades unionism in the struggle for progressive social change.

The important question was how to draw the correct political conclusions from what was happening, and apply these to changing industrial and social conditions. For Ramelson the elephant in the room, to which Hobsbawm had failed to give sufficient weight, was the impact of the records of Labour governments on the political consciousness of the working class. In reality and without exception, every Labour government since 1945 had to one degree or another been a failure and the extent of this failure had increased exponentially with every successive Labour administration. By 1978 broad swathes of traditional Labour support were alienated from the political process altogether (the politicians apparently had no answers to the issues concerning working people). Millions of others were now voting instrumentally for policies which appeared to benefit them personally (e.g. tax cuts) rather than out of class loyalty for a party which when in government continuously failed to meet their aspirations for higher living standards and job security.[5]

By the time Hobsbawm's lecture appeared as an article in *Marxism Today*, Ramelson had been retired for a year from his National Industrial Organiser's position. [6] Uncharacteristically, he decided to take no direct part in the debate that subsequently opened up in the journal. Perhaps he felt that it was too soon after his retirement to intervene, and that it was for others within the Party's national leadership to take up the baton. In retrospect this was a mistake, which was not repeated later, as Ramelson sought to influence debates on the big questions facing the movement, nationally and internationally, right through the 1980s and early 1990s. He did, however, try to persuade others to draft replies critical of Hobsbawm's thesis. Both Ken Gill and Gordon McLennan told us that Gill's reply was prepared following pressure from Ramelson.[7] Gill's reply is perfectly adequate on most levels, and reflected some of Ramelson's thinking on the issues raised by Hobsbawm. It lacked, however, the incisive quality so characteristic of Ramelson's pamphlets, and his ability to concede your opponent some points before going on to dismantle their main argument.

Ramelson did express views on the Hobsbawm article after the event. In his pamphlet *Consensus or Socialism*, published in 1987, he took Hobsbawm to task for arguing that the post-1945 consensus had been based on the unity of the right and left in the Labour Party. Ramelson argued that, at the beginning of the 1945 Labour government, 'Keynesianism combined with the Beveridge philosophy of the Welfare State was the common ideology of big business and right-wing Labour'; and it was this which had underpinned the post-war political settlement.[8] The implications of this were not spelt out in the pamphlet, but it is clear that when this consensus began to be challenged, particularly by sections of big business, right-wing Labour had nothing to put in its place; and it is at this stage that the level of Labour's mass electoral support begins to weaken. Of course Ramelson valued labour movement unity as much as Hobsbawm, but he was always insistent that it could only be sustained by a leadership which was committed to pro-working-class policies and determined to implement them in government.

Despite Ramelson's best efforts, the Hobsbawm thesis proved to be very influential in the years that followed. Labour leaders, beginning with Neil Kinnock, were impressed, and drew conclusions which were later to be part of New Labour's thinking. As usual the overriding concern was electoral – how could the decline in traditional working-class support be replaced by support from new sections of the working class, particularly those increasingly adopting consumerist 'middle-class' life styles? Following the debacle of Labour's 1979 election defeat and the emergence of a strong right-wing Tory government, Labour tacked with the prevailing wind to distance itself from the trade union movement and from the policies – such as full employment and a growing welfare state – that had underpinned support for its version of social democracy.

Ramelson spent much of the 1980s arguing that this was a tragically mistaken strategy, and that its essentially defeatist premise that only by accommodating a neoliberal approach could Labour return to office would in fact condemn Labour to electoral failure.[9] The alternative was set out in the Alternative Economic and Political Strategy which Ramelson had done so much to develop during the 1960s and 1970s. This offered a programme of left policies which if taken together could challenge the power of the giant companies and improve the living standards of all working people, thus providing the basis for electoral success and radical political change in a socialist direction.[10]

No sooner had Hobsbawm given his lecture than there began an intense period of industrial action, with workers determined to recover the ground lost during the Social Contract years. The start of the strike wave now known as the 'winter of discontent' was at Fords, and by the end of September 1978 all twenty-three plants were idle as a wage demand well in excess of the 5 per cent norm was pursued. After two months Ford gave in and awarded a 17 per cent pay deal. This encouraged other groups to press their demands, particularly low-paid workers in the public sector. The TGWU led the way, with lorry drivers and oil tanker drivers taking action in January 1979.[11] The government tried to fix it, but it was all too late. The lorry drivers won their dispute by 19 January 1979, with rises of between 17 and 20 per cent. This was followed by the 24-hour strike on 22 January of public service workers in NALGO and NUPE (National Union of Public Employees) mainly in local government. Local strikes of health workers, dustmen and gravediggers came thick and fast. As the BBC news reported: 'Public sector strike paralyses country: Tens of thousands of public sector workers have taken part in a day of action - the biggest mass stoppage since 1926 - in support of a claim for more pay. The four major public service unions angry at the government's attempt to impose a 5% pay ceiling called out their 1.5 million members. They included hospital workers, rubbish collectors, school caretakers, grave diggers and airport staff. Mass demonstrations have been held in London, Cardiff, Edinburgh and Belfast, bringing many services to a standstill. Services in the North East of England have also been badly affected'.

On 14 February a deal was reached for 9 per cent pay rises, but more strikes by civil servants and local authority groups continued in March. A deal with the TUC looked hollow and was seen as such. On 28 March the government lost a vote of no confidence by one vote, the first time since October 1924 that such an event had happened. So came to an end a weak and limited Labour government that had sought to control inflation and growth through wage restraint, and had succeeded only in creating mass opposition and disillusion.

This 'Winter of Discontent' became a slogan and legend for much of British politics for the next thirty years. Indeed in 2011, as we write, the 'popular experts' are predicting another 'Something of Discontent' as a response to coalition government public spending cuts. There is no seminal account of this great illusion, but several commentators have sought to analyse, explain and recount events.[12] The position of the communists was that it represented part of the wage militancy legacy, that it showed the folly of incomes policies by any other name, and that it illustrated what happens when the left is weak and divided, leaderless and full of self-doubt. Namely, industrial unrest on a mass scale, but without political gain as the working-class as a class sought to hold back the international forces of the rising tide of finance capital.[13]

On 3 May 1979 Margaret Thatcher won the election for the Tories with nearly 44 per cent of the popular vote (13,697,923 votes), securing 339 seats against Labour's 269. Some traditional working-class Labour voters had deserted them and turned Tory. This result had been foretold by the communist leadership since it hinged on workers abandoning a right-wing Labour government out of frustration and disappointment. Writing in 1977 Ramelson had warned of the electoral consequences of cuts in real wages and services: although 'a Labour government is preferable to a Tory government, let alone one led by Mrs Thatcher', the Labour government would be held responsible by many working-class voters for 'bringing about mass unemployment and drastic cuts in living standards through the erosion of wages'; and all of this had 'increased the chances of the return of a Tory Government whenever the next election takes place'.[14]

ON THE INTERNATIONAL SCENE

Though Ramelson's position on the editorial board of *World Marxist Review* was nominally full-time, he managed to negotiate a special arrangement which typically involved spending one week a month in Prague to attend editorial board and other business meetings (including international seminars on topical theoretical issues), while the rest of the month could be spent in Britain, where he would liaise with the printers and distributors of the English language edition and commission articles from British contributors.

Ramelson quickly adapted to his new life style and enjoyed the new freedom it offered him. He liked nothing better than a serious political discussion, whether on matters of Marxist theory, current political developments, and the international labour movement. He quickly established himself as a formidable figure in the *WMR* collective, and his clear views were constantly reported in the journal as he fought to make his contribution to the understanding of a rapidly changing world in which many of the traditional communist positions were under scrutiny. His views were often controversial, particularly on questions like the form and practice of democratic centralism and the relationship between the Soviet Party and the world communist movement. Because they were always based on sound Marxist principles – for example rejecting non-class categories such as the universal human values later popularised by Gorbachev – Ramelson was always given a platform for his views and listened to with respect. In the small group of international communists based in Prague Ramelson enjoyed an active life centred around political discussion and good food and wine. He was always a welcome guest with his energy and humour at the many small dinner parties hosted by English and Russian speaking comrades. Not that these occasions were without tension. Many a conversation developed into a heated discussion as Ramelson broke bread with the comrades. Eye-witness accounts report shouted arguments going long into the night to be repeated the following month with friendship and mutual respect retained.[15] The crux of these arguments usually centred on the role of the Soviet Union and certain aspects of inner-party democracy, particularly democratic centralism. The reality was that in his later years Ramelson became increasingly critical of Soviet theory and practice, arguing that the particular experiences of the Soviet revolution were in many respects non-exportable, and that the failure to build an advanced socialist democracy was both worrying and frustrating.

Ramelson argued that after seventy years of power, albeit in a difficult and mainly hostile international environment, surely the CPSU should have been able to build a democratic society that was in advance of the very limited social and democratic gains made by the struggles of working people in the major imperialist powers. Yet in several respects the reverse was the case. In particular civil liberties in the first workers' state lagged behind those achieved by the progressive movement in advanced bourgeois societies. At the same time it was clear by the end of the 1970s that the Soviet Union's economic model, based on centralised planning and top-down command management techniques, had failed to produce the results that had been predicted in the 1950s and 1960s. While full employment was maintained, productivity was low compared to other advanced industrial countries, and major problems such as inadequate housing provision and agricultural shortages remained intractable.

While Ramelson rejected the notion that it was necessary to have competing political parties as a basis for a democratic polity, he did argue in his later years that democratic centralism had in practice led to an ossified political culture and to a badly informed Communist leadership. His view was that in socialist societies one-party systems could only be democratically viable if there was a vibrant democratic culture allowing for vigorous debate and alternative positions within the party and in wider society. Only then could mistakes, which are inevitable in every system, be corrected and the leadership be constantly refreshed by new ideas and new people. At every stage the CP had to work for the respect of the people and for their full involvement in decision-making in every social activity and at every level. Simply proclaiming the leading role of the Party and enshrining this in a nation's constitution led to all sorts of corruption and abuse of power. Failure to develop democratic structures based on people's power rather than Party edicts resulted in ill-informed decision-making at the top and political cynicism at the grass roots.[16]

That Ramelson made a considerable impact in Prague is confirmed by Essop Pahad, who represented the South African Communist Party on the *WMR* editorial board. He wrote to tell us how much he had gained from Ramelson's company in Prague:

> As a member of the editorial board Bert participated in all those debates and discourses fearlessly, authoritatively bringing to bear his immense experience of working-class struggles in the UK and Europe … He had serious reservations about the relevance of the

theoretical and practical significance of the dictatorship of the proletariat. For him the notion of dictatorship was anathema. Following the position and policies of the CPGB one must say that whilst Bert was highly critical of existing Socialism, a position many of us in Prague disagreed with, he was never anti-Soviet or anti the CPSU.

Although I disagreed with a number of theoretical and ideological positions taken by Bert and the CPGB at that time, Bert and I got on very well … Bert had a phenomenal experience of working within the communist movement as well as the labour movement … I am grateful that I was able to learn a great deal from Bert Ramelson, who remained true and loyal to his party, the working class movement and international solidarity to his last breath.[17]

No doubt these heretical ideas arose partly from what Ramelson saw around him during his Prague years. For example, he told Tom Sibley about the chats he had with his window cleaner, an ex-professor and CP EC member who had lost his job and political position because of his support for the Dubcek reforms. In a letter written in 1990 to Stellan Hermannson, who represented the Swedish Young Communist League on the *WMR* board, Ramelson recalled his mixed feelings about the Prague experience – of living and working with leading communists from all over the world, some of whom were exemplary revolutionaries, while at the same time far too many, particularly from the socialist countries, were time-serving opportunists and conformists. For his part Hermannson wrote to Ramelson after the demise of the *WMR* to say: 'I will always remember you and your discussions often with a whisky in your hand. You are an example for the New Left. I admire your strength, clear mind and attitude to people'.[18]

During the 1980s, relationships between Ramelson and the CPGB leadership deteriorated as the '*Marxism Today* group' increasingly gained ground at the top of the British Party. Yet Ramelson's position as the British representative on the *WMR* editorial board was apparently never challenged. This is particularly surprising given the bitterness of the struggle concerning the Party/*Morning Star* Management Committee relationship, in which Ramelson played a leading role as a critic of the Party's EC strategy and tactics. It may be that by the mid-1980s the CPGB leadership simply did not care about its relationship with the international communist movement, or it may have been that they had enough trust in Ramelson's integrity to know that he would loyally protect and represent the British Party's interests in the international arena. Whichever it was, Ramelson was able to use his official position to campaign, with due care and discretion, for what he considered to be the policies of the Party Congress (at least until the 1985 Congress), and the strategy set out in the 1977 *British Road to Socialism*. This can be seen in the various discussion groups called by the *WMR* on theoretical questions.[19] The positions adopted by Ramelson on incomes policy, industrial democracy and nationalisation in *WMR* channels and publications contrasted sharply with the editorial line of *Marxism Today*. Ramelson argued, correctly, that his views were fully in line with Party policy, while those expressed as the dominant voice in *Marxism Today* were often clearly at variance with majority decisions that had been taken at successive Congresses.

AFGHANISTAN

Ramelson's role as a sort of Minister without Portfolio attached to the Party's international department was about to take a new and important turn. During the 1970s the communist movement in Afghanistan had made significant advances and established a strong base among young officers within the armed forces. By 1978 these elements were strong enough to win state power through a military coup, and to establish a progressive regime guaranteeing new social and economic rights for the people. At the same time links at state level were established with the neighbouring Soviet Union, and these were formalised in treaties pledging military and economic aid.

This educated and progressive section of Afghan society was determined to modernise the country and to tear down centuries of religious obscurantism. Perhaps its most striking reforms were in the field of women's rights and girls' education, where for the first time in decades genuine attempts were made to guarantee equal opportunities regardless of gender and religious differences. Such reforms met fierce resistance from religious leaders and the regionally based warlords, and from Islamic fundamentalists with political power in neighbouring countries such as Pakistan and Iran. As resistance to reform developed so divisions in the communist movement widened. Arms and other forms of support for the Mujahedeen and the warlords poured into the country from within the region and from the United

States, which was anxious to embarrass the Soviet Union and halt the spread of progress. Then, over Christmas 1979, the Soviet Union intervened militarily to overthrow the government, install its own preferred leader, and quell the armed revolt that had been led by the Mujahedeen with considerable outside support. There began a long-term and disastrous military commitment which eventually led to withdrawal, and set back for years to come the prospects for progressive change in Afghanistan.[20]

Ramelson was sent to Afghanistan in the early days of communist rule to attend a Solidarity Conference called by the Afghan government. His first reports were extremely positive, analysing both the achievements and difficulties facing the new regime. These difficulties included the continuing incidents of border skirmishes, initiated by dissident elements and mercenaries, sometimes trained by agents of the CIA and based in Pakistan and Iran. Speakers representing the government were confident that, with assistance from the international community, particularly the Soviet Union, these counter-revolutionary forces could be contained, and that they had no substantial base of support from within Afghanistan itself. Ramelson recognised that the stakes were high. If Afghan communists could make a success of their attempts to move towards a more equal society with the fraternal assistance of the Soviet Union, this would have a positive demonstrative effect among millions of the Muslim poor throughout the world, including within the Asian Republics of the Soviet Union.[21]

The Soviet military intervention was to change all this. In Ramelson's eyes it offended the principles of international law and relationships between socialist states. It was clear to Ramelson that Soviet military power had been used to change the political leadership of a neighbouring state in order to install a government to suit Moscow's wishes. The principle of non-interference in the affairs of sovereign nations had been blatantly ignored, as it had during the Prague Spring in 1968. It was therefore beholden on communists to protest and campaign against the Soviet Union's actions, and to seek an end to all foreign interference in Afghanistan. Ramelson made his and the British CP's views absolutely clear – publicly in a letter to the *Morning Star*,[22] and privately within the channels open to him as an editorial board member of *World Marxist Review*.

The stance taken by the Party's Executive Committee provoked a lively correspondence in the *Morning Star*. Many of the published letters were critical of the British Party's position and in support of the Soviet military intervention. Perhaps the letter from Jack Gaster, a former Communist Councillor in London and highly respected veteran activist, best sums up the opposition position. In this Gaster argued:

> There is a principle, not the so-called principle of non intervention but the principle of international class solidarity. Long before December the USSR had made it clear that it could not stand by and let external aggression threaten its allies. [23]

After several letters of similar bent, Ramelson felt it necessary to intervene in the debate. His letter was characteristically robust in tone. It argued that the critics dodged the real issue, which was whether Afghanistan was threatened with outside imperialist aggression that the Afghans could not deal with themselves and whether it was the Afghan government that had asked for military intervention by the Red Army. He recalled the solidarity conference in Kabul which he had attended in August 1979, where it had been made clear that the Afghan government felt confident that with Soviet assistance (not military occupation) it could handle imperialist-inspired raids. Ramelson concluded his letter as follows:

> No satisfactory explanation has yet been given as to what catastrophic change took place in the following [after August] months to make intervention necessary ... Nor had it been established that a legitimate Afghan authority asked for such intervention. [24]

This was, however, a much more difficult case to make within the British CP than had been the situation at the time of the 1968 Czech intervention. In Afghanistan reactionary forces supported by US money and arms were clearly at play, and if they were to be successful then the prospects of social progress for the whole of the region would be seriously and adversely affected. So it is no surprise that many within the British Party argued for support for the Soviet Union's professed claim of protecting the legitimate Afghan government from internal and external military threat. Others argued for a more circumspect line in the special circumstances facing progressives in Afghanistan: to

condemn the Soviet action but to use it as a lever to secure the demili-
tarisation of the country, perhaps with UN involvement.

In essence the critics of the Party leadership were saying that it
was one thing to apply the principle of non-interference to
Czechoslovakia in 1968, where the elected government was intent on
a programme of reform which in no way threatened the interests of
the Soviet Union and which had widespread support within the CP.
It was quite another to condemn Soviet actions in support of a
socialist regime that was introducing progressive reforms in the teeth
of opposition from profoundly reactionary forces that were openly
supported by the major imperialist power. Within the Party groups
of members strongly supported the Soviet action. This included some
people who did so on a reflexive basis, seeing the world as a straightforward struggle between the forces of socialism and those of
imperialism, in which the Soviet Union, by definition, could and
should not be criticised. Other groups – for example communist
sympathisers of Asian origin based in Southall and Leicester – felt
particular bonds of solidarity with Afghan Communists and strongly
argued the need to protect progressive groups in the country, partly
in order to change the balance of forces in favour of socialist advance
in the region as a whole.

When this issue was debated at the British CP Congress in 1981,
the leadership line prevailed, but for a CP Congress it was a close run
thing (60 per cent to 40 per cent), and at least one very experienced
insider at the time has told us that the leadership had to pull out all the
stops to secure its thin majority.[25] The same observer is of the view that
this was a turning point for the Party's General Secretary, Gordon
McLennan. Concerned by what he saw as a threat from pro-Soviet
elements to capture the Party and thus compromise its position as an
independent movement in the eyes of British progressive opinion, he
determined to throw his lot in with the neo-Gramscians organised
around *Marxism Today*. In the years that followed, and much to
Ramelson's chagrin and frustration, McLennan steadfastly continued
to support these elements, and as General Secretary he ensured that
Party loyalists followed his line. The irony is that Ramelson was among
the strongest advocates of the principle of non-interference, recognising that failing to do so undermined efforts to build peaceful
co-existence in the world, while helping to legitimise imperialist
adventurers around the globe. On the crucial issue of the role of the

organised working class in the revolutionary process, the neo-Gramscians, with McLennan's support, increasingly distanced themselves from Ramelson's classic Marxist position and helped create the conditions for the CPGB's liquidation in the 1990s.

POLAND

No sooner had the furore over the Soviet military intervention in Afghanistan died down somewhat than a new crisis for the international communist movement reached fever point. Not for the first time in Poland, an attempt to cut subsidies and impose price increases in order to reduce government debt and rebalance the economy had led to hardship and opposition. As in 1970 and 1976, this provoked mass opposition, culminating in the strikes and the occupation of the giant Gdansk shipyards, a major source of foreign exchange earnings for the Polish economy. What started as an industrial dispute allied to demands for new independent trade union structures developed to become a mass social movement of workers and intellectuals campaigning for fundamental political change. The Solidarnosc trade unions rapidly grew, and by the end of the 1980s clearly represented an alternative power to the Communist government and the state it headed.[26] Under great pressure, the Polish Party leadership made considerable concessions to the workers' demands in order to settle the industrial dispute at Gdansk. As Ramelson pointed out a few months later, the crisis went much deeper than purely economic or trade union grievances. The Polish people were profoundly dissatisfied with the existing regime. Many had longstanding grievances concerning democratic rights, and these overlaid deep-seated ideological differences, based on the mass nature of the Catholic Church and Poland's historical enmity with Russia. Writing in *Marxism Today* and replying to a piece by a leading neo-Gramscian, Martin Myant, Ramelson outlined the chronic nature of the crisis and stressed that its solution would neither be quick nor tidy:

> I have heard four Polish representatives from the current leadership in Havana, Prague and twice in Sofia at international gatherings, speaking to a not always sympathetic audience. Yet all of them stressed precisely the fact of the genuinely spontaneous and under-

standable eruption of the movement of discontent, and minimised as of not great significance the existence of indigenous and foreign provocative elements in it. [27]

At this stage Ramelson was clearly of the view that the Communist leadership in Poland had both the will and the ability to reach a negotiated compromise with its critics. As on other occasions, in his fervent hope that the Party would step up to the challenge his optimism was not rewarded. By mid-December 1981 the authorities had declared martial law, arrested the Solidarnosc leadership and put troops on the streets. Not for the first time Ramelson had clearly put optimism of the will above pessimism of the intellect, but the evidence suggests that the doubts he felt about important features of government and society in the Soviet bloc were now beginning to multiply.

GROWING DIVISIONS WITHIN THE CPGB

The CPGB's influence peaked during Ramelson's watch as industrial organiser. If there was a turning point that can be identified as marking the time when CP influence began to decline, perhaps it was the acceptance by wide sections of the trade union left of the Social Contract in 1974/5. The good fight was fought but the balance of forces within the labour movement was such that the battle was lost, and the left since has not been able to recover. This was linked to and compounded by the abject failure of successive Labour governments, which prepared the way for a resurgent right-wing Toryism in an international situation that was increasingly unfavourable for the progressive movement. In this environment it is hardly surprising that the CPGB suffered setbacks, including substantial membership decline. The events that followed the 1979 watershed, epitomised by Thatcher's election in Britain, were cataclysmic for the Party – and in some ways self-induced.

As we have seen, the Party leadership had survived the 1981 Congress challenge, shaken but not seriously threatened by a coherent threat to its authority. Bubbling away just under the surface was the *Marxism Today* question. Under the energetic editorship of Martin Jacques, the journal had been transformed from a serious communist publication into an eclectic journal with a bent for radical sociology rather than political economy, and a feel for contemporary political debate on the left. By its own lights it was very successful, and it enjoyed constantly rising sales – though commercially it still relied on a significant financial subsidy from the Party to keep afloat.[28] The biggest problem was that it divided opinion in the Party. Many, like the General Secretary, saw *Marxism Today's* success as an important breakthrough for the Party, enabling it to reach out to a new audience and to bring new energy to the development of Marxism in a British context. To others, like Ramelson, it appeared that McLennan was grasping at straws, particularly since it was evident by the mid-1980s that the Party was losing influence among organised workers and labour movement activists – where it mattered most. For Ramelson, by the early 1980s the journal was no longer reflecting the main thrust of Party policy as determined by successive Congresses. In particular, in a letter to Gordon McLennan, he cited articles supporting incomes policy and attacking the Party's alternative economic strategy as being outdated.[29] Of course Ramelson argued his corner. In Klugmann's time as editor he had been a regular contributor to *Marxism Today* of articles on a range of issues, particularly economic and industrial questions, and Middle East politics. He had also written most of the editorial comment on trade union developments in the late 1960s and early 1970s. As Jacques's position became more secure, he was able to sideline Ramelson's influence. When Ramelson submitted an article jointly authored with Jim Mortimer, the former General Secretary of the Labour Party, Jacques promised to publish it at a later date but then proceeded to sit on it for a year. That these two doyens of the labour movement, both Marxists, both highly experienced, might have had something important to say about contemporary developments in the labour movement was apparently less important to Jacques than the need to promote his world view and to fill the pages of *Marxism Today* with articles from new and often non-Marxist perspectives. After several letters politely requesting that Jacques run the article as he had originally promised, Ramelson received a scruffy almost illegible handwritten note indicating that the article was still being considered for publication – space allowing.[30]

The differences in the Party about the role of *Marxism Today* became a major contributory factor in the organisational splits of the1980s. In September 1982, a week before the start of the annual TUC Congress, a gathering to which the Party accorded great importance, *Marxism Today* published an article by Tony Lane, a university lecturer who had spent a few months on secondment to the TGWU.[31] It purported to illustrate the failure of the trade union movement to respond to the changing industrial geography of Britain. Perhaps more damagingly, it focused on what Lane described as the creation of a new working-class elite sharing in the perks of the expense account syndrome. Here he was referring to full-time union convenors bargaining at company level on behalf of workers often spread across several industrial locations. The implication, not fully spelt out, was that such union representatives were in fact morphing into company men or women, travelling together with the plant managers to high level company-wide meetings, usually in London. Such behaviour, alleged Lane, led to rank-and-file cynicism and resentment, and fuelled uncertainty about 'whether the unions were worth fighting for'. All this is based on assertion, with practically no evidence from primary or even secondary sources. Any article that included the statements that 'The city too has a large and diverse population and this bestows on the individual a certain social invisibility', and that 'the unions are continuously making shabby compromises where equity is subordinated to expediency' – without a single example or piece of research to back up these assertions – should have been referred back for rewriting. But it was not.

It was then that the editor of the *Morning Star* Tony Chater, already at loggerheads with the Party leadership over the relationship between the paper's Management Committee and the CP's Executive Committee, decided to act. After a short and hurriedly arranged discussion with Party national industrial organiser Mick Costello, Chater published a news item in the paper, describing Costello's disquiet about the timing and content of the *Marxism Today* piece. The *Morning Star* story went on to point out that sections of the press had used Lane's article to discredit the Party and the shop stewards movement.[32]

There followed an unholy row in the top echelons of the Party, which ended up with the Political Committee, by a narrow majority, strongly criticising Chater and Costello, arguing – with some justification – that the points at issue should have been discussed within Party structures before any individual statements were made. Within a few weeks Costello had resigned his Party position and returned to the *Morning Star* as its industrial editor, while the gulf between Chater and McLennan developed into what was to prove to be an unbridgeable chasm.

Ramelson watched these events with dismay. He had not been consulted by Chater and Costello, and, while he shared many of their views, particularly in relation to the role of *Marxism Today*, he felt that their actions were precipitate and damaging. He also recognized that the publication of the Lane article was a provocation. In Ramelson's eyes it illustrated and emphasised that the *Marxism Today* tendency was out of Party control, and that the editor was determined to use his considerable influence to challenge Congress policy and the basic tenets of the *British Road to Socialism* concerning the leading role of the working class in the revolutionary process. The Lane affair was symptomatic of the deep divisions that had developed since the neo-Gramscians had won leading positions in the Party, and had begun using their newly-gained power to steer the Party's approach in new directions.

It was Ramelson's assessment that developments within *Marxism Today* were a far greater danger to Party unity and influence than was the abrogation of Party practice committed by Chater and Costello. What Ramelson could not fully anticipate at the time was that the single-minded determination of Jacques to drive out all those in opposition to their tendency would lead to his own temporary exclusion from the Party a few years down the line. In the struggle for hegemony within the Party the neo-Gramscians now turned their attention to the *Morning Star*, the 'Party's' newspaper and the only daily socialist publication in Britain. The paper was widely read by Party members and had considerable influence in the broad left of the labour movement.

THE CRISIS AT THE *MORNING STAR*

The formal relationship between the Party and the paper was complicated. Since 1946 the paper (then the *Daily Worker*) had been a co-operative owned by shareholders – the People's Press Printing Society (PPPS) – on a one share-holding one vote principle – thus a reader with a single one-pound share had as many votes as a big union with 2,000 such shares. The shareholders elected a Management Committee at AGMs in a secret ballot, and this Committee ran the paper, including the appointment of the editor. Formally speaking the CP stood outside of this process. In practice, until the rupture in relations, the editor had always been a member of the CP's Political

Committee, and shareholders had regularly reaffirmed that the paper's editorial line should be guided by the principles and strategy outlined in the *British Road to Socialism*.

During 1982 and 1983 the relationship became increasingly strained as the CP Executive Committee began to interfere in Management Committee affairs. This interference ran from the petty to the fundamental. In late 1982 the EC – though it did not have the facts on which to make such a decision – queried the Management Committee decision to introduce a price rise, counter-proposing a somewhat larger one. At around the same time it insisted that Beatrix Campbell, who was in the neo-Gramscian camp, should be given the right of reply to an article by Management Committee member Barbara Switzer, in which Switzer had criticised an anti-union piece by Campbell that had been published in the *Guardian*.

The EC insisted that Campbell be given 1,500 words to reply. The editor was prepared to offer 500 words, in line with previous practice, but no agreement could be reached.[33] In both these cases the Management Committee declined to accept the proffered advice from the Party leadership. There then followed the sort of circular argument which sometimes occurs within democratic centralist structures. The Party EC insisted that the editor, who was of course one of their number, should fight for their decisions at the Management Committee even though he disagreed with them personally. Clearly the editor was in an impossible position if he wanted to continue the existing editorial line of the paper and carry out the wishes of the elected Management Committee. He could of course have resigned, but unless the Management Committee had capitulated before CP tutelage this would have solved nothing. So impasse was reached.

At the Party Congress in November 1983, the EC adopted a course which ensured that the breach would be permanent. The Party's EC was elected by Congress delegates, who were presented with a recommended list of candidates to vote for by the outgoing EC. This list was then 'defended' against suggestions for changes during the Congress by the Election Preparation Committee (EPC), which was appointed by the outgoing EC. Individual delegates supporting particular candidates, all of whom had to be nominated by the branches, could make representations to the EPC that their candidate should be included on the list, but the EPC had the final decision. This belt and braces approach ensured that the recommended list rarely varied from that first proposed by the EC, and it was rarer still for candidates not on the list to be successful candidates in the voting for the EC. At the 1983 Congress, rather than keeping doors open for further discussions between a new EC and the Management Committee, the EC decided to exclude Tony Chater from its recommended list, almost guaranteeing his defeat in the elections at the Congress. In the event, even without being on the list Chater secured 106 votes, against the average vote of 150 for successful candidates, despite the highly managed nature of the process involved. At the PPPS AGM, the majority of votes were decisively cast for Management Committee-backed candidates, including Chater; there was little doubt that the majority of *Morning Star* readers supported the editor's position.

These developments deeply worried Ramelson. Gordon McLennan later recalled that he had given Ramelson a lift home following the Congress, which Bert had attended as a Consultative Delegate. During the journey Ramelson had expressed serious disquiet at what he now saw as an unbridgeable rift, following the EC-inspired move to remove Chater from the Party leadership.[34]

Ramelson was less than happy about some of the actions of the Management Committee and Chater. He thought the *Star*'s criticism of *Marxism Today* during the Lane affair was precipitate and exaggerated, while the description of the CP as an 'outside' body by Costello had been politically inept as well as inaccurate, except in the narrowest literalist way. His main criticism was reserved for the CPGB's EC and its refusal to reach an understanding with the *Morning Star*'s Management Committee rather than seeking to impose its own position. The exclusion from the EC of Tony Chater had effectively closed the door to the possibility of a rapprochement. Ramelson saw that the rupture was likely to become permanent, since rules and administrative methods were being used to cement divisions, instead of political discussion being initiated that was aimed at mending fences. He was to be proved right.

During 1984, the rift between the CP leadership and the Management Committee of the *Morning Star* deepened. To Ramelson this was a symptom of a deep malaise, and a clear sign that the Party was taking a revisionist path, and deserting key concepts of its revolutionary strategy as outlined in the *British Road to Socialism*. On 17 January 1985 the *Morning Star* published a 1000-word letter addressed to the EC by Ramelson, in a major feature article spread over two pages. In this he identified four areas of particular concern: the Executive Committee's resort to widespread administrative measures that were quite alien to the Party's practice since 1956 if not earlier; its disregard or at best arbitrary use of the rules; its general handling of the problem of the 'special relationship' with the *Morning Star*; and its acquiescence over a long period with *Marxism Today*'s being out of tune with Party policy on a number of policy issues, and failure by the leadership to put forward the Party's position in the journal.

The Party's house journal *Focus* printed a long reply to this letter penned by Dave Priscott, who had succeeded Ramelson as Yorkshire District secretary in the 1960s. Priscott paid tribute to Bert's record – he could do no less, but he went on to say that 'the strategy and tactics which Bert applied with such energy, skill and success in that period [mid-1960s to mid-1970s] are manifestly not working now in this very difficult period in which ruling class strategy has entered the new phase we call "Thatcherism".[35]

Ramelson was far from convinced that what *Marxism Today* identified as 'Thatcherism' had tilted the balance of forces to such a dramatic extent that traditional forms of class struggle, whether industrial or political, had become problematic. For Ramelson 'Thatcherism' was very much within the Tory tradition; it was in many ways akin to Heath's 'Selsdon man' approach, which had seen the introduction of anti-union laws and cash limits in the public sector at the beginning of the 1970s. The mass movement had seen off Selsdon Man and forced Heath to retreat, and in Ramelson's view, given the same determination and political leadership it could and should have challenged Thatcher's government.

Ramelson's article in the *Star* had little to say about policy questions or strategic issues, except in his argument that the editorial policy of *Marxism Today* was consistently straying from Party Congress decisions and consistently giving space to articles which understated the leading role of the working class in the revolutionary process. At this stage Ramelson was more concerned to prevent the rift with the *Morning Star* from becoming permanent, and to halt the growing number of expulsions of Party members who were critical of the EC, which was threatening to destroy the Party as an organised force. Within a few years his fears would become realities, and older comrades such as Priscott would see the liquidation of the Party they had given their life's work to building. They had defended the Party's rules and democratic centralism like pre-1956 Bolsheviks, only to be outmanoeuvred by the *Marxism Today* tendency and led down a cul-de-sac of extra-labour movement single-issue politics.

Ramelson's attempts to build bridges failed as the Party EC continued to campaign against the elected *Morning Star* Management Committee. At the June 1985 PPPS AGM, the Party's attempt to elect a new Management Committee packed with EC supporters was soundly defeated.[36] Shareholders, mainly CP members, packed the Wembley Conference Centre and at the biggest ever AGM voted overwhelmingly for the Management Committee's nominees. For example, incumbent Management Committee member Tom Sibley received 3,017 votes, while Ron Halverson, CPGB Executive Committee nominee, got 1,965 votes.[37]

The internal dispute was still in full flow when, in 1984-5, Britain's miners took on the government and the state apparatus in a determined campaign to prevent pit closures and save their communities, in a dispute which was to become the biggest class confrontation in Britain since the 1926 General Strike. This struggle was to expose still further the inner-party differences that had emerged during the previous decade.

THE 1984-1985 MINERS' STRIKE[38]

As we have seen, Ramelson was still regularly consulted by both CP and trade union leaders well after his retirement as national industrial organiser. He continued to take a close interest in trade union questions and was supplied with copies of TUC General Council papers by his trade union comrades for most of the 1980s. It is no surprise, therefore, that from the start of the overtime ban and then the first day that the miners came out on strike Ramelson became deeply engaged in support for their cause. It was after all with the Yorkshire miners that he had first developed the broad left strategy which was to transform the NUM and to lead to positive developments in many other unions. As we have seen during the 1970s, on Ramelson's watch as CP National Organiser, the miners had won two national disputes, the second of which had effectively brought down the Tory government in 1974. During these struggles – in Yorkshire and nationally – Ramelson had won the respect and confidence of the NUM left leaders who were in the forefront of the 1984-5 dispute. In particular he had a good working relationship with Arthur Scargill, Mick McGahey and Peter Heathfield, the three senior officials in the union.

The Thatcher government, whose popularity had been boosted during the Falklands war, had won a second election victory in 1983 and was now intent on taking on the miners and running down the publicly owned coal industry.[39] From an economic standpoint such a strategy would remove the modest central government subsidy that was necessary to keep open the less profitable pits, and help prepare the most profitable for privatisation. In political terms the Thatcher government saw the strike as an opportunity to break the industrial strength of the NUM, a union which in recent history had been strong enough to bring down the Heath government, and to frustrate her earlier pit-closure plans in 1982. For the Tories the political imperative was to weaken trade union power, and the NUM, led by the left, was a key target in carrying through such a strategy.

Ramelson made no public statements during the strike and there were no articles or speeches from him in this period. He did comment later, and there are several letters and memos in his personal papers which show how he felt at the time. Not surprisingly, Ramelson started in optimistic vein. He saw the dispute as eminently winnable and therefore as a political opportunity to seriously damage a right-wing Tory government which was presiding over mass unemployment, introducing anti-union laws, and, in alliance with the US, undermining proposals for world peace and nuclear disarmament. In Ramelson's view the stakes were very high: the battle required a completely united labour movement response in solidarity with the miners if the Tories were to be defeated. If such solidarity was forthcoming, possibilities would emerge for the miners who were still working – mainly in the profitable Nottinghamshire Coalfield – to join the strike, thus healing the rift in the NUM and quickly reducing the coal stocks available to the electricity supply industry.[40]

As the dispute went on and it became increasingly clear that the necessary industrial solidarity was not forthcoming, Ramelson became concerned to find a way out which would at least protect the NUM's position, by means of a revised Pit Closure Review procedure and a new *Plan for Coal* which would keep existing production levels. In this situation Ramelson felt that some concessions would have to be made to the NCB's position if a negotiated settlement protecting jobs and communities was to be achieved.

In November 1984, six months into the strike, Ramelson was asked by CP General Secretary McLennan to intercede with Scargill. By this time it was clear that the TUC General Council was unable (or unwilling) to mobilise the movement's industrial power in support of the miners, and that in these circumstances the current strategy was unlikely to force the NCB and the government to back down. This state of affairs was underlined in early October when NACODS (National Association of Colliery Overmen, Deputies and Shotfirers) withdrew its strike threat on being offered a revised Pit Closure Review procedure which fell far short of the NUM's ambitions. Had NACODS members joined the strike no pit in the Nottingham coalfields could have continued production, since they were responsible for health and safety issues in the mines.

Ramelson's view at this stage was that the NUM leadership needed to change tack and put more emphasis on finding a pit closure agreement which would fit in with a new Plan for Coal (with increased output targets); and it looked as if it would have to concede that, in the most extreme cases, there could be an economic case made for closure (as opposed to closure on the grounds of exhaustion of reserves, or on health and safety or geological reasons). Building on research carried out on behalf of the Scottish NUM, Ramelson argued that pits showing consistently large financial deficits should be put into the review process; and if it could then be shown that future additional investment in such pits would be uneconomic, and that the overall costs to the community in terms of loss of jobs, unemployment benefit, and social security payments would be less than the subsidy needed to keep such pits open, in these conditions, and these conditions only, a case for closure could be made on economic grounds. Such cost-benefit analysis, taking into account all relevant social as well as economic factors, could underpin the case for increased state subsidies, particularly at a time when alternative sources of energy were costly or beyond the government's ability to control. In other words, argued Ramelson, a genuine national interest case could be made for subsidising coal production at higher levels, which would both protect jobs and communities and guarantee secure energy supplies.[41] If the dispute could not be won industrially, which was Ramelson's judgement after the NACODS decision not to strike, then political pressure on the Tories had to be turned up. The key was to find an economic argument for increased coal production while conceding that in some circumstances pit closures could be justified on economic grounds.

Through McGahey's good offices Ramelson met Scargill on 12 December 1984. Although we have no exact account of what occurred, it is clear that there was no meeting of minds. According to notoriously unreliable Secret Service sources, based on bugged recordings at the CP headquarters, Ramelson reported, presumably to McLennan, that he had found the miners' leader 'tired and strained' and 'unable to admit that his current strategy is wrong'. According to the bugged evidence Ramelson, ever the optimist, expressed the hope that Scargill would read seriously the document presented to him and that a further meeting between the two men might ensure.[42] There is no evidence that a further meeting took place, however, and the NUM's tactics did not change until the return to work without agreement in March 1985. The Secret Service version of events broadly corresponds to that of Paul Routledge, who interviewed Ramelson while researching his biography of Scargill, and these two accounts do appear to capture the essence of Ramelson's role.[43]

In retrospect it is clear that Ramelson's intervention, which essentially was McGahey's attempt to put pressure on Scargill, was too late to be fruitful. No doubt Ramelson expressed his views throughout the dispute, and would have discussed the issues involved with McLennan, McGahey and Pete Carter, who was the Party's industrial organiser at the time. The Party leadership was therefore aware of Ramelson's views, and McGahey clearly felt that Ramelson might make more progress with Scargill than he himself had managed. The meeting with Scargill was not Ramelson's initiative: it was a desperate attempt by the CP, and in particular McGahey, to convince Scargill that a new more flexible approach to pit closures was required.[44] By this time it was probably the case that no amount of fancy footwork would have moved the government. A trickle of miners was by now slowly returning to work, the government was confident that coal stocks would last the winter, and that the strike would not spread to Nottinghamshire. Ministers knew that they had the whip hand, and, short of effective industrial action by the TUC and the power station workers, that was likely to remain the case until all the miners were forced back to work. And so it proved.

When the miners' strike began Ramelson was seventy-four and had been retired from full-time Party work for seven years. He was still widely consulted, and in private would let all who would listen have the benefit of his views. But, like the CP itself, he was only a bit part player in the great drama that was the miners' strike. That things came to such a pass, with the CP isolated and ineffective during a massively important dispute, is what really matters for this biography of Ramelson. This goes a long way towards explaining how Ramelson could become estranged from the Party he loved, and why that Party, with its proud record of leadership and involvement in industrial struggles, was to self-destruct less than a decade later.

The Secret Service files show that as early as July 1984 Ramelson was expressing strong criticism of industrial organiser Pete Carter's analysis of the strike, and was trying to persuade the CP leadership 'to extend their influence in the Miners' Strike'.[45] This criticism was expressed in Ramelson's writings after the strike. At issue were the differing approaches to securing political progress and revolutionary change. For Ramelson the key dynamic was class struggle and the ability of a revolutionary Party to influence this with its socialist perspective. So in the miners' dispute the number one priority was to make it possible for the miners to win the dispute by bringing key sections of the organised working class – in this case the power workers, the steelworkers and the transport workers in particular – into solidarity action with the miners. If this could be done, then, together with the miners' picketing efforts, the NCB and the government could have been forced to renegotiate the pit closure programme. The miners had to fight for their industry and their communities. The rest of the movement had a vested interest in doing all within its power to ensure that the miners were successful.

All this is made clear in Ramelson's correspondence with Pete Carter. In a sharply worded letter, dated 20 April 1985, he said:

> All my criticisms I made of the first draft … are even more valid of the 2nd draft [of Carter's position on the miners' strike]. It is an unmitigated all-out attack (though unnamed) on the Miners' leadership. The major weakness – the failure of developing more solidarity industrial action – is ignored. It was the absence of continuous campaigning at factory, local and national levels involving the shop stewards, local r&f committees, actions etc. The impact of the pamphlet is defeatist, demoralising, mesmerised by Thatcher's invincibility. Can only inhibit struggle unless there is almost a priori

guarantee of victory based on having won the vast majority of the people to support it.[46]

Ramelson's analysis of the strike is set out in his 1986 pamphlet *Consensus or Socialism*. In this he argues:

> … the miners had no choice but to take on MacGregor [the newly appointed chair of the NCB] when, in collusion with, and on behalf of, the Tory government, he decided to launch his attack on the jobs and communities. They could not wait for prior guarantees of solidarity from the movement before engaging in the battle. No doubt the miners' leaders have made mistakes. No great battle has ever been fought without mistakes. But these did not decide the outcome. As with any major class confrontation, the outcome was decided by the existing balance of forces. Someone ought to tell *Marxism Today* and the Communist Party's industrial department this elementary fact. They should be reminded about the total mobilisation of all the state agencies. They should be told about the mobilisation of the media to lie and to slander the miners – with one honourable exception, the *Morning Star*.
>
> And on the other side of the balance, they should be told about the failure of Kinnock, the majority of the TUC General Council and the Communist Party to mobilise solidarity action on the scale required, particularly in the power industry and transport. In saying that, I do not in any way underestimate the extent of popular support for the miners that developed during their long strike. But it was not mobilised in the decisive sectors.
>
> The outcome was determined by this unfavourable balance of forces, which could only have been changed by mobilising massive solidarity in the course of the strike, and this was not done.[47]

What is noteworthy here is the open and public criticism of the CP leadership at a time when Ramelson was still a member, and had some residual influence, particularly among industrial comrades. In private Ramelson was also critical of aspects of the NUM's campaign. His heavily annotated copy of Frank Watters's memoirs indicates that he was most critical of the approach adopted early on in trying to win over the Nottingham miners to the national union's campaign.[48] In the margins of the book there are dozens of notes in Ramelson's untidy handwriting. Why, he asks, did the union use Yorkshire pickets in Nottingham? Why not use the Nottingham miners who supported the strike to picket Nottingham pits still working? Why was there so much confrontation with fellow miners rather than a more patient approach combining picketing (with Nottingham NUM members on picket duty) and a broader political campaign of meetings, leaflets and so on to make the case?

The priorities and assessment of the neo-Gramscian/Eurocommunist wing of the Party, spearheaded by *Marxism Today*, were substantially different from Ramelson's. In essence they were intent on playing down the leading role of the working class in the revolutionary process in order to promote the growing importance, as they saw it, of various movements and social groups who were objectively oppressed by monopoly capitalism and could be at the centre of new alliances to challenge the hegemony of the capitalist state. Thus during the strike the CP leadership gave greater priority to the question of alliance building and winning broad public support than it did to mobilising effective industrial solidarity with the miners. As was claimed during the pre-1985 Congress discussions, during the dispute not a single industrial advisory meeting was called of CP union members in a position to influence events.

In a letter to Pete Carter dated 6 October 1986, Ramelson expressed both his frustration with the leadership and the reasons why, despite this, he continued to offer advice and guidance. The letter was as follows:

> Dear Pete, You asked me to put down in writing a) a description of the pre-automatic system of GC election to the TUC, b) an assessment of it, c) a criticism of the current system and d) proposals for change. In reply to your request I am enclosing a 'paper' covering your requests. Though I wonder why you asked me, since you ignore any advice I've given you, in my view harming the Party's standing in the TU movement. I suppose I've done so, because I continue to stick to the 'guiding principle' I have set myself in this difficult period we are going through, namely, to respond to anyone seeking my views and opinions, on issues they consider my opinion worth having, and what I believe will benefit the movement. Yours, Bert Ramelson.[49]

It was now clear to Ramelson that the *British Road to Socialism*, in John Foster's words, had been hijacked by the *Marxism Today* section of the Party leadership.[50] This was a bitter pill for Ramelson, a man who had worked all his political life in Britain guided by a revolutionary strategy which recognised the basic Marxist positions concerning the primacy of class division and conflict, and the consequences which flowed from this, particularly the leading role of the working class. Now he saw the Party's industrial work being downgraded, and the public voice of the Party, *Marxism Today*, being used to downplay the role of the unions while questioning the credibility of the Alternative Economic Strategy that Ramelson himself had made a major contribution to formulating. While he would never give up the struggle, Ramelson must have realised in 1986 that the prospects for communist renewal had seldom been bleaker. Despite Ramelson's best efforts to find a way forward avoiding continuing division and inner-party strife, it now appeared that a formal split was the most likely outcome.

A POSTSCRIPT TO THE MINERS' STRIKE

After the strike Ramelson and Scargill corresponded regularly. Whatever happened at the December 1984 meeting does not appear to have seriously affected their relationship, which was based on mutual respect. Ramelson admired Scargill's commitment to his members and his fearless advocacy of socialist policies and approaches. Above all he recognised Scargill's qualities as a class warrior – as a leader who saw the necessity of promoting and organising mass struggle to defend and advance working-class interests. In Ramelson's view, Scargill's approach had much more to recommend it in the struggle for socialism than did the rather cautious and reactive responses of most trade union leaders during this period. Ramelson was not blind to the problems caused by Scargill's inability to work with others in leadership positions as equals with valid contributions to make to collective decision-making. Neither was Ramelson uncritical, in private, of some of the tactics employed during the 1984-85 strike. These negative features were for him far outweighed by the positive aspects of Scargill's leadership – his ability to convince members of the need to fight for their jobs and communities rather than to leave it to their union leaders and Labour politicians, while consistently arguing for socialist solutions to problems caused by capitalist exploitation.

That the Ramelson-Scargill relationship remained cordial despite the strain of the miners' strike was evident a few years later in a very public way. In early 1988 a group of comrades began to plan a 'Tribute to Bert Ramelson' event. The invitations were sent out by Ken Brett, Assistant General Secretary of the AEU, and some 150 comrades came together on 28 April in a central London pub. The food was good and the band was excellent, encouraging dozens of couples to show their paces on the dance floor. The highlight of the evening was the speeches. Ramelson himself was in fine form, his voice undiminished in power and his message still clear and undiluted. He argued as forcefully as ever that struggle was the key to advance and that socialism was the only guarantee of human progress. He drew lessons from recent struggles and reminded his audience that 'the seamen's strike started a cycle of struggle which lasted a decade and achieved more than anything else in breaking the grip of the right wing';[51] and that 'the unity of the working class can compel a government to declare, "we surrender"'. After outlining the struggle and solidarity which had led to the defeat of Edward Heath he declared: 'That's the way you get rid of Thatcher'.

Arthur Scargill presented Ramelson with a miner's lamp and paid a warm tribute: 'He has been a leader to many of us in the labour movement, a constant inspiration, guide and comrade'.[52] Messages of appreciation were also received from other trade union activists and parliamentarians, including Tony Benn and Joan Maynard. One of the longer messages came from a group of retired Yorkshire USDAW members, who remembered that, despite his many responsibilities in the movement, Ramelson had always found time to 'pop into most of our Branch meetings, if only to squeeze a bit more activity out of us'. All present recognised the truth of the statement in the invitation letter that 'Bert Ramelson's contribution to our movement is enormous'. As Tony Benn's message put it, 'Bert has made a formidable contribution to the development of Socialism in Britain and has devoted his life to the strengthening of the labour movement'. AEUW Assistant General Secretary Bob Wright wrote: 'I regard Bert as a great Marxist and socialist. His knowledge and wisdom have on many occasions been an inspiration'.[53]

THE *BRITISH ROAD TO SOCIALISM* AND *MARXISM TODAY*

The growing divisions in the Party arising from Tony Lane's attack on the shop steward movement had quickly widened and were soon to assume crisis proportions. The central question that had been at issue during the 1977 congress debate on the *British Road to Socialism* – the level of relative importance in the movement for socialism of the working class and other social forces, and of the industrial struggle in comparison to other battles – simply would not go away. A serious reading of the final document of that Congress, and the speeches made at the time by Jack Woddis and Gordon McLennan, strongly supports the position that Ramelson advanced as Chair of the Congress *British Road to Socialism* Committee.

Put simply, Ramelson, McLennan, Woddis and the Congress supported a view that the organised working class was the only force capable of building and bringing into action a broad alliance of anti-capitalist forces. This would include all those sections of the people oppressed or exploited by capitalist property relations and the ruling class ideological superstructure. Left to themselves, these social movements had neither the organisational capacity nor the political clarity to seek alliances or to recognise that the roots of their oppression were class-based. The task facing revolutionaries was to convince the organised working class to take up and champion the cause of such movements, recognising of course that many of its own members were oppressed by gender, race and other forms of discrimination. The opponents of this position (represented by the neo-Gramscians and increasingly in the pages of *Marxism Today*) wanted to emphasise the trade union movement's weaknesses and to upgrade the significance of the various social movements (e.g. the women's movement, and black people's organisations).

After bubbling under the surface for a number of years, the issue re-emerged in early 1985. By then the neo-Gramscians were prepared to highlight the divisions in the Party and to accuse *Morning Star* supporters, including Ramelson, of denying that the 1977 Congress represented a fundamental break from the Party's traditional class-based approach. Furthermore, they argued that events since had presented a new challenge in the form of Thatcherism. As we have seen, Ramelson had strongly opposed the *Marxism Today* position that Thatcherism was something new in the ruling-class armoury. He had argued that Thatcher's response to the crisis for the British ruling class (which had arisen mainly from the growing strength and combativeness of the organised working class) was in most important respects a continuation of the policies followed by every Labour and Tory government since the mid-1960s. In a letter to *Focus* in July 1984 he put his position thus: 'Serious Marxists would locate the current phase as beginning in the mid-1960s when the post-war consensus era was eroded. It was then that the attacks on the unions, the welfare state and local government started'.[54]

In Ramelson's view the term 'Thatcherism' was journalese, and it was an unhelpful and ahistorical concept. Throughout the 1980s he came back to this argument: it had been the Wilson/Callaghan/Healey administration of the 1960s and 1970s which had first abandoned full employment and adopted monetarism as their overarching economic strategy. The election of Thatcher had not marked the beginning of a new direction for British capitalism. Rather, it was a continuation of policies followed since the 1960s, albeit in a somewhat more extreme form.

Arguments highlighting the divisions and accusing the *Morning Star* group of being disloyal to Party policy were first fully deployed by Party national organiser Dave Cook, in an article in *Marxism Today*.[55] The following month, John Foster, a *Marxism Today* editorial board member who opposed the line promoted by its editor, wrote in support of the approach put forward by Woddis and Ramelson at the 1977 Congress, as outlined above. With some justification he accused Cook of dividing the broad democratic alliance into social and class elements: 'What is so damaging is the fact that this formulation abstracts them [the social elements] from the class character of our society and thereby changes the ultimate relationship to the working class as a revolutionary class'. The article goes on to show that at least one of the groups identified by Cook as the enemy within was not culpable:

> It is not that Chater, Costello and Ramelson, to name but a few, finally came into the open as enemies of the *British Road*. On the contrary, these comrades were those most identified, practically as well as theoretically, with the creative development of strategy in the 1970s. It was precisely in this period that the working class, and in particular the shop stewards' movement, opened up crucial new areas of struggle and alliance.

Foster and Ramelson had clashed at the 1977 Congress about the replacement of the notion of the anti-monopoly alliance (Foster's preferred formulation since it emphasised a clear class position) by one of broad democratic alliance (a position that Ramelson accepted since it advocated the leading role of the working class while recognising the importance of all forms of oppression). Now they were united against what Foster called the hijacking of the *British Road to Socialism* by *Marxism Today* and its neo-Gramscian supporters.[56]

THE END-GAME AND NEW TIMES

The end of the CPGB was not long in coming. In March 1988 the neo-Gramscians in the leadership of the Party turned their attention to strategic issues. In their eyes it was necessary to abandon the approach of the *British Road to Socialism* with its emphasis on class struggle and the labour movement. What they required was an entirely new way forward that stressed the role played by the various social movements outside of the labour movement. The Party's EC set up a Commission with the task of preparing a discussion document ahead of the 1989 National Congress. The Commission was dominated by the leading lights of the *Marxism Today* group, with Martin Jacques very much in the driving seat. It worked quickly, and in September 1988 the document *Facing up to the Future* was published. This received a mixed reception. The document's overall drift was too much for some members of its drafting group. Monty Johnstone, Marian Darke and Bill Innes, who had each stuck with the CPGB with varying degrees of enthusiasm, now resigned, on the grounds that the document 'failed to recognize the centrality of the class struggle in capitalist Britain today'. Johnstone was uncompromising in his criticisms: 'the document's definitions of class were un-Marxist and confused – it is … unsustainable from any point of view'.[57]

Ramelson was quick to join the attack. In a 500-word article published in the Party's journal *Seven Days* he pulled no punches. He mocked the term post-Fordism as mere jargon, and predicted that by 2010, many, indeed most, commodities would still be mass produced by giant multinational companies and sold in look-alike high streets by giant hypermarkets. Indeed Ramelson's predictions rather than those of *Marxism Today*'s post-Fordist world seem to have better stood the test of time. As Ramelson went on to point out, even if there had been major changes in the forces of production, 'changes in the forces of production do not of themselves change the nature of the society if the social relations of production remain unchanged'. The article became increasingly sharp in tone as it progressed: 'we are asked to believe that class identity is not objectively determined ... but [is based on] what we subjectively believe oneself to be ... since Marx's days Marxists have combated this capitalist claptrap'. Finally: 'this document has no strategy for socialism at all. The objective is to defeat Thatcher not as a step towards socialism but towards a "New Order". Its shape and essence is a mystery that only time will divulge'. This is classic Ramelson. Insisting on the verities of Marxist analysis and focusing on revolutionary aims, he was exposing the vacuity of the alternatives to the *British Road to Socialism* that were being presented by those who claimed at the time to be renewing Marxism while offering a 'realistic' way forward. [58]

At a Special Congress in 1990, the leadership prepared the ground for winding up the Party; it would be succeeded, following discussion around a new constitution, by the Democratic Left – which subsequently became a loosely based organisation that gave great weight to the formation of networks and specialist groups. Before this process had been completed Martin Jacques and Beatrice Campbell, two leading members of the neo-Gramscian group, resigned, not wishing to be associated any longer with the communist movement. The pretext was the revelations concerning 'Moscow Gold', a modest subsidy provided by the Soviet Union which had ended in the 1970s.[59] This expression of practical solidarity with sister parties, which was widely assumed to be current practice by active Party members, provoked a show of moral outrage, led by Martin Jacques, on the grounds that, limited though it was, such a subsidy was likely to influence political decisions. That the payments were still being made in 1968 when the British Party condemned in forthright terms the Soviet intervention in Czechoslovakia did not apparently give Jacques pause for thought.

By 1991 the CPGB was no more. There was to be one final legacy – a new strategy document *The Manifesto for New Times*, which was drafted to replace the *British Road to Socialism*. *The Manifesto for New Times* brought together many of the ideas and analyses developed in the columns of *Marxism Today* over the previous ten years. Its general emphasis was on 'all conquering' Thatcherism, post-Fordism, and the need for new electoral alliances to challenge the Tories, all of which was predictable enough, based as it was on the *Facing the Future* document. Ramelson's views are shown in his heavily annotated copy of the document.[60] His notes and comments make it clear that he viewed *The Manifesto for New Times* as a utopian document which failed to explain how revolutionary social change was to be brought about. He was particularly critical of the document's treatment of the role of the unions and the structure and practices of the Labour Party.

All of this was taking place at the same time as the world-shattering events in the Soviet Union and in the other Eastern European countries in the Soviet camp. A coup in August 1990 to remove President Gorbachev from power was quickly followed by the disintegration of the Soviet Union. The 1917 Revolution and the People's Democracies established following the defeat of fascism in the Second World War were no more. All of this represented a disastrous setback for the world communist movement, and this was bound to be reflected in the considerations of the British communists. Ramelson made few public pronouncements on these developments, but privately he argued that what mattered in Britain was the continuation of a Marxist presence in the labour movement, and that the organised form that this would take was a secondary question.

In one of the last interviews he gave Ramelson is quoted as saying: 'In the end we are going to have socialism. There is no capitalist way of life for the majority of the world's population. But I know of no socialist political party which has yet even tried to build socialism'. The same interview has Ramelson describing the 1989/1990 events as a 'setback' and the 'result of serious mistakes' that could nevertheless be put right.[61] In a sense these last two sentences reveal a certain ambiguity in Ramelson's views. By the mid-1980s he had come to the view that the CPSU had sidelined the socialist project, but in public he had continued to argue that socialism (however limited by its specific application) was too deeply embedded in Soviet life for it to be abandoned.[62]

ASSESSING RAMELSON'S INTERVENTION

Ramelson has been criticised for not taking a more upfront public position during the disputes which eventuated in the split and the dissolution of the CPGB.[63] This criticism is difficult to justify. Here was a man by now in his late seventies, suffering from indifferent health. Since the early 1980s he had, however, eschewed the habits of a lifetime to publicly express serious misgivings about the Party's direction of travel since the neo-Gramscians had taken over. Critical articles by Ramelson in the *Morning Star* and letters to *Focus* and *Seven Days* were fairly frequent, and to Party activists Ramelson's position on these issues was well known.

The underlying problem was that Ramelson felt that a formal split was probably the worst possible outcome. For this reason, as Mary Davis told us, Ramelson saw his role to be that of a mediator, and he hoped that, as a senior Party figure, he could help persuade the two sides to co-exist. In a letter to the *Morning Star*, jointly signed by Ramelson, Bill Alexander and Nora Jefferys, he urged patience, arguing that events and struggle could enable the Party's rank and file to reverse the policies of the current leadership, restore membership to those expelled, and rebuild the relationship with the *Morning Star*. [64] The letter pointed out that 'nowhere have such splits furthered the cause of Communism'; and that 'it is defeatism to suppose that the developing capitalist crisis, the impact of class struggles will have no effect in exposing the bankruptcy of the policies of *Marxism Today* and thus changing the views of CPGB members to give a majority for the policies of the *Morning Star*'.[65]

Not for the first time Ramelson proved to be over-optimistic. He had underestimated the decline in Party activity and the impact on rank-and-file morale caused by implosion of the socialist countries in combination with the constant inner-party battles. Many of the industrial comrades who had provided bedrock support for Ramelson's strategy in the 1960s and 1970s had tended to be semi-detached communists who, despite Ramelson's constant pleading, failed to operate within basic Party units. The result was that Party leadership at branch and district level was in many cases controlled by supporters of the *Marxism Today* tendency, and the semi-detached members had neither the drive nor the organisational base to challenge this. The many good comrades Ramelson had in mind were too often world-weary and in their retirement years. They had little stomach for a long drawn out struggle to win back the Party.

The publication of the Ramelson, Alexander and Jefferys letter did nothing to halt the split from becoming formalised. For their trouble, the authors were publicly rebuked by *Star* editor Tony Chater, who rather disingenuously denied any involvement of the paper in the formation of an alternative Communist Party.[66] Chater and the paper's Management Committee Secretary Mary Rosser were soon to become leading members of the alternative organisations that were set up, the Communist Campaign Group and the Communist Party of Britain.[67]

Ramelson's approach was two-pronged. He took what opportunities there were to discuss issues with Gordon McLennan, and the archive shows that there were several unminuted meetings between the two, and a long discussion at the end of 1988.[68] From Ramelson's notes it is clear that there was no meeting of minds. He clearly felt that McLennan was a superb organiser but had insufficient grasp of Marxism. He also, in Ramelson's view, enjoyed basking in the reflected glory of *Marxism Today*, which during this period was widely praised by the non-Marxist left, mainly from the intellectual strata but also by Labour politicians such as Neil Kinnock. For a Party which had largely been ostracised by the liberal establishment since the early days of the Cold War, such praise was seductive, especially to a Communist leader anxious to be associated with a successful enterprise. Ramelson thought that McLennan was over-inclined to accept the arguments advanced by George Matthews, who by now had become a supporter of the *Marxism Today* group, Martin Jacques, and his own son Gregor McLennan (a university lecturer). On all the key issues during this period, McLennan gave support to the neo-Gramscian position. The archives include a note prepared by Ramelson before one of his periodic meetings with McLennan, dated 30 April 1986. Among its headings were:

- the Party spreads confusion – at best the Party often acts like a debating society for the elite
- much of *Marxism Today's* content is not in line with Congress policy
- need for wisdom in the use of rules. Lenin argued that politics is not only a science it is also an art.

We have no record of how the meeting went.

As ever, Ramelson was not content to limit himself to discussions and letter writing. He also saw the need to organise and to plan further actions with a group of like-minded comrades. Graham Stevenson recalls what he describes as a tightly organised meeting in early 1987, involving among others Ramelson, Bill Alexander and Frank Watters, who took handwritten notes of the meeting.[69] These comrades had decided to work for the best attainable vote against the EC's position on the *Morning Star* at the November Congress, and to re-assess the position after the Congress.

The evidence suggests that Ramelson worked hard to prevent a split and to win back the CPGB for what he considered to be a Marxist position. He failed, however, and we can now see that his estimates were always over-optimistic. The reality is that the neo-Gramscians, backed by McLennan, had a firm grasp on the Party machine, and the majority of the membership had neither the energy nor the conviction to win back the Party for its traditional approach. It is not as if Ramelson was not warned of the likely outcome. Some of his long-standing and closest comrades were not convinced by his call for caution and patience. During 1985 Ramelson was in regular (and long) correspondence with Norman Berry, who brought to his attention the proposed disciplining of his Halifax branch for having publicly expressed its disquiet about leadership's criticism of the NUM leadership following the 1984-1985 strike. Ramelson replied:

> The real problem is what to do about it. And here I think I'm of the same view as Bill [Alexander] – the worse thing at the moment is to allow ourselves to be provoked into a split. Patience, principled struggle for one's point of view and a degree of tolerance and a measure of confidence that what is happening politically today and every day will demonstrate the correctness of our view and how wrong some of the views propagated by the leadership. [70]

Berry was not won over:

> I appreciate what you mean when you say that when serious debate takes place in the Party we must be there to take our part in a rational and comradely exchange and comparison of ideas etc, etc, etc. But you know, it isn't going to take place is it? And, if and when it does, the scenario will be stage managed by those who own the theatre, won't it?
>
> And the 'advice' we might get, without the slightest evidence to validate it, is to stay in the Party and fight. And the expulsions will go on, as and when the EC decide, and we are out there like sitting ducks. Is it really practical to think in terms of having the support

within the Party by next Congress to replace the Euro-communists and their disastrous policies and outrageous conduct? Bert, you are a realist![71]

By May 1986 Ramelson must have come to understand more fully the import of Berry's warnings, for his own Sydenham branch was also facing disciplinary action by a higher Party Committee. In November 1984 Gordon McLennan had peremptorily closed the London District Congress, fearing that it was about to elect a leadership with a majority against the Eurocommunist direction being taken at national level. However, Sydenham's two representatives, along with the majority of delegates, defied McLennan's order to leave the Congress immediately, and were subsequently expelled from membership, despite the support they received from their branch colleagues. Throughout 1985 the branch had met monthly, with the two expelled members in attendance. After protracted correspondence the national leadership responded by dissolving the branch (in May 1986) and requiring all members to re-apply for their Party card, thereby reserving the right to exclude individual members.

Ramelson re-applied for membership, but under protest. In a letter to Ian MacKay, then National Organiser, he put it like this:

> Of course I accept ... the Constitution of the Party and all its rules, and therefore expect to be re-registered ... The procedure ... for the re-registration of the Sydenham Branch membership is, in my view, a wrong interpretation of rule by the EC ... annual re-registration has always been treated as a routine administrative act and not an application to retain membership requiring the approval of a Higher Committee ... I conclude by drawing your attention to rule 16(d) which recognises the right of members to have disagreements with decisions of the Party and their right to reserve their dissenting opinion.[72]

Thus after several months without a Party card Ramelson maintained his membership of some forty-eight years, but it was not a happy or satisfying reconciliation.[73]

These developments helped to reinforce Ramelson's growing conviction that democratic centralism was a system prone to corrupt misuse by Party leaderships anxious to stifle debate and repress opposition trends. Speaking at a *WMR* seminar in autumn 1986 on *The Communist Movement in a Changing World*, he argued that division had arisen as a result of dashed expectations concerning the collapse of capitalism, despite the chronic crisis of that system, and the failure of the socialist system to resolve many of the problems of developing a new society. These factors had led many to question the 'validity of aspects of Marxism-Leninism, leading to inner-party tensions and divisions',

> However, the need is not only to understand the processes which cause division, but to seek ways for overcoming disunity, to recreate and maintain unity through frank but comradely discussion of the differences, within the framework of democratic centralism – which to be of constructive assistance must be exercised with a considerable degree of tolerance.[74]

Here are Ramelson's first open expressions of doubts about democratic centralism, along with a plea for tolerance. Later came a full condemnation of the universal application of such procedures across the world communist movement. By 1989 Ramelson had clearly become totally disenchanted by the way the principles of democratic centralism had been distorted throughout the communist movement. As Ramelson put it, in practice 'democratic is the adjective and centralism the noun with the emphasis laid on the latter'.[75]

At a *WMR* Commission on the International Communist Movement held in autumn 1989, Ramelson was typically forthright in his analysis:

> All power corrupts, and absolute power corrupts absolutely [a familiar misquote from Lord Acton]. Over the past half century in the Party, I do not recall any important changes, including changes in the leadership that have originated with rank-and-file Communists in any party, in the international communist movement. Often there are bureaucratic decisions at the top, and *democratic centralism is used as a sort of sword of Damocles*, with a system of personal coteries and loyalties operating everywhere.[76]

This was linked to an observation about the situation in Czechoslovakia, where, after the events of 1968, thousands of communists had been expelled from the Party: 'when so many people are expelled, those who remain become the majority and the leadership becomes unchallenge-able; the minority are deprived of the chance to fight for their views to turn them into majority views'.

Later in the same meeting Ramelson spelt out what he saw as the essential features of communist democracy. These included the right of every Party member to take part in decision-making, as well as the duty of each member to implement decisions agreed by the majority. For Ramelson communist democracy also involved the possibility for minorities to put forward their views, and should include checks and balances on the leadership to ensure that it was fully accountable to the membership. His basic position was that the emphasis on centralism arose from the specific conditions of the revolutionary process in Russia, and that the level of democracy depended on the concrete historical and political conditions facing each Party. This being so:

> do we need centralism in the form it has been distorted over the decades? Why not be content with 'democracy'? I hope that I will not be regarded as a revisionist for my call to abandon this term (democratic centralism) which in real life, in diverse parties with diverse histories, has always led to harmful distortion.[77]

We can see that a lifetime's experience in the leadership of a commu-nist movement had by the end of the 1980s convinced Ramelson that a radical reappraisal was necessary. He was probably convinced of the need to speak out both by his recent experience in the British Party, and his witnessing at first hand of inner-party life in Czechoslovakia. His was almost a lone voice in the late 1980s and early 1990s. The neo-Gramscians who had so much to say about the limitations of inner-party democracy before they gained the leadership majority, now found democratic centralism an extremely useful tool for disci-plining and expelling opponents – such as communists on the *Morning Star* Management Committee. Ramelson thought that the CPGB's disciplinary measures against those opposed to the majority line were an un-Leninist application in a country like Britain, with its long-established labour movement traditions and democratic structures, since Lenin had always insisted on taking into account specific condi-tions when applying general principles. For example, in *State and Revolution*, Lenin had pointed out that, unlike the rest of Europe, in 1871 Britain had no militarist cliques and therefore it was possible to conceive of a people's revolution 'without the precondition of destroying the ready-made state machinery'. [78]

Writing to his great friend and comrade Colin Siddons in June 1990, Ramelson linked the shortcomings in the way democratic centralism had operated in the Soviet Union with its failure to build socialism:

> I was a great believer for nearly 47 of my 53 years membership in democratic centralism, with its corollary of the 'vanguard Party' based on military structures and discipline. If you read *WMR*, you may have read … in the last couple of years my criticism of 'democratic centralism' and Lenin's culpability for an important ingredient of Stalinism which in turn led to the 'Soviet model' … a model stripped of democracy – an essential element of 'socialism'. Without democracy whatever name you may call the system, it is not socialism.
>
> Socialism has yet to be built anywhere. I believe the potential for a socialist system emerged in 1917, but in about the mid-twenties, the 'socialist project' was abandoned. It is of course with hindsight – it was not till mid-eighties that my views radically changed in this orientation.

This was written at a time when the collapse of the Soviet Union was imminent following the earlier demise of Party rule throughout the Peoples Democracies of Eastern Europe. It should not therefore be seen as a fully formed view on the struggle to build socialism in the Soviet Union. Nonetheless, there can be no question that Ramelson clearly felt that the failure to develop democratic structures and practices lay at heart of the collapse of the Soviet Union; it helped to explain why the Party had been paralysed by the crisis, and unable to mobilise support for the considerable gains that had been made in the economic, social and cultural lives of the working people. [79]

TOWARDS THE END

While he was still engaged in the struggle to save the CPGB, Ramelson's health continued to give him problems. Although he had a strong physical constitution, years of good living and lack of exercise had taken their toll, while the legacy of his Spanish civil war wound to his right leg remained. In June 1985, at seventy-five, he had had a further operation on his leg to bypass an arterial blockage or thrombosis. Nonetheless, he continued to remain politically involved. For example, he shared a platform with Arthur Scargill in Barnsley during the May 1987 General Election campaign, where, addressing a packed meeting, he urged the audience to 'go out and fight for Labour' and to go on after the election campaigning for socialist policies.[80]

He also attended every London District Congress between 1988 and 1991, either as a Consultative Delegate, a branch delegate or as an approved Visitor. At the 1985 National Congress Ramelson had been a branch delegate, and had intervened in the main political debate to strongly criticise the EC's abandonment of key aspects of the Alternative Economic Strategy. Until the final demise of the Party in 1991 he carried on engaging MacLennan and readers of the Party press in debate and discussion; and whatever their differences the General Secretary always treated Ramelson with respect and courtesy. Despite deepening political differences with the leadership Ramelson also stayed actively involved in the work of the CPGB. He regularly attended and made important contributions to the work of the Party's Middle East Committee, often presenting reports and position papers.[81] His speaking and writing abilities were barely diminished. For example, he presented the first Sam Kahn Memorial Lecture in May 1988. His talk on the 'Causes and solutions of the Palestinian Problem' was well received, and showed that he kept himself abreast of developments in the struggle against imperialist intrigues in the region.[82]

As well as keeping abreast of political developments, intervening in debates from time to time and attending meetings, Ramelson was still very open to new ideas – perhaps unusually for an old Bolshevik. The British CP might have been in a mess but the struggle went on, and new movements emerged to reflect this. Ramelson was particularly interested in the newly formed Socialist Society, and attended their annual discussion conferences in 1987 and 1988, taking extensive handwritten notes.[83] The journey to Chesterfield for a weekend of intensive political debate that this involved was quite a commitment for a person of his age and in his state of health.

It was in this period that Ramelson produced his last pamphlet, *Consensus or Socialism?* This was based on the text of a lecture given in Halifax in November 1986 – The Ralph Fox Memorial Lecture.[84] The pamphlet had a print run of 2,000 and received generous support in the form of advertising from the TGWU, NUM and TASS. Its main theme was that in a period when capitalism was in crisis it was more necessary than ever to organise for struggle and class confrontation. His message to the Labour leadership was: 'You can't be for both consensus politics – i.e. managing capitalism – and for Socialism'. (Since that time, of course, the Labour leadership has made it abundantly clear that it is in the business of managing capitalism). In making the case for struggle whatever the objective difficulties, Ramelson cited the Spanish experience. After listing some of the problems that had faced the anti-fascist forces he continues: 'But despite all these difficulties it was right to stand up to Franco, Hitler and Mussolini, because of the contribution it made in the longer term to the defeat of fascism in 1945'.[85]

Throughout 1988 and 1989 Ramelson also continued with his *World Marxist Review* responsibilities – by this time as editor of the English edition – and travelled to Prague for a week each month. The *Review's* British circulation was around 1,700 each month, and the journal was distributed to seventy Communist Parties in forty different language editions. However, the problems developing in the socialist countries, including Czechoslovakia, were shaking its whole political and financial base. As a result it ceased publication in May 1990, and at the age of eighty Ramelson finally became unemployed.[86]

In January 1990 Ramelson suffered a stroke. In a letter to Colin Siddons he said, 'the stroke is affecting my speech, memory of some words and mixing up words. I can still read but only slowly'.[87] In spite of these difficulties, however, Ramelson remained politically active until his death. For example, he attended and gave a paper to a CP conference in June 1990. His speech may have been slow but his brain remained sharp.

None of this continuing activity would have been possible without the support and nursing care Ramelson received from his wife Joan. As Ramelson's GP was to tell Joan after his death, 'You kept him alive and active for the last ten years'.

Ramelson had married Joan Smith in December 1969. A twice bereaved widow with three children, Joan had known Bert since his Leeds days, and the two had been longstanding comrades and friends for many years before their marriage – which was an extremely happy one. By the time they married Joan's children were in their twenties, but Ramelson had a close relationship with them, and with his step-grandchildren. He enjoyed a rich family life with them, especially after his retirement as industrial organiser; he took a close interest in family activities, and was very proud of their many accomplishments. To a person, their love and respect was reciprocated, as Bert adapted to the role of favourite granddad and wise counsellor within the family.[88] Joan had also seen to it that for the first time in his life Ramelson began to eat regular meals, and to make room for a fulfilling family life. When Ramelson became ill, Joan became his full-time carer, enabling him to continue his political activities right up to his final illness. As Joan put it: 'I would not have had it any other way. I could see that Bert was such an important figure in the communist movement and he was such a lovely man and companion'.[89]

REFLECTING ON THE PAST: STALIN AND THE *BRITISH ROAD TO SOCIALISM*

It came as quite a shock to Ramelson's political equilibrium when in 1991 his old comrade and lunchtime companion George Matthews, who for many years, with Ramelson and John Gollan, had been part of the intellectual powerhouse within the full-time Party apparatus, published an article that discredited its revolutionary programme, *The British Road to Socialism*.[90] The essence of Matthews's revelations was that Stalin had personally overseen key drafting points in the 1951 *British Road*, and that this had been confirmed by Khrushchev in 1963 when addressing the Congress of the GDR Communists. Ramelson was by now in poor health but he could still spot a phoney argument. One immediate question was why, if Matthews had known about this in 1963, he had kept quiet about it for thirty years. For Ramelson the revelation was a dishonest manoeuvre, part of a wider process of destroying the CPGB, in order to launch a new political force divorced from any historical baggage relating to the international communist movement.

In a later interview with Kevin Morgan, Ramelson attempted to deal with the changes that had taken place in his relationship with Matthews:

> … the odd part of it is that in all the political policies that divided the Party, I never, never, never … I can't remember in all the years on the Political Committee where we disagreed on fundamental poli-

cies. I still cannot understand when George suddenly started more or less sponsoring Jacques. The one who sponsored Jacques in the last few years was George, I'm pretty sure, and just the same I haven't any doubt in mind that George influenced Gordon. Gordon was influenced you see. He'd be influenced by anybody … until I started spending too much time in Prague, Gordon used to more or less consult with George and myself … That's why I could never understand when it all started changing with *Marxism Today* obviously being influenced, it must have been influenced by George … When Johnnie [Gollan] had to go I went to argue with George for him to become the general secretary, and Johnnie agreed to it … I tried to get George but he wouldn't do it. 'See if you can talk him into it' – which I tried to do, but he wouldn't have it.[91]

In drafting his reply to Matthews's article, Ramelson enlisted the help of Tom Sibley, with whom he had remained in touch since they had first met at Ruskin College in the early 1970s. (In the period following the winding up of *WMR* Ramelson and Sibley had met monthly to talk about current political and industrial questions over a long lunch.) It took two difficult days to write the reply, during which Ramelson would often be frustrated, about his inability to articulate a line of argument and Sibley's failing to immediately understand the points being made. Eventually they got there and a lengthy letter duly appeared in *Changes*.[92] The gist of Ramelson's argument was, firstly, that it was hardly a surprise that Pollitt had consulted Stalin: this was a hangover from the old Comintern days but it was also recognition that the Soviet Party still had a special position and influence, based on its achievements which at that time had recently been strengthened by the Soviet Union's post-war role as a political as well as military superpower. Secondly, Harry Pollitt, the Party's general secretary in 1951 and the leading force behind the programme, could well have been up to some of his old tricks here: by using the authority of Stalin he could have been guarding the new line against the possible opposition of some members of the Political Committee, including Dutt. If Stalin was using Pollitt to popularise a 'parliamentary' road to Socialism internationally, then Pollitt was using Stalin to sideline possible critics of the new line in Britain.

Ramelson – who doubted that Stalin had any major, let alone decisive, role in the drafting – argued that what mattered in all this was whether the outcome had benefited the Party and the working class generally. In other words, if Stalin did give advice, was it good advice? Matthews was trying to frighten the horses by mentioning Stalin's name and almost certainly exaggerating his input – and it could be that Khrushchev had had similar motives in 1963, in the midst of his campaign to de-Stalinise the Soviet Union. (In the event the 1951 version of the *British Road* had been very well received initially, selling 150,000 copies in the first few weeks after publication, but in the Cold War conditions of the early 1950s it had failed to usher in a period of Party growth in membership or influence).

In order to underline that the Matthews article should be seen as an opportunist gambit, Ramelson drew attention to previous occasions when Matthews had stressed the Britishness of the Party's revolutionary strategy. In an article for *World Marxist Review* published in August 1979 he had specifically demonstrated that the *British Road* had been foreshadowed by Pollitt in his CP pamphlet *Looking Ahead* as early as 1947:

> A major step forward in developing such a strategy was taken by the British Party in 1951 with the publication of the first edition of *The British Road to Socialism*. This had been foreshadowed earlier by Harry Pollitt … in a pamphlet published in 1947 called *Looking Ahead*. In a chapter headed 'The British Road to Socialism' he wrote that 'the progress of democratic and socialist forces throughout the world had opened out new possibilities of transition to socialism by other paths than those followed by the Russian Revolution.[93]

There can be no doubt that in all essential matters the British Road was made in King Street not the Kremlin.[94] Matthews knew this but chose to greatly inflate Stalin's role in the process in order to discredit the CPGB's past revolutionary strategy.

In a further revisiting of old questions, Ramelson also spoke at a conference organised to discuss what '1956' had meant to the British CP, focusing in his contribution on debates about the *Reasoner*. Monty Johnstone summed up a broad swathe of opinion at the conference when he argued that the British Party had suffered greatly from its leadership's failure to adequately analyse the CPSU's Congress. He put forward the following critique of the British Party's leadership:

There was a totally un-Marxist refusal to allow structural analysis of the bureaucratic system which had produced Stalinism ... The terror was an extreme manifestation of Stalinism rather than its essence: a system where capitalism has been overthrown but power is exercised not democratically by the working people, but is concentrated in the hands of a small leading group in a ruling Party. This top elite acts in their name but is not accountable to or removable by them.

In 1956 Ramelson had been loyal to the Party line – indeed he had played a leading role in shaping it. In looking back in the early 1990s he took a more nuanced view of these events.[95] He accepted Monty Johnstone's view on the nature of Stalinism as outlined above, but remained insistent that the line on Hungary had been correct (i.e. that it was a fascist-inspired counter-revolution that exploited genuine grievances of the people that had been fed by the grievous errors made by the Party leadership); and he continued to believe that the democratic issues raised by Saville and Thompson in the *Reasoner* dispute could have been adequately accommodated were it not for the Hungarian events and the intransigence of the two comrades involved.

The central issue arising from the CPSU Twentieth Congress was whether Stalin's crimes arose, as Khrushchev had argued, as a result of the 'cult of the personality', or whether, as most argued at the 1992 Conference, the lack of democratic accountability had been systemic. Ramelson's view on this had changed over the years. In 1956 he had taken the pragmatic view – the Soviet leaders had promised to rectify this situation by introducing democratic changes, and British communists, who could do little to influence these events, were best advised to accept this at face value. To do otherwise would have opened up serious divisions in the British Party and strengthened the hands of those who were already questioning the necessity of a CP in British conditions, while others were raising doubts about the value of being part of the international communist movement. Better, Ramelson thought in 1956, to trust that democratic progress in the Soviet Union would be forthcoming in a period when the Cold War appeared to be thawing. Better to argue that the *British Road to Socialism* was based on a profoundly democratic process leading to a new democratic state – a socialist society where power had been transferred from the wealthy few to the common people. British conditions in 1956 were after all entirely different from those in Stalin's Russia.

At some time during the 1980s Ramelson's assessments changed. He came to the view that the Soviet Party had effectively abandoned the socialist project sometime in the mid-1920s, opting instead to protect its leading position in the society and state it had created by all means available, and elevating this objective above all others. It was this that explained the crimes, and not Stalin's personality. He did not accept all the views of contemporary CP critics of the Soviet Union. His view was that at the time the response they made had appeared to be the best available if the Party was to be held together. It was simply not the case, as many had claimed, that the Party had declined in either size or influence as a result. On the contrary the immediate membership losses had been quickly reversed, and the period between 1957 and 1968 had seen a steady but very slow rise in Party membership. Contrary to the myth, there was no golden period for the Party before 1956 – apart from the brief interlude of the war years. Indeed, it is now clear the Party's influence was at its highest during the 1960s and 1970s, particularly in the mass trade union movement.

SOLIDARITY FOREVER

As 1993 progressed Ramelson found it increasingly difficult to read or to express himself, whether verbally or in writing. Nonetheless, he continued with his taped interviews with Rodney Bickerstaffe, and he always made visitors welcome, anxious as he was to keep abreast of political developments. He remained in good spirits and retained his optimism about possibilities for social and political advance in Britain and the world. By the second half of the year he was relying on others to read to him. Comrades who lived nearby popped in to ensure that Ramelson was kept informed. Two of his readers, Carolyn Jones and Phil Clark, both recall that Ramelson never tired of discussing trends and events, and that he always had something forceful and pertinent to say, even if he sometimes had difficulty in finding the words he wanted. During most weeks in this period Ramelson spent several hours with Jim Mortimer, who read to him from books dealing with theoretical questions from a Marxist perspective. The book which engaged them most was Alec Nove's *The Economics of Feasible Socialism*,[96] with Ramelson, though critical of some aspects of the book, supporting Nove's argument that within the context of state ownership of the main industrial and financial centres, socialism could best be developed through decentralised forms of ownership (e.g. co-ops in agriculture), and that regulated markets rather than rigid central planning were the best way of allocating resources in commodity production and exchange. He believed that if it had been possible to continue Lenin's policies of the 'New Economic Policy' period (as opposed to the forced collectivisation in agriculture and breakneck industrialisation), the Soviet Union would have seen higher living standards and less central control over people's lives at work. [97]

Early in 1994 Bert Ramelson was taken ill with what was diagnosed as respiratory failure. In April he was admitted to Lewisham Hospital, where he died on 13 April 1994. On the day before he died he asked Joan Ramelson to be sure to post a donation to the African National Congress Election Fund in South Africa to assist the liberation movement's triumph at the first post-apartheid elections.

Ramelson's funeral took place on a bright early spring day, with hundreds flocking to Lewisham Crematorium to salute the life of an outstanding leader whose influence had been felt right across the British labour movement and the international communist movement. There were many elements of the traditional socialist funeral – political speeches, Paul Robeson's recording of the 'Ballad of Joe Hill', and as a finale the 'Internationale'. There were also some Ramelson-specific features. The song of the International Brigade, commemorating those who had fought for democracy and freedom in Spain, was introduced by Bill Alexander, the leader of the British Battalion. The duet from Bizet's 'Pearl Fishers' was played, at Bert's request, partly because of its expression of aspiration for friendship between peoples the world over.

Monty Meth, who had worked as the YCL organiser in Yorkshire during the 1950s, recalled Ramelson's leadership during that time:

> The foundation of Bert's quite unique contribution to the ending of years of right-wing domination of labour movement policies were laid in Yorkshire, and they paved the way for a whole series of left victories through to the 1980s.
>
> … I was fortunate to see at close hand Bert's inspiring leadership in Yorkshire: his total dedication to the job, day after day, his supreme optimism, which in turn gave all sections of the left the confidence to believe that advances could be made.

Commenting that 'people who never really knew Bert thought that he was just a hard Party man, but beneath that steely veneer was a man full of humanity with a loving concern for those closest to him', Meth also singled out Ramelson's wicked humour, recalling that he had once described the local MP Alice Bacon, whose constituency included a large Jewish population, as ham-fisted. During a subsequent election campaign, one of Ramelson's slogans had been 'Don't Vote for Bacon – Vote Kosher – Vote Ramelson'.

In his contribution Bill Alexander touched on both Ramelson's internationalism and his work in his local Party branch. As Alexander stressed, Ramelson's internationalism had had deep roots, and was based on his own experiences, particularly in Palestine and Spain. From Spain Ramelson had taken the inspiration provided by the International Brigade and the Spanish people, drawing the lesson that people from many different countries, many philosophies, could co-operate and struggle together for liberty and peace, and that racism and violence are not an integral part of human nature. [98]

Lengthy obituaries appeared in all the broadsheets as well as the *Jewish Chronicle,* ranging in tone from eulogistic to respectful; all recognised the passing of a leading communist who had made a substantial contribution to working-class struggles and labour move-ment politics. In the *Morning Star*, LCDTU leader Kevin Halpin, one of the most influential rank-and-file leaders of his generation, paid tribute to 'an outstanding Communist', and gave especial recognition to Ramelson's role as an innovator and strategist, acknowledging that it had been his drive and ideas that had led to the formation of the LCDTU. [99]

Seumas Milne in the *Guardian* summed up Ramelson's contribu-tion to the industrial struggles of the 1960s and 1970s: 'Ramelson was a master strategist with a powerful intellect who gave the Communist Party influence far beyond its membership and supporters and trained a whole generation of industrial militants'. But as he also pointed out, 'Ramelson was a strong believer in building organisation from the shop floor and the strategy paid off handsomely'.[100] The *Times* obitu-arist (anonymous) recognised Ramelson as 'a brilliant organiser' and a man who made a 'great contribution to the Communist Party and labour movement militancy'.[101]

Common themes emerged in many of the dozens of messages received by Joan. Some recognised the loving nature of her relationship with Bert, and the great strength and pure enjoyment that he had drawn from his marriage and his family. Most valued his courage, determination and commitment in the socialist cause. All who knew him at all well saw the enormous intellectual energy which he had brought to all his political work. A letter from Monty Johnstone, one of the leadership's strongest critics during the period of Ramelson's greatest influence, tells us much about his humanity and charismatic qualities. Johnstone, a widely respected historian of the international communist movement, wrote:

> A discussion with Bert was always a stimulating experience. Far from resenting disagreement, he seemed to warm to one when one was putting an opposing view to his with equal conviction. This was certainly my experience with him over many decades and not a few disagreements! I particularly appreciated the way he braved a storm in 1979 when he proposed that I should go with him from the CPGB to a *World Marxist Review* conference in Hungary on Revolution and Democracy. And I recall, after the storm had subsided somewhat, the happy week we spent together at the conference sharing a flat and defending our conceptions of the British Road and socialist pluralism against their many Soviet and East European critics.

Norma Bramley, a close friend for over twenty years, wrote: 'Through all my remembrances shines Bert's wonderful faith in human nature, despite all the setbacks and disappointments. He was a wonderful, special person who never ever lost his enthusiasm for life and politics'.

Arthur Scargill said of Ramelson: 'For some 40 years he has been a central figure in my life, a constant point of reference, whether struggling with ideas or engaged in the struggle of direct action'. From Moscow came a note from his nephew Volodya: 'From his first coming to Moscow in 1956 ... he was the main bond of our big family Rachmilevitch'.

Elsie Gollan, widow of former Communist Party General Secretary John Gollan, remembered both his wit and commitment to the socialist cause: 'Bert was a great Communist who devoted his whole life to the movement, yet though his commitment was total and serious, he had a ready wit and gave us all many a good laugh'. Roger Simon, General Secretary of the Labour Research Department throughout Ramelson's period of national office, remembered their days in the Party's Economic Committee, commenting that, 'He had the gift of making me feel that what we were doing was important'.[102] Bill Moore, an old comrade and fellow Party full-time worker in Yorkshire, remembered Ramelson as a tough but fair and understanding leader, 'a magnificent Communist, a world-class leader and the most powerful Communist of the second half of the century in Britain'.[103]

NOTES

1. Mick Costello and Gordon McLennan interviews, 2009.
2. The lecture was subsequently reproduced, Hobsbawm, E. 'The forward march of labour halted?', *Marxism Today*, September 1978, pp. 270-286; and again in Jacques, M. and Mulhearn, F. (eds.) *The Forward March of Labour Halted?*, Verso, London 1981.
3. Trade union membership grew from 7.8 million in 1945 to 13.2 million (the highpoint) in 1979, and is 7.4 million in 2010 – see annual reports of the trade union Certification Officer.
4. This broadened agenda owed much to the work of the CP Industrial Department, whose 'Needs of the Hour' promoted draft motions for union conferences, many of which were subsequently adopted as TUC and Labour Party policy. Perhaps the best example of this are the AEUW-TASS motions opposing the Social Contract submitted in 1974 and 1975.
5. See Coates, D. *The Crisis of Labour*, Oxford 1989, pp.105-112; and see the series of studies published by Goldthorpe, J., Lockwood, D., Bechhofer, F., and Platt, J. as *The affluent worker: political attitudes and behaviour*, Cambridge University Press 1968; *The Affluent worker: industrial attitudes and behaviour*, CUP 1968; *The Affluent Worker in the Class Structure*, CUP 1969. These studies were available to Hobsbawm. They concluded that the political choices made by working class voters are 'to some degree … attributable to the fact that the political leaders of the working class chose this future for it'. *The Affluent Worker in the Class Structure*, p. 195.
6. The *Marxism Today* article and the written responses it provoked were subsequently published in Jacques and Mulhearn, op.cit., 1981.
7. Ken Gill interview 2008; Gordon McLennan interview, 2009.
8. Ramelson, B. *Consensus or Socialism*, The 1986 Ralph Fox Memorial Lecture, p. 16.
9. Chomsky 1999, op.cit.
10. See Ramelson, *Bury the Social Contract*, op.cit, March 1977, for the most succinct outline of the Alternative Economic Strategy, for both the inter-linked nature of the demands raised and the dynamic process involved.
11. Smith, P. '"The Winter of Discontent": The Hire and Reward Road Haulage Dispute, 1979', *Historical Studies in Industrial Relations*, 1999 No. 7, pp. 27-56.

12. Hay, C. 'Narrating Crisis: the Discursive Construction of the "Winter of Discontent"', *Sociology*, 1996 30: 253-277; Rodgers, W. 'Government Under Stress; Britain's Winter Of Discontent 1979', *Political Quarterly*, 1984 55(2): 171-179.

13. McIlroy, J. and Campbell, A. 'The High Tide of Trade Unionism: Mapping Industrial Politics, 1964-79', in McIlroy et al 1999, op.cit., pp. 110-119.

14. Ramelson, March 1977, op.cit., pp. 17-18.

15. Noel Harris was a WFTU official based in Prague in the early 1980s, interview, 2010.

16. CP Archives, Ramelson's personal papers.

17. E-mail November 2010.

18. CP Archive CP/IND/RAM/14/04.

19. Over the dozen or so years Ramelson was involved he took part in over twenty such group discussions/seminars, e.g. 'An International Symposium on Trade Union Problems and the Attitudes of Communists', *World Marxist Review* 1982, No.12; and 'Can the Transnationals be Controlled', a round table discussion, *World Marxist Review* 1988, No.6.

20. Halliday, F. 'The War and Revolution in Afghanistan', *New Left Review*, 1980, 119: 20-41.

21. *Morning Star*, 14/9/79.

22. *Morning Star*, 18/2/80.

23. *Morning Star*, 31/1/80.

24. *Morning Star*, 18/2/80.

25. Mick Costello interview, 2009.

26. Staniszkis, J. 'The Evolution of Forms of Working-Class Protest in Poland: Sociological Reflections on the Gdansk-Szczecin Case, August 1980', *Soviet Studies*, 1981 XXXIII: 204-231.

27. *Marxism Today*, 'Poland', July 198, p. 25.

28. The subsidy varied but was always in terms of thousands of pounds, a heavy drag on a small party's income. One estimate puts the subsidy at £43,000 per annum although it must have varied year on year. See Andrews 2004 op.cit., p. 225; and Fishman, N. 'The British Road is Resurfaced for New Times', in Bull, M. and Heyward, P. (eds.), *West European Communist Parties after the Revolutions of 1989*, Macmillan 1994, pp. 145-177.

29. CP Archive: CP/IND/RAM/06/03.

30. CP Archive: CP/IND/RAM/04/02.

31. Lane, T. 'The Unions Caught on the Ebb Tide', *Marxism Today*, September 1982, pp. 6-13.

32. *Morning Star*, 26/8/82.

33. Tony Chater, letter, Pre-Congress Discussion 1983, *Focus* No. 12, 1983.

34. Gordon McLennan interview, 2009.

35. *Focus*, 24/1/85.

36. This was the CPGB's Publicity Officer Nina Temple's response. Temple

later became General Secretary of the CPGB and it was on her watch that the CPGB was liquidated.

37. *Morning Star*, 11/6/85.

38. There have been numerous articles on this epic strike from various perspectives. For a general review see Howell, D. 'Goodbye to all that?: A Review of Literature on the 1984/5 Miners' Strike', *Work, Employment & Society*, September 1987, pp. 388-404; for an account of the strike in Yorkshire see Winterton, J. and Winterton, R. *Coal, Crisis, and Conflict*, Manchester University Press 1989; and for an excellent contemporary analysis see Towers, B., 'Posing larger questions: the British miners' strike of 1984-85', *Industrial Relations Journal*, 1985, 16: 8-25.

39. The Tory victory in 1983 was partly attributable to the split in the Labour ranks due to the setting up of the Social Democratic Party by the so-called 'gang of four' – rightwing ex-leaders who felt the Labour Party had shifted too far left.

40. Bert Ramelson's personal papers – annotated copy of Frank Watters' book.

41. Ramelson's personal papers.

42. Andrew 2009 op.cit., p.680.

43. Routledge P., *Scargill: the unauthorized biography*, Harper Collins, 1992; and Routledge's shorthand notes sent to the authors.

44. Mike Seifert interview, 2009.

45. Andrew 2009 op.cit., p. 969

46. CP Archive CP/IND/RAM/11/04.

47. Ramelson 1986 op. cit., pp.6-7.

48. Frank Watters, *Being Frank*, Doncaster, 1992. Annotated copy in Bert Ramelson's personal papers.

49. CP Archives: CP/IND/RAM/11/04.

50. Foster, J. 'Moving the Goalposts', *Marxism Today*, March 1985, pp. 43-4.

51. In retrospect this was to overstate the advances made unless it is limited to the period 1966-1976 before the Social Contract.

52. *Morning Star*, 2/5/88.

53. Ramelson's private papers.

54. *Focus*, No. 23, July 1984, p. 3. The welfare state consensus referred to was the state's commitment to full employment and an expanding welfare state, underpinned by Keynesian policies to promote economic growth.

55. Cook, D. 'No Private Drama', *Marxism Today*, February 1985, pp. 25-9.

56. Foster 1985, op.cit., p. 44.

57. *Daily Telegraph*, 24/8/88.

58. *Seven Days*, 1/10/88, p. 8.

59. Reuben Falber, *Changes*, 16-29 November 1991.

60. Ramelson private papers.

61. *Observer Magazine*, 21/10/90.

62. Richard Craven interview, 2002.

63. One interviewee strongly expressed this view and linked the neo-

Gramscian faction's dominance in the Party to the 1977 'compromise' on the British Road to Socialism, which essentially replaced the 'anti-monopoly alliance' with the 'broad democratic alliance' with the emphasis on social movements. Ramelson accepted the 'broad democratic alliance' position as long as everyone understood that within it the organised working class remained the leading force.

64. *Morning Star*, 11/12/87.
65. Mary Davis interview, 2010. Mary often met Ramelson and she put it to Ramelson that 'it was time for him to give a clear lead by supporting a reconstitution of the Party since the current leadership was no longer acting as a Communist leadership and, on the contrary, was expelling "good" comrades and attacking the *Morning Star*'.
66. *Morning Star*, 11/12/87.
67. In an e-mailed note John Foster told us, 'no-one was allowed as a member of the CCG unless they had been expelled or excluded and this was rigidly enforced. The CPB was founded in 1988 and did take existing CPGB members. Its own membership on re-establishment was 2,200'.
68. CP Archive, CP/IND/RAM/06/03.
69. See Communist Party of Britain website, Graham Stevenson, *Short History of the Communist Party*.
70. Ramelson to Berry, 8/7/85. Ramelson's private papers.
71. Berry to Ramelson 18/7/85. Ramelson's private papers.
72. Letter dated 2 June 1986, personal papers
73. This account is based on a discussion with Ramelson circa 1989. For an account which is sympathetic to McLennan's position but broadly confirms the facts, if not the interpretation, as recounted by Ramelson, see Thompson, W. *The Good Old Cause: British Communism 1921-1991*, Pluto Press, London 1992, pp. 193-4.
74. Reproduced in *World Marxist Review* 10/86, 'The Communist Movement in a Changing World'.
75. 'Discussing democratic centralism', *World Marxist Review* 01/90, p. 41.
76. Ibid., p. 39.
77. Ibid., p. 40.
78. Lenin, *State and Revolution*, op.cit., p. 36.
79. Ramelson's personal papers.
80. *Morning Star*, 16/5/87.
81. Middle East Committee Minutes, 29/4/86; and 15/5/86. CP Archives, CP/IND/RAM/09/01.
82. CP archive: CP/IND/RAM/09/01.
83. The Socialist Society was founded in 1981 by a group of Marxist academics, including Ralph Miliband and Raymond Williams. Its political objective was to provide a link between socialists in the Labour Party and those in other organisations. It concentrated on socialist education and research. Its last AGM was in 1993. CP Archive: CP/IND/RAM/14/02.

84. Ralph Fox, like Ramelson, had been an International Brigader in Spain, and had given his life to the cause at Lopera.

85. Ramelson 1986, op.cit., p. 6.

86. CP Archive: CP/IND/RAM/14/04.

87. Letter to Colin Siddons, 15/6/90. Ramelson's personal papers.

88. Anne and Richard Craven interviews, 2008.

89. Joan Ramelson. interview, 2008.

90. *Changes*, 14-27 September 1991.

91. Kevin Morgan interview with Bert Ramelson.

92. *Changes*, October 1991. It is regrettable that in Andrews 2004, op.cit., p.74, the Matthews claim is recorded as if it was incontrovertible, and no mention is made of correspondence, particularly Ramelson's letter which strongly challenged it.

93. *World Marxist Review*, August 1979, p. 84.

94. This is confirmed by an article by Kitty Cornforth (sister of James Klugmann and married to communist philosopher Maurice) 'The British Road to Socialism', *Communist Review*, April 1947, pp. 113-8, in which she argues, 'Recent developments in various countries have brought home the fact that there is no set formula for the road to Socialism, and that different countries are going in the direction of Socialism in different ways according to their special circumstances'. It was published three years before Pollitt's discussion with Stalin and there is no evidence to suggest that Cornforth benefitted from Stalin's words. Others have confirmed this and noted the original contribution Kitty Cornforth made to the debate; see Laybourn, K. *Marxism in Britain: dissent, decline and re-emergence 1945-c.2000*, Routledge, London, 2006, p. 37; and Chester, A. 'Uneven development: communist strategy from the 1940s-1970s', *Marxism Today* September 1979, p. 278.

95. Conversations with Tom Sibley in the early 1990s, and correspondence with Colin Siddons.

96. Nove, A. *The Economics of Feasible Socialism*, Allen and Unwin, London 1983.

97. NEP – the New Economic Policy, whereby the free market was reintroduced for peasant production and state requisitioning was replaced by a tax in kind after the Tenth Party Congress in 1920. See Dobb, M. *Soviet Economic Development since 1917*, International Publishers, New York 1966.

98. Taped transcript of funeral service.

99. *Morning Star* 14/4/94.

100. *Guardian*, 16/4/94,

101. *Times*, 16/4/94.

102. All above quotes from Joan Ramelson's personal papers.

103. Bill Moore interview, 1999.

8. Themes from a life

A LIFETIME OF STRUGGLE

As we have seen Bert Ramelson lived a life of a revolutionary at work. He was deeply influenced by his roots and early experiences in the Ukraine, Canada, Palestine, and later fighting in the Spanish civil war and the Second World War. These events and activities created in him a burning sense of the need and possibility to remove injustice and inequality through the overthrow of the state that kept them alive, the capitalist state. Ramelson was never negative, and saw that replacing like with like was of no use, and that what was needed therefore was a socialism built on liberty, equality, solidarity and democracy. This was no idle sentiment, and his whole adult life was dedicated to its achievement through the development of styles of work, strategic consideration of British conditions, and the need to act in a disciplined as well as a principled way inside a revolutionary party working with the wider labour movement. He died believing that socialism was the best possible system, and that struggling for such an outcome was to live the best possible life.

ON BEING JEWISH

When asked by Rodney Bickerstaffe about being Jewish, Ramelson replied that for many decades he did not think about this question. Though his early education and experiences, when he had lived in a Jewish ghetto in the Ukraine, had had a profound influence on his thinking, Ramelson had eschewed both his father's religion and Jewish nationalism or zionism when in his twenties. As a communist he saw himself first and foremost as an internationalist and as such he became a fierce opponent of zionism and of Israel's expansionist approach to its own nation building, which resulted, as it was bound to do, in the denial of Palestinian rights and the oppression of the Palestinian people.

316

Many of Ramelson's closest friends – such as Michael Seifert, Monty Meth, Arnold and Margot Kettle – were Jewish, but the basis of these friendships was largely that they were all active politically, on the left and mainly in the CP. Within the Party, particularly in big urban centres like London, Leeds and Manchester, Jews were a lively and proportionately over-represented section of the Party (they were often the sons and daughters of immigrants from East and Central Europe). In Leeds in particular Bert had enjoyed their comradeship and support. He was in more than one sense one of them, and they were mostly proud of his achievements and of the standing he enjoyed in the local labour movement. However, there is some evidence that Bert's fierce anti-zionism and his strong conviction that the evil of anti-semitism could only be resolved by assimilation – not least in the Soviet Union – did upset some Jewish CP members in Leeds.[1]

Given his background it is no surprise that Ramelson was appointed Chairman of the Party's Jewish Committee in 1959. As we have seen, the Khrushchev revelations had shown that Jews had been persecuted by Stalin's secret police in the years between 1948 and 1953 – as had many other ethnic minority communities, as well as intellectuals. Ramelson had been part of the British Party's formal meetings to discuss these matters with the Soviet leadership. While in Moscow, the subsequent delegation received certain assurances that in the process of de-Stalinisation these barbarities would cease and anti-semitic ideas among the people would be controlled and combated. Some actions were taken to rectify the situation, but the problem – particularly in the realm of ideas and culture – never really went away. Prominent British Communists continued to monitor the international press closely, and many examples were found to confirm or suggest bad practice by the Soviet authorities – some true and others manufactured.

In response to the unease felt by some prominent British communists in the Jewish community, Ramelson, on behalf of the Party leadership, took a number of initiatives. Firstly, as was his wont, he took the theoretical arguments head on. He refused to accept any part of zionism, and would have nothing to do with ideas about the Jewish nation. In his eyes 'Jewishness' was defined by religion, not nationality. From this he refused to accept that Israel was a Jewish country – Israeli Arabs had an equal claim in every sense to Israeli Jews.

Because in practice the Israeli government had since 1948 refused to accept Arab rights, and furthermore had allied itself with Western imperialism against the legitimate rights of Arab nationalists (e.g. at Suez), then it was perfectly understandable and correct that the Soviet Union should condemn these actions.

In late 1957 Hyman Levy, who had been a prominent member of the delegation sent by the British Party to the Soviet Union in 1956, published a generally well-received and scathing attack on Soviet policy.[2] Ramelson's review in the *Daily Worker* took no prisoners.[3] He argued that Levy's approach was un-Marxist and zionist, and that the 'Jewish question' could only be resolved through assimilation not through separation. Only socialism, by ending class division, could undermine the material basis of anti-semitism. In dealing with cultural rights for minorities in the Soviet Union, Ramelson was equally forthright if less convincing. This failure to adequately address the issue stemmed partly from his own personal experiences. In his eyes, his upbringing had been educationally restrictive – he had been taught only in Yiddish until he was twelve, and had been formally separated from all other cultural influences. In later life he resented this. For example, during the Spanish Civil War he had been asked to act as interpreter for the leading Soviet general, but had quickly realised that the smattering of Russian he had picked up on the streets of Cherkassy was totally inadequate to the task.

There was plenty to criticise in Soviet policy towards its Jewish citizens, but in 1957 Ramelson was not prepared to concede any ground to critics of Soviet practice beyond acknowledging the crimes of the 1948-1953 period, which he argued had not been anti-semitic as such, since they had been visited on every minority population. As the years went by, however, while never abandoning his basic position, particularly concerning assimilation, Ramelson increasingly argued that special means to keep languages and traditions alive did have merit, and that administrative measures to attack religions and other rights were to be condemned.

In an article for *Marxism Today* in 1959 Ramelson had much more to say on the position of Soviet Jewry. He argued that 'the revelations that amongst the victims of the gross abuse of socialist democracy and legality in the Soviet Union during the period of 1948-1953 were many leaders of Jewish cultural life … were heaven-sent opportunities, unscrupulously used by zionists and anti-Soviet

Jewish elements, to spread the vilest slanders about the position and status of Jews in the Soviet Union'. [4] On the language issue and assimilation he argued:

> Yiddish developed over the centuries as the mother-tongue of Jews in Central and Eastern Europe, owing to the persecution of Jews and the enforced segregation in Ghettoes. This compulsory isolation developed a common way of life, tradition and behaviour, and this in turn gave rise to a specific Yiddish culture, whose essence was the depicting of Ghetto life and a yearning for revolt against such intolerable conditions.
>
> Wherever the Ghetto walls were broken down ... Yiddish ceased to develop and was gradually replaced by the language of the country where the Jews lived.
>
> ... In the period immediately following the socialist revolution ... every facility was given to them in the Soviet Union for the development of Yiddish culture. Freed from the shackles of Tsarism, the new opportunities offered by socialism were fully grasped, the Yiddish culture flourished.
>
> ... With the further development of socialism and the complete emancipation of the Jews, the conditions and memories of the Ghetto disappear into the past. Yiddish ceases to be a living tongue and the basis for a specific culture (expressing a specific Jewish life which no longer exists) rapidly crumbles.[5]

However the issue would not go away. At the 1965 Party Congress the Prestwick Branch tabled a motion critical of the treatment of Soviet Jewry and calling for the British Party to again intercede with the Soviet authorities. This was remitted to the incoming Executive Committee, and subsequently, in a long letter to General Secretary Gollan, Ramelson sketched out the basis of a possible approach. He disputed many of the arguments concerning the preservation of Jewish culture, but stressed the importance of using persuasion and education rather than administrative means to advance the cause of assimilation – which he saw as part of the development of 'socialist persons' within a socialist society. He did also acknowledge that synagogues were being closed even in areas where there was still a demand for them, and that much of the anti-religious and anti-zionist propaganda used by the authorities was 'very crude indeed'.[6] He further argued that this issue should be taken up with the CPSU, pointing out that the use of such propaganda was wrong in principle and was likely to be counter-productive in practice. The inner-party debate on this issue continued through 1966, with special weekend schools being arranged in a small number of Party Districts, and Ramelson was the preferred tutor and leading speaker.

These debates were complicated by differing attitudes to zionism, and this became the main issue after June 1967, when, in the Six Days War, Israel attacked Egypt, Jordan and Syria, winning a swift victory and occupying territory in all three countries. In a 40,000 word pamphlet produced a few months later, Ramelson strongly condemned the Israeli action, labelling it as a threat to world peace.[7] He saw zionism as a weapon used by imperialism in its struggle against socialism, and linked the war to what he described as a zionist-inspired anti-Soviet campaign:

> The campaign was waged in the foreknowledge that the Soviet Union would support the Arab victims of Israeli aggression and this would help to undermine the belief in Socialism as the answer to discrimination, leaving no alternative but support for a zionist Israel.[8]

Ramelson, on the contrary, argued that 'the Jewish problem could only ultimately and permanently be solved by the victory of socialism, by ending capitalist class society, which was the root of the problem'. He did, however, acknowledge that: 'There are undoubtedly remnants of anti-semitism in the Soviet Union, as there are remnants of many other prejudices, attitudes and behaviour rooted in the class society of pre-1917 Russia'. This was not the main issue. He finished with a clear statement of the Communist case:

> Our championing of the Jewish people in their struggle against discrimination and injustice is part of the Communists' championing of the struggle of all peoples against discrimination and injustice, as is our support of the national liberation movement, of which the Arab liberation movement is an integral part. Rectification of one injustice cannot and must not be achieved by creating another injustice …
>
> It is our task to expose British imperialism which has so often and for so long been ready to sacrifice the lives of Jews and Arabs and

even risk world war in its attempts to secure the rich profits of the oil monopolists out of their vast investments in the Middle East.[9]

The evidence is that the Soviet Union had, to say the least, an erratic record on anti-semitism, and this became unnecessarily complicated by its hostile relationship with Israel from the 1950s onwards. Whilst Ramelson's writing and actions partly reflected this, he failed to take on board the insights which the civil rights movement in the United States and to a lesser extent the anti-racism movement in Britain brought to the struggle for equality. Ever anxious to stress the benefits that only socialism could bring, he understated the need to campaign for the democratic and cultural elements of a group that – like black people in the US and Britain – had no separate nationality but did feel alienated from aspects of the society in which they lived. To provide an adequate critique of Soviet practice more was needed than opposition to administrative means to 'falsely advance' the cause of socialist assimilation.

STYLE OF WORK

Ramelson understood that politics was both an art and a science. The ways in which leaders worked influenced events and shaped outcomes. His style of work was distinctive – for example he was acutely aware of the need not to be seen as interfering in union affairs but at the same time he was determined to maximise communist influence. This section describes and considers his priorities and methods, taking account of a wide range of activities over the period 1965 to 1977. In most cases his power of argument, allied with tactical flexibility, carried the day in his dealings with labour movement leaders and activists. But it was not always so.

Throughout Ramelson's political life in Britain, CP full-time workers were generally held in great respect by most members. They were badly underpaid, and if they did the job well they worked long and anti-social hours.[10] For Ramelson, and most other full-time Party workers of his generation, the compensations were substantial. They were after all deeply involved in organising a revolutionary movement created to build a new social system governed by principles of equality, liberty and solidarity, and in many parts of the world replacing capitalist exploitation and colonialist oppression.

A month in a life

Joan Ramelson told us how happy they were in their London years, from 1969 onwards. She recalled that they were both involved in rewarding work, and they had a circle of political friends whose company they enjoyed. Joan worked as a Senior Social Worker overseeing professional standards in the London Borough of Westminster.

Though Ramelson did not keep a diary, it is possible to put together a typical month in his life, from discussion with people who knew him, knowledge of CP procedures and reading the Party press for the period. Below we have assembled an outline of Ramelson's activities for the month of January 1977.

From Monday to Friday each week Ramelson would work in the Party's headquarters in King Street, being dropped off and picked up by Joan. Most of his out of town engagements were at weekends, and these included reports to District Committees and lectures at weekend schools, particularly to industrial comrades. About twice a month he would speak at an evening public meeting, and around five times a year at a students' meeting, usually during the daytime. His social life revolved around the Party. Most months there would be a London Embassy function to celebrate – October 1917, Victory in Europe Day, May Day, International Women's Day, Liberation Days in the various Eastern European countries, and the appointment of a new ambassador. These functions were well provisioned, and in the 1970s at least attracted a good many trade union leaders. They were an opportunity to meet, to socialise and to engage in private political discussions on friendly neutral ground. Ramelson rarely missed such events.

At the beginning of January 1977 Ramelson attended a two-day Executive Committee meeting, and throughout the month he attended the weekly meeting of the Political Committee – usually for two hours on a Thursday night, and preceded during the afternoon with discussions among the senior full-time staff. Ramelson, with his hands-on experience and day-to-day contact with the organised labour movement, often took the lead at the EC meetings, and according to Roger Bagley, who as the *Morning Star*'s political correspondent regularly attended and reported on EC meetings, Ramelson's contributions were usually the liveliest, the most substantial, and the most relevant to the struggles of the British people.[11] The EC met five times a year, and on average Ramelson gave the main report at two of these meetings.

During this month Ramelson gave a talk on zionism at Brunel University in west London; he spent a weekend in Glasgow at the Festival of Marxism, where he addressed an audience of over two hundred on the socialist revolution; he prepared articles for the *Morning Star*; and he wrote comments on the Israeli Party Congress, which he had attended in December 1976, and on the Bullock Report on industrial democracy. This was a punishing schedule for a man in his sixty-seventh year with a history of respiratory and other health problems, but he enjoyed almost every moment of it, and, with Joan's unstinting support, appeared to take the burdens placed on him in his stride.

Most of the time at the office was spent in preparing reports and articles, as well as a number of meetings with District Secretaries, Advisory Committee Officers, and occasionally with trade union leaders. Lunchtimes would involve wide-ranging discussions with fellow full-time workers. In John Gollan's time, the intellectual powerhouse of the Party at national level – Ramelson, Matthews and Gollan – often lunched together. Once Gollan had died it was left to Ramelson and Matthews to form the main theoretical nucleus of the Party, McLennan not being as interested in this as Gollan, or as capable a Marxist theoretician. Indeed it is ironical, given the later history of bitter disagreement, that Ramelson and Matthews should have been so close at this time.

The Ramelsons' social life at this time revolved around close friends in the CP, most of whom lived in the Sydenham area. All were members of the same local branch, including the Alexanders, the Jefferys, and the Cromes.[12] This group spent a great deal of time in each other's company, usually around well-stocked dinner tables and with a rich diet of political discussion. For a period in the early 1970s, particularly in the run-up to the AUEW amalgamation, Ramelson would also meet with leaders from all four sectors of the proposed amalgamation (TASS, CEU, AEU, and the Foundry workers), usually accompanied by their wives, for a 'social' drink in a South London pub. Ken Gill's partner Norma Bramley told us that the 'social' quickly degenerated into a detailed discussion about the problems involved in integrating four unions' rule-books: Ramelson's legal brain was deeply appreciated by trade union leaders during such discussions.[13] After a few of these Friday night socials, Joan Ramelson turned to Bert and said, 'if you carry on like this I'm bloody well leaving and you can walk home'.[14]

As he had done throughout his career, Ramelson made a point of attending his own Party branch meetings. When addressing industrial comrades at Industrial Advisory meetings he would stress the importance of Party branch activity, knowing full well that many of his senior industrial comrades were not in touch with their basic Party units.[15] Ramelson was a well known local figure in Sydenham, often seen on the local High Street selling the *Morning Star*, addressing open air meetings, collecting signatures for CND petitions, and helping out at the annual *Morning Star* Christmas Bazaar. These activities were part of Ramelson's life despite the enormous burdens placed on him by his national and international responsibilities in the communist movement. Simon Steyne, a TUC official who lived in Sydenham during this period, clearly remembers on many Saturday mornings seeing Ramelson, then well into his seventies, engaging in public work for the CP and peace movement.[16] As Bill Alexander stressed, 'with Bert there was no question of telling others what to do – he set an example, inspiring others to join the struggle'.[17]

Though Ramelson was a political activist all his life, his duties reduced as he got older and he had more time for family and social life as a result. This meant that during the 1980s he was able to see much more of the family he had 'inherited' on marrying Joan. There was now more space in his life for family holidays, for long leisurely weekends, and for involving himself in his children and grandchildren's lives.[18] In turn they loved Bert and deeply appreciated his interest in them, with its unfailing good humour and unflagging energy.

Ramelson and trade unions

Ramelson had good personal relations with a number of trade union leaders on the left.[19] They recognised his unique experience, breadth of knowledge, and integrity – and they also knew that he commanded an effective, if relatively small, army of militants that were capable of influencing their organisations' policies and approaches. For his part Ramelson worked hard to understand the particular constraints placed on trade union leaders either by the circumstances of the industries in which they were working or by the balance of political forces within their own organisations. He also knew and respected the difference between 'on' and 'off' the record discussions.

Many people we interviewed for this book remarked on Ramelson's style of work.[20] These included a number of trade union leaders, in particular Ken Gill, who told us that Ramelson always listened carefully and offered a variety of options when giving advice. Before Ramelson's arrival at the national level the Party leadership had tended to hand down a general line which it was expected that comrades would follow, albeit adapted to the particular circumstances of their union or industry. Ramelson's advice was usually much more specific, based on his knowledge of the relevant and concrete conditions, and his understanding of the political balance of forces within a particular union. He was also a very good organiser, with a great eye for detail and an understanding of the importance of pre-planning and preparation. Vic Allen, who, with Ramelson's encouragement and support, did so much to organise a national broad left organisation within the NUM, remarked on Ramelson's ability to inspire others to undertake what were often daunting tasks. For example, according to Allen, it was at their very first meeting in 1966 (at a funeral!) that Ramelson had persuaded him – and he was not then a Party member – to take on the task of organising a national broad left in the NUM, a union which until then had been marked by acute regional rivalries.[21]

Ramelson's work with activists in the NUM offers one of the best examples of the way in which he operated. Evidence in Lawrence Daly's archive papers shows how deeply Ramelson was involved in the process of building an effective national broad-left organisation in the NUM, and of Vic Allen's key role as an intermediary between the CP (Ramelson and McGahey) and Daly in this exercise. This work was to be the decisive factor in winning the General Secretary's position for Daly, thus greatly strengthening the broad left's ability to determine union strategy. Among Daly's papers is a letter from Vic Allen in which he says:

> I saw Bert Ramelson last week ... we discussed the organisation of the meeting and agreed that either Jock Kane or Mick McGahey should be Chairman ... the gist of Ramelson's proposals were that: efforts should be made to get into Durham ... he suggested this course of action – [organising] a weekend school for which all branches are requested to send delegates; the establishment of a sort of Reference of Trade Union Committee in Yorkshire by miners, say the Doncaster Panel which would organise meetings to which you [Daly] would be invited ... and that you [Daly] should visit Yorkshire at least once a quarter.[22]

This was very much 'hands-on' leadership, drawing on years of experience and knowledge of the NUM. However Ramelson did not restrict himself to organisational advice. On 5 March 1968 he sent Daly a three-page letter with a friendly critique of a draft pamphlet (probably written by Daly, and possibly including input from Royden Harrison and John Hughes). Although the over-all approach of Ramelson's letter is highly supportive, the analysis is at times quite cutting.

Ramelson's main criticism was that Daly's draft did not 'lay sufficient stress on the cost to the community of pit closures'. He also comments: 'I would argue that all indications are that the only way to save the Labour Government from certain defeat in 1970 is by compelling changes of policy. To acquiesce in the present policies would be doing them [Labour] a disservice'. [23] This is also a good example of Ramelson's broad approach, and his sense of the need to build alliances – which predated by a decade the concept of a broad democratic alliance as developed in the CPGB's 1977 programme for *The British Road to Socialism*. In describing his work with Ramelson in the Broad Left Allen commented: 'he never seemed to follow a strict Party line in terms of the people he mixed with, though the policies he pursued were always consistent with CP aspirations. He wanted to make sure that only one left candidate stood for election'. [24] This non-sectarian and broad approach was characteristic of Ramelson's work at all times, and it was one of the secrets of his success: the Broad Left went on to secure complete ascendancy in the NUM. This approach was in stark contrast to that of other prominent left-wing (non-NUM) activists – especially ex-CP members involved in developing education programmes for miners. Partly for careerist reasons, many of them attempted to undermine the CP's influence within the union. Royden Harrison, a Professor at Warwick University in the 1970s, was probably the most active in pursuing this line. John McIlroy quotes approvingly an NUM member's recollection that Harrison had played a leading role 'in pointing out the negative aspects of the CP's role'. [25]

We have seen that Ramelson played an important role during the 1966 seafarers' strike and its aftermath, during which time the left made considerable gains in democratising the union and winning elected positions, as well as in policy terms. Bill Edwards, a London seafarer and prominent NUS activist at that time, recalled one episode in particular when Bert gave important assistance to these positive developments.

Following the death of the union's right-wing General Secretary Bill Hogarth in 1974, Ramelson led a discussion about who to back as the broad left candidate at a well attended meeting of CP members. The choice was between Jack Coward, a CP member with an outstanding record of militant leadership, not least during the 1966 strike, and Jim Slater, a Labour party member on the left who was respected by the CP members in the union. After a long debate, in which Ramelson held the ring while pointing out the possibilities of the union establishment and the press running an intensive, no-expenses-spared, anti-communist campaign against Coward, the comrades opted to campaign for Jim Slater as a broad left candidate. Ramelson's judgement was that Slater was in the better position to win the election, and that the Party, including himself, could work with the broad left to strengthen the struggle for progressive change in the unions. Slater subsequently won the election, beating two right-wing candidates, including Sam McCluskie, who later became Labour Party treasurer. [26]

Ramelson took care not to intervene in the democratic structures of the union, and to ensure that decisions were made by activists and not predetermined by a small group of leaders. He was also there to offer advice, based on a great wealth of experience, and in the knowledge that he usually had the support and respect of those he was trying to influence. He trod the delicate line between political leadership and party tutelage with great accomplishment. Ken Gill also recalled how Ramelson was able to synthesise factions and strategy in order to optimise progress for the broad left in the movement. This would often involve a short-term compromise in order to advance the medium-term objectives. According to Gill, Ramelson 'was the person above all who could explain the necessity for choosing the best that could be achieved tactically as part of a strategic approach to building left unity, left influence and left leadership of mass organisations. This was a quality that I've rarely seen in people who are advising others on how to take the world nearer to socialism, which was always Bert's main preoccupation'. Gill clearly relied heavily on Ramelson's judgement. Speaking as a former trade union General Secretary he told us:

when the great issues came up it would be crazy to go to your executive with ideas without having a word with Bert – he often initiated discussions on the big issues, anticipating that the union would need to take a view – and furthermore to learn from his trade union contacts what particular circumstances had to be taken into account so that the best possible outcome could be achieved.[27]

There were some nuts which even Bert Ramelson could not crack. For example, he could never find a way of building a close working relationship with Jack Jones, the most formidable and effective trade union leader of his generation. Ken Gill told us the story of a very public display of distancing which occurred at a Soviet Embassy function in the early 1970s. Jones, in a voice which could be heard right across a large room, told Ramelson 'to keep his Party out of my union'. So taken aback was Ramelson that he was temporarily speechless, and he was seen a little later in a corridor nurturing a large whiskey and with a packet of cigarettes for company. At first glance this apparent frostiness, which was entirely on Jones's side, is surprising. Both men had fought and been wounded in Spain. Both were working for the return of a Labour government and for a stronger more effective trade union movement, not least at shop steward level.

We also know that Ramelson had a great respect for Jones. This was confirmed in recent Secret Service revelations, which tell of hidden microphones picking up Ramelson's remarks in 1969 that assessed Jones as 'sound politically with courage and guts'.[28] All this was before the Social Contract years, however, in which Jones played a pivotal role in selling wage restraint to the movement, during which period Ramelson was unreservedly critical of Jones's approach. The same bugging device in 1969 picked up his next remark: 'the only dishonest thing about Jack was that he gave the impression that he was never in the Communist Party'. Geoffrey Goodman, who knew both men well, told us that at a gathering of Jewish comrades held at Arnold Kettle's house in Milton Keynes sometime in the late 1960s, Ramelson had told him that Jones had been a Party member in Spain, and that Jack knew that Ramelson was aware of this.[29] It appears that Jones left the Party in 1939, the year the CP instructed all secret members to 'come out' or leave. In that year Jones was appointed TGWU District Organiser in Coventry, leaving behind his CP comrades in Liverpool. Later, in 1945, he faced the anti-communist witch hunt in the TGWU initiated by Arthur Deakin, and chose not to talk about his CP past.[30] In these circumstances Jones preferred to bide his time rather than tackle head-on the undemocratic anti-communist bans and proscriptions introduced by Deakin.

After Jones retired in 1978, the relationship improved somewhat, once neither man was actively in a leadership position in his respective organisation. Ramelson recalled a discussion with Jones at a social function some time in the early 1980s.[31] Here Jones strongly defended the Social Contract, arguing that it had been sabotaged by Healey, through a mixture of IMF inspired cuts in the social wage and the imposition in 1978 of a 5 per cent limit on wage increases, at a time when inflation was running at around 10 per cent. Ramelson's argument was that if Healey had not done so someone else in the Labour Cabinet would have ensured that the Treasury's orders were carried out. You could not construct a social contract within capitalism that was favourable to workers and working people generally. There would always be disappointment for supporters of the Social Contract like Jones and Lawrence Daly: a Labour government led by the right would never deliver a bigger social wage in exchange for wage restraint at workplace level. Jones's support for the Social Contract never wavered, despite the unhappy record of the Wilson-Callaghan governments. Writing in the *Forward March of Labour Halted* he argued: 'for all of its deficiencies the idea of a social contract has quite a lot to recommend it. It means committing national union leaders to a definite immediate policy and if the policy is a right one it can enthuse to give cohesion to what is now a disunited army'.[32] Jones could never answer the crucial question of what happens if Labour reneges. Though the obvious answer would be to pull out of such a contract as soon as it appeared to be degenerating into a mechanism for wage restraint and nothing more, but Labour leaders knew full well that the political price of such an action would too high for trade union leaderships. Ramelson had no objection in principle to a voluntary agreement with a progressive government, but such agreements had to be underpinned by political trust and sound judgement. It was Ramelson's judgement that Healey could not be trusted; that the Cabinet were in thrall to Treasury and IMF thinking and policies; and that they had neither the intention nor the ability to deliver on their side of the social contract.

The importance of struggle

In his speeches and articles Ramelson returned time and again to the importance of struggle to the development of the progressive movement, particularly its revolutionary wing. Perhaps more than any other communist leader of his generation, he made the link between involvement in struggle and the growth of a socialist consciousness as opposed to class consciousness. In capitalist society, Ramelson argued, workers had to organise and struggle for better working conditions broadly defined – such as tenants for fairer rents, women for equal rights, and trade unionists for the freedom to collectively bargain and take strike action. Nothing would be handed out on a plate or through parliamentary action alone. In the course of these struggles, those involved could learn important lessons about the nature of the employment relationship, the role of the capitalist state in upholding property rights, and the approach of the capitalist class to radical social change encompassing fundamental human rights. On a more prosaic level, struggle promoted organisation and, where successful, gave confidence in the potency of collective action as well as developing individual cadres. The willingness of workers to take action also forced employers to take their demands seriously or face a serious threat of disruption to their operations. It also assisted trade union leaderships in their negotiations with companies and governments. In a pluralistic society the extent to which the law and the state permitted effective struggle determined the amount of progress reached in the continuous campaign to protect and extend democratic rights.

Ramelson always argued strongly for normal collective bargaining as the best environment in which to strengthen the unions and advance living standards. He made the point time and again that if workers and unions were not prepared to fight for wage increases then they would not be prepared to mobilise behind more advanced demands. When convinced of the need to challenge the employer on the basic issue of wages, workers were more likely to broaden their demands and the scope of the bargaining agenda. For Ramelson the demand for a 'socialist incomes policy', where national trade union leaders talked to national government and traded wage increases for public service improvements, tax cuts, and limitations on management rights, was 'pie in the sky'. Furthermore, policies like the Social Contract were demoralising and undemocratic because they removed the point of decision away from the workplace and into Whitehall boardrooms. While on a very practical level, the results of wage restraint policies were uniformly bad from a working-class perspective. In Ramelson's view the wages struggle mobilised workers, thereby giving them a sense of their own power and ability to change aspects of their working lives.

On humanism and equality

Lecturing to a factory branch conference in the mid-1960s, Ramelson spelt out his views on the political role of the industrial working class and what it meant to be an active, committed communist. His notes begin with his analysis of the impact on factory work on class consciousness: 'factories are where workers meet and understand their common problems, can best appreciate their power and where they can most efficiently bring this collective strength to bear'. He goes on to outline what he saw as the attributes that being a communist conferred on individual members. These included the ability to see each struggle on immediate issues as a step on the path to socialism, and to see socialism as a system which corresponded to the developing needs of humankind. It was therefore a system which was intensely human, which could provide for cultural as well as material needs, and which could provide humankind with the solution to such intractable problems as war, disease, and poverty. He urged those attending the conference 'to have humility towards the Party which makes different people of us', and summed up the role of the CP factory branch as being 'to agitate, to arouse, to raise both confidence in the ability to win advances and anger at the inequities of capitalist property relationships including power relations at work'.

He finished his lecture by outlining what he saw as 'the main sources of deep satisfaction you get by being a communist'. These included gaining an understanding that cruelty, greed and prejudice are not in fact part of human nature, but the product of a specific environment which we have power to change; and that

> because of this understanding, a communist never despairs, is never pessimistic. Communism is a philosophy of optimism, of boundless confidence in the future. Communists are agents of change.[33]

Here Ramelson is expressing the profound humanism which guided his conduct and whole approach to life.

There can be no question about Ramelson's commitment to issues of equality and human and social rights. Though it was not his role to be centrally involved in developing campaigns on these questions, he was aware of the work being carried out by others in the Party, and gave helpful advice about how best to work with the trade union movement in advancing work on equality.[34] Thus he would ensure that the Party's *Needs of the Hour* bulletin reflected the demands of the broad movement in campaigning for gender and racial equality.[35] However it was, for example, the Party's Race Relations Advisory Committee, rather than Ramelson's industrial department, that, through its work with organisations such as Trade Unionists to Combat Racism and Liberation, played the most important part in advancing the anti-racist agenda in the 1970s trade union movement.

The same observation can be made about the interface with the Party's International Department. While the increased attention to international issues at TUC level can partly be explained by the CP's input into congress resolutions through *Needs of the Hour*, it was mainly left to comrades active in such movements as Anti-Apartheid and Chile Solidarity to advance the Party's approach and priorities within the labour movement. Ramelson was deeply interested in the international scene and was always up to speed on the varying issues, but generally he left campaigning strategies to those comrades most deeply involved in solidarity movements.

Ramelson the public speaker

Ramelson was a gifted public speaker and readily accepted invitations to speak to a variety of audiences, despite the heavy pressures imposed by his main Party responsibilities. A number of ex-students recall Ramelson addressing university and college meetings on a variety of topics. Mike Squires remembered Ramelson's visits to Swansea University to talk about the Middle East, and Mitch Howard recalled lively meetings of the Socialist Society at Sheffield University in the 1960s.[36]

Perhaps more surprisingly, Ramelson also spoke to the senior boys at Eton College and to senior officers at the Police College. The Eton schoolmaster Mr J.E. Garlinski wrote a short thank you note in November 1978, in which he referred to Ramelson's energetic address and went on, 'I sincerely hope that you found it as worthwhile an experience as we did. May I wish you every success'.[37] A letter from the Director of Command Courses at the Police College was even more remarkable:

Your lecture to the senior course at the college entitled 'The Communist Goal in the UK' was exactly what we had in mind when we invited you to Bramshill earlier this year. It is most unusual for a speaker here to deliver a formal lecture for fifty minutes, and then enter into questions and discussions for something approaching a further two hours, but the interest that you were still maintaining at the end of the morning spoke volumes for the way you stimulated the students, and captured their imagination.

We all found the experience extremely worthwhile and I must thank you for giving up your time and coming to the college to help us in this respect. We appreciate your help and hope to see you here on some future occasion.[38]

Ramelson loved debate and discussion and saw the importance of taking socialist ideas into areas of British life where they were rarely heard, hoping they would influence future generations of state cadres, whether they were civil servants, police officers or teachers.

Paul Dunn, an ex-miner, remembers Ramelson addressing large audiences at Oxford Town Hall, mainly of students, each year during his period of office as Chair (1972-3) of the Oxford Com-Club, which was organised by the Oxford University Student Branch of the CP.[39] Tom Sibley recalls a packed meeting in the Buxton Hall, Ruskin College, in 1971, at which Ramelson held forth against the iniquities and dangers to the labour movement of the Tory Industrial Relations Bill. What was memorable about the meeting, beside Ramelson's *tour de force*, was the warmth with which Ramelson greeted old associates (in some cases the children of Party stalwarts) from Yorkshire. These included Paul Brodetsky, then a politics tutor at Ruskin; Martin Kettle, son of Margot and Arnold Kettle and a leading light in the Oxford Student Branch (now a leader writer on the *Guardian*); and Simon Mohun, now a Professor at London University.

This somewhat surprising and extensive record of attention to the student body is explained by Ramelson's conviction that it was from here that the next generation of Marxist intellectuals would be largely drawn. Student politics might be limited, but the creation of an intellectual cadre force was essential to the building of an effective revolutionary party. That this was Ramelson's approach was confirmed by former Birmingham University student and now university lecturer John Corcoran. Corcoran states that Ramelson told him after a series of lectures, 'the National Union of Students is not that important, but Party members who will become active trade unionists in the professions and the public sector learn their trade union stripes in the NUS'. Corcoran also observed of Ramelson: 'He was always thinking strategically and said that what made "The Party" different was its ability to engage and recruit people to produce a lifelong commitment … "lifers", he wryly said, "he was interested in"'.[40]

The Labour Party

Ramelson had somewhat different views from most members of the CP leadership on the nature of the British labour movement. For example, he had no illusions about the possibilities of building a mass CP in the Italian mould, nor was he convinced by arguments for a widespread Communist electoral strategy. He remained committed to Pollitt's view that the CP would only make an electoral impact as an affiliated body of the Labour Party, and later recalled discussions before the 1959 edition of the *British Road to Socialism* where he had been defeated on the question of campaigning for affiliation to the Labour Party.[41] At this stage he had seriously considered voting against the whole draft, but on reflection had decided that, since apart from this one issue he was content with the draft, he could therefore vote for it. Ramelson argued the same position in the run up to the 1977 revision of the *British Road*. He clearly did not favour the concept of a mass party competing widely against Labour in the electoral field. He felt that this led to certain defeat and disillusionment among active Party members, as well as making relations with the Labour and trade union left more difficult. He preferred a party of Marxist activists working alongside the Labour left in the mass organisations, and seeking to move such bodies towards a socialist perspective.

It is now some thirty-five years since Ramelson was at the height of his political powers and the notion that the Labour Party could be at the centre of the struggle for socialism seems more unlikely year by year. Yet Ramelson always argued that what gave Labour its socialist potential was that it remained a federal party with significant trade union affiliation and participation. It also continued to attract considerable electoral support, dwarfing that of the extra-parliamentary left. As long as this remained the case, the line that the trade unions held the key and that Labour still had the potential to become a party of the left with mass support remained valid. Today the debacle of New Labour has left the movement at a crossroads – including those supporting revolutionary change. As yet a viable alternative to a trade-union supported Labour Party has not emerged. Until it does Ramelson's strongly held views remain viable, namely to work to win left policies in the unions, to build workplace organisation, and to propagate socialist ideas as well as supporting those in struggle against the employers and the state.

The ultra-left

Much of Ramelson's attitude to the ultra-left can be seen in his 1977 response to Jim Nichol's letter on behalf the SWP Central Committee to the Political Committee of the CP, which called for the 'unity of the Communist Party, ourselves and left-wing members of the Labour party … [because it] … could rapidly reverse the tide of defeats in industry'.[42]

Ramelson's detailed reply in the *Morning Star* reflected the experience of many communists working at rank-and-file level, particularly in developing the work of the LCDTU. He made a number of points critical of the SWP's approach. For example: 'your disregard of decisions adopted by meetings of the left in which you participate is further evidence … that you create disunity and play into the hands of the right wing of Tories'. He also took to task the failure of the SWP to offer anything on policy issues other than criticism of labour movement leaders. This, he argued, was not enough to develop and mobilise the movement: 'It is also essential to propose an alternative policy credible for working people and assisting the process of them moving into action for left, socialist change. Yet the alternative policy our Party advocates is constantly misrepresented and attacked in your press and meetings'. In sum: 'In our view, and indeed in our experience, your activity and propaganda is divisive and disruptive, making more difficult the development of united mass struggle'. It is fair to conclude from this that Ramelson had little time for ultra-left groups, whether Trotskyists or militant syndicalists – which probably most accurately describes the rather inchoate politics of the SWP in this period. Nonetheless, in a limited number of areas there is some evidence of co-operation with left activists outside of the Labour Party; for example, the Building Workers' Charter movement, although clearly led by the communists, did involve SWP activists, who generally made a positive contribution to the struggle.[43]

Ramelson's views on ultra-leftism had been partly shaped on the battlefields of the Spanish Civil War, where, in general, anarchist and Trotskyite leaders were divisive in their politics and actions, though many of their followers were brave anti-fascist soldiers. He also had some views on Trotskyism as a political ideology. In notes prepared for a Party school, Ramelson described Trotsky as a 'great Marxist'.[44] He went on to observe that Trotsky had not joined the Bolsheviks until July 1917, and that before that he had been a centrist with no allies, while his post-1917 life had been spent in constant opposition to the Party, and in opposing Lenin on nearly all issues.

Ramelson went on to note that the Trotskyist movement was characterised by a lack of confidence in the working class – that they reflexively oppose across-class alliances, fearing that the working class will be incorporated or led astray by potential allies. This view of the nature of the SWP and its style of political polemic had been influenced by Ramelson's experiences during the seafarers' strike, as well as by the way Paul Foot had, in the summer of 1977, abused the opportunity given him by the *Morning Star* to contribute to a discussion on the future prospects for socialist advance. Paul Foot – then editor of the *Socialist Worker* and constant critic of the CP and all its works – did acknowledge the positive role played by individual communists in a number of campaigns, but had damning words for the Party as a whole. He argued that 'so many years slavish support for Russian policies had deprived the old communists of the habit of argument'.[45] He went on to emphasise that the CP was 'past it', stating that 'during the 1950s, the CP shed much of its pre-war revolutionary politics and aspirations, by adopting an electoral strategy tending towards reformism'.[46]

Ramelson's reply centred on recent and current campaigns,[47] he argued that no other sect or Party would have had the 'will or the influence' to launch the LCDTU's campaign against *In Place of Strife* and the Industrial Relations Act, a campaign which some months later was powerful enough to persuade the TUC General Council to call a General Strike and procure the release of the Pentonville Five. Foot might assert that the CP was finished – Ramelson could cite living proof that it was very much alive and kicking. Whatever might be claimed, Ramelson had certainly not lost the habit of argument.

Internationalism

In every sense Ramelson was a child of the Russian Revolution and a fully fledged member of the international communist movement. He was an internationalist who took great inspiration and satisfaction from the role played by the Soviet Union and the British Party in helping to bring about the ending of colonialism. He saw the Soviet Union as the emancipator of the Jewish people in 1917, 1945 and 1948 with the support it gave to the formation of Israel. He recognised the positive role that the Soviet Union played in promoting the objectives of a world free from nuclear weapons. He was no abstract moraliser. He recognised that in the life and death struggle to defend the socialist state against its enemies' mistakes and crimes could occur under the pressure of events, no matter how vigilant and farsighted the Party leadership. Unlike some Communists, Ramelson was not afraid to voice – often privately and sometimes publicly when he felt it to be necessary – his disquiet about action and practices which violated the norms of socialist democracy.

For Ramelson, like many of his generation, the fight against fascism was pivotal in the quest to build a better world, free from exploitation, oppression and poverty. In this the Soviet Union, both in Spain and in the Second World War, was the lynchpin of the anti-fascist forces. By showing that it was possible to organise a huge and relatively backward country along socialist lines, the CPSU became a beacon of progress for people across the globe. The Khrushchev revelations about the enormity of the crimes that had been committed in the name of socialism during Stalin's years raised very difficult questions for communists everywhere, but Ramelson shared the Italian leader Togliatti's general view: 'it is in nobody's interest for these criticisms to become the rallying-cry for the usual champions of anti-Communism'.[48] Furthermore, while the British Party had been forthright in its criticism of aspects of Soviet policy, at least since 1956, its main responsibility was for its actions as a revolutionary force in Britain and not as a commentator on developments in the Soviet Union, which it had little or no chance of influencing.

Ramelson's life was almost coterminous with that of the Soviet Union. He saw the Bolsheviks come to power, ending the ghettoisation of Jews and outlawing anti-semitism. He fought in Spain with Soviet weapons and served with Soviet generals. He saw that it was only the Soviet Union in the 1930s that had worked to build alliances of peace and against Nazi expansionism. As a soldier in the British Army he recognised that it was the Soviet Red Army which had, in Churchill's words, 'ripped the guts' out of the Nazi war machine. In sharp contrast, however, his beloved sister Rosa had been a victim of the Stalinist terror, and spent nearly ten years in a labour camp where her husband died.

It is a lazy commonplace of anti-communist political analysis that all the key decisions made by the British Party for most of its existence were in fact made in Moscow, in order to advance Soviet foreign policy objectives. John McIlroy goes as far as to claim that communists of Ramelson's generation were complicit in Stalinism's crimes against humanity – presumably on the grounds of association rather than participation.[49] A less extreme view, often voiced by older members of the Labour Party with a record of consistent left activity, is that CP members would fight injustice wherever they came upon it but would not speak out against Stalin's crimes or the demise of democratic and civil rights in the Soviet Union.

The suggestion that Ramelson and his generation of British Communists were in any way morally culpable or responsible for Soviet crimes against human rights is dangerously and mischievously wrong. It is on a par with the comments of professional anti-communist Denis MacShane, who once remarked that 'Bert Ramelson used to joke that he shot more Trotskyists in the back then fascists in the front'.[50] MacShane, who could not have made such a statement during Ramelson's lifetime, should have known that Ramelson did not make jokes about such matters. Similar but no less egregious remarks have been made by the SWP historian Chris Harman. Without a shred of evidence and quoting not one source, he alleged that in May 1937 Ramelson was sent by Stalinist leaders to shoot anarchists and Trotskyists who were fighting against the government's anti-Franco forces in Barcelona. This is a total fabrication. Ramelson did not arrive in Spain until April 1937, and spent his first few months there in training camps.[51] Harman also claimed that Ramelson was directly responsible for the expulsion from the CP of Saville and Thompson in 1956. As we have seen, the two men were not expelled but resigned, after Ramelson had worked very hard to persuade them to stay in the Party, while persuading others on the EC to desist from taking disciplinary action (see p62-66).

There was much that British Communists did not know about in the Soviet Union, particularly in the 1930s. They respected the achievements of the Soviet system, and they knew that every criticism they made would be picked up and magnified ten-fold to discredit socialism as a system of government and theoretical base for supplanting capitalism. More could and should have been done to critically analyse Soviet developments but this was a political judgement, not a morality test. Fred Westacott, a longstanding Party full-time worker who died in 2002, put it like this: 'I accepted that there were weaknesses and that mistakes were made, but the ones we knew about paled into insignificance compared with the achievements and the historical importance of a new socialist society in the process of being created'.[52]

First and foremost Ramelson was a British Communist. Like Party activists everywhere he took strength from being part of the international movement which he saw as a powerful force striving for peace and social justice all over the world. Being associated with the international movement alongside parties who had taken and exercised state power was not always comfortable. No other section of the British labour movement, from the Labour Party to the ultra-left, had a comparable network of solidarity links, or such a consistent record of opposition to British imperialism and colonialism. In an interview in the late 1950s Nelson Mandela was asked to comment on the fact that there was never any criticism of the Soviet Union in his speeches or articles. His reply was: 'In the whole world they're our only friends. You don't attack your friends'.[53]

OVERVIEW

In many respects Bert Ramelson was a modest man not known for making claims about his personal contribution to the struggle for social and economic advance. For Ramelson it was the Party and the movement which mattered, and any gains made were achieved as a result of collective efforts. Nonetheless, political biographers are called upon to make assessments about the role of the individual. It is clear that Bert Ramelson was the most significant figure in the British Communist Party between 1965 and 1979, and that he made one of the most important contributions to strategic thinking across the whole labour movement during this period.

Ramelson was a well-read Marxist whose deep understanding of theory enabled him to successfully apply this to the practice (both art and science) of the class struggle. He brought this understanding both to the Party and to his work in the trade union movement. As a member of the national Party leadership since 1953 he made an important contribution to the process of developing the Party's programme the *British Road to Socialism*, which for a small Party was a major achievement. It added greatly to the understanding of the need for revolutionary change in Britain as well as raising awareness in the international labour movement of the possibilities of winning and defending state power through a combination of parliamentary and extra-parliamentary struggle. Ramelson was proud of the Party's achievement in drafting such a programme and in updating it periodically over nearly three decades of rapidly changing economic and political developments.

Ramelson's main and considerable contributions were in the field of industrial strategy. Above all he was interested in movement building and, within that, of linking militancy and trade union struggle to the development of a mass socialist consciousness. Like generations of British communists before him, Ramelson saw the organised working class as the core of any revolutionary movement. He recognised that the official trade union movement, with its direct links to the Labour Party and the workplace, was the main political expression of the working people, and therefore the key area of ideological and political struggle. Above all Ramelson provided the strategic thinking which linked progressive changes in the official movement, which for decades before the mid-1960s had been dominated by right-wing reformist leaders, to the development of an effective rank-and-file movement. This meant working with rank-and-file communists and others on the left, including progressive trade union officials, to strengthen broad left organisation in all major unions, which, in Ramelson's view, involved the vital first step of building CP organisation at workplace, industry and union level.

His central conclusion was that only through struggle could the basis be laid for building class consciousness. Rank-and-file activity allied to political clarity could force trade union leaders to the left and 'keep them honest'. The election of left trade union leaders and the subsequent possibility of changing Labour Party policy was not the alternative to building workplace organisation and activity: the two developments were mutually reinforcing. This approach enabled

Ramelson, working with a small group of CP rank-and-file senior activists led by Kevin Halpin, to play a significant role in promoting the LCDTU – arguably the most successful workplace based national organisation in the history of the British trade union movement.

Ramelson also provided strong ideological leadership in the CP's broad campaign against wage controls, including his debates within the Party's economic committee against the neo-Gramscians, where he succeeded in showing the basic flaw in their argument for critical support for a social contract. Here he argued that wage restraint in any guise would demobilise a main engine for progressive social change – the organised trade union movement, particularly at workplace level. This would hold back the struggle to achieve redistribution in the short term and socialism in the longer term. He also argued that the Labour leaders of the 1970s were not interested in progressive social change, but only in using the Social Contract to underpin wage restraint and falling living standards for working people. With a left government things would be different. It could then be possible to discuss a voluntary incomes policy together with normal collective bargaining. Ramelson's view was that the two were not mutually exclusive.

Besides being an innovator in strategic thinking, Ramelson also helped to bring new approaches to the means of struggle, as, for example, with his promotion of the flying picket strategy in the Yorkshire coalfield, and the LCDTU – the first national rank-and-file movement which had the prime strategic objective of forcing the official unions to the left rather than becoming an alternative centre of power. He was also a formidable propagandist and advocate for socialism, both in his speeches and his writings, particularly his pamphlets.

In the end the Party to which Ramelson gave his life's work disintegrated. Critics have explained the CP's failure as an inability to establish an independent political identity. They argue that the Party's revolutionary strategy was too dependent on the Labour Party and left trade union leaders in delivering a socialist parliamentary majority backed by extra-parliamentary struggle. As part of the international communist movement it was seen to be subservient to the interests of the Soviet Union. In all essentials these critics present the CP as a reformist fringe Party without a distinctive role to play, and without either the ambition or ability to have made a significant contribution to progressive politics in Britain. Once the temporary successes of the 1960s and 1970s, mainly in the trade union field, had been overtaken by changes in industrial structures, which marginalised traditional industries and undermined the position of skilled manual workers, the demise of the Party began to seem a possibility; and the collapse of the Soviet Union in 1990 ensured that the death throes were short and dramatic. This argument is put forward by both Geoff Andrews and John Callaghan in their contributions to the series on the history of the Party published by Lawrence & Wishart.[54]

Ramelson did not accept any part of this analysis. In his view the Party's contribution was important and distinctive. It supplied the working-class movement with a realistic revolutionary strategy and Marxist perspective, which provided an understanding of how society worked, at home and internationally. It was linked with a vast international movement giving it the knowledge and experience other sections of the labour movement did not have, and enabling it to play an important role in the anti-colonial movement and in anti-imperialist solidarity work. Despite its small size it was able to sustain Britain's only socialist daily newspaper over the last sixty years of its existence, and to provide generations of activists with a political education which was often used to benefit the whole of the labour movement.[55] This is a formidable legacy to which Ramelson made a considerable contribution.

Analysing the decline of the Party

A central question remained about the CP's failure to build on the industrial successes of the 1960s and 1970s in order to create a bigger, more influential organisation, and a stronger left movement in Britain. Above all the problem was that the Party failed to create a new generation of CP industrial activists, as Kelly sums up: 'it was failing to sustain its organisation at the union base. Contrary to some claims, this was not the inevitable by-product of the broad left strategy; rather it was a result of the Party's failure to recruit among young workers and to replenish its activist core'.[56] As McIlroy shows, however, this was not for the want of trying.[57]

The failure to recruit was partly due to the impact of the Cold War. As Ramelson observed in 1987: 'Anti-communist hysteria has been with us for four generations and it would be non-Marxist to believe that anti-communism in the West has not struck deep roots in politics, ideology and consciousness'.[58] At the start of the 1960s it was the industrial activists who had been trained in the 1940s – before the Cold War had really taken hold – who were in influential positions. By the mid-1970s many of them were retired, past their best, or had become union full-time officials. The cold-war generation, who had been young workers in the 1950s, came into the movement at a time when the Party was isolated and vilified by the right wing. It is this 'lost generation' which was by the mid-1970s in shop floor leadership positions. Their experiences and attitudes were then passed onto younger activists, some of whom were attracted by the energies of the new left – as well as being repelled by some of the developments in Eastern and Central Europe.

As we have shown such a stream of misrepresentations had been well illustrated by Paul Foot's piece on the 1966 seaman's strike, in which, without a shred of evidence, he had accused Ramelson of advocating a return to work.[59] This was part of the ultra-left's argument that the CP was itself part of the reformism of the labour movement and was 'focused on bread and butter issues and on the union hierarchies at the expense of ideological struggle to make Marxists'.[60] There is, however, no evidence that the kind of strategy urged by the ultra-left – a more adventurist or syndicalist strategy, based mainly on rank-and-file struggle, with independent structures in opposition to the official movement – would have been any more successful as a means to build a revolutionary Party. On the contrary, the ultra-left groups which adopted such strategies were spectacularly unsuccessful industrially and made very little progress in recruiting to their own ranks.[61]

In fact the CP made every effort to 'make Marxists', through extensive Party literature and education programmes and it is unclear why there should be an assumed conflict between this and influencing union hierarchies. During these years the CP helped publish a daily newspaper which regularly included articles on Marxist theory, a fortnightly magazine *Comment*, with regular features of a theoretical nature, and a monthly theoretical journal *Marxism Today*. Industrial schools were also a regular feature of the Party's education work. Indeed, in his evidence to the Donovan Commission, respected trade union education specialist John Hughes stated: 'Communist Party "servicing" of its members, in the sense of provision of information, education and training, has often been relatively efficient where much union servicing has been deficient'.[62] All of this 'servicing' had ideological content.

The reality is that the material and, more importantly, political conditions changed after 1979, with the election of Thatcher's right-wing Tory government, such that the balance of class forces moved sharply against the organised working class; and the union left were simply not strong enough to resist. The effects of deindustrialisation and mass unemployment were compounded by anti-union laws and a renewed iron-willed determination to defeat any major public sector strike; and the defeat of the miners in 1985 effectively put the lid on any possibility of an early union recovery. New Labour's response to this was to continue the strategy begun in the 1960s and 1970s, and to resolve that they too would marginalise union power – as was fully demonstrated, for example, during the 2002-4 fire fighters' dispute.[63] Initially, as Ramelson had fully expected, the industrial struggles of the 1960s and 1970s had brought with them political gains for the left, and the Labour Party had moved sharply to the left during the early 1980s. In the face of splits and electoral unpopularity, the Labour Party once more began to shift towards the right after the election of Neil Kinnock as leader in 1983.

At some stage in the mid-1970s Ramelson had probably expected to see a left Labour government in power during his lifetime, with a progressive programme that opened out possibilities for a socialist transition in the future. It was clear by the end of the 1980s that this was not going to happen. For Ramelson this was a serious setback but not a mortal blow to the cause of socialism: he remained convinced that socialism was the future for humankind, including the British people.

As well as the problems of the wider labour movement and left during the 1980s, the CP also had to face the development of a world crisis for the international communist movement. Ramelson's views on the overall failure of the Communist movement to sustain, let alone take forward, the advances that had been made in many parts of the world between 1945 and the late 1960s are not recorded at any length. However, it is clear from various contributions he made to seminars and discussion groups at the *World Marxist Review*, that he attributed great importance to subjective factors in producing this failure; in general he argued against regarding objective factors – such as changes within the working class and production methods in the capitalist world – as the catalyst for communist decline. For Ramelson the working class was always in a state of change, but one fundamental remained unchanged – *relations* of production within capitalism would ensure that workers remained exploited economically and oppressed politically. The failure of the existing socialist countries to realise their potential, and the tenacity and strength of the capitalist world in spite of its regular economic crises, had led to frustration, disappointment and impatience in Communist ranks: 'The truth is that we have tended to underestimate capitalism's capacity to adapt to the chronic crisis … while overrating our expectations of the speed with which socialism would spread its influence'.[64] In reaction to these developments many people, particularly but not exclusively those newer to the movement or from non-working class backgrounds and experiences, started to call into question basic Marxist-Leninist precepts and categories. This in turn led to enervating discussions within the international communist movement, presaging organisational splits, electoral decline and a weakening of its working-class base.

It is now also clear that Ramelson had by the late 1980s come to the view that 'actual existing socialism' was not socialism at all. He had already in previous years recognised the failure of the Soviet Union to extend democratic liberties and create opportunities for the people to control their working, social and cultural lives, but he had also argued that the commanding heights of the economy were in public ownership, a fundamental feature of any society calling itself socialist. During the 1980s the doubts of previous years began to multiply. He saw that in country after country, the ruling CP had lost touch with the people and that when challenges arose it was unable to mobilise its members – let alone the masses – in defence of the cultural and social gains that had been made over several decades. The experiences and habits of a lifetime had to be re-evaluated in the light of these developments. While the Soviet Union in Gorbachev's time remained in the broadest terms a progressive force on the international stage, it was no longer a reliable ally in the struggle against imperialism, nor a champion of socialism as a world system. Many of the pressing reasons for Communist defence of the Soviet Union against ideological and political attacks were long gone. Very soon afterwards they were to become matters for historical analysis rather than current political discourse, as the Soviet Union collapsed and a form of unregulated and frequently criminal capitalism spread rapidly across the former Socialist Republics. In all of this China was seen as of growing importance for the world communist movement, but Ramelson like many other comrades in Europe, made few references to Chinese developments and showed little interest in Chinese communism at the time.

Some critics

David Purdy was probably the most consistent and persistent critic of Ramelson's economic and political strategy. Purdy argued for a socialist incomes policy as part of a democratically planned economy as the best way of advancing the living standards of working people and opening up possibilities for revolutionary change.[65] His argument was that this project, which was consistent with the approach advocated at the time by senior trade union figures such as Jack Jones, Hugh Scanlon and Lawrence Daly, could force the Labour leadership to the left. It would enable the labour movement as a whole to present itself as the leading force in a broad democratic alliance of objectively anti-capitalist class and social interests.

Ramelson strongly disagreed with this approach, arguing that it was essentially 'pie in the sky', since at the time Labour's leadership was interested only in wages control, not in democratic planning to challenge capitalist interests; and that in these circumstances any form of incomes policy would disarm the working class. What is more, argued Ramelson, the rank-and-file movement simply would not accept wage restraint over any extended period, so that even if it was desirable (which it was not), a 'socialist incomes policy' was not sustainable, because it would not command mass support. Of course in different circumstances – with a left Labour government seen to be actively pursuing policies undermining capitalist interests and transferring wealth and power to working people – it might be possible to agree an approach on wages that preserved normal collective bargaining but in reaching wage settlements took into account the government's policies.

Despite their differences, Purdy seems to have respected Ramelson personally and enjoyed the cut and thrust of the debate on the Party's Economic Committee while Ramelson was its Chairman. He also made comments about Ramelson and the norms of communist democracy that appear quite wrong-headed, including the claim that Ramelson committed the 'egregious' sin of censorship when he convinced the Party leadership in 1976 not to publish a text that had been drawn up by the members of the Economic Advisory Committee. As Purdy explains, 'The main reason for cancelling the project was that the chapter dealing with the economics of State monopoly capitalism expressed views on the causes of inflation and the need for an incomes policy which were at odds with the official Party line'.[66] It is, however, hardly surprising that a pamphlet critical of the Party's approach to one of the most important issues of the time should have been denied its approval and resources.

Andrews claims that in the Party's Economic Committee the intellectuals and industrial and political leaders were constantly at loggerheads. He goes on to argue, correctly, that there was substantial support for incomes policy on the committee and arguably majority support. In fact the argument was much more nuanced than this. For example, academics such as Ron Bellamy and Ben Fine strongly supported Ramelson's position of total opposition to government imposed incomes policy. Furthermore, the Economic Committee was not there to make Party policy. It was an Advisory Committee, whose attendance was by invitation and extremely variable. In this context, to talk of majority support is irrelevant. What mattered was the position adopted by the Executive Committee, and to suggest that the Party's refusal to publish a textbook consisting of a series of contributions arguing against Party policy was an act of censorship rather than political judgement shows how far Andrews and Purdy are from understanding normal democratic practices or the political culture of the communist movement.[67]

Writing in 1995, Andrews portrayed Ramelson as a member of the old guard of what in his view was by the 1970s a moribund Party. He puts Ramelson in the same camp as McLennan and Falber, and claims that together these comrades had 'presided over an internalised culture of decline and routinism which in its own logic could justify the freezing out of invention'.[68] For the sake of accuracy it is important to note that Ramelson had retired from the Party leadership at the 1977 Congress, and the 'old guard' still in the leadership in the 1980s included people like George Matthews, who by the end of the 1970s was very much in the camp of the 'reformers'. McLennan too, though his position was more complicated, by the end of the 1970s was totally supportive of the *Marxism Today* tendency. Thus it is clear that the alleged division between the old guard and the 'young Turks' does not bear serious scrutiny. Indeed there were many intellectuals of similar vintage to Martin Jacques who strongly opposed the *Marxism Today* 'inventors'. [69] In fact Ramelson had an appetite second to none for debate, the clash of opinions and the development of theory, and he is the last person that could be accused of 'routinism'. If new ideas were good ideas he welcomed them, but he fought bad ideas and bad inventions with a great ferocity. Not for him the calculation of political advantage nor the need to lie low in case a potential future ally was lost. To those who knew him Ramelson was the antithesis of Dennis Healey's Comintern official and Andrews' servant of the Party machine (see p15).

At a conference organised by the Democratic Left in 2000, its secretary, Nina Temple, made a scathing attack on Ramelson's work for the communist movement.[70] She claimed that Ramelson's period as industrial organiser was 'dedicated to the creation of a manipulative, secretive and bureaucratic machine'; and that the industrial department had been operating as a secretive Leninist organisation, with its industrial organisers being more interested in keeping in touch with the officials of the hierarchy of the union movement than in attempting to win large numbers of ordinary trade unionists to new positions. This attack was totally baseless: Ramelson wrote countless pamphlets and articles addressed to 'ordinary trade unionists', attempting to win them to new positions. He was always available to speak at public meetings and always preferred to meet – on a one-to-one or group basis – rank-and-file activists. Where necessary he openly challenged and criticised union leaders both of the right and the left. *Needs of the Hour* was drawn up after consultation with industrial advisory elected officials and with CP Heads of Department. Time and time again Ramelson returned to the need to build rank-and-file unity, broad left organisation and activity, and CP workplace branches. These were in Ramelson's eyes complementary and linked activities.

Temple's line of argument can be seen as representative of the neo-Gramscian attack on established Party policy and practice. These matters were never raised openly, least of all at Party Congresses in the 1960s and 1970s. Indeed the Party was proud of its industrial work and its achievements in mobilising struggle, advancing left policies in the movement and building broad left organisation at rank-and-file level. Thus at the July 1977 EC, when it had become clear that union conferences had rejected the Social Contract, General Secretary McLennan proclaimed: 'This is a great victory for the working class movement. We are immensely proud of what we have done along with others on the left to bring it about'.[71]

In essence the neo-Gramscians wanted the industrial department to concentrate on party building, at the expense of attempting to work alongside others on the left to mobilise mass struggle and change union and Labour Party policy. In particular, national organiser Dave Cook had argued that the Party's workplace branches should come under the aegis of the industrial department rather than that of the organisation department. Ramelson had an entirely different view: it was the job of the Districts and local branches to nurture existing and build new factory branches, and it was impossible to do this from national headquarters even if it were given extra resources within the range of possibilities available to a small party. Ramelson worked tirelessly to increase the Party's influence, but he realised that this was inextricably linked to the development of left policies and socialist ideas in the broad labour movement. The British Party could not build socialism on its own; and neither should it try. In the end the neo-Gramscians fell between every possible stool. On their watch during the 1980s the Party's influence quickly dwindled in the labour movement, and wider civil society was oblivious to the Party's presence once its industrial base had gone.

Ramelson's socialist vision

Monty Meth's funeral oration described Ramelson as the most important figure to emerge from the Yorkshire labour movement since the war. Gordon McLennan in his interview with Rachel Seifert acknowledged that in the collective national communist leadership of the 1960s Ramelson had made the biggest all-round contribution. His knowledge and involvement spread far wider than trade union and labour movement politics and he was acknowledged as an authority on many international issues. He could more than hold his own in any forum on a wide range of topics, including complex theoretical issues related to developments within Marxism. In Geoffrey Goodman's assessment, in any small discussion group of labour movement leaders during the

1960s and 1970s Ramelson's voice would have been the clearest and most authoritative. From this, and from all that we know about his political practice, it is reasonable to conclude that Ramelson was – as Bill Moore put it – Britain's leading communist for at least two decades. He was a man of total integrity who was absolutely committed to the struggle to build socialism in Britain as part of a better world for human-kind. As we have seen, in some respects he died a disappointed man.

It is clear that most of the world-shattering developments of the late 1980s and early 1990s were totally outside of Ramelson's field of influ-ence – and that of the British communist movement as a whole. The breaking up of the Soviet Union, the unification of Germany within the NATO alliance and the ending of Communist rule in Central and Eastern Europe clearly affected the morale of British communists and their status in the wider labour movement. Life would never be the same for the Communist movement. As far as Britain was concerned, Ramelson remained convinced that a socialist revolution was neces-sary to release the creative potential of the people while guaranteeing social and economic rights for all; and that such a revolution was achievable given the growth of a revolutionary party and the unity of anti-capitalist forces. He thought that these preconditions could best be realised through the affiliation of the CP to a genuinely federal Labour Party, which presupposed a long campaign to transform the political orientation of the trade union movement.[72]

Whilst he was opposed to the split in Communist ranks when it occurred, the Communist Party of Britain has tried to continue with a Ramelsonesque set of policies and strategies, and by and large adopted the *British Road to Socialism* that he did much to fashion over four decades. While all trace of the neo-Gramscians as an organised force has gone, yet *The Morning Star*, the paper that they battled bitterly and unsuccessfully to control remains as a daily expression of the political tradition that they tried to destroy. Bert Ramelson, who saw every struggle against capitalist injustice as a victory, would have taken quiet satisfaction in the fact that the *Morning Star* remains a living voice for peace and socialism long after those responsible for the Party's dissolution have left the political stage.

To the end Ramelson remained an optimist, with a materialist outlook on historical development. He saw how human society had progressed over the centuries and how generations of the dispossessed had fought to obtain economic security and democratic rights.

Problems had been confronted and overcome in the search for a better life. Ramelson saw no reason to doubt that such progress would continue, although he recognised that there would be many a setback along the way. In late 1986 he looked back and observed:

> Not very long ago the Communists believed that the twentieth century would be one of world-wide triumph for socialism. It is now clear that, however great the revolutionaries' natural desire to bring on the hour of victory, this goal has receded into a more distant future. The truth is that we tended to underestimate capitalism's capacity to adapt to the chronic crisis, and its viability, while over-rating our expectations of the speed with which socialism would spread its influence.[73]

In Ramelson's view the big challenges facing late twentieth-century humankind – including environmental sustainability, eliminating mass poverty in all its forms, securing world peace, and developing people's rights – could only be successfully tackled by socialist means. Imperialist oppression and capitalist exploitation were at the root of the problems and had no part to play in the solutions. In the end, rationality demanded that mankind take the co-operative road rather than a path that led to a future of conflict and uncontrollable market forces. In the end, Ramelson argued, rationality would triumph, if only because the people's struggles for economic and social justice will be too powerful to resist. Bert Ramelson's life was dedicated to this struggle.

NOTES

1. Ethel Shepherd interview, 2009.
2. Levy, H. *Jews and the National Question*, Hillway, London 1958.
3. Ramelson, B. Review of Levy's book, *Daily Worker*, 11/3/58.
4. Ramelson, B. 'An old problem re-discussed', *Marxism Today*, January 1959, pp. 21-27.
5. Ibid., p. 24.
6. CP Archives: CP/IND/RAM/02/05.
7. Ramelson, B. *The Middle East Crisis*, CP 1967, p. 1.
8. Ibid., p. 7.
9. Ibid.
10. Wages were half the average industrial male wage.
11. Roger Bagley interview, 2010.

12. Nora Jefferys was National Women's Organiser and a member of the CPGB's Political Committee; Len Crome was a doctor who pioneered new treatment in field hospitals during the Spanish civil war and later was a major figure in setting up the NHS.
13. Norma Bramley interview, 2008.
14. Joan Ramelson interview, 2008.
15. Derek Perkins interview, 2009.
16. Simon Steyne interview, 2008.
17. Bill Alexander's oration at Bert's funeral.
18. Joan Ramelson and Anne Craven interviews. Joan remembers visits to Cuba and the Soviet Union particularly.
19. These included Labour Party members such as Ray Buckton (ASLEF), Alan Sapper (ACTT), Doug Grieve (Tobacco Workers Union), Hugh Scanlon (AEU), Bob Wright (AEU) and Ron Todd (TGWU).
20. Interviewees commenting on this aspect included Barry Bracken, Bill Moore, Joan Bellamy, Monty Meth and Beryl Huffingley.
21. Vic Allen interview, 2008; the broad left in the 1960s consisted mainly of communists and left-wing members of the Labour Party.
22. *Lawrence Daly Papers*, Modern Records Centre, University of Warwick.
23. Ibid.
24. Vic Allen interview, 2008.
25. McIlroy, J. and Halsford, J. 'A Very Different Historian: Royden Harrison, Radical Academics and Suppressed Alternatives', *Historical Studies in Industrial Relations* No.15 Spring 2003, pp. 113-143.
26. Letter from Bill Edwards to Charles Lubelski, April 1999.
27. Ken Gill interview, 2008.
28. Andrew 2009 op.cit., p. 657.
29. Goodman interview, 2009.
30. Evidence of Jones's dual membership of the CP (as a secret member) and the Labour Party between 1930 and 1939 has recently been provided by Richard Baxell, quoting from a Spanish CP document which includes a signed application from Jones dated 5 September 1938, giving his political affiliations in England. See M. O'Riordan, *The Vindication of Brigadista and Union Man Jack James Larkin Jones*, Bevin Society pamphlet, Dublin 2010.
31. Beckett interview with Ramelson, 1992.
32. Jack Jones cited in Jacques, M. and Mulhern, F. (eds.) *The Forward March of Labour Halted?*, Verso 1981, pp.157-158.
33. Draft lecture notes in personal papers.
34. Joan Bellamy interview, 2008.
35. *Needs of the Hour* was a compendium of model motions drawn up by the Party's Industrial Department and fed into union decision-making processes.
36. Mike Squires interview, 2010; Mitch Howard interview, 2010.

37. Ramelson personal papers.
38. Ramelson personal papers.
39. Paul Dunn interview, 2010.
40. E-mail received 21/8/2009.
41. Interview with Kevin Morgan 1991.
42. *Morning Star*, 1/7/77.
43. Darlington and Lyddon, 2001, op. cit., pp. 184-207.
44. CP Archive: CP/IND/RAM/02/01.
45. Note the use of 'Russian' implying imperialist and 'old', relegating the Party to the past.
46. *Morning Star*, 2/7/71.
47. *Morning Star*, 6/7/71.
48. Agosti op.cit. 2008, p. 234.
49. McIlroy, J. and Campbell, A. 'Histories of the Communist Party: A Users Guide', in *Labour History Review*, Vol. 68(1) 2003, pp. 33-59.
50. *New Statesman*, 6/6/05.
51. Harman, C. 'The Storm Breaks the Crisis in the Eastern Block', *International Socialism*, Spring 1990.
52. Westacott, F. *Shaking the Chains*, Joe Clark, Chesterfield 2002, p. 299.
53. Cited in Maharaj, M., Nicol, M., Coward, R., Frense, A. and Parkin, K. *Mandela: The Authorised Portrait*, Bloomsbury 2006, pp. 92-93.
54. Andrews 2004, op. cit., p. 15; Callaghan 2003, op. cit., p. 305.
55. Hughes, J. 'Evidence to the Donovan Commission', reproduced in W.M. McCarthy (ed.), *Trade Unions*, Penguin 1972, chapter 11.
56. Kelly, J. Review of Callaghan's book, op.cit. 2003, *Historical Studies in Industrial Relations* 2004 No. 17: 155-160, p. 159.
57. McIlroy, J. 1999, 'Notes on the Communist Party and Industrial Politics', McIlroy et al 1999 op.cit., p. 225.
58. *World Marxist Review*, May 1987, p. 85.
59. Foot 1967, op.cit.
60. McIlroy 'Notes on the Communist Party and Industrial Politics', 1999, op.cit., p. 247.
61. McIlroy, J. 'Always Outnumbered, Always Outgunned; The Trotskyists and the Trade Unions', in McIlroy et al 1999 op.cit., pp. 259-296.
62. Hughes, J. 'Evidence to Donovan', *Research Paper No.5*, 1967, p. 74.
63. Seifert, R. and Sibley, T. *United They Stood*, Lawrence & Wishart, London 2005; and Seifert, R. and Sibley, T. 'It's politics, stupid: the 2002-4 UK firefighters' dispute', *British Journal of Industrial Relations*, Vol 49(S2): 332-352, July 2011.
64. *World Marxist Review*, op.cit., October 1986.
65. Prior, M. and Purdy, D. *Out of the Ghetto*, Spokesman, Leicester 1979.
66. Purdy commented on this when favourably reviewing Andrew's book, op.cit. 2004, *End Games and New Times* in 2005. See *Communist History Network Newsletter*, Issue 18, Autumn 2005.

67. Andrews, G., Fishman, N. and Morgan, K. (eds) *Opening the books ... essays on the social and cultural history of British Communism,* Pluto Press, London 1995, p. 237.
68. Ibid, pp. 225-45.
69. For example, writing in 1985, such a group published a lengthy pamphlet, Fine, B., Harris, L. and Mayo. M. *Class Politics. An Answer to Its Critics,* which strongly attacked the 'pessimism' inherent in the term 'Thatcherism' and concluded: 'we must reject the ways in which they [the Marxism Today group] have raised these issues, for they inevitably lead to defeatism and collaboration with capital', p. 63.
70. Nina Temple was General Secretary of the CPGB when with her support it was liquidated in 1991.
71. McLennan's statement to the CP EC 'Prices, wages, EEC – the communist role' *Comment,* 23/7/77, p. 259.
72. Interview with Ramelson by Kevin Morgan 1991.
73. Ibid.

Bibliography

Aaronovitch, S. 'Forward or Back? Prospects for the Movement', *Marxism Today*, January 1967 pp. 6-12

Aaronovitch, S. 'Where next for Britain's economy', *Comment* 11/12/76, pp. 387-8

Aaronovitch, S. *The Road from Thatcherism: the Alternative Economic Strategy*, Lawrence & Wishart, London 1981

ACAS *Industrial Relations Handbook*, HMSO, London 1980

Agosti, A. *Palmiro Togliatti, a Biography*, I.B. Taurus, London 2008

Alexander, W. *British Volunteers for Liberty – Spain 1936-1939*, Lawrence & Wishart, London 1982

Alexander, W. 'George Orwell and Spain' in Norris, C. *Inside the Myth: Orwell: Views from the Left*, Lawrence & Wishart, London 1984

Allen, V. 'Trade Unions in Contemporary Capitalism' *Socialist Register* 1964, pp. 157-174

Allen, V. 'The Centenary of the British Trades Union Congress, 1868-1968', *Socialist Register* 1968 pp. 231-252

Allen, V. *The Militancy of British Miners*, Moor Press, Shipley 1981

Ali, T. *The Coming British Revolution*, Jonathan Cape, London 1972

Anderson, P. 'The Left in the Fifties' *New Left Review* 1965 29: 3-18

Anderson, P. 'The Limits and Possibilities of Trade Union Action' in Blackburn and Cockburn op. cit. 1967 pp. 263-80

Andrew, C. *The Defence of the Realm: the Authorized History of MI5*, Allen Lane, London 2009

Andrews, G. *Endgames and New Times: the final years of British Communism 1964-1991*, Lawrence & Wishart, London 2004

Andrews, G., Fishman, N. and Morgan, K. (eds) *Opening the books ... essays on the social and cultural history of British Communism*, Pluto Press, London 1995

Arnison, J. *The Shrewsbury Three: Strikes, Pickets and 'Conspiracy'*, with foreword by Bert Ramelson, Lawrence & Wishart, London 1974

Arnison, J. *The Million Pound Strike*, with foreword by Hugh Scanlon, Lawrence & Wishart, London 1970

Arrow, K. 'The utilitarian approach to the concept of equality in public expenditure' *Quarterly Journal of Economics*, 1971 85(3): 409-415

Atkinson, A. 'How progressive should income tax be?' in Parkin, M. (ed.) *Essays on Modern Economics*, Longman, London 1972;

Attfield, J. and Williams, S. (eds) *1939 The Communist Party and the War*, Lawrence & Wishart, London 1984

AUEW-TASS *British Leyland Cars: Collapse or Growth – An Alternative to Edwardes*, TASS, London 1978

Bailey, V. *Forged in Fire: the History of the Fire Brigades Union*, Lawrence & Wishart, London 1992

Bain, G. *The Growth of White-Collar Unionism*, Oxford University Press, Oxford 1970

Baran, P. and Sweezy, P. *Monopoly Capital*, Penguin 1966

Barnett, A. 'Class Struggle and the Heath Government', *New Left Review*, 1973 77: 3-41

Barou, N. *British Trade Unions*, Victor Gollanz, London 1947

Bateman, D. 'The Trouble with Harry: A memoir of Harry Newton, MI5 Agent', *Lobster*, Issue 28, 1994

Beeching, C. *Canadian Volunteers – Spain 1936-1939*, Canadian Plains Research Centre 1989

Beck, T. *The Fine Tubes Strike*, Stage1, London 1974

Bellamy, J. 'Politics and Race', *Marxism Today* October 1969, pp. 311-318

Bellamy, R. 'Trends in British Capitalism in the 1970s', *Marxism Today*, January 1973, pp. 22-30

Bellamy, R. 'More on inflation', *Marxism Today* November 1974, pp. 340-349

Bellamy, R. *Getting the Balance Right – An Assessment of the Achievements of the CPGB*, Socialist History Society, June 1996

Benn, T. *Against the Tide: Diaries 1973-1976* Hutchinson, London 1989

Beynon, H. *What happened at Speke?* TGWU, Liverpool 1978

Biggs, K. 'Coventry and the shop stewards' movement 1917', *Marxism Today*, January 1969, pp. 14-23

Blackburn, R. and Cockburn, C. (eds) *The Incompatibles: trade union militancy and the consensus*, Penguin 1967

Branson, N. *History of the Communist Party of Great Britain 1927-1941*, Lawrence & Wishart, London 1985

Brasher, J. 'The Trico equal pay dispute', *Labour Monthly* 1976 58(12): 547-9

Braverman, H. *Labor and Monopoly Capitalism*, Monthly Review Press, New York 1974

Bridges, G. 'The Communist Party and the Struggle for Hegemony', *Socialist Register*, 1977, pp. 27-37

Broadway, F. *State Intervention in British Industry 1964-8*, chapter six 'New agencies of intervention' pp. 60-7; Associated University Press, New Jersey 1970

Brown, A. *Profits, Wages and Wealth*, Lawrence & Wishart, London 1961

Brown, G. *The Industrial Syndicalist*, Documents in Socialist History No. 3, Spokesman, London 1974

Buckton, R. 'The sort of social contract we really want', *Labour Monthly* 1974 7(56): 349-52

Bullock Report: The *Report of the committee of inquiry on industrial democracy*, HMSO, London1977, Cmnd 6706

Bunyan, T. 'From Saltley to Orgreave via Brixton', *Journal of Law and Society*, 1985, 12(3): 293-303

Burns, E. *Right Wing Labour: Its Theory and Practice*, Lawrence & Wishart, London 1961

Burns, E. 'Problems of Inflation', *Marxism Today*, December 1964, pp. 370-4

Callaghan, James *Time and Chance* London: Collins 1987

Callaghan, J. *Rajani Palme Dutt, a Study in British Stalinism*, Lawrence & Wishart, London 1993

Callaghan, J. *Cold War, Crisis and Conflict: a History of the CPGB 1951-1968*, Lawrence & Wishart, London 2003

Callaghan, J. 'Industrial Militancy, 1945-79: The Failure of the British Road to Socialism?' *Twentieth Century British History* 2004, 29: 388-409

Callaghan, J. and Phythian, M. 'State Surveillance of the CPGB Leadership', *Labour History Review*, 2004 69(1): 19-33

Campbell, J. *Some Economic Illusions in the Labour Movement*, Lawrence & Wishart, London 1959

Campbell, J. *Hands off the Trade Unions*, CP Pamphlet, London 1965

Campbell, J. 'The Development of Incomes Policy in Britain', *Marxism Today*, March 1965 pp. 69-75

Campbell, J. and Ramelson, B. 'British State Monopoly Capitalism and Its Impact on Trade Unions and Wages', *Marxism Today* January 1968, pp. 7-14, and February 1968, pp. 50-59

Campbell, J. 'The Movement and the Commission: Delusions About Donovan', *Marxism Today*, September 1968, pp. 264-272

Carr, E. *The Bolshevik Revolution*, Penguin 1973

Castle, B. *The Castle Diaries 1974-1976*, Weidenfeld and Nicolson, London 1980

Chalfont, A. *The Shadow of My Hand: a Memoir*, Weidenfeld & Nicholson, London 2000

Chester, A. 'Uneven development: communist strategy from the 1940s-1970s', *Marxism Today* September 1979, pp. 275-282

Childs, D. 'The Cold War and the "British Road", 1946-53', *Journal of Contemporary History*, 1988 23: 551-572

Chomsky, N. *Profit over People: Neo-liberalism and the world order*, Seven Stories Press, New York 1999

Clegg, H. *Industrial Democracy and Nationalization*, Blackwell, Oxford 1951

Clegg, H. *How to run an incomes policy, and why we made such a mess of the last one*, Heinemann, London 1971

Cliff, T. and Gluckstein, D. *Marxism and Trade Union Struggle: the General Strike of 1926*, Bookmarks, London 1986

Cliff, T. *The Crisis: Social Contract or Socialism*, Pluto Press, London 1975

Coates, D. *The Crisis of Labour*, Oxford 1989

Coates, K. 'AEU Elections' *New Left Review* 1964 25: 26-8

Coates, K. 'Socialists and the Labour Party', *Socialist Register* 1973, pp. 155-178

Coates, K. and Topham, T. (eds.) *Industrial democracy in Great Britain:*

a book of readings and witnesses for workers' control, Spokesman Books, Nottingham 1975

Cohen, G. *Karl Marx's Theory of History: A Defence*, OUP, Oxford 1978

Cohen, G. *History Labour and Freedom*, Clarendon, Oxford 1988

Cole, G. *The World of Labour*, G. Bell & Sons, London 1913

Cole, G. *Practical Economics*, Penguin 1937

Cole, G. *British Trade Unionism To-Day*, Methuen, London 1938

Cook, D. 'No Private Drama', *Marxism Today*, February 1985, pp. 25-9

Costello, M. *Defeat the Anti-Union Laws*, CP 1980

Conservative Party *Fair Deal at Work*, Conservative Political Centre, London 1968

Cornforth, K. 'The British Road to Socialism', *Communist Review*, April 1947 pp. 113-8

Coward, J. *We Want 40*, CP pamphlet, London 1966

Crosland, A. *Socialism Now*, Jonathan Cape, London 1975

Crossman, R. *The Diaries of a Cabinet Minister 1964-1966*, Book Club Associates, London 1975

Crouch, C. *The Politics of Industrial Relations*, Fontana, London 1979

Darlington, R. and Lyddon, D. *Glorious Summer: Class struggle in Britain 1972*, Bookmarks, London 2001

Dash, J. *Good Morning Brothers!*, Lawrence & Wishart, London 1969

Dash, J. 'The Pentonville Five', *Labour Monthly*, September 1972, pp. 407-8

Dobb, M. *Economic Growth and Underdeveloped Countries*, Lawrence & Wishart, London 1963

Dobb, M. 'Inflation and All-That', *Marxism Today*, March 1965, pp. 84-87

Dobb, M. *Soviet Economic Development since 1917*, International Publishers, New York 1966

Donovan Report of the Royal Commission on trade unions and Employers' Associations 1965-8 (Chairman: Lord Donovan), HMSO, London 1968, Cmnd 3623

Dorfman, G. *Government Versus Trade Unionism In British Politics Since 1968*, Macmillan, London 1979

Doughty, G. 'The Donovan report', *The Trade Union Register*, Coates, K., Topham, T. and Barratt Brown, M. (eds), Merlin Press, London 1969

Dromey, J. and Taylor, G. *Grunwick: The Workers' Story*, Lawrence & Wishart, London 1978

Duncan, D. *Mutiny in the RAF: The Air Force Strikes of 1946*, Social History Society Occasional Paper No.8, 1998.

Durkin, T. *Grunwick: Bravery and Betrayal*, Brent Trades Council, London 1978

Egelnick, M. 'Non-manual Workers in the Sixties', *Marxism Today*, August 1964 pp. 239-245

Ellman, M., Rowthorn, B., Smith, R. and Wilkinson, F. *Britain's Economic Crisis*, Cambridge Political Economy Group, Spokesman Pamphlet, Nottingham 1974, No.44

Engels, F. *The Condition of the Working Class in England*, Leipzig 1845

Fagan, H. *Nationalisation*, Lawrence & Wishart, London 1960

Falber, R. 'The 31st CP Congress and the Fight Against Monopolies', *Marxism Today* February 1970, pp. 40-49

Falber, R. 'The 32nd Congress of the CPGB', *Marxism Today*, January 1972, pp. 4-10

Falber, R. 'The 1968 Czechoslovakia crisis: inside the British CP', Socialist History Society Occasional Paper No. 5 1995, p. 51

Fawcett, M. *Political Economy for Beginners*, Macmillan, London 1884

Fine, B., Harris, L. and Mayo. M. *Class Politics. An Answer to Its Critics*, London 1985

Fishman, N. 'The British Road is Resurfaced for New Times', in Bull, M. and Heyward, P. (eds.) *West European Communist Parties after the Revolutions of 1989*, Macmillan, London 1994, pp. 145-177

Fishman, N. *Arthur Horner: A Political Biography*, Lawrence & Wishart 2010

Flanders, A. *Management and Unions*, Faber & Faber, London 1970

Foley, T. *A Most Formidable Union: the history of DATA and TASS*, TASS 1992

Foot, P. 'The Seaman's Struggle' in Blackburn, R. and Cockburn, A. (eds.) *The Incompatibles: Trade Union Militancy and the Consensus*, Penguin 1967

Forbes, A. 'In the Wake of Grunwick', *Marxism Today*, December 1978, pp. 386-391

Foster, J. 'Moving the Goalposts', *Marxism Today*, March 1985, pp. 43-4

Foster, J. and Woolfson, C. *The Politics of the UCS Work-in*, Lawrence & Wishart, London 1986

Foster, J. and Woolfson, C. 'How workers on the Clyde gained the capacity for class struggle: the Upper Clyde Shipbuilders' work-in, 1971-2' in McIlroy et al 1999, op. cit, pp 297-325

Frankenberg, R. *Communities in Britain: Social Life in Town and Country*, Penguin 1966

Frow, E. and Frow, R. 'The Petticoat Rebellion: a review', *Marxism Today*, 1967 11(5): 146-8

Frow, E. and Frow, R. *Shop Stewards and Workshop Struggles*, Working Class Movement Library, Manchester 1980

Fryer, R 'The politics of industrial relations in the public sector' in Mailly, R.; Dimmock, S. and Sethi, A. (eds.) *Industrial Relations in the Public Services*; Routledge, London 1989, pp. 17-67

Fyfe, H. *Keir Hardie*, Duckworth, London 1935

Galbraith, J. *The Affluent Society*, Penguin 1958

Gallacher, W. *Revolt on the Clyde*, Lawrence & Wishart, London 1936

Gallacher, W. *Marxism and the Working Class*, Lawrence & Wishart, London 1943

Gallacher, W. *The Tyrants' Might is Passing*, Lawrence & Wishart, London 1954

Gill, K. 'Marxism and the Trade Unions', *Marxism Today*, June 1974, pp. 163-174

Gill, K. 'Review of "Social contract" by Bert Ramelson', *Comment*, 1975 13(3)

Glyn, A. and Sutcliffe, R. 'Labour and the Economy', *New Left Review* 1972 No.76, 91-6

Glyn, A. and Sutcliffe, R. *British Capitalism, Workers, and the Profit Squeeze*, Penguin 1972

Gold, M. 'Worker mobilisation in the 1970s: revisiting work-ins, co-operatives and alternative corporate plans', *Historical Studies in Industrial Relations* 2004 no 18, 65-106

Goldthorpe, J., Lockwood, D., Bechhofer, F., and Platt, J. *The Affluent worker: political attitudes and behaviour*, Cambridge University Press, Cambridge 1968

Goldthorpe, J., Lockwood, D., Bechhofer, F., and Platt, J. *The Affluent worker: industrial attitudes and behaviour*, Cambridge University Press, Cambridge 1968

Goldthorpe, J., Lockwood, D., Bechhofer, F., and Platt, J. *The Affluent Worker in the Class Structure*, Cambridge University Press, Cambridge 1969

Goldthorpe, J. 'Industrial Relations in Great Britain: A Critique of Reformism', 1974, in Clarke, Tom and Clements, Laurie (eds), *Trade Unions under Capitalism*, Fontana, London 1977

Gollan, J. 'Which Road?', *Marxism Today*, July 1964, pp. 198-216

Gollan, J. *What is the Socialist Way Forward?*, CP pamphlet, 1970

Gollan, J. 'Marxism and the Political Organisation of the Workers', in *Marxism Today*, May 1972, pp. 136-142.

Gollan, J. 'Parliament, Anti-Monopoly Alliance and Socialist Revolution', *Marxism Today* September 1975, pp. 260-264

Gollan, J. *Socialist Democracy – some problems*, CP Pamphlet, London 1976

Gollan, J. 'The 20th congress of the CPSU in retrospect', *Marxism Today*, January 1976, pp. 4-30; reprinted as *Socialist Democracy – some problems*, CP Pamphlet 1976

Goodman, G. *Awkward Warrior: Frank Cousins, his life and times*, Davis-Poynter, London 1979

Goodman, G. *From Bevan to Blair*, Pluto, London 2003

Goodwin, D. 'Shop Stewards – Past, Present, and Future', *Marxism Today*, April 1964, pp. 109-114

Goodwin, D. 'Profits from the seamen', *Comment*, June 1966

Goodwin, D. 'In Defence of Trade Union Rights', *Marxism Today*, September 1966, pp. 261-271

Graham, H. *The Spanish Civil War*, Oxford University Press, Oxford 2005

Gramsci, A. *Selections from the Prison Notebooks 1929*, Lawrence & Wishart, London, 1971 edition

Greaves, C. *The Life and Times of James Connolly*, Lawrence & Wishart, London 1961

Griffith, J. *The Politics of the Judiciary*, Fontana, London 1977

Haldane, J. *The Inequality of Man*, Penguin 1937

Hallas, D. 'How Can We Move On?', *Socialist Register* 1977, 14: 1-10

Halliday, F. 'The War and Revolution in Afghanistan', *New Left Review*, 1980, 119: 20-41

Harman, C. 'The Storm Breaks the Crisis in the Eastern Block', *International Socialism*, Spring 1990

Harris, L. 'Healey's panic squeeze', *Comment* 1976 14(22): 339-340

Harrison, M. *Trade Unions and the Labour Party since 1945*, Allen & Unwin, London 1960

Hart, F. *The CP and the Trade Unions*, CP 1958

Hay, C. 'Narrating Crisis: the Discursive Construction of the "Winter of Discontent"', *Sociology* 1996 30: 253-277

Healey, D. 'The Cominform and World Communism', *International Affairs*, 1948 24: 339-349

Healey, D. *The Time of my Life*, Penguin 1989

Hobbes, T. *The Leviathan*, first published 1651, this edition Everyman, London 1914

Hobsbawm, E. (ed.) *Labour's Turning Point 1880-1900*, Lawrence & Wishart, London 1948

Hobsbawm, E. 'Parliamentary Cretinism?' *New Left Review* 1961 12: pp. 64-6

Hobsbawm, E., *The Crisis and the Outlook*, Birkbeck College Socialist Society and London Central branch of the CP, London 1975

Hobsbawm, E. 'Gramsci and political theory', *Marxism Today*, July 1977, pp. 205-213

Hobsbawm, E. 'Forward march of labour halted?', *Marxism Today*, September 1978, pp. 279-286

Hobsbawm, E. *Age of Extremes: the short twentieth century 1914-1991*, Michael Joseph, London 1994

Howell, D. 'Goodbye to all that?: A Review of Literature on the 1984/5 Miners' Strike', *Work, Employment & Society* September 1987, pp. 388-404

Huberman, L. *Man's Worldly Goods*, Victor Gollanz, London 1937

Hughes, J. 'British trade unionism in the sixties', *Socialist Register* 1966, pp. 86-113

Hughes, J. 'Evidence to the Donovan Commission', reproduced in W.M. McCarthy (ed), *Trade Unions*, Penguin 1972, chapter 11

Hughes, J. 'Trade union structure and government', Donovan report, op. cit., *Research Paper No.5*, 1967

Hughes, J. *The TUC: a Plan for the 1970s*, Fabian tract 397, London 1969

Hughes, J. and Moore, R. (eds), A *Special Case? Social Justice and the Miners*, Penguin 1972

Hull NUS 1967, *Not Wanted on Voyage: the Seaman's Reply to the First Report of the Court of Inquiry into Certain Matters Concerning the Shipping Industry*, Cmnd. 3025, with an introduction by Charlie Hodgins and John Prescott

Hunt, A. *Class and Class Structure*, Lawrence & Wishart, London 1977

Hunt, J. 'The fight for wages goes on', *Comment* 1976 14(10): 147-150

Hutt, A. *The Post-War History of the British Working Class*, Victor Gollanz, London 1937

Hutt, A. *British trade unionism: a short history*, Lawrence & Wishart, London 1975

Hyman, R. *Marxism and the Sociology of Trade Unionism*, Pluto Press, London 1971

Hyman, R. 'Industrial Conflict and the Political Economy: Trends of the Sixties and Prospects for the Seventies', *Socialist Register* 1973, pp. 101-153

Hyman, R. *Industrial Relations: A Marxist Introduction*, Macmillan, London 1975

Johnstone, M. 'Marx and Engels and the Concept of the Party', *Socialist Register* 1967, pp. 121-158

Jones, J. *Jack Jones: Union Man*, Collins, London 1986

Jones, M. *Choices, an Autobiography*, Verso, London 1987

Kane, J. *No Wonder We Were Rebels*, autobiographical notes compiled by Frank Watters in 1978, published in 1994

Kelly, J. *Trade Unions and Socialist Politics*, Verso, London 1988

Kelly, J. Review of Callaghan's 2003 book op. cit., *Historical Studies in Industrial Relations*, 2004 no. 17, pp. 155-160

Kelly, J. *Ethical Socialism and the Trade Unions: Allan Flanders and British Industrial Relations Reform*, Routledge, London 2010

Kerrigan, P. 'Trade Unions and Amalgamations', *Marxism Today*, June 1964, pp. 166-170

Kessler, S. and Bayliss, F. *Contemporary British Industrial Relations*, Macmillan, London 1998

Kettle, A. 'The Future Of The Left: An Open Letter To A Non-Communist Left Winger', *Marxism Today*, January1966, pp. 5-10

Kiernan, V. 'Gramsci and Marxism', *Socialist Register* 1972, pp. 1-33

Kilroy-Silk, R. 'Donovan research papers', *Parliamentary Affairs* 1968, Vol. 22: 82-7

Kisch, R. *The Days of the Good Soldiers: Communists in the Armed Forces WWII*, Journeyman Press, London 1985

Klugmann, J. 'The Revolutionary Ideas of Marx and the Current Revolt', *Marxism Today*, June 1969, pp. 165-175

Klugmann, J. *The History of the Communist Party of Great Britain, Formation and early years 1919-1924*, Lawrence & Wishart, London 1969

Klugmann, J. *The History of the Communist Party of Great Britain, The General Strike 1925-1926*, Lawrence & Wishart, London 1969

Labour Research Department *New Tory Attack on Union Rights*, LRD, London 1981

Lane, T. and Roberts, K. *Strike at Pilkingtons*, Fontana, London 1971

Lane, T. 'The Unions Caught on the Ebb Tide', *Marxism Today*, September 1982, pp. 6-13

Laybourn, K. *Marxism in Britain: dissent, decline and re-emergence 1945-c.2000*, Routledge, London, 2006

Lenin, V. *The State and Revolution: The Marxist Theory of the State and the Tasks of the Proletariat in the Revolution*, Lawrence & Wishart, London 1969 edition, original 1917

Lenin, V. *What is to be Done?*, OUP, Oxford 1902

Lenin, V. (1895) 'Engels and English Socialism', in *British Labour and British Imperialism*, Lawrence & Wishart, London 1969

Lenin, V. *The Re-organization of the Party*, 1905

Lenin, V. *Trade Union* Neutrality, 1908

Levy, H. *Jews and the National Question*, Hillway, London 1958

Leyland Combine Trade Union Committee, *The Edwardes Plan and Your Job*, London 1979

Leys, C., *Politics in Britain from Labour to Thatcherism*, Verso, London 1989

Lindop, F. 'The Dockers and the 1971 Industrial Relations Act, Part 1: Shop Stewards and Containerization', *Historical Studies in Industrial Relations*, 1998, 5: 33-72

Lindop, F. 'The Dockers and the 1971 Industrial Relations Act, Part 2: the Arrest and Release of the "Pentonville Five"', *Historical Studies in Industrial Relations*, 1998 6: 65-100

Locke, J. *Two Treatises of Government*, first published 1689

Lozovsky, A. *Marx and the Trade Unions*, Martin Lawrence, London 1935

Lumley, R. *White-Collar Unionism in Britain*, Methuen, London 1973

Maharaj, M., Nicol, M., Coward, R. Frense, A. and Parkin, K. *Mandela: The Authorised Portrait*, Bloomsbury 2006

Mahon, J. 'The record of the labour government 1964-1968', *Marxism Today*, August 1968, pp. 231-245

Mahon, J. *Harry Pollitt: A Biography*, Lawrence & Wishart, London 1976

Mann, T. *Tom Mann's Memoirs*, McGibbon & Kee, London 1923

Marlow, J. *The Tolpuddle Martyrs*, Grafton Books, London 1985

Marx, K. *Capital: A Critical Analysis of Capitalist Production*, Swan Sonnenschein, Lowrey & Co., London 1887

Matthews, G. 'The Wilson Government and Britain's Crisis', *Marxism Today*, February 1975, pp. 35-46

Mathews, G. 'Report to the EC on the crisis and the left', *Comment*, 20/3/76, pp. 83-6

Mathews, J. *Ford Strike: The Workers' Story*, Panther, London 1972

Maynard, J. 'No "stage three"', *Labour Monthly*, May 1977, pp. 203-4

McCarthy, W. 'Shop stewards in British industrial relations', Donovan op. cit Research Paper 1, 1966

McCormick, B. *Industrial Relations in the Coal Industry*, Macmillan, London 1979

McKersie, R. 'The British Board for Prices and Incomes', *Industrial Relations* 1967, 6(3): 267-284

McIlroy, J. 'Notes on the Communist Party and Industrial Politics', in McIlroy et al op. cit. 1999, pp. 216-258

McIlroy, J. 'Always Outnumbered, Always Outgunned; The Trotskyists and the Trade Unions', in McIlroy et al 1999 op. cit., pp. 259-296

McIlroy, J. and Campbell, A. 'Organizing the militants: the Liaison

Committee for the Defence of Trade Unions, 1966-79', *British Journal of Industrial Relations* 1999 37(1): pp 1-31

McIlroy, J. and Campbell, A. 'The High Tide of Trade Unionism: Mapping Industrial Politics, 1964-79', in McIlroy et al 1999 op. cit., pp. 93-132

McIlroy, J. and Campbell, A. 'Histories of the Communist Party: A Users Guide', in *Labour History Review*, Vol. 68(1) 2003, pp. 33-59.

McIlroy, J., Fishman, N. and Campbell. A. (eds.) *British Trade Unions and Industrial Politics: The High Tide of Trade Unionism, 1964-79*, Ashgate, Aldershot 1999

McIlroy, J. and Halsford, J. 'A Very Different Historian: Royden Harrison, Radical Academics and Suppressed Alternatives', *Historical Studies in Industrial Relations* No.15 Spring 2003, pp. 113-143

McLennan, G. 'Report to EC on mass struggle for left policies', *Comment*, 18/9/76, pp. 291-5

Miliband, R. 'What Does The Left Want?' *Socialist Register* 1965, pp. 184-194

Miliband, R. 'The Labour Government and Beyond', *Socialist Register* 1966, pp. 11-26

Miliband, R. 'Lenin's State and Revolution', *Socialist Register* 1970, pp. 309-319.

Miliband, R. *The State in Capitalist Society*, Quartet, London 1972

Miliband, R. and Saville, J. 'Labour Policy and The Labour Left', *Socialist Register* 1964, pp. 149-156

Minkin, L. *The Contentious Alliance: Trade Unions and the Labour Party*, Edinburgh University Press, Edinburgh 1991

Mennell, W. *The British Economy*, Lawrence & Wishart, London 1964

Moffat, A. *Smash the Pay Pause*, CP pamphlet, London 1962

Morgan, K. *The People's Peace: British History 1945-1989*, Oxford University Press, Oxford 1990

Morgan, K. 'The Wilson Years 1964-1970' in Tiratsoo, N. (ed.) *From Blitz to Blair*, Phoenix, London 1997

Morgan, K. *Callaghan: A Life*, Oxford University Press, Oxford 1997

Morgan, K. *Against Fascism and War*, Manchester University Press, 1989

Mortimer, J. 'The Structure of the Trade Union Movement', *Socialist Register* 1964, pp. 175-191

Morton, A. *The English Utopia*, Lawrence & Wishart, London 1969

Moss, J. *Wages – The Tory Attack*, CP London 1961

NBPI Report No 16, *Pay and conditions of busmen*, Cmnd 3012, HMSO, London 1966

NBPI Report No 29. *The Pay and Conditions of Manual Workers in Local Authorities, the National Health Service, Gas and Water Supply*, Cmnd 3230, HMSO, London 1967

NBPI report 123 *Productivity Agreements*, HMSO, London 1969, Cmnd. 4136

Nicholson, F. 'Student Perspectives', *Marxism Today*, October 1969, pp. 295-301

Nove, A. *The Economics of Feasible Socialism*, Allen and Unwin, London 1983

O'Connor, K. *Passionate Socialist* Politicos, London 2003

Palme Dutt, R. *Problems of Contemporary History*, International Publishers 1963

Panitch, L. 'Socialists and the Labour Party: a Reappraisal', *Socialist Register* 1979, pp. 51-74

Paynter, W. *British Trade Unions and the Problem of Change*, George Allen & Unwin, London 1970

Paynter, W. *My Generation*, Allen & Unwin, London 1972

Pearce, B. 'The Strategy of Socialist Revolution in Britain', *Marxism Today*, January 1971, pp. 6-18

Pelling, H. *A History of British Trade Unionism*, Penguin 1976

Phillips, A. 'The Relationship between Unemployment and the Rate of Change of Money Wages in the United Kingdom 1861-1957', *Economica*, 1958, 25 (100): 283-299.

Phillips, J. 'The miners' strike: popular agency and industrial politics in Britain', *Contemporary British History*, 2006 20(2): 187-207

Piratin, P. *Our Flag Stays Red*, Lawrence & Wishart, London 1948

Piratin, P. *Cut Arms Not Houses – Raise Wages Not Profits*, CP 1949

Piratin, P. *Defend Trade Union Rights*, CP 1949

Pitt, M. *The World on our Backs: the Kent Miners and the 1972 Miners' Strike*, Lawrence & Wishart, London 1979

Pollitt, H. *Serving my Time*, Lawrence & Wishart, London 1940

Pollitt, H. *Looking Ahead*, CP, London 1947

Pollitt, H. *Selected Articles and Speeches*, Volume II 1936-9, Lawrence & Wishart, London 1954

Preston, P. *A Concise History of the Spanish Civil War*, Fontana, London 1996

Prior, M. and Purdy, D. *Out of the Ghetto*, Spokesman, Leicester 1979

Priscott, D. 'The Communist Party and the Labour Party', *Marxism Today*, January 1974, pp. 5-15

Priscott, D. 'Problems of Communist Labour relationships', *Marxism Today*, October 1977, pp. 294-301

Purdy, D. 'Some Thoughts on the Party's Policy Towards Prices, Wages and Incomes', *Marxism Today*, August 1974, pp. 246-252

Purdy, D. 'British capitalism since the war – origin of the crisis', *Marxism Today*, September 1976, pp. 270-277

Purdy, D. 'British capitalism since the war – decline and prospects', *Marxism Today*, October 1976, pp. 310-318

Ramelson, B. 'An old problem re-discussed', *Marxism Today*, January 1959, pp. 21-27

Ramelson, B. 'Truth about that deficit', *Labour Monthly*, October 1966

Ramelson, B. 'Incomes Policy in Britain: Its Theory and Practice', *World Marxist Review* July 1966, Vol.9 (7): 11-15

Ramelson, B. *Incomes Policy: the Great Wage Freeze Trick*, CP 1966

Ramelson, B. *The Middle East Crisis*, CP 1967

Ramelson, B. *Donovan Exposed: A Critical Analysis of The Report of The Royal Commission On Trade Unions*, CP 1968

Ramelson, B. 'Workers' Control? Possibilities and Limitations', *Marxism Today* October 1968, pp. 296-303

Ramelson, B. *Keep the unions free*, CP February 1969

Ramelson, B. *Productivity Agreements: an Exposure of the Latest and Greatest Swindle on the Wages Front*, CP January1970

Ramelson, B. *Carr's Bill and How to Kill It: a Class Analysis*, CP November 1970

Ramelson, B. 'The Industrial Fight: the Docks and the Act', *Comment*, August 1972, pp. 259-261

Ramelson, B. 'Strategy of socialist revolution in Britain', in *Marxism Today*, October 1972, pp. 318-320

Ramelson, B. *Heath's War On Your Wage Packet: The Latest Tory Attack on Living Standards and Trade Union Rights*, CP February 1973

Ramelson, B. *Smash Phase III: the Tory Fraud Exposed*, CP December 1973

Ramelson, B. 'The crisis, the government attacks, and the way to fight back', *Comment*, 26/1/74, pp. 18-21

Ramelson, B. *Social Contract: Cure-all or Con-trick?* CP December 1974

Ramelson, B. 'The role of general strikes today', *Marxism Today*, July 1976, pp.216-220

Ramelson, B. *Bury the Social Contract: the case for an alternative policy*, CP March 1977

Ramelson, B. 'Discussion on workers' control', *World Marxist Review* 1978, pp. 92-5

Ramelson, B. *Consensus or Socialism*, 1986 Ralph Fox Memorial Lecture

Ramelson, B. 'The communist movement in a changing world', *World Marxist Review*, October 1986

Ramelson, B. 'Discussing democratic centralism', *World Marxist Review*, January 1990, pp. 36-43

Ramelson, M. *The Petticoat Rebellion: a Century of Struggle for Women's Rights*, Lawrence & Wishart 1976

Reid, B. 'Trotskyism in Britain Today', *Marxism Today*, August 1964, pp. 274-284

Rideout, R. 'The Industrial Relations Act 1971', *The Modern Law Review*, 1971 34(6): 655-675

Roberts, B. *Trade Union Government and Administration in Great Britain*, G. Bell & sons, London 1956

Robinson, D. 'Leyland workers and the social contract', *Labour Monthly*, April 1977, pp. 156-7

Robinson, D. *Incomes Policy and Capital Sharing in Europe*, Croom Helm, London 1973

Rodgers, W. 'Government Under Stress; Britain's Winter Of Discontent 1979', *Political Quarterly* 1984 55(2): 171-179

Rolph, C. *All those in favour? The ETU trial*, Andre Deutsch, London 1962

Rousseau, Jean Jacques, *The Social Contract*, first published 1762

Routledge, P. *Scargill: the unauthorized biography*, Harper Collins, 1992

Rowbotham, S. *Hidden from History*, Pluto Press, London 1973

Rude, G. *Wilkes and Liberty*, Clarendon Press, Oxford 1962

Runciman, W. *Relative Deprivation and Social Justice*, Penguin 1970

Samuel, R. 'The Lost World of British Communism', *New Left Review*, 1985 No. 154, pp. 3-53

Samuel, R. 'Staying Power: The Lost World of British Communism, Part Two', *New Left Review*, 1986 No. 156, pp. 63-113

Samuel, R. 'Class Politics: The Lost World of British Communism, Part Three', *New Left Review*, 1987 No. 165, pp. 52-91

Sassoon, D. *One Hundred Years of Socialism*, Fontana, London 1997

Saville, J. 'Labourism and the Labour Government', *Socialist Register* 1967, pp. 43-71

Saville, J. *The Labour Movement in Britain*, Faber and Faber, London 1988

Saville, J. *Memoirs from the Left*, Merlin Press, 2003

Scanlon, Hugh 'The Role of Militancy', *New Left Review*, 1967 No. 46: 3-15

Seifert, R. and Sibley, T. *United They Stood: the story of the UK firefighters' dispute 2002-4*, Lawrence & Wishart, London 2005

Seifert, R. and Sibley, T. 'It's politics, stupid: the 2002-4 UK firefighters' dispute', *British Journal of Industrial Relations*, Vol. 49 (S2): 332-352, July 2011

Sen, A. *The Idea of Justice*, Harvard University Press, Harvard 2009

Short, R. 'Dilution the road to disaster', *Labour Monthly* 1974 7(56): 300-4

Sibley, T. *Anti-Communism: Studies of its Impact on the UK Labour Movement in the Early Years of the Cold War*', PhD. dissertation, Keele 2008

Silver, E. *Victor Feather*, Gollantz, London 1973

Simon, R. 'Gramsci's concept of hegemony', *Marxism Today*, March 1977, pp. 78-86

Skinner, D. 'Clay Cross and the Social Contract', *Labour Monthly*, November 1974

Smith, B. 'Thoughts on Shrewsbury', *Labour Monthly*, July 1974

Smith, P. (1999) '"The Winter of Discontent": The Hire and Reward Road Haulage Dispute, 1979', *Historical Studies in Industrial Relations*, No. 7, pp. 27-56

Staniszkis, J. 'The Evolution of Forms of Working-Class Protest in Poland: Sociological Reflections on the Gdansk-Szczecin Case, August 1980', *Soviet Studies*, 1981 XXXIII: 204-231

Stieber, J., McCarthy, W., Marsh, A. and Staples, J. 'Three studies in collective bargaining', Donovan op. cit, Research Paper 8, 1967

Tawney, R. *The Acquisitive Society*, G. Bell and sons, London 1926

Tawney, R. *Religion and the Rise of Capitalism*, Penguin 1937

Taylor, R. *The Fifth Estate*, Pan Books, London 1978

Taylor, R. *The Trade Union Question in British Politics*, Blackwell, Oxford 1993

Taylor, R. *The Future of the Trade Unions*, Andre Deutsch, London 1994

Taylor, R. *The TUC – From the General Strike to New Unionism*, Palgrave, Basingstoke 2000

Taylor, R. 'The Rise and Fall of the Social Contract' in A. Seldon and K. Hickson (eds.) *New Labour. Old Labour*, Routledge, London 2004, pp. 87-103

Thatcher, M. *The Downing Street Years*, Harper Collins, London 1993

Thompson, E. *William Morris: Romantic to Revolutionary*, Merlin Press, London 1977

Thompson, W. *The Good Old Cause: British Communism 1921-1991*, Pluto Press, London 1992

Thompson, W. *The Long Death of British Labourism: Interpreting a Political Culture*, Pluto Press, London 1993

Thompson, W. and Hart, F. *The UCS Work-In*, Lawrence & Wishart, London 1972 with a foreword by Jimmy Reid

Thorpe, A. 'The Labour Party and the Trade Unions' in McIlroy et al op. cit. 1999, pp. 133-150

Thorpe, K., 'The "Juggernaut Method": The 1966 State of Emergency and the Wilson Government's Response to the Seamen's Strike', *Twentieth Century British History* 2001 12(4): 461-485

Tobin, J. 'On limiting the domain of inequality', *Journal of Law and Economics*, 1970 13(2): 263-277

Topham, T. 'Dockers Want Workers' Control', in Monthly Broadsheet of IWC, November 1968

Topham, T. and Coates, K. 'Workers' Control', *Marxism Today*, January 1969, pp24-8

Torr, D. *Tom Mann and his Times*, Lawrence & Wishart, London 1956

Towers, B., 'Posing larger questions: the British miners' strike of 1984-85', *Industrial Relations Journal*, 1985 16, pp8-25

Tressell, R. *The Ragged Trousered Philanthropists*, Monthly Review Press, New York 1962, first published 1914

TUC, *Reason: the case against the Government's proposals on Industrial Relations*, TUC, London 1970

Turner, H. *Do Unions Cause Inflation?*, Cambridge University Press 1972

UCATT: 'UCATT and the Shrewsbury Trials', London 1973

Wainwright, W. 'Labour What Next?', *Marxism Today*, September 1965, pp. 4-9

Waters, M. (ed) *Rosa Luxemburg Speaks*, Pathfinder Press, New York 1970

Watters, F. *Being Frank,* Doncaster, 1992

Wedderburn, W. *The Worker and the Law*, Penguin 1986

Weiler, P. *British Labour and the Cold War*, Stanford University Press 1988

Westacott, F. *Shaking the Chains: a Personal and Political* History, Joe Clark, Chesterfield 2002

Whitehead, P. *The Writing on the Wall – Britain in the 1970s*, Michael Joseph, London 1985

Wilberforce: Report of a Court of Inquiry into a Dispute Between the National Coal Board and the National Union of Mineworkers, under the chairmanship of Lord Wilberforce, HMSO, London 1972

Williams, R. 'The British Left', *New Left Review* 1965 30: 18-26

Williams, R. *Culture and Society*, Chatto and Windus, London 1958

Wilson, D. *Dockers*, Fontana, London 1972

Wilson, H. *The Labour Government 1964-1970: A Personal Record*, Weidenfeld and Nicolson, London 1971

Winterton, J. and Winterton, R. *Coal, Crisis, and Conflict*, Manchester University Press 1989

Woddis, J. *New Theories of Revolution*, Lawrence & Wishart, London 1972

Woddis, J. 'The State – some problems', *Marxism Today*, November 1976, pp. 331-343

Woddis, J. '"A single gigantic flood": reflections on the democratic alliance', *Marxism Today*, September 1977, pp. 260-269

Woddis, M. 'Some Problems of Poverty in Britain Today', *Marxism Today*, December 1967, pp. 357-363

Worsley, P. 'Frantz Fanon and the "lumpen proletariat"', *Socialist Register* 1972, pp. 193-230

Wright, R. 'The lessons Labour governments never learn', *Labour Monthly* March 1977, pp. 111-3

Wright Mills, C. *The Sociological Imagination*, OUP 1959

Index